Microprocessor Based Systems
for the Higher Technician

Microprocessor Based Systems for the Higher Technician

R.E. VEARS

Heinemann Newnes

Heinemann Newnes
An imprint of Heinemann Professional Publishing Ltd
Halley Court, Jordan Hill, Oxford OX2 8EJ

OXFORD LONDON MELBOURNE AUCKLAND SINGAPORE IBADAN
NAIROBI GABORONE KINGSTON

First published 1988

© R.E. Vears 1988

British Library Cataloguing in Publication Data
Vears, R.E.
    Microprocessor based systems for the higher technician.
    1. Microprocessor systems. Design.
    Applications of microcomputer systems
    I. Title
    004.2′56′0285416

ISBN 0 434 92339 7

Printed and bound in Great Britain by
Butler & Tanner Ltd, Frome and London

Contents

Acknowledgements viii
Preface ix

1 System development design cycle 1
   Introduction 1
   Design sequence 1
   Program writing 4
   Program testing 9
   Microcomputer development system 10
   Problems 11

2 Operating systems 13
   Introduction 13
   Standard operating systems 13
   CP/M-80 14
   Organisation of CP/M 2.2 15
   Disk storage 17
   Disk files 18
   Disk directory 19
   CP/M filenames 20
   CP/M file types 21
   Specifying the drive associated with a file 22
   Built-in commands 22
   Transient commands 25
   Problems 27

3 Text editors 28
   Introduction 28
   Creating and saving new files 29
   The edit buffer 30
   Opening and closing files 30
   Files created during editing 33
   Types of text editor 33
   Summary of ED operations 36
   WordStar 38
   Installation 38
   Commands 40
   Typical WordStar menus 41
   Problems 42

4 Assemblers 43
Introduction 43
Nature of an assembler 43
CP/M assemblers 45
Assembling a program 46
Assembly language statements 48
Assembler directives 52
Errors 58
Assembly language documentation 59
Assembly language examples 60
Problems 66

5 Macros 70
Introduction 70
Macro pseudo-ops 70
Stored macros 76
ENDM and EXITM pseudo-ops 83
LOCAL pseudo-op 86
MACLIB statement 89
Road intersection—traffic light sequence 90
Problems 100

6 Linking and loading 101
Introduction 101
Linking source code 101
Linking object code 104
M80 relocating assembler 105
M80 command line 106
Switches 107
M80 file format 107
M80 assembler directives 108
Linking loaders 122
Loading 126
Relocatable file library manager 127
Cross-referencing of symbols 129
Problems 129

7 Debuggers 133
Introduction 133
Debugging programs 133
Loading ZSID 135
ZSID commands 136
Sample debug run 145
Symbol tables 157
Utility programs 157
Problems 162

8 Hardware design 164

Introduction   164
Design considerations   164
Z80 MPU circuits   167
Z80 CPU technical data   167
ROM/RAM   186
Z80 PIO technical data   187
Z80 SIO technical data   199
Z80 CTC technical data   222
Address decoding   239
Interrupts   239
Problems   243

9 Hardware/software integration   244

Introduction   244
Principle of in-circuit emulation   244
DICE in-circuit emulator   246
Memory mapping   248
Typical emulation sequence   249
Real time trace and hardware trace   253
Breakpoint monitor   254
Program storage in EPROM   254
EPROM programming   257
EPROM erasure   258
Problems   258

10 Fault location   259

Introduction   259
Typical faults in microprocessor based systems   259
Conventional fault-finding techniques   261
Special test equipment   262
Logic analyser   265
Signature analysis   269
Software diagnostics   273
Problems   276

Solutions to problems   280

Index   285

Acknowledgements

I am grateful to Zilog (UK) Limited for permission to include in Chapter 8 technical data relating to Z80 MPU based systems.

In Chapter 9, information relating to the DICE in-circuit emulator is reproduced by permission of DUX (UK) Limited and details of logic test equipment, on pages 262–5, are included by permission of Hewlett-Packard.

The displays shown on pages 266–9 were obtained using a Philips logic analyser.

R.E.V.

Preface

The aim of this book is to provide the theoretical and practical information necessary for the development of software and hardware associated with microprocessor based systems. It provides coverage of the BTEC level 4 unit in Microprocessor Based Systems (syllabus U80/674), however it can be regarded as a textbook for a much wider range of studies.

Each topic considered in the text is presented in a way that assumes in the reader only the knowledge attained at BTEC level 3 Microelectronic Systems (syllabus U79/604), i.e. a basic knowledge of microprocessor principles and machine code programming.

This book concentrates on the development of 8-bit microcontrollers specifically constructed around the ever popular Z80 microprocessor. For many industrial applications this microprocessor is still more than adequate, and capable of giving excellent performance.

The design cycle for the development of such a microprocessor based system and the use of a disk-based development system (MDS) as an aid to design are both described in detail.

The commonly used CP/M operating system is described, and background information concerning file handling is included where appropriate for the benefit of readers unfamiliar with disk based equipment.

The use of professional software development tools is comprehensively covered, including a full chapter on macros which shows how these may be used to advantage to simplify program writing.

Hardware development may be carried out with the minimum of basic electronics knowledge, particularly if devices from the Z80 family are chosen. This topic is therefore dealt with by including basic circuits for each stage, together with appropriate data sheets, such that microprocessor based systems may be readily constructed from these basic building blocks. The all important process of software/hardware integration using emulation techniques is also presented.

The final chapter deals with the topic of fault location. This has obvious significance when dealing with systems under development which may never have worked satisfactorily. The equipment needed, and principles of operation and basic techniques are described, but of course the location of faults in electronic equipment is an acquired skill.

I am indebted to all companies who have created and developed microprocessor technology for providing the inspiration and tools for writing a book of this type, and acknowledge in particular those firms who have generously given permission to publish their material.

Finally, I wish to express thanks to colleagues who have provided the necessary encouragement, and to my wife Rosemary for her patience during the preparation of this book.

R. Vears

1 System Development Design Cycle

Introduction

The introduction of microprocessors into electronic systems offers many advantages in terms of flexibility, lower costs and shorter development times. Since most of these advantages owe much to the programmable nature of microprocessors, it is no longer possible to rely entirely on traditional circuit design techniques. The major part of the design of a microprocessor based system therefore follows two distinct paths:

(i) hardware design, and
(ii) software design.

Hardware design basically consists of selecting appropriate components and interconnecting them to form an electronic circuit.

Software design consists of writing a program which, when installed in the hardware circuit, causes the complete system to function in the intended manner.

This is, of course, an over-simplification, but does highlight the additional problems encountered when incorporating microprocessors into a new design, which are:

(i) deciding which system functions are to be implemented in hardware or software,
(ii) writing software, and
(iii) integrating separately developed software with the hardware.

The organisation of these additional items with respect to hardware design is shown in Fig. 1.1.

Design sequence

A logical design sequence is required to enable efficient system design to take place. A typical sequence includes the following stages:

(i) initial specification for the complete system
(ii) formulation of measures of cost effectiveness
(iii) derivation of system flowchart
(iv) definition of hardware/software implementation
(v) selection of necessary electronic devices, controllers etc and the necessary interfacing devices

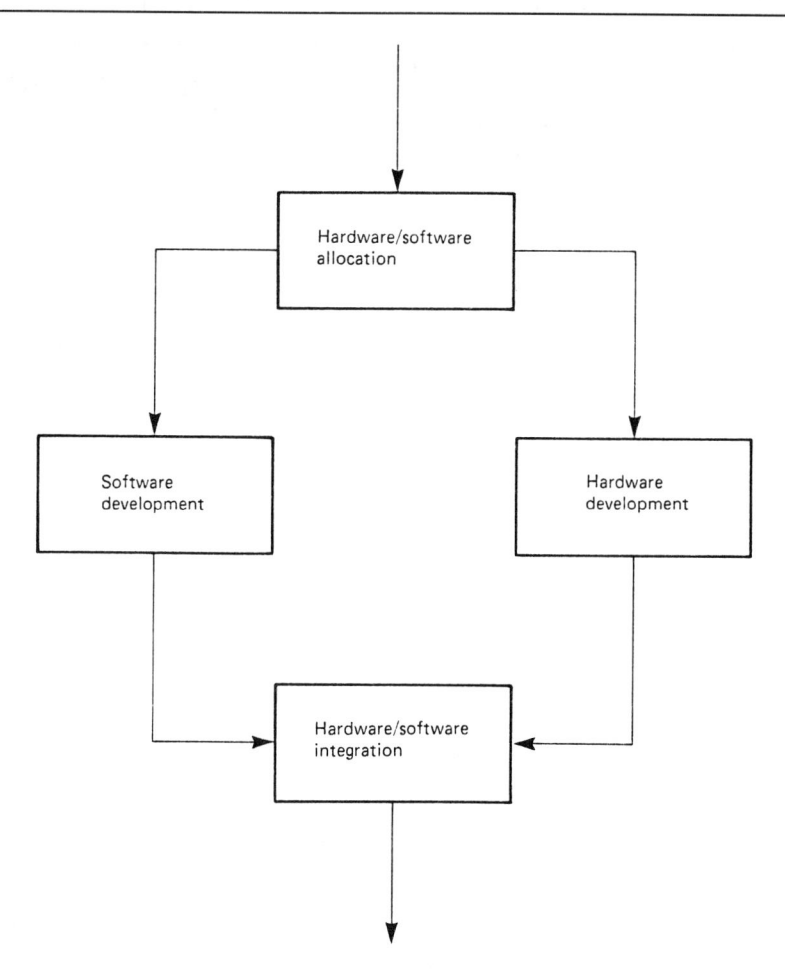

Fig. 1.1

(vi) definition of boundary constraints for the microcomputer program, e.g. timing, address space
(vii) develop a system flowchart
(viii) write program
(ix) test program
(x) modify where necessary
(xi) emulation of system
(xii) modify further if necessary
(xiii) run hardware and firmware prototype
(xiv) iteration as necessary

Initial specification

It is essential to obtain a specification for the complete system before any development work can proceed. Without this, the wrong solution to a problem may be devised (see Fig. 1.2).

System development design cycle 3

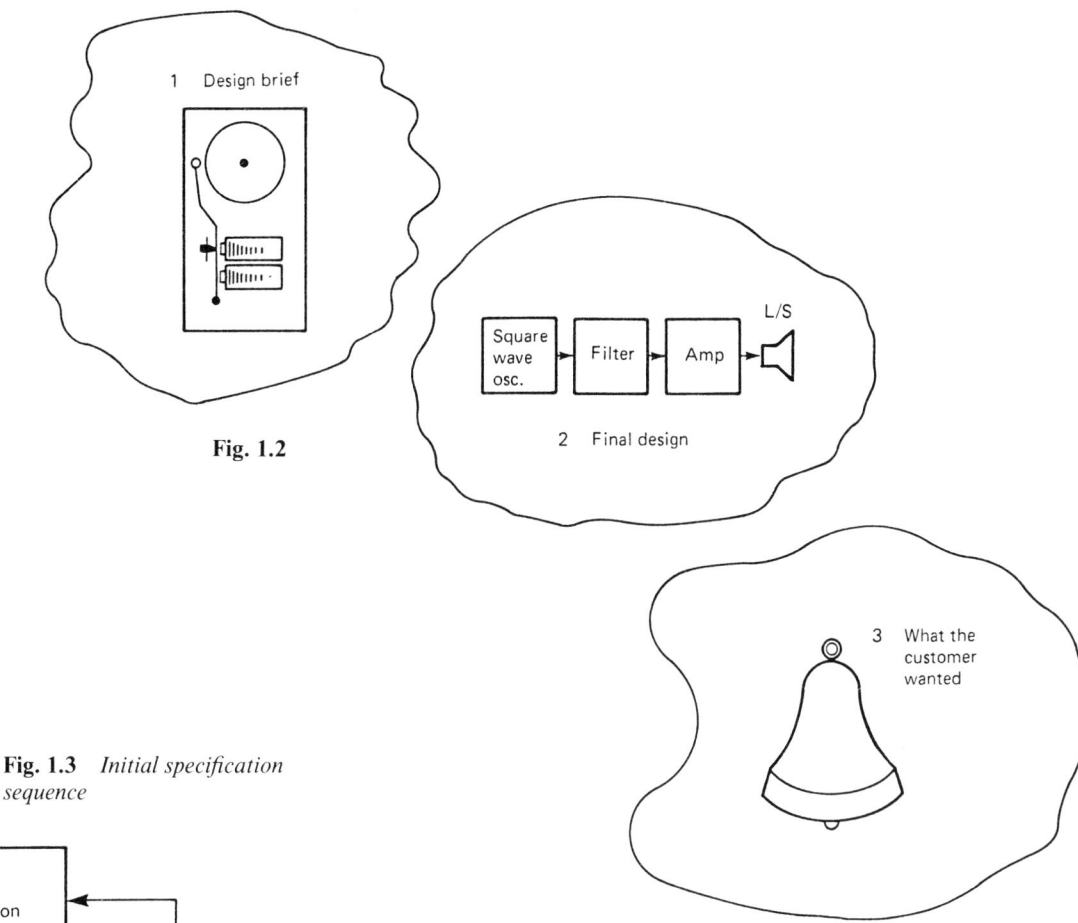

Fig. 1.2

1 Design brief

2 Final design

3 What the customer wanted

Fig. 1.3 *Initial specification sequence*

An initial specification may be produced in consultation with the customer, but this will probably require further details and refinement as development work proceeds. This sequence is shown in Fig. 1.3.

Cost effectiveness

A designer has the choice of implementing specific functions within a system in hardware or in software. The choice of whether to use hardware or software is often determined by cost/performance considerations. In general it is cheaper to implement functions using software rather than hardware. Initial development costs may be higher for software, but once written it is a one-off expense, whereas hardware implementation adds cost to each item manufactured. In some cases the required performance can only be achieved by the use of hardware, e.g. where the speed of a microcomputer is not great enough for satisfactory operation. In such cases, the microcomputer is often used to control the hardware in a supervisory capacity.

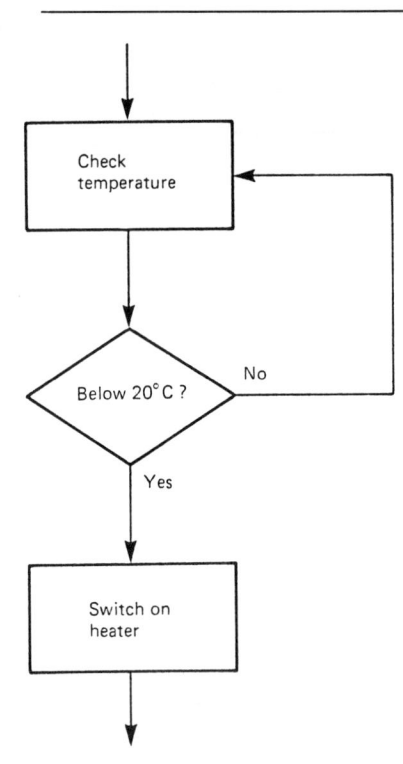

Fig. 1.4 *Part of system flowchart*

System flowchart

The flowchart for a system gives the designer a complete overview of the system and its operation. This may enable decisions to be made regarding hardware/software trade-offs and component selection. An example of a system flowchart is shown in Fig. 1.4.

Selection of electronic devices

A designer must be able to make decisions regarding the partitioning of hardware and software tasks for the complete system, and select appropriate electronic devices. Since many of the components used are programmable, their choice inevitably influences the software design stages. For example, the software designer needs to know which microprocessor and which programmable I/O devices will be used in the final design. The choice of these components will depend upon a number of different factors, and may often be determined by the investment already made in development equipment.

Program boundary constraints

A programmer needs to know the boundaries within which the system must operate in order to write a program that will be compatible with the final system. It is necessary to know, for example, what address space is available for ROM and RAM, what I/O addresses are proposed, and what timing constraints are imposed upon specific sections of program.

Program flowchart

Once the software specification for a system has been defined, it becomes necessary to develop logical sequences of operations which provide solutions to the particular problems presented by each section of the software. The approach adopted to solve a particular problem is known as an 'algorithm', and a choice of different algorithms often exists. An algorithm may be represented graphically as a program flowchart and from this flowchart it is possible to produce program statements directly. An example of a program flowchart is shown in Fig. 1.5.

Program writing

This is the actual program writing stage during which a programmer translates a flowchart into program statements. The form of these statements depends upon the level of programming adopted. There are basically three levels of programming, and these are:

(i) machine language,
(ii) assembly language, and
(iii) high level language

A program development sequence is shown in Fig. 1.6.

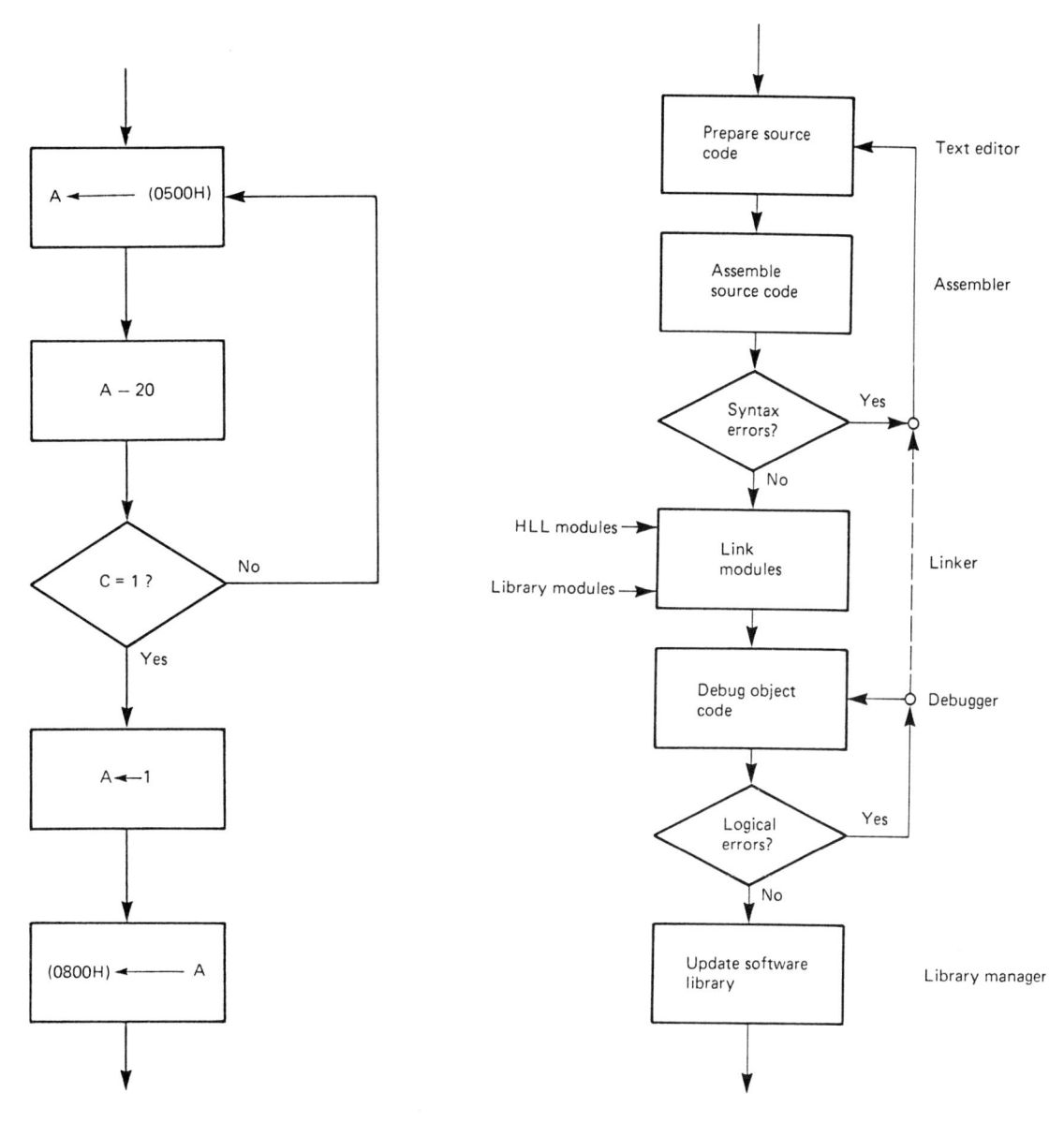

Fig. 1.5 *Part of program flowchart*

Fig. 1.6 *Software development sequence*

Machine language

Machine language, or machine code, is the term given to sequences of binary coded instructions which form the basic instructions understood by a microprocessor. Since long sequences of binary codes are rather tedious for humans to handle, and therefore prone to errors, most programmers use the more convenient hexadecimal representation. The benefits of using hexadecimal representation may be seen in the following example:

Binary machine code		Hexadecimal equivalents	
Address	Instruction	Address	Instr.
0000 0001 0000 0000	0011 1110	0100	3E
0000 0001 0000 0001	1000 0000	0101	80
0000 0001 0000 0010	0011 1101	0102	3D
0000 0001 0000 0011	0010 0000	0103	20
0000 0001 0000 0100	1111 1101	0104	FD

Although it is possible to write complete programs at machine language level, it is unlikely to be used for serious development since it is very time consuming and difficult to detect errors introduced at the program writing stage. Neither form of code indicates the nature of the instructions that they represent.

Assembly language

When using assembly language, machine code instructions are represented in a much more readable form by using mnemonics and symbols for each instruction rather than hexadecimal codes. Each assembly language statement represents one machine code instruction and is therefore still considered as a low level language. For example, the sequence of binary and hexadecimal codes in the previous example could be written in assembly language in the following manner:

```
         LD    A,80H
LOOP:    DEC   A
         JP    NZ,LOOP
```

In this form, a program has more meaning to a human operator, since the mnemonics indicate the function of each instruction, i.e. LoaD, DECrement and JumP if Not Zero.

For many microprocessor applications, assembly language is preferred since:

(i) it provides a reasonable compromise between the efficiency of machine code and the readability of a high level language
(ii) compared with a high level language, the machine code that it generates executes faster and uses much less memory space

At some stage, assembly language statements must be converted into their machine code equivalent if they are to be executed by a microprocessor, and for this purpose it is best to use an assembler program (see

Chapter 4), since this provides rapid and accurate conversion from instruction mnemonics into binary machine codes.

Even when an assembler is not available, it is usually better to write programs in assembly language and then 'hand assemble' by looking up the relevant opcodes in the manufacturer's instruction set.

Programming at both machine code and assembly language level requires a detailed knowledge of the internal architecture of a microprocessor, and programs may not be transportable from one machine to another, since each different microprocessor has its own unique language.

High level language

A high level language is oriented towards the user or the user's problems rather than towards the microprocessor. For this reason, programs are usually written in a more readable form, and consist of mathematical or English language type statements, each of which may generate long sequences of machine code.

Numerous different high level languages have been devised, each with its own particular strengths and weaknesses that make it more suitable for some applications than for others. Commonly used high level languages include BASIC, PASCAL, and FORTRAN, and the following short program examples show the nature of each of these languages:

(i) BASIC

```
10 REM THIS PROGRAM ADDS TWO NUMBERS
20 A=5
30 B=4
40 C=A+B
50 PRINT C
60 END
```

(ii) PASCAL

```
PROGRAM sum;
VAR total,number1,number2: INTEGER;
BEGIN
    number1:=5;
    number2:=4;
    total:=number1+number2
    WRITE(total)
END.
```

(iii) FORTRAN

```
C       THIS PROGRAM ADDS TWO NUMBERS
        A=5
        B=4
        C=A+B
        WRITE (5,100)C
100     FORMAT (I6)
        STOP
        END
```

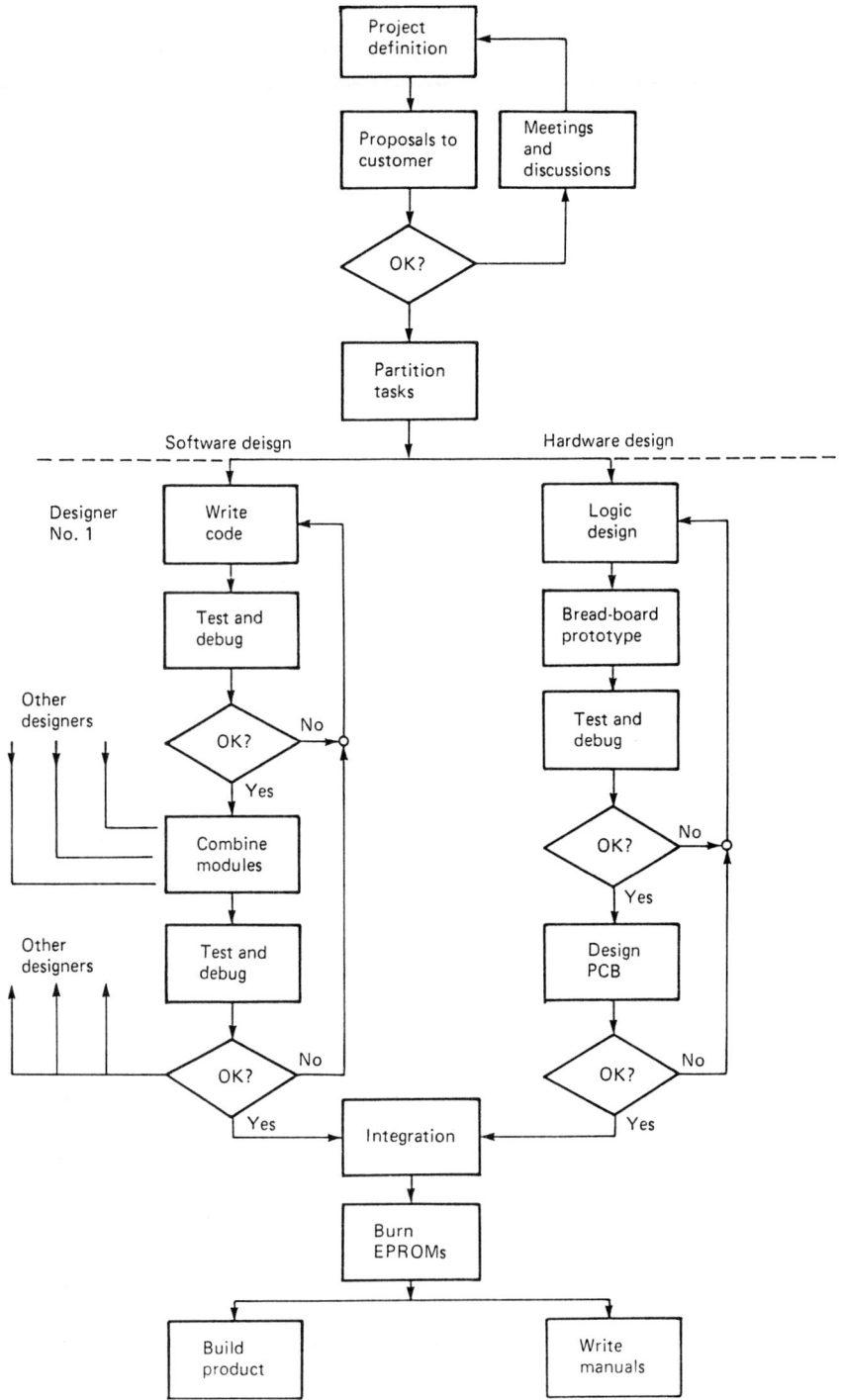

Fig. 1.7 *Microprocessor based system design cycle*

All three examples perform the identical function of calculating the sum of 4 and 5 and printing the result.

Since high level languages are user or problem oriented, they are much less dependent upon the type of microprocessor used than machine code, and are therefore readily transportable from one machine to another. All high level languages require the use of an interpreter or a compiler to convert each statement into its machine code equivalent. This is not always very efficient, particularly the interpreting process, hence programs written in a high level language usually execute much slower than those written directly in machine code. Also more memory space is required in which to run such programs, particularly where an interpreter is used e.g. for BASIC, since this must always be present if the program is to run.

Program testing

Few programs function as intended at the first attempt. It is therefore necessary to 'debug' a newly written program, and this is a process which involves testing a program under different conditions and with various parameters until all logical errors have been removed and satisfactory operation obtained.

In order to carry out this very necessary process, a comprehensive set of debugging tools are required which allow a program to be executed and tested in a controlled manner. The debugging tools should ideally include both software and hardware trace facilities which allow full monitoring of the microprocessor registers and busses during the testing phase (see Chapter 7).

Emulation

Once the separate hardware and software development stages have been successfully completed, it becomes necessary to integrate the software and hardware to form a complete system.

Although the hardware and software may both have performed satisfactorily when tested independently of one another, this is no guarantee that the same will be true once the two are integrated. Should the final system not perform as intended, it may not be possible to determine the cause, since the system probably does not possess the debugging facilities needed for this purpose, in fact it may not even have a keyboard or display.

The use of an emulator helps to solve this problem, since it is arranged that the software runs initially in the hardware environment of the emulator which has previously been set up to be identical to that of the hardware of the system under development, i.e. to emulate it. It is also arranged that the hardware functions performed by the emulator may be gradually taken over by the new system as each section is developed.

Microcomputer development system (MDS)

The complete design cycle for a microprocessor based system is shown in Fig. 1.7, and much of this development work is carried out with the aid of a 'microcomputer development system' or MDS.

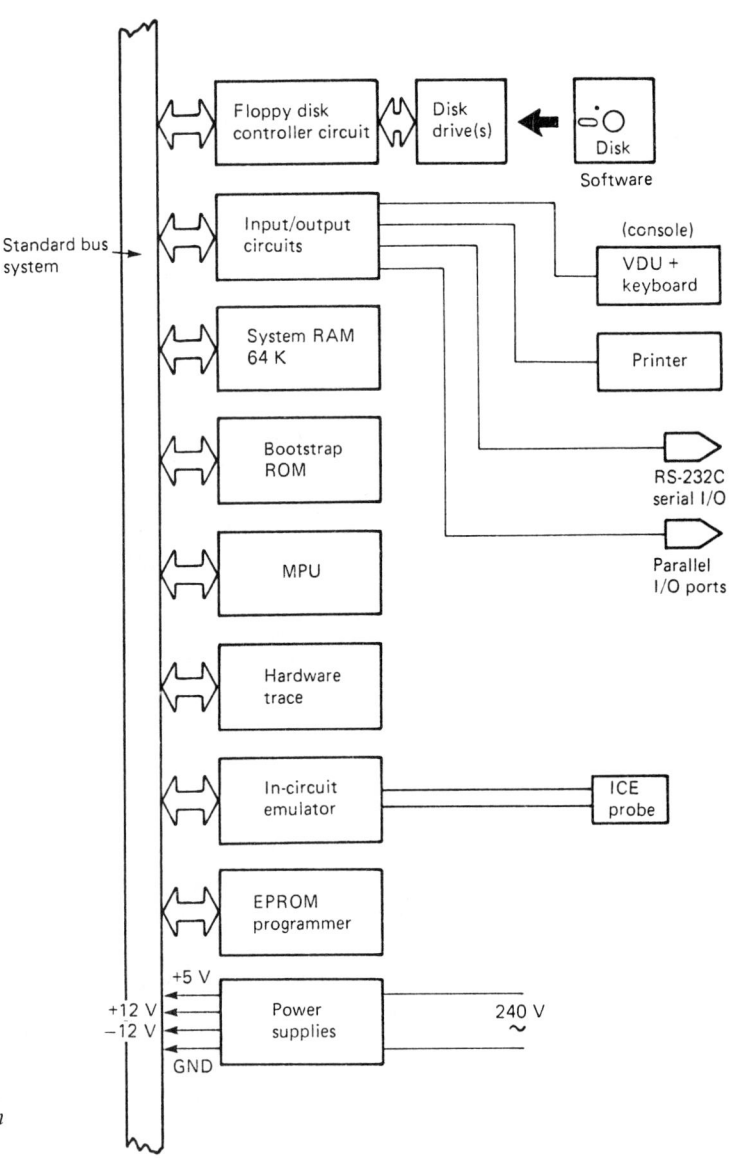

Fig. 1.8 *MDS block diagram*

A microcomputer development system, or MDS, is a computer system which may be used to develop both hardware and software for a new microprocessor based system. For effective development to take place, an MDS should offer the following facilities:

(i) Software, consisting of:
    (a) an operating system
    (b) a text editor
    (c) an assembler
    (d) a debugger
    (e) a linker
    (f) a loader
    (g) EPROM programming routines
    (h) high level languages
 (ii) Memory for:
    (a) an operating system
    (b) development software
    (c) applications program development
    (d) non-volatile bulk storage e.g. floppy or hard disk
(iii) Hardware consisting of:
    (a) a keyboard and VDU (user's console)
    (b) a printer
    (c) an EPROM programmer
    (d) I/O facilities
    (e) an in-circuit emulator (ICE)

In theory, almost any computer could be used as a development system, but difficulties would inevitably arise due to the manner in which a general purpose computer is constructed and organised. A purpose-built MDS is usually constructed in more modular form to facilitate development work. This enables the I/O of the MDS (host system) to be configured in an identical manner to that of the system being developed (the target system). It is also advantageous if the MPU and its control circuits are located separately from the remainder of the system so that development work for systems using other types of MPU may be carried out by a simple change of MPU card and disk. The internal organisation of a typical MDS is shown in Fig. 1.8.

Problems

1. A customer has commissioned the design of a microprocessor-based temperature controller. Make a list of the additional information required before a complete design specification could be produced.
2. A microprocessor-based motor speed controller is required to simultaneously perform the following tasks:
   (i) scan a matrix keyboard for data entry,
   (ii) measure the speed of the motor,
   (iii) calculate the motor speed in rev/min,
   (iv) display motor speed on four 7-segment LEDs,
   (v) provide multiplexing signals for the display, and
   (vi) maintain the selected motor speed over a wide range of loads.
   It is discovered that the selected MPU cannot satisfactorily perform all of these tasks within the time available. Explain how this problem may be solved.

3. (a) State the advantages of using a High Level Language (H.L.L.) for software development,
   (b) Explain why it may be necessary to use embedded machine code routines when using a H.L.L. for real-time control purposes.

2 Operating Systems

Introduction

A microcomputer spends much of its time transferring data betwen its MPU and various other parts of the system, such as the keyboard or VDU. A typical computer system is shown in Fig. 2.1 and the relevant data paths may be readily identified using this diagram.

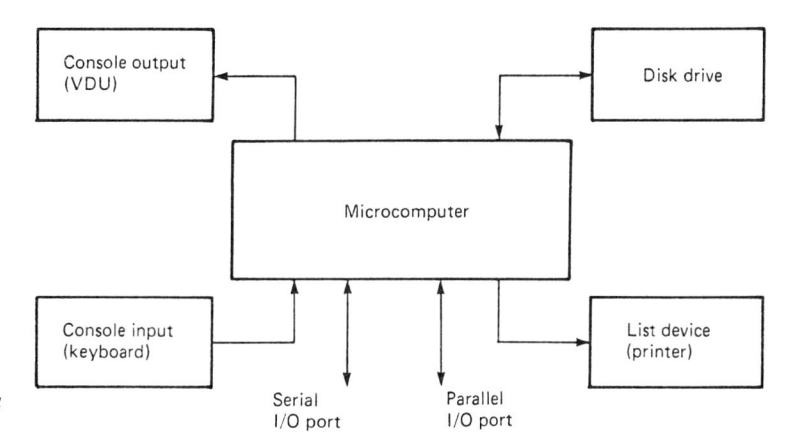

Fig. 2.1 *Microcomputer data paths*

Each of these data paths requires its own simple program to enable transfers of data to take place under software control. An organised collection of these programs is known as an 'operating system' or 'monitor program'.

Standard operating systems

All computers need an operating system which effectively acts as a software interface between the user, the user's programs and the computer. All applications programs interact with a computer and its resources via the operating system, therefore it must always be present whenever the computer is used. This may be achieved in one of the following two ways:
  (i) in non-disk systems, the operating system is stored in ROM which is mapped into the microcomputer memory system so that it takes control immediately after power up or reset,
  (ii) in disk based systems, a short program in ROM (the boot ROM) is used to read a short loader program (the cold boot loader) from disk.

This loader program then proceeds to read the operating system from the disk and places it in the computer's memory. Once fully loaded, control is then handed over to the operating system.

When writing software for a microcomputer, it is necessary to know the exact address of each routine in the operating system and how it may be incorporated into applications programs. Unfortunately, many different operating systems are used (even in the same make of microcomputer!) which often means that programs written for one microcomputer are unlikely to run on a different type of computer, although both using identical microprocessors.

There is, therefore, an obvious advantage in developing a standard operating system for each microcomputer so that software may be exchanged between different machines without the need to modify it. One such system, which was originally developed for the 8080 microprocessor, is called 'CP/M®' (Control Program/Monitor). Since 8085 and Z80 microprocessors are also capable of executing 8080 machine code, CP/M is also suitable for systems which use these types of microprocessor.

The Z80 is widely used for industrial control purposes, therefore CP/M has in many ways become an 'industry standard' for 8-bit microprocessors. Much software is available to run under CP/M, including assembly language development tools and high level languages. All of the software described in this book is CP/M based, therefore a more detailed look at this system will be useful, but for more comprehensive information concerning CP/M, the reader is advised to consult one of the many specialist publications on CP/M.

CP/M-80

CP/M is an operating system which has been designed for disk-based microcomputers. It therefore contains all of the routines required for communications between the various physical parts of a microcomputer system, including the management of disk storage and running of applications programs. The problem associated with different microcomputers having widely differing I/O arrangements is solved by the fact that CP/M does not communicate directly with physical devices, but instead communicates with logical devices which are accessed via the same address in all CP/M systems. This means that, broadly speaking, programs that are written to execute under CP/M will function correctly in all microcomputers which use this operating system, the exception being that some newer programs require CP/M version 2.2 or later.

CP/M 3 (or CP/M Plus) is an enhancement of CP/M 2.2, and is designed for computers with memories larger than 64K i.e. computers with memory 'banking'. Consequently, although CP/M 3 offers many new features, most applications programs written for the early CP/M 2.2 still function correctly under this system.

The manufacturer of each microcomputer system is responsible for ensuring that correct logical to physical translation takes place within the system, and this forms part of the installation procedure.

Organisation of CP/M 2.2

CP/M 2.2 consists of approximately 5.5K bytes of standard code plus a further 1K to 8K bytes of machine dependent code which is loaded into the topmost addresses of RAM. A typical CP/M installation for an MDS consists of 6.5K bytes of code.

Although CP/M is located at the top end of memory, it is arranged such that the absolute addresses used are unimportant, thus enabling CP/M to operate in microcomputers with differing sizes of memory. A minimum size memory of 20K bytes must be provided, however.

CP/M is divided logically into the following five sections:
 (i) BIOS   (Basic Input/Output System),
 (ii) BDOS   (Basic Disk Operating System),
 (iii) CCP   (Console Command Processor)
 (iv) TPA   (Transient Program Area)
 (v) Base Page (system parameters)
which are arranged in memory as shown in Fig. 2.2.

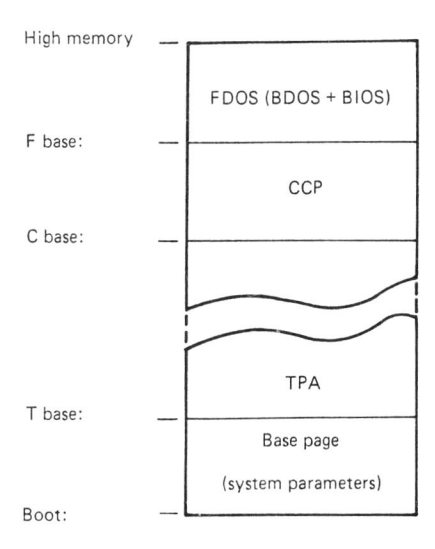

Fig. 2.2 *Organisation of CP/M in memory*

The function of each of these sections may be briefly summarised as follows:

(i) BIOS

The Basic I/O System contains all of the routines required to access the disk drives and to communicate with the peripheral devices such as the keyboard, printer and VDU. Since I/O arrangements in a microcomputer are machine dependent, this part of CP/M is not supplied as part of the operating system, but must be written by the manufacturer of each different microcomputer system. The BIOS is expected to contain certain routines which are used by the other sections of CP/M and which are accessed via a 'jump table' at the start of the BIOS. The jump table contains jumps to the following routines which must be arranged in the order shown:

ORG	CCP+1600H	;start of BIOS
JP	COLD	;complete restart of CP/M
JP	WARM	;re-enter CP/M
JP	CONST	;check console status
JP	CONIN	;read console (keyboard) input
JP	CONOUT	;write to console (VDU) output
JP	LISTOUT	;write to list device (printer)
JP	PUNCH	;write to punch output
JP	READER	;tape reader input
JP	HOME	;reset disk drive read/write head
JP	SELDSK	;select disk
JP	SETTRK	;select track
JP	SETSEC	;select sector
JP	SETDMA	;select DMA address for disk read/write
JP	READ	;read current disk sector
JP	WRITE	;write to current disk sector

Part of the logical to physical translation is performed by the BIOS, and in particular, information concerning the disk system is included so that CP/M may operate with different types of disk drive. The BIOS is the only part of CP/M that need be altered for different microcomputers.

(ii) BDOS

The Basic Disk Operating System acts as an interface between the user's programs and the operating system, and provides disk management facilities for up to 16 independent disk drives. All I/O activity is processed through the BDOS which in turn accesses the physical devices of the system via the BIOS. Each I/O routine is assigned a function number, and is accessed by loading register C with the appropriate number and performing a subroutine call to the primary BDOS entry point at address 0005H.

(iii) CCP

The Console Command Processor provides a symbolic interface between the user's console and the remainder of the CP/M system. All commands entered via the keyboard are interpreted by the CCP and are executed immediately if the CCP contains the necessary routine. Such commands are known as 'built-in' commands, and included in this category are commands to erase, rename or print the contents of certain disk files. Valid commands for which no corresponding routines exist in the CCP are known as 'transient' commands, and these may only be executed after the appropriate routine has been read in from disk and stored in the memory of the microcomputer.

(iv) TPA

The block of memory from address 0100H up to the start of the CCP is known as the 'transient program area' or TPA. The TPA is used to store and execute programs that are loaded in from disk under the control of the CCP, and to provide essential work space in which the user may develop and test software.

(v) Base Page

The first 256 bytes of memory from address 0000 to 00FFH are reserved for use by CP/M and are generally unavailable to the user. Alteration of the contents of these addresses should not be attempted unless the user has considerable knowledge of the CP/M system, since this will invariably cause system 'crashes'.

Fig. 2.3 shows the various communication paths that exist between the main sections of CP/M.

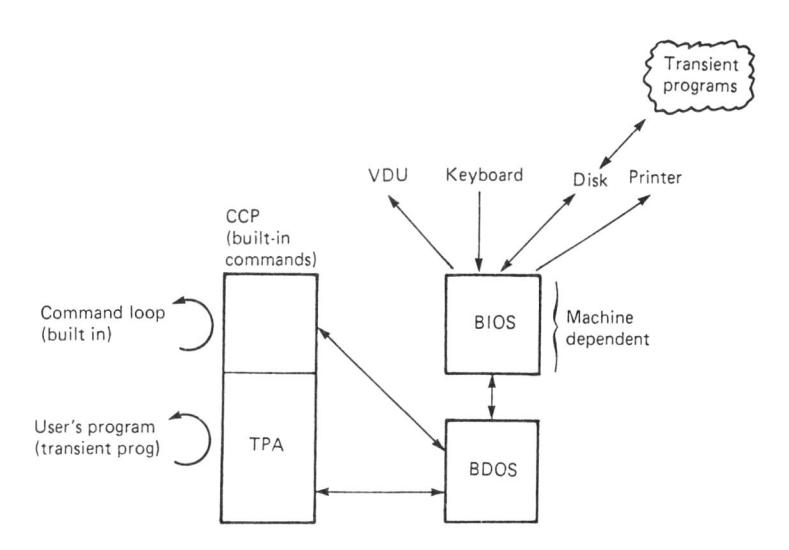

Fig. 2.3 *CP/M communications paths*

Disk storage

The development of software on a microcomputer system usually involves many hours of work, spread out over a period of weeks or even months. It is therefore essential to have some form of non-volatile storage available so that previous work may be quickly retrieved to allow further development work to take place. One commonly used form of data storage are floppy disks which are available in 3 in, 3½ in, 5¼ in and 8 in diameters. Each disk is made from a flexible plastic material upon which is deposited a very thin layer of magnetic material. Programs and data are stored, in serial form, as a magnetic pattern on the surface of the disk. The magnetic patterns are arranged in the form of tracks and sectors, as shown in Fig. 2.4.

The exact number of tracks and sectors may vary considerably from one disk system to another, but the IBM standard of 77 tracks, each divided into 26 sectors, may frequently be found in practice.

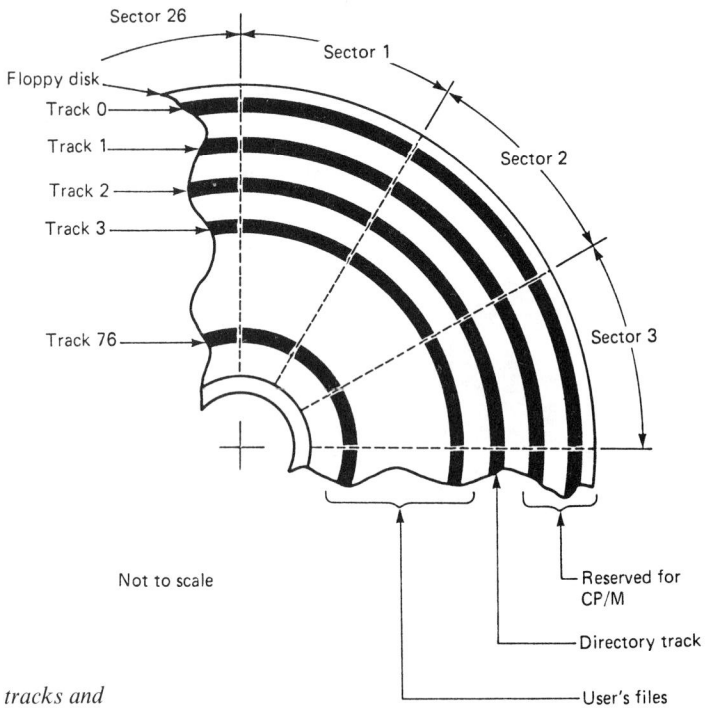

Fig. 2.4 *Floppy disk tracks and sectors*

It is seldom necessary for the average user of an MDS to be aware of physical organisation of a disk, however, since such variations are taken care of by the use of disk parameter tables which are stored in the BIOS. The outer two tracks are reserved for the storage of CP/M itself (system tracks), and are not available to the user for any other purpose. This applies even though a disk may be used for data storage rather than program storage and therefore not require an operating system of its own.

Disk files

A file consists of a collection of ASCII characters, instructions or data which share a common identifier called the 'filename'. A CP/M file consists of a collection of 128 byte 'records' which may be referenced by a single filename. The physical size of sectors on a disk is often 128 bytes, although sectors larger than this are commonly used e.g. 512, 1024 or 2048 bytes. In a CP/M system, however, the logical size of each sector is always considered to be 128 bytes or one 'record'. This unit is too small for efficient management by the BDOS, and in any case, is generally insufficient for storing complete programs. Disk space is therefore allocated in 'blocks' of 1K, 2K, 4K, 8K or 16K consecutive bytes, and each block has an identifying number (the 'block number'). The actual size of each block is defined by disk parameters which are stored within the BIOS. A whole number of blocks must be allocated to each file, and although a file may only require one or two bytes of a particular block, the remainder of that block is not available for use by other files. This may appear to be a rather wasteful use of disk storage, but it does enable the operation of the BDOS to be simplified.

Disk directory

A part of each disk is reserved for use as a directory for files stored on it. The contents of a directory track may be read and displayed on the user's console in the following form:

```
A: DATE    COM : DDHP7470 PRL : DEVICE  COM : DUMP    COM : GENCOM  COM
A: GET     COM : HEXCOM   COM : HIST    UTL : INITDIR COM : LIB     COM
A: LINK    COM : MAC      COM : PALETTE COM : PATCH   COM : PUT     COM
A: RMAC    COM : SAVE     COM : SID     COM : TRACE   UTL : XREF    COM
```

The directory normally occupies the whole of track 2 and possibly part of track 3 of each disk. Each entry in the directory contains a *filename* which acts as an identifier for a specific file, and associated with each filename are the numbers of the blocks which are allocated to it. The block numbers are translated into specific track and sector numbers so that the correct sectors may be located for performing read and write operations. A hex dump of a small part of the directory of a disk appears as follows:

```
  active=00                              no. of 128
  erased=E5     filename      extent     byte logical sectors
     |            |             |          |
     ↓            ↓             ↓          ↓
    00 44 41 54 45 20 20 20 20 43 4F 4D 00 00 00 17   ,DATE    COM,,,,
    02 03 04 00 00 00 00 00 00 00 00 00 00 00 00 00   ,,,,,,,,,,,,,,,,
    ↑  ↑  ↑
    blocks used

    00 44 44 48 50 37 34 37 30 50 52 4C 00 00 00 56   ,DDHP7470PRL,,,V
    05 06 07 08 09 0A 0B 0C 0D 0E 0F 00 00 00 00 00   ,,,,,,,,,,,,,,,,

    00 44 45 56 49 43 45 20 20 43 4F 4D 00 00 00 3A   ,DEVICE  COM,,,:
    10 11 12 13 14 15 16 17 00 00 00 00 00 00 00 00   ,,,,,,,,,,,,,,,,

    00 44 55 4D 50 20 20 20 20 43 4F 4D 00 00 00 08   ,DUMP    COM,,,,
    18 00 00 00 00 00 00 00 00 00 00 00 00 00 00 00   ,,,,,,,,,,,,,,,,
```

It can be seen that each directory element consists of 32 bytes, therefore four directory elements may be stored in each logical sector. The maximum number of directory elements permitted on a disk is defined by disk parameters that are stored in the system BIOS. A single directory element can identify up to 16 blocks or one 'extent' on the disk. An extent is therefore a group of groups, and defines a unit of disk storage of 16K (or multiples of 16K, depending upon block size).

For example, the directory entry for the file DATE.COM shows that it consists of 17_{16} (or 23_{10}) logical 128 byte sectors. The total size of the file is therefore 23×128 bytes or 2.94K. Blocks of 1K are used in this system, therefore three blocks are required (blocks 02, 03 and 04).

Should a file be so large that it requires more storage space than that provided by 16 blocks, then a second directory entry or second extent is created for the file which has the same filename as that used for the first extent. This arrangement is shown in the following example:

```
                                    full 128
                         extent 0   sectors
                            ↓         ↓
00 49 4E 49 54 44 49 52 20 43 4F 4D 00 00 00 80   .INITDIR COM,,,.
33 34 35 36 37 38 39 3A 3B 3C 3D 3E 3F 40 41 42   3456789:;<=>?@AB
 ↑  ↑  ↑  ↑  ↑
all blocks used            extent 1   122 sectors
                              ↓          ↓
00 49 4E 49 54 44 49 52 20 43 4F 4D 01 00 00 7A   .INITDIR COM,,,z
43 44 45 46 47 48 49 4A 4B 4C 4D 4E 4F 50 51 52   CDEFGHIJKLMNOPQR
 ↑  ↑  ↑  ↑  ↑
all blocks used in second extent


00 4C 49 42 20 20 20 20 20 43 4F 4D 00 00 00 38   .LIB     COM,,,8
53 54 55 56 57 58 59 00 00 00 00 00 00 00 00 00   STUVWXY,,,,,,,,,


00 4C 49 4E 4B 20 20 20 20 43 4F 4D 00 00 00 7B   .LINK    COM,,,{
5A 5B 5C 5D 5E 5F 60 61 62 63 64 65 66 67 68 69   Z[\]^_`abcdefghi
```

CP/M filenames

A filename identifies a particular file or group of files on a disk controlled by the CP/M operating system. References to filenames may be either 'unambiguous' (*ufn*) or 'ambiguous' (*afn*). An unambiguous filename uniquely identifies a single file, whilst an ambiguous file name is satisfied by a number of different files on the disk. A complete filename consists of two parts; a primary filename (eight characters or less) which may be used to identify a group of related files, and an optional file type (three characters or less) which is used to indicate the nature of the named file. The primary filename and type are separated by a '.' in the following manner:

filename.typ

An unambiguous filename consists of a mixture of alphabetic, numeric and other characters, which should ideally indicate the contents of the file. The following filenames demonstrate this point:

(i) BASIC-80 *BASIC interpreter*
(ii) BASCOM *BASIC compiler*
(iii) TEXTED *text editor*
(iv) DEBUG *debugger program*
(v) LOAD *loader program*

Certain characters may not be used in filenames since they have special meanings for the system, and these are:

< > . , ; : = ? * [ ] − % | ( ) / \

All other characters are allowed.

An ambiguous filename is used for directory search and pattern matching purposes. The form of an ambiguous filename is similar to that used for unambiguous filenames, except that the symbol '?' may be used to represent any character in the filename in that position, and the character '*' may be used to represent all characters in the filename following its use. These two characters are known as 'wildcard' characters. Therefore the ambiguous filename A?B?C?D? could represent unambiguous filenames A1B2C3D4, or AZBYCXDW, and the ambiguous filename ABC* could represent unambiguous filenames ABCDEF or ABCD1234. The * character may be used to replace all characters in the filename, thus the filename ???????? may be replaced by *.

CP/M file types

An optional file type consisting of up to three valid characters may be added to the filename to indicate the intended function of the file. Certain file types have evolved, and the use of such file types is advisable, and in some cases is mandatory. Examples of some of the commonly used file types are as follows:

(i) .ASC *file containing ASCII text*
(ii) .BAK *back-up file*
(iii) .BAS *BASIC language source file*
(iv) .COM *executable (command) program*
(v) .HEX *Intel HEX format object code file*
(vi) .PRN *assembly language print listing file*
(vii) .REL *relocatable object code file*
(viii) .TXT *document (text) file*
(ix) .ZSM *Z80 source code file*
(x) .$$$ *temporary file*

Ambiguous file types may be used, thus the file ambiguous file type .B?? may represent .BAS or .BAK . A filename without a file type is allowed and is treated as having a file type consisting of three spaces.

Specifying the drive associated with a file

Most development systems will be fitted with at least two disk drives. It is therefore important for the system to know which drive to access to locate a particular file. At any point in time, one drive is active and therefore immediately ready for disk transactions. This drive is known as the 'currently logged' drive or the 'default' drive, which in CP/M is always drive A after a cold start, and this is indicated by an A> prompt on the VDU screen. A user may access other drives in one of two ways: either change the default drive, or precede the filename with a drive reference. The default drive may be changed at any time when the CCP is waiting for console input by typing the disk drive reference (any of the letters A to P) followed by a colon (:), assuming that such a drive selected exists. Suppose for instance that the default drive is A, and the A> prompt is present on the left hand side of the console (VDU screen). The default drive may be changed to B in the following manner:

A>B: [RETURN]
B>   ←————console response

The source drive may also be specified in a command line by preceding the filename with a drive reference as shown in the following examples:

A:*filename.typ*   or   B:*filename.typ*

It is not necessary to specify a drive if the file exists on the default drive (although it does no harm), but in most cases the drive must be specified if the file is located on any other drive.

Built-in commands

Built-in commands are those commands which are included in the CCP and which are available whenever CP/M is loaded into the system. Further disk access is not required in order to execute these commands, although the commands themselves may access the disk system. The following built-in commands are available:

   (i) ERA   *erases specified files*
  (ii) DIR   *lists filenames in the directory*
 (iii) REN   *rename a specified file*
 (iv) SAVE *save memory contents as a file*
  (v) TYPE *display contents of a file*
 (vi) USER *partition disk into user areas*

The operation of each of these commands may be summarised as follows:

ERA

The ERA (*erase*) command removes files from the default disk. Files are not actually erased, but the first byte in the directory element relating to each file is changed from its active value of 0X (00 for user 0) to $E5_{16}$ which indicates that the file is inactive or erased. The files erased are those which satisfy the ambiguous file reference *afn*. The following examples illustrate the use of the ERA command:

ERA MYFILE.TXT *The file named MYFILE.TXT on the default drive is removed from the directory and the corresponding disk space is freed.*

ERA X.* *All files with the primary name X are removed from the default disk.*

ERA *.ZSM *All files with the secondary name .ZSM are removed from the default disk.*

ERA *.* *Erase all files on the default disk. In this case the CCP prompts with the message:*
ALL FILES (Y/N)?
and requires a 'Y' response before all files are actually removed.

ERA B:*.PRN *All files on drive B that satisfy the ambiguous file reference ????????.PRN are deleted from whichever default drive is used.*

DIR

The DIR (directory) command causes the names of all files that satisy the ambiguous filename *afn* to be listed at the console output (VDU). As a special case, the command:

DIR

lists all files on the default disk (the command 'DIR' is equivalent to the command 'DIR *.*'). Valid DIR commands are:

DIR MYFILE.TXT
DIR X?Z.C?M
DIR ??.Y

Similar to other CCP commands, the *afn* can be preceded by a drive reference. The following DIR commands cause the selected drive to be addressed before the directory search takes place:

DIR B: *display all filenames on disk B*
DIR B:MYFILE.TXT *display just this filename*
DIR B:*.ZSM *display all .ZSM files on disk B*

If no file on the selected disk satisfies the directory request, the message 'NO FILE' is printed at the console output.

REN *ufn1* = *ufn2*

The REN (rename) command allows the user to change the names of the files on a disk. The unambiguous file reference *ufn2* is changed to *ufn1*. The default disk is assumed to contain the file to rename (*ufn2*). Since the REN command merely makes changes to directory entries and does not perform any copy operations, *ufn1* and *ufn2* must have the same drive reference. Examples of the use of the REN command are:

REN NEW.TXT = OLD.TXT   *the file OLD.TXT is renamed NEW.TXT*
REN XYZ.COM = XYZ.XXX   *the file XYZ.XXX is renamed XYZ.COM*

The operator may precede either *ufn1* or *ufn2* with a drive reference. If *ufn1* is preceded with a drive reference, then *ufn2* is assumed to exist on the same drive. The same drive must be specified in both cases if *ufn1* and *ufn2* are preceded by drive references. The following REN commands demonstrate this:

REN A:X.ZSM = Y.ZSM   *file Y.ZSM is changed to X.ZSM on drive A*
REN B:NEW.BAS = OLD.BAS   *file OLD.BAS is renamed NEW.BAS on drive B*
REN B:A.ZSM = B:A.BAK   *file A.BAK is renamed A.ZSM on drive B*

If *ufn1* is already present, the REN command will respond with the error message 'FILE EXISTS' and not perform the change. If *ufn2* does not exist on the specified disk, the message 'NO FILE' is printed at the console output.

SAVE *n ufn*

The SAVE command stores '*n*' pages (256 byte blocks) of memory, starting from TPA address 0100H, onto disk and names this file with a *ufn* specified by the user. The value of '*n*' must be the number of pages in decimal. Examples of the use of this command are as follows:

SAVE 5 MYFILE.COM   *copies TPA addresses 0100H to 05FFH into a file called MYFILE.COM*
SAVE 40 XYZ   *copies TPA addresses 0100H to 28FFH into a file called XYZ*

The SAVE command can also specify a disk drive in the *ufn* portion of the command as shown in the following example:

SAVE 10 B:MYFILE.COM   *copies 10 pages (0100H to 0AFFH) into a file MYFILE.COM on drive B*

TYPE *ufn*

The TYPE command displays on the console output the contents of an ASCII source file, *ufn*, which is located on the default disk. Valid TYPE commands are:

TYPE MYFILE.TXT
TYPE X.ZSM
TYPE SEG7

The TYPE command may also include a drive reference:

TYPE B:X.PRN

Note that ctrl-P toggles the printer on and off, and may be used to simultaneously direct output to the printer. This facility enables hard copy of programs to be obtained.

USER

The USER *n* command allows maintenance of separate groups of files in the same directory, and takes the form:

USER *n*

where 'n' is an integer value in the range 0 to 15. Therefore each user number gives access only to those files in its own particular area. The first byte in the directory element is allocated the number 00, 01, 02 etc and indicates to which user the file is assigned.

Transient commands

Transient commands are stored on a disk as .COM files. When a command is issued which is not one of the built-in commands, the read/write head of the disk drive is stepped across the surface of the disk until the directory track is located (track 2). The directory is searched for a filename that matches the name of the file requested, and once located in the directory, the block numbers for the file are read from the directory and are copied into the RAM of the microcomputer. These block numbers are then translated into actual track and sector numbers by CP/M and the read/write head is stepped across the surface of the disk to the first sector of the file. Data is then read sequentially from the disk and is transferred into the TPA of the microcomputer. Once the complete file has been loaded (or as much loaded as necessary), the command is executed from address 0100H. This process is shown in Fig. 2.5.

If the name of the file requested cannot be traced in the directory, the message 'NO FILE' is displayed on the console output. The following examples are typical transient commands executed by CP/M:

STAT   *list the number of bytes of storage remaining on the default disk, provide statistical information about particular files, and display or alter device assignments.*

ZASM	*load the Z80 assembler and assemble the specified program from disk.*
ZSID	*load the Z80 debugger program into the TPA and start execution.*
PIP	*load the peripheral interface program for subsequent disk file and peripheral transfer operations.*
FORMAT	*initialise a new disk by laying down track and sector positions.*
SYSGEN	*create a copy of CP/M on a newly formatted disk.*

Transient commands are specified in the same manner as that used for built-in commands.

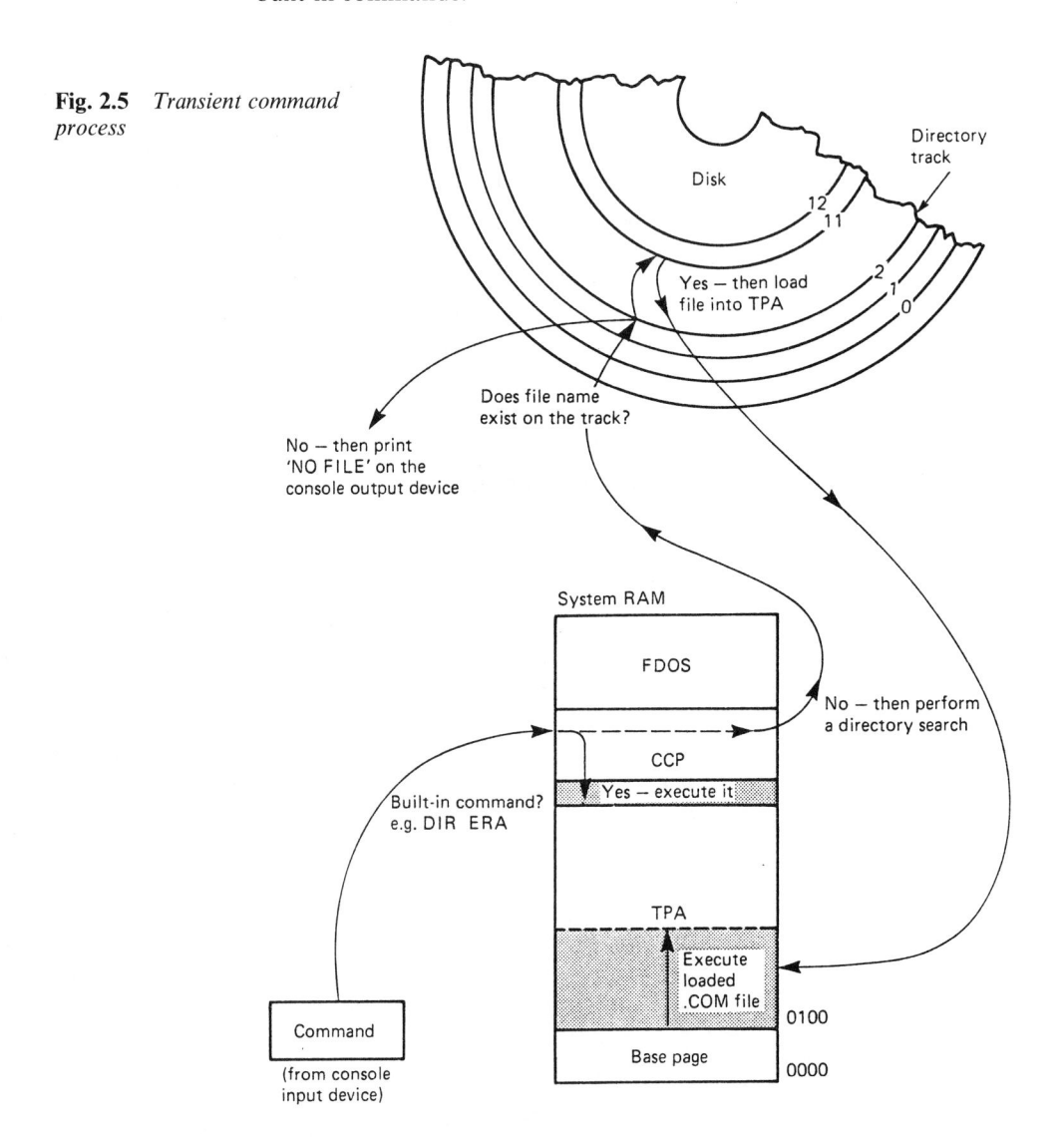

Fig. 2.5 *Transient command process*

Problems

1. (a) Explain why it is necessary for all microcomputers to have some form of operating system,
   (b) List *four* routines that are required in the operating system of a disk-based microcomputer.
2. Describe the advantages of having a standard operating system, e.g. CP/M, for all microcomputers.
3. With reference to a CP/M operating system, explain the difference between 'built-in' and 'transient' commands.
4. (a) With the aid of a diagram, show how CP/M is organised in a microcomputer with 64 K of memory, naming each section, and indicating typical addresses.
   (b) Explain how CP/M is organised so that programs may be written without considering the actual hardware configuration used.
5. (a) Explain how CP/M operating system routines may be incorporated into user's programs,
   (b) Write simple assembly language routines to enable CP/M routines to be used to carry out the following operations:
      (i) get input from the keyboard (console input),
      (ii) display an ASCII character (console output),
      (iii) print a text string.
6. With reference to a disk system, define the following terms:
   (i) physical sector,
   (ii) logical sector,
   (iii) track,
   (iv) block,
   (v) extent, and
   (vi) default drive.
7. (a) Explain what is meant by the term 'file',
   (b) describe how CP/M files are identified, and
   (c) show how a directory of files is maintained upon each disk.

3 Text Editors

Introduction

The initial stages in writing an assembly language program involve the preparation of 'source code'. Source code consists of a sequence of ASCII characters or text that represent instruction mnemonics, symbolic addresses and data for an assembly language program, and is usually stored as a disk file which is subsequently accessed by an assembler to generate the equivalent machine or object code.

Initially, source code must be entered via the keyboard in the usual way, but of course, errors may be inadvertently introduced which need subsequent correction. These errors may be obvious e.g. simple typing errors, and require correcting at the time the source code is being entered, or they may be errors which do not become apparent until after the program has been assembled or debugged.

In the case of simple typing errors, these may frequently be corrected by means of keyboard controls such as 'backspace' or 'delete' provided that this is carried out before the 'return' or 'enter' key is pressed to transfer the text from the keyboard buffer into the microcomputer.

For errors which are only discovered after the source code has been stored in a microcomputer, it is obvious that a facility is required which enables the contents of a text file to be altered or 'edited', since the alternative would be the tedious and time-wasting process of re-entering the whole of the work.

This facility, provided by a transient program known as a 'text editor', may also be used to create the original text file. A 'word processor', which may be considered as a more comprehensive text editor, may also be used to create assembly language source code, although when used for this purpose, many of its facilities will never be used.

The range of facilities found in different text editors varies considerably, but as a minimum requirement should enable the following processes to be carried out:

   (i) create and save new files
  (ii) open and close existing text files
 (iii) insert, delete or alter text in new or existing files
 (iv) print text files

Creating and saving new files

The use of a text editor implies that a text file already exists which requires correction or modification in some way. However, text files cannot be edited unless they have been created in the first place, therefore one of the functions of a text editor must be to create and save new files. From the user's point of view there is little difference between creating a new file and opening an existing file for editing purposes, save for the fact that the new file contains no text.

Some editors make a distinction between creating a new file and opening an existing file, and require slightly different commands, but for the majority of text editors, a command line is entered which has the following format:

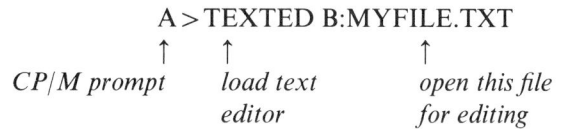

```
         A>TEXTED B:MYFILE.TXT
         ↑       ↑         ↑
CP/M prompt   load text   open this file
              editor      for editing
```

This command first causes the text editor (TEXTED.COM) to be loaded into the TPA. Next, a directory search is performed (in this case on drive B), and if a directory entry for MYFILE.TXT is found, this file is opened for editing.

If the filename requested is not found in the directory, a new file is opened on the disk with, in this case, the filename MYFILE.TXT, and an appropriate entry is made in the disk directory. The message 'NEW FILE' will probably appear on the VDU, then the editing facilities may be used to enter new text.

Eventually the user will wish to save the text created, and although it would appear that the proper time to do this is when all editing work has been completed, it is a good idea to save partially completed work at regular intervals, especially when creating very large files. This procedure avoids losing large amounts of work should the system crash or the mains supply be interrupted, since all work up to the last save operation will still be intact on the disk.

The method used to terminate an editing session will depend upon the type of text editor, but typically the following options are provided:

(i) abandon the work—nothing is saved
(ii) save the text and return to CP/M
(iii) save the text and select a different file to edit
(iv) save the text and continue to edit the same file

The first option is used mainly when an existing file is reviewed, but it is decided that changes are not required. This avoids the necessity of re-saving an unchanged file. This option may also be used when it is decided that a newly created file is not required after all.

The second option is used when completion of editing a particular file terminates an editing session completely. If this option is selected, the editor returns control to CP/M which then allows other programs to be run.

The third option is selected when the user wishes to terminate editing of one file, but wishes to start editing a different file. In this case, the current work is saved, the text editor remains loaded in the microcomputer, and the user is invited to select a further file for editing.

The final option is used when the user wishes to continue editing the same file, but wishes to update the disk file to safeguard against losing the newly edited version of text should the system crash or the mains supply be interrupted. After saving all work, the editor allows the user to continue from the point.

The edit buffer

Before the text in a disk file can be edited, it must first be loaded into the microcomputer's RAM i.e. into the TPA. The text editor itself resides in the TPA, therefore the amount of free RAM space is limited. Usually a fixed amount of RAM (4K to 12K bytes) is set aside as editing workspace, and this is known as the '*edit buffer*'. The size of the edit buffer should not itself impose a limit on the maximum size of the file that may be processed (although it does so with certain editors). The system is therefore arranged so that the edit buffer contains only a small segment of the file, i.e. that part currently being edited.

When the user wishes to edit text which lies outside the limits of the edit buffer, the disk file must be accessed. The current contents of the edit buffer are written back onto disk, and the next segment of text is loaded into the edit buffer to replace its previous contents. This process may appear to be a little complicated, but it is the responsibility of the person who devised the text editor to ensure that the software causes this process to occur automatically whenever necessary. All that the user should notice is that disk drive activity occurs upon reaching certain points in the text.

Opening and closing files

In order to start editing the contents of a disk file, the file must first be '*opened*', and upon completion of this process, the file must be '*closed*'. Files are usually opened and closed automatically when a text editor is used, but a better understanding of the operation of a text editor may be obtained by studying the processes involved.

Information concerning all file operations is stored in a 36 byte block of memory called a '*file control block*' or FCB. In CP/M, addresses $005C_{16}$ to $007F_{16}$ are frequently used for this purpose, and are known as the '*default file control block*'. When the user wishes to edit a file, the filename which forms part of the command line is stored in the FCB by the BDOS. A BDOS '*open file*' operation is then performed, which causes CP/M to scan the directory of the default disk for a matching entry with the filename stored in the FCB. If found, information concerning that file, i.e. block numbers, are copied from the directory into the FCB. If there is no match, then a BDOS '*make file*' operation is performed to create a new directory entry.

Typical FCB and buffer information is illustrated by the following memory dumps:

```
005C: 0D 43 48 41
      .  C  H  A
0060: 50 33 20 20 20 54 58 54 00 00 00 00 00 20 20 20
       P  3           T  X  T  .  .  .  .  .
0070: 20 20 20 20 20 20 20 20 00 00 00 00 00 00 00 00
                               .  .  .  .  .  .  .  .
```

(i) *File control block prior to directory search*

```
                                        total no,
         Drive                          of records
           ↓                               |
005C: 0D 43 48 41      extent no,      |  block no,
      .  C  H  A           ↓           ↓  ↓
0060: 50 33 20 20 20 54 58 54 00 02 80 05 31 00 00 00
       P  3           T  X  T  .  .  .  |  .  .  .
0070: 00 00 00 00 00 00 00 00 00 00 00 00 01 00 00 00
       .  .  .  .  .  .  .  .  .  .  .  . ↑ .  .  .
      ←space for 15 more blocks→         current
                                         record no,
```

(ii) *File control block after directory search*

```
1000: 54 68 65 20 69 6E 69 74 69 61 6C 20 73 74 61 67
       T  h  e     i  n  i  t  i  a  l     s  t  a  g
1010: 65 20 69 6E 20 77 72 69 74 69 6E 67 20 61 6E 20
       e     i  n     w  r  i  t  i  n  g     a  n
1020: 61 73 73 65 6D 62 6C 79 20 6C 61 6E 67 75 61 67
       a  s  s  e  m  b  l  y     l  a  n  g  u  a  g
1030: 65 20 70 72 6F 67 72 61 6D 20 69 6E 76 6F 6C 76
       e     p  r  o  g  r  a  m     i  n  v  o  l  v
1040: 65 73 20 74 68 65 20 0D 0A 70 72 65 70 61 72 61
       e  s     t  h  e     .  .  p  r  e  p  a  r  a
1050: 74 69 6F 6E 20 6F 66 20 27 73 6F 75 72 63 65 20
       t  i  o  n     o  f     '  s  o  u  r  c  e
1060: 63 6F 64 65 27 2E 20 20 54 68 65 20 73 6F 75 72
       c  o  d  e  '  .        T  h  e     s  o  u  r
1070: 63 65 20 63 6F 64 65 20 63 6F 6E 73 69 73 74 73
       c  e     c  o  d  e     c  o  n  s  i  s  t  s
```

(iii) *Buffer dump after reading first 128 byte record*

```
005C: 0D 43 48 41
      .  C  H  A
0060: 50 33 20 20 20 54 58 54 00 02 80 05 31 00 00 00
       P  3           T  X  T  .  .  .  .  1  .  .  .
0070: 00 00 00 00 00 00 00 00 00 00 00 00 02 00 00 00
       .  .  .  .  .  .  .  .  .  .  .  .  ↑  .  .  .
                                          current
                                          record no. (updated)
```

(iv) *File control block after reading first record*

```
1000: 20 6F 66 20 61 20 73 65 71 75 65 6E 63 65 20 6F
          o  f     a     s  e  q  u  e  n  c  e     o
1010: 66 20 0D 0A 41 53 43 49 49 20 63 68 61 72 61 63
       f  .  .  . A  S  C  I  I     c  h  a  r  a  c
1020: 74 65 72 73 20 6F 72 20 74 65 78 74 20 74 68 61
       t  e  r  s     o  r     t  e  x  t     t  h  a
1030: 74 20 72 65 70 72 65 73 65 6E 74 20 69 6E 73 74
       t     r  e  p  r  e  s  e  n  t     i  n  s  t
1040: 72 75 63 74 69 6F 6E 20 6D 6E 65 6D 6F 6E 69 63
       r  u  c  t  i  o  n     m  n  e  m  o  n  i  c
1050: 73 2C 20 73 79 6D 62 6F 6C 69 63 20 0D 0A 61 64
       s  ,     s  y  m  b  o  l  i  c     .  .  a  d
1060: 64 72 65 73 73 65 73 20 61 6E 64 20 64 61 74 61
       d  r  e  s  s  e  s     a  n  d     d  a  t  a
1070: 20 66 6F 72 20 61 6E 20 61 73 73 65 6D 62 6C 79
          f  o  r     a  n     a  s  s  e  m  b  l  y
```

(v) *Buffer dump after reading second 128 byte record*

It can be seen that one byte of the FCB is reserved as a '*record*' counter, that is automatically updated by the BDOS as each logical sector is read from the disk. This particular file (first page of this chapter) consists of five 128-byte records.

Records are usually read by means of a BDOS '*read sequential*' operation. Therefore, each time that editing progresses beyond the current limit, the system writes the edited buffer contents to disk and is then able to read the next record in sequence into the buffer for further editing. An edited file may well be larger or smaller than the original version, since text may have been inserted or deleted, therefore it is necessary to update the directory. This is carried out by means of a BDOS '*close file*' operation which copies updated FCB information back onto the directory track of the disk, i.e. performs the reverse of an '*open file*' operation.

Files created during editing

When editing a text file, of necessity there are frequent transfers of text between disk and edit buffer. If the user edits the original or main file, changes will be made to that file each time that the edit buffer is written back onto the disk. This is not an ideal situation, since it is possible for parts of the file to become corrupted, or worse still, accidentally erased. The obvious solution to this problem is to make a copy of the main file, and edit this file. Should this file become corrupted or erased, the user still has the original main file, and has only lost work carried out between the current and previous edits. In most text editors, this process takes place automatically, although it does take a certain amount of organisation on the part of the person who devised the text editor program. It is usual for a text editor to read the main file only, and store the edited version in a completely different file. The previously edited version of the file is then retained as a 'back-up' copy should there be anything wrong with the edited version. Three different file types may be created when the source code for an assembly language program is edited, and assuming that the primary file name is 'MYFILE', these are:

MYFILE.ZSM   *assembly language source file (latest version)*
MYFILE.$$$ *temporary file, used during editing only*
MYFILE.BAK   *back-up file (version before latest edit session)*

Each time that MYFILE.ZSM is opened for edit, a new file called MYFILE.$$$ (temporary file) is automatically created on the disk. Unedited text from MYFILE.ZSM or edited text from MYFILE.$$$ is read into the edit buffer for processing. All write operations are to the temporary file MYFILE.$$$. At the end of the editing session, the text is located in three different places. Completely edited text is contained in the temporary file MYFILE.$$$, partially edited text remains in the edit buffer, and text which is to remain unchanged is still in the original file MYFILE.ZSM. The editing process is terminated by transferring the contents of the edit buffer, followed by the remaining text from the original file MYFILE.ZSM into the temporary file MYFILE.$$$. The original file MYFILE.ZSM is then renamed as MYFILE.BAK, and the temporary file MYFILE.$$$ is renamed as MYFILE.ZSM. This process is shown in Fig. 3.1.

Types of text editor

There are basically two types of text editor, the *'line'* editor and the *'on-screen'* editor.

The line editor identifies each line of text with a line number, and each character with a character pointer. Text is called into the edit buffer by number and is displayed, one line at a time, for editing. The character pointer may be an imaginary pointer, or may be a visible marker on the VDU screen, i.e. a cursor. If the character pointer is imaginary, then it must be moved to the appropriate position in the text by means of a command

Fig. 3.1 *Editing a new source file*

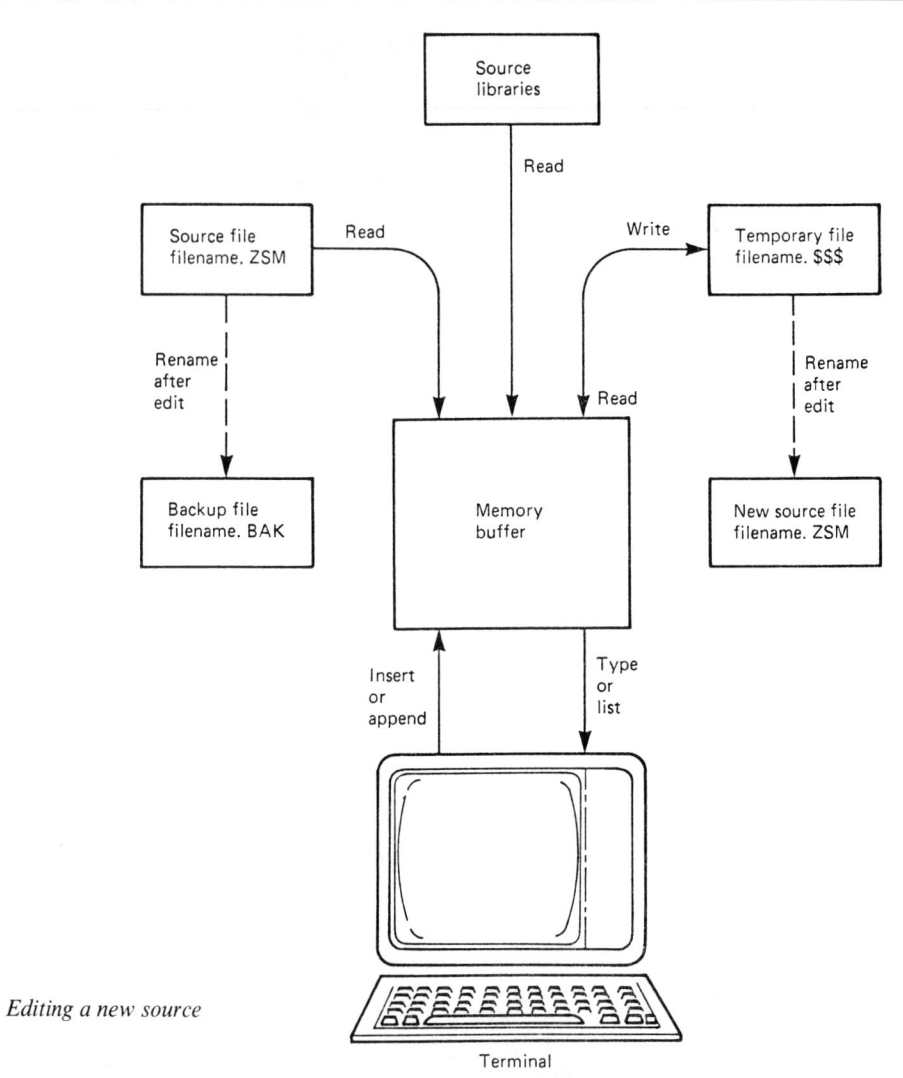

containing a position reference number. If a visible cursor is used, then it must be moved to the desired position for editing by means of cursor control commands or cursor positioning keys. Some editors require the whole line to be re-entered if changes are required, others allow individual characters or words to be inserted, changed or deleted. After the necessary changes have been made, the edited line replaces the original line in the text file.

The on-screen editor displays a segment of the edit buffer continuously on the VDU screen, and a movable cursor is positioned on the displayed text to indicate the point at which corrections are to be made. When alterations are made to the text in the edit buffer, these changes are also echoed to the VDU screen, thus allowing the user to see the overall effects of such changes. If an attempt is made to move the cursor off the top or bottom of the VDU screen, the screen scrolls and a different part of the text buffer is displayed. If the user attempts to display text which is outside the limits of the edit buffer, then disk operations take place which transfer text from the edit buffer into the temporary file (the .$$$ file), and read further text into the edit buffer (see Fig. 3.2).

On-screen editing is generally simpler to use since the operator can view much more of the text, and the VDU screen shows text exactly as it will be stored in the disk file. Frequently, keyboards are set up to have special keys for editing functions so that it is not necessary to remember special control key sequences.

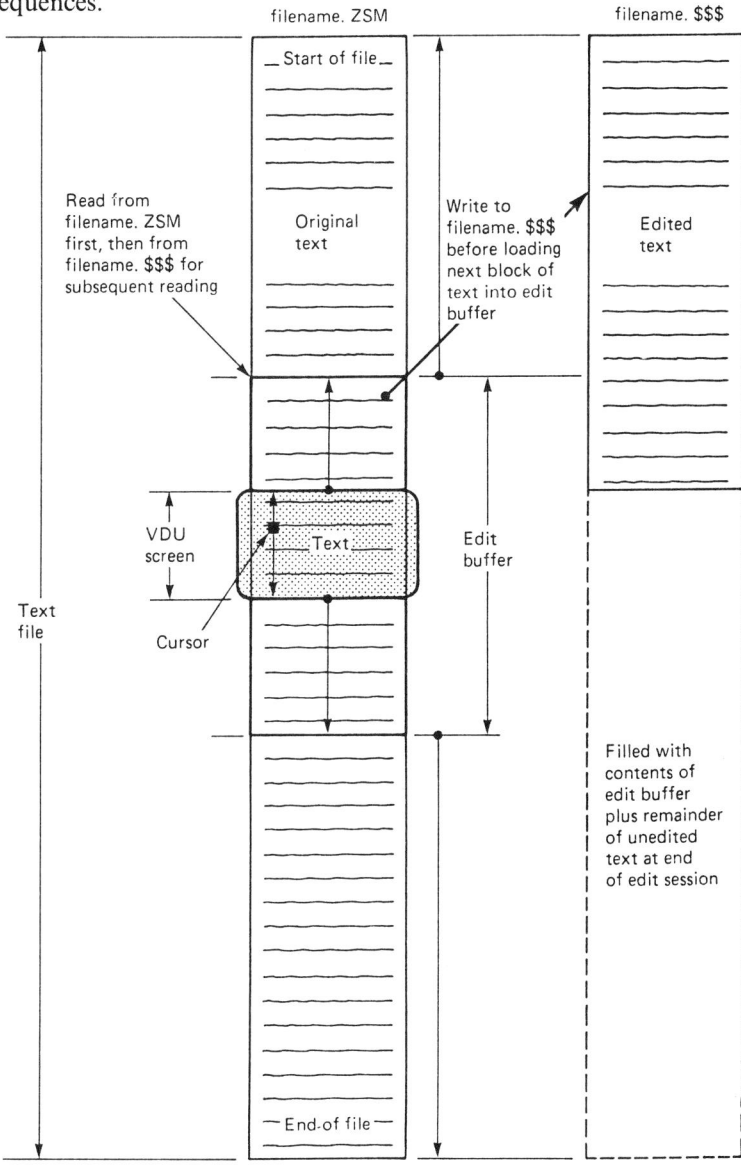

Fig. 3.2 *Relationship between VDU screen, edit buffer and text file*

Practical text editors

Sometimes an editor is included with a particular item of software. This is often the case with certain high level languages, but for most assembly language writing a separate text editor is required. A wide range of different text editors are available to the user of CP/M based systems, but selection of a particular text editor should be based upon ease of operation, and whether text files produced by it are capable of being read by an assembler.

Sophisticated text editors are available which are intended to replace dedicated word processing systems for business and commercial applications. Such word processors may often be suitable for producing assembly language source files, although many of the facilities provided will be unused in this particular application. A problem may arise with certain word processors, since they introduce special non-printable codes into the text which are used to control the way in which the text is displayed or printed. Some of these may be unsuitable for editing assembly language statements and may cause confusion in an assembler unless they also possess facilities for creating '*non-document*' files, in which case such codes are eliminated.

Since each text editor has its own different set of operating instructions and commands, only a brief description of the facilities found in two contrasting types of editor is included in this chapter. Detailed operating instructions are normally in the documentation accompanying a text editor program disk, and reference should be made to this source for complete details of available commands.

ED text editor

This is a line and character oriented text editor which is issued with CP/M. Unfortunately ED was developed prior to VDU based computers becoming widely available when communication with a microcomputer largely took place using a Teletype™ machine. This has caused ED to acquire a poor reputation for ease of use, and certainly editing and reviewing text is a rather difficult process with the obscure commands provided. Except for certain jobs, few programmers would use ED by choice if an alternative on-screen editor were available. It is therefore intended to include here only brief information about ED so that it may be compared with the alternative on-screen editors. Those users wishing to use ED seriously will find full documentation in the relevant CP/M manuals.

Summary of ED operations

(i) Invoking ED:
   A > ED *filename.typ* [RETURN]
   :* *command*

This applies to editing new files or creating new files. The ED prompt '*' indicates that an edit command may be entered. Type 'E' to end the edit.

(ii) Command groups:
   (a) *transfer text*
   (b) *work on edit buffer*
   (c) *search and change text*

A number of individual commands may be combined and entered as a single command line.

(iii) Commands:

nA	*append n lines from source file to ED workspace*
0A	*append lines from source file until workspace is half full*
#A	*append lines from source file until workspace is full or end of file*
B, —B	*move WP to beginning (B) or end (—B) of workspace*
nC	*move WP n characters forwards (backwards if n is negative)*
nD	*delete n characters after WP (before if n is negative)*
E	*save file, return to CP/M*
F string↑Z	*find string in workspace beyond WP position*
H	*save current file, re-open and use this file as source*
i	*enter insert mode, use ↑Z to exit*
i string↑Z	*insert string at position of WP*
nK	*delete n lines after WP (before if n is negative)*
nL	*move WP n lines forward (backwards if n is negative)*
0L	*move WP to beginning of current line*
nMcommands	*execute given command n times*
n	*move WP n lines forward (backwards if n is negative) and display that line*
n:	*move WP to line n and display that line*
O	*abandon editing, return to original for re-editing*
nP	*move WP forwards (backwards if n is negative) through workspace and display all lines*
Q	*abandon edit and return to CP/M*
Rfilespec↑Z	*read named file into ED workspace, append it to whatever is already there,*
nSold-string↑Z	*new-string*
	replaces n occurrences of old-string with new-string, the search carried out forwards from WP
nT	*displays n lines after WP (before if n is negative) leaving WP in original position*
nW	*write first n lines in workspace to destination file, and*
nXfilespec	*writes n lines from workspace into named file, appending them to any other lines already there due to a previous nXfilespec command.*

(WP = workspace pointer)

WordStar®

MicroPro's WordStar is high quality software which turns any CP/M based computer into a wordprocessor. It makes full use of the on-screen facilities, and allows the user to configure or 'install' it so that it may operate on a wide range of different terminals and printers. CP/M-80 computers running WordStar therefore became very popular for business word processing applications, and for a long time remained supreme.

The current range of word processors running on 16-bit microcomputers with more advanced terminals now make the original WordStar look a little dated in terms of its business applications.

For the preparation of assembly language source code, however, the original WordStar is still more than adequate, and many of the features provided, mostly with business applications in mind, are unlikely ever to be used. WordStar has had considerable influence on the design of text editors generally, and many are now available which are basically simplified versions of it. This has the obvious advantage that once learnt, commands used for WordStar are equally applicable to a much wider range of software. The following descriptions consider only those aspects of WordStar which are of general use to the assembly language writer and are therefore mostly applicable to the general range of text editors which are based on WordStar.

Installation

Most on-screen text editors must be 'installed' so that they function correctly in their intended environment. Basically this means that certain parts of a text editor program must be altered to take into account the characteristics of different types of terminal (keyboard and VDU) and printer.

Text editor software is usually written so that all peripheral-dependent variables are stored in one block of memory, therefore installation essentially consists of entering appropriate data bytes into this block. Although it is possible to patch this block manually, it is more usual to make use of an '*install*' program which is supplied as part of the text editor package. An install program prompts the user for answers to a series of questions which it poses regarding the characteristics of the peripheral hardware. The answers to these questions determine what is stored in the table of variables and upon completion of the installation process, the text editor program is modified accordingly.

Libraries of data for the more popular peripherals are usually supplied to simplify the installation procedure, but if the intended peripheral is not listed, then it becomes necessary to carry out a full installation, after which the user is normally given the option of adding this peripheral data to the library.

A typical installation sequence consists of the following steps:

(i) **Select terminal type**

The user will normally be presented with a terminal selection menu, having typically the following format:

******   TERMINAL MENU   ******

1. Lear-Siegler ADM-3A
2. Hazeltine 1500
3. Wyse WY-50
4. Lear-Siegler ADM-31
5. Volker-Craig VC4404
6. None of the above

SELECT NUMBER REQUIRED

If the terminal used is not listed in the menu, then 'None of the above' (option 6) is selected, and the user is asked a sequence of questions to which answers concerning the terminal must be given. Typically the following questions are included:

How many screen columns?
How many screen rows?
Cursor position lead-in sequence?
Is the row sent before the column (Y/N)?
Offset for column?
Offset for row?
Clear screen sequence?
Clear to end of line sequence?

The current settings are usually displayed after each question, and the user either supplies a new setting or [RETURN] to leave unchanged.

(ii) **Select printer type**

The user may also be presented with a printer selection menu, having typically the following format:

******   PRINTER MENU   ******

1. Any 'Teletype-like' printer
2. 'Teletype-like' with BACKSPACE
3. QUME Sprint 5 daisy wheel
4. DIABLO 1610/1620 daisy wheel
5. NEC Spinwriter
6. None of the above

SELECT NUMBER REQUIRED

(iii) **Re-defining commands**

Although the commands to perform the various text editing functions are pre-defined, some text editors allow these commands to be re-defined during installation. This allows the commands to be set up to suit the personal preferences of the user, for example to give compatibility with other software, or to simplify keyboard operation.

Commands

The WordStar commands which are likely to be of most use when preparing assembly language source code may be grouped as follows:

(i) **Cursor moving commands**

Right/Left	character	[CTRL]-S / [CTRL]-D
Right/Left	word	[CTRL]-F / [CTRL]-A
Tab right		[CTRL]-I
Start/End	line	[CTRL]-S / [CTRL]-D
Start/End	file	[CTRL]-QR / [CTRL]-QC
Up/Down	line	[CTRL]-E / [CTRL]-X
Up/Down	screen	[CTRL]-C / [CTRL]-R

(ii) **Text insert/delete commands**

Toggle INSERT (ON/OFF)	[CTRL]-V
Delete line	[CTRL]-Y
Delete character left/right	[DEL] / [CTRL]-G
Delete word right	[CTRL]-T
Delete to end/start of line	[CTRL]-QY / [CTRL]-Q[DEL]

(iii) **Block commands**

Mark start/end of block	[CTRL]-KB / [CTRL]-KK
Copy/move marked block	[CTRL]-KC / [CTRL]-KV
Delete marked block	[CTRL]-KY
Read file (insert at cursor)	[CTRL]-KR
Write marked block to file	[CTRL]-KW

(iv) **Search and replace commands**

Find string	[CTRL]-QF
Find and replace all	[CTRL]-QA
Find/replace next occurrence	[CTRL]-L

(v) **Saving files**

Save and continue edit	[CTRL]-S
Save, edit finished	[CTRL]-D
Save, exit to CP/M	[CTRL]-X
Save, abandon edit	[CTRL]-Q

Most assembly language writers will find that this abbreviated list of WordStar commands is quite adequate for most purposes, and in any case, is probably all that will be provided with the majority of text editors based upon this word processor.

Word processors and text editors are usually well documented, with on-screen '*help*' menus which considerably assist users during the initial learning stages. WordStar is particularly helpful in this respect, with the option of displaying full on-screen help most of the time.

Typical WordStar menus

When starting WordStar without specifying a file name, or when editing is terminated, a 'no-file' menu is displayed which allows the user to select from the list of options presented by entering a single command letter. A typical no-file menu is displayed as follows:

```
             editing no file

   D = create or edit a Document file       H = set Help level
   N = create or edit a Non-document file   X = eXit to system
   M = Merge print a file                   P = Print a file
   F = File directory off (ON)              Y = delete a file
   L = change Logged disk drive             O = cOpy a file
   R = Run a program                        E = rEname a file

   DIRECTORY of disk A:
```

For the creation of assembly language source code, the 'Non-document' option should be used.

After selecting the appropriate option, further instructions are printed on the screen to prompt the user for the necessary inputs. For example, if the 'L' option (change logged disk drive) is selected, the following display is obtained:

```
      L          editing no file

      The LOGGED DISK (or Current Disk or Default Disk) is the
      disk drive used for files except those files for which
      you enter a disk drive name as part of the file name.
      WordStar displays the File Directory of the Logged Disk.

      THE LOGGED DISK DRIVE IS NOW A:

      NEW LOGGED DISK DRIVE (letter, colon, RETURN)?

      DIRECTORY of disk A:
```

Once a file has been opened for editing, or a new file has been created, a screen display of the following type appears:

```
           A:MYFILE.TXT   FC=1 FL=1 COL 1        INSERT ON

CURSOR:  ^A=left word     ^S=left char    ^D=right char   ^F=right word
         ^E=up line       ^X=down line
SCROLL:  ^Z=up line       ^W=down line    ^C=up screen    ^R=down screen
DELETE   DEL=char left    ^G=char right   ^T=word right   ^Y=entire line
OTHER:   ^V=insert off/on ^I=tab          RETURN=end para ^U=stop
         ^N=insert a RETURN ^B=reform to end para    ^L=find/replace again
HELP:    ^J displays menu of information commands
PREFIX KEYS      ^Q ^J ^K ^O ^P display menus of additional commands

                          space for text
```

Other similar help menus may be selected by the use of ^Q, ^J, ^K, ^O and ^P keys, and the level of help is controllable according to the experience of the user. The highly experienced user has the option of suppressing all help menus to give a greater screen area for text.

Problems

1. Explain why a text editor is required in order to create a Z80 assembly language source code file.
2. Describe five essential features of a text editor suitable for producing Z80 source code programs in a disk-based microcomputer.
3. Describe the main differences between 'line' and 'on-screen' editors.
4. Explain how it is possible for a text editor to edit files which are much larger than the available memory in a microcomputer.
5. (a) Explain why it is usual for a text editor to maintain a temporary file during the editing process, and
   (b) explain why a 'back-up' file may be produced upon terminating an editing session.
6. Explain why it may be necessary to 'install' an on-screen text editor before it can be used with a given microcomputer.

4 Assemblers

Introduction

Many people find their introduction to programming at machine code level a rather tedious process, since initial attempts invariably make use of 'hand assembly'. This is a process which requires a programmer to spend much time looking up opcodes for each instruction, performing various calculations in binary or hexadecimal, and simultaneously keeping track of many different addresses. Unfortunately this often creates the impression that programming microprocessors at machine code level is an almost impossible task. In fact it soon becomes obvious that a better method must be found if writing of serious programs is to be contemplated, since hand assembly is inevitably both time consuming and error-prone. Such a method consists of writing programs at 'assembly language' level, and using an assembler program to generate all necessary machine code for the microprocessor. Assembly language consists of a sequence of instruction mnemonics, labels and symbolic addresses which make programs much easier to follow. Hand assembly is normally used only for very minor alterations to existing programs, i.e. for 'patching'.

The advantages of writing programs in assembly language rather than machine language using hexadecimal codes become very obvious, and may be summarised as follows:

(i) shorter program writing time
(ii) no need to look up instruction opcodes
(iii) less error-prone
(iv) symbolic addresses may be used to eliminate the need to keep track of absolute addresses
(v) labels may be assigned to addresses in the program as references for jumps and calls
(vi) relative jump offsets are calculated automatically at assembly time
(vii) references to addresses are automatically readjusted when instructions are added or deleted or when the program is assembled at a new starting address.

Nature of an assembler

An assembler is a program which has been written to perform the specific task of converting assembly language source code for a given microprocessor into its equivalent machine or object code.

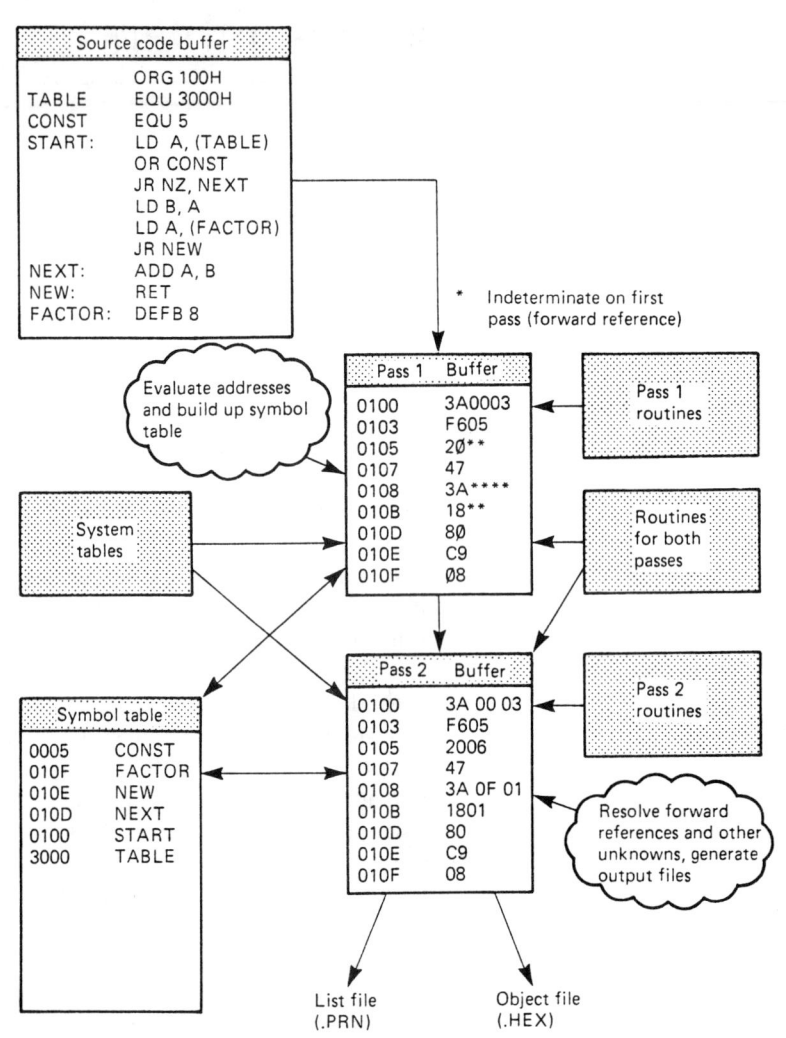

Fig. 4.1 Basic operation of an assembler

```
Source code buffer
            ORG 100H
TABLE       EQU 3000H
CONST       EQU 5
START:      LD A, (TABLE)
            OR CONST
            JR NZ, NEXT
            LD B, A
            LD A, (FACTOR)
            JR NEW
NEXT:       ADD A, B
NEW:        RET
FACTOR:     DEFB 8
```

Evaluate addresses and build up symbol table

* Indeterminate on first pass (forward reference)

Pass 1 Buffer
0100	3A0003
0103	F605
0105	20**
0107	47
0108	3A****
010B	18**
010D	80
010E	C9
010F	08

Pass 1 routines

System tables

Routines for both passes

Symbol table
0005	CONST
010F	FACTOR
010E	NEW
010D	NEXT
0100	START
3000	TABLE

Pass 2 Buffer
0100	3A 00 03
0103	F605
0105	2006
0107	47
0108	3A 0F 01
010B	1801
010D	80
010E	C9
010F	08

Pass 2 routines

Resolve forward references and other unknowns, generate output files

List file (.PRN) Object file (.HEX)

Each assembler generally assembles code for the same type of microprocessor as that on which it runs, but since its main task is essentially one of processing numeric and textual data, it may equally well be written to act as an assembler for a different type of microprocessor. In this case it is then known as a 'cross-assembler'.

Since each assembler program operates in a manner determined by its creator, it must not be assumed that all assemblers require identical source code formats. Certain assembly language conventions are defined by the manufacturer of each different type of microprocessor, and although, for the sake of compatibility, it makes sense to adhere to these conventions, software writers often have other ideas. Frequently the differences are only of a minor nature, but in extreme cases, totally non-standard mnemonics may be encountered. Some assemblers are written such that they are flexible enough to accept most of the commonly used source code variations. It therefore follows that reference to software manuals regarding the precise operating details of a given assembler is a pre-requisite for performing successful assembly. An assembler typically performs two passes through source code which has previously been read from a disk file. On the first pass, each line of source code is scanned by the assembler, and values are assigned to labels and mnemonics in so far as this is possible. A location counter is initialised by an ORG (origin) directive in the source code, and as each instruction is processed, this location counter is incremented according to the number of bytes required for that particular instruction. Using the location counter, a symbol table is built up which associates each label in a program with the address that it represents. This process is illustrated in Fig. 4.1.

Labels and expressions which are used as operands are also evaluated, although it is not always possible for an assembler to fully evaluate all operands during the first pass, since references may be made to parts of the program which are yet to be processed. Such references are known as 'forward references', and these can only be resolved once the symbol table is complete, thus necessitating a second pass through the source code.

After completion of the second pass, object code is optionally written to disk. Errors detected in the source code during either pass may prevent correct assembly from taking place and will lead to the generation of error messages.

CP/M assemblers

Although originally devised to run on machines using the 8080 microprocessor, nowadays CP/M is more often used with Z80 based microcomputers. Assemblers such as ASM, MAC and RMAC are frequently supplied with CP/M for assembly of 8080 machine code programs which are fully compatible with the Z80 microprocessor at object code level, but to make full use of the Z80 instruction set, a full Z80 assembler is required.

A number of different Z80 assemblers are available to run under CP/M, e.g. ZASM, Z80ASM, GEN80, PASM and M80. Some assemblers generate relocatable code (.REL files) which is an essential requirement where programs are developed in modular form, for example when linking assembly language routines to code produced by high level languages. This chapter concentrates on assemblers which produce non-relocatable code, since these produce object files which may be debugged without the need for linking, and are in general much simpler for the beginner to use. Once this type of assembler has been mastered, it is then quite straightforward to concentrate on the different techniques required for relocatable assemblers. Consequently, these are considered along with linking in Chapter 6.

The following descriptions should be considered as being of a general nature rather than specific to one particular assembler. They indicate the types of facilities available on most assemblers, but variations in detail will most certainly be encountered.

Assembling a program

A non-relocating assembler reads Z80 language source files from disk, and generates Z80 machine code, usually in Intel hex format. The assembler itself is a transient command, with a file name such as ZASM.COM, and is brought into operation by entering a command line of the following format:

ZASM *filename*

Some assemblers allow a file type to be specified, but often a fixed file type is assumed, e.g. ZSM. In this case the assembler assumes that a file exists on the current logged drive with the name:

filename.ZSM

and which contains Z80 assembly language source code. Upon receipt of this command, the assembler is loaded into the TPA, and a sign-on message is printed at the console to alert the user that the assembler has been loaded. This message typically has the following format:

ZASM Z80 ASSEMBLER V3.0A

Copyright © 1979 by Research Machines

The assembler then reads assembly language source code sequentially from a disk file, and performs its assembly processes. Upon completion of this task, output files may be optionally written back onto the disk, but it is usual to postpone writing these output files to disk until an error-free assembly has been achieved. There is little point in storing errors onto disk, particularly where large files are concerned, due to the length of time taken to store them. The following files may be created by the assembler:

filename.HEX

which is a machine code program (object code) in Intel hex format corresponding to the original source program, which may be used for debugging and testing purposes, and:

filename.PRN

which is a print file which contains a fully annotated listing (source and object codes) which may be used for documenting a program and for tracing errors. In addition, some assemblers produce the file:

filename.SYM

which is a sorted symbol table listing which may be used in conjunction with symbolic debuggers. Alternatively, the sorted symbols may appear at the end of a PRN listing.

Examples of all three types of file are as follows:

Source program (SAMPLE.ZSM)

```
                ORG   100H         ;transient program area
        BDOS    EQU   5            ;BDOS entry point
        WCHAR   EQU   2            ;write character function
        ;             enter with CCP's return address in the stack
        ;             write a single character (?) and return
                LD    C,WCHAR      ;write character function
                LD    E,'?'        ;character to write
                CALL  BDOS         ;write the character
                RET                ;return to the CCP
                END   100H         ;end address is 100H
```

Assembler HEX output file (SAMPLE.HEX)

```
:080100000E021E3FCD0500C9EF
:00010000FF
```

Assembler listing file (SAMPLE.PRN)

```
0100                    ORG   100H         ;transient program area
0005=           BDOS    EQU   5            ;BDOS entry point
0002=           WCHAR   EQU   2            ;write character function
                ;             enter with CCP's return address in the stack
                ;             write a single character (?) and return
0100 0E02               LD    C,WCHAR      ;write character function
0102 1E3F               LD    E,'?'        ;character to write
0104 CD0500             CALL  BDOS         ;write the character
0107 C9                 RET                ;return to the CCP
0108                    END   100H         ;end address is 100H
```

Assembler sorted symbol file (SAMPLE.SYM)

```
        0005 BDOS        0002 WCHAR
```

Assembly language statements

Programs written using assembly language consist of a sequence of statements, and each statement consists of between one and five fields. A field is a group of characters, and fields are separated from each other by at least one space. The fields of a typical assembly language program are as follows:

Line No.   Label   Mnemonic   Operand(s)   Comment

and these fields may be identified in the following program segment:

```
Line     Label     Mnemonic  Operand(s)   Comments

0000     START:    LD        HL,0200H     ;outer loop counter
0001               LD        C,0          ;inner loop counter
0002     DELAY:    DEC       C            ;count down inner loop
0003               JP        NZ,DELAY     ;loop until timed out
0004               DEC       HL           ;count down outer loop
0005               LD        A,H          ;test for HL=0,(DEC HL
0006               OR        L            ; does not set flags)
0007               JP        NZ,DELAY     ;loop until timed out
```

Line numbers

Line numbers may be required in an assembly language source program when using certain assemblers, are not permitted in others, but are optional in most. The range of numbers allowed is usually 0000 to 9999 decimal. It may often be helpful to number each line of assembly language for cross-referencing of labels, particularly in large programs. Where line numbers are not permitted in the source code there is often the option to add them automatically at assembly time.

Labels

A label is a sequence of characters which act as an identifier, and represent an instruction address which may need to be referenced by other instructions within a program. Labels are used instead of the hexadecimal addresses that they represent for two reasons,

(i) at the time of writing the source code, the actual address is probably unknown, and

(ii) the use of meaningful labels is an aid to following the flow of a program

As an example of the use of a label, consider the following segment of machine code:

```
0125    0D              DELAY:    DEC    C
0126    C2 25 01                  JP     NZ,DELAY
```

At the time of writing the source code, the address of the DEC C instruction is unknown, but is assigned the label DELAY. During the assembly process, the actual address of the DEC C instruction is evaluated, and the label is recorded as being equivalent to address 0125H. This information is stored by the assembler in a 'symbol table'. When a subsequent reference is made to this label, as in the case of the instruction JP NZ,DELAY, the assembler searches the symbol table for an entry DELAY, and once found, determines the address represented by the label and substitutes this as the operand for the JP instruction. In this case, JP NZ,DELAY is equivalent to JP NZ,0125H.

The number and type of characters permitted in a label varies from one assembler to another. As a general guide, labels may contain up to 8 characters, the first of which must be alphabetic. Most assemblers allow the use of the dollar ($) symbol as a label which is assigned the current value of the location counter at the point where it is used. Some assemblers require a colon (:) as a terminator for each label.

Mnemonics

This field must be included in all lines in which an operand is specified. The mnemonic field consists of Z80 instruction mnemonics or assembler directives. Instruction mnemonics are two to four characters in length and describe in abbreviated form the type of operation performed by each instruction. Each mnemonic must be separated from its operand(s) by at least one space. Assembler directives or pseudo-ops are instructions for the assembler rather than for the microprocessor, and in general they define the manner in which assembly takes place. Examples of assembler directives are ORG, EQU and DEFB, and these are described later in this chapter.

Operands

Many instructions require one or more operands which define the data (or location of data) to be operated on by the instruction. The operand may be a constant, a label or an expression. An example of each of these types of operand is as follows:

LD A,0CFH   — *numerical constant*
LD A,(SWITCH)   — *label*
LD A,(PORT*5+2)   — *expression*

Z80 instructions usually require source and destination operands, although either may be implied in the instruction mnemonic. Where two operands are specified, they must be separated by a comma (,). The contents of external addresses may be used as operands provided that references to them are enclosed in brackets, e.g. direct reference—(0200H) or indirect reference—(HL). Expressions are formed by combining a number of simple operands (labels and constants) using arithmetic and logic operators. These are evaluated during assembly, and each expression must produce a 16 bit value. Furthermore, after evaluation, the number of significant digits must not exceed the number required for its intended use, i.e. the eight most significant digits must evaluate to zero if the operand is data destined for an eight bit register.

Numeric constants

A numeric constant is a 16 bit value which may be expressed in one of several different bases. The base or radix is denoted by a following radix indicator, and those used are:

B	*binary constant*	*(base 2)*
D	*decimal constant*	*(base 10)*
H	*hexadecimal constant*	*(base 16)*
O	*octal constant*	*(base 8)*
Q	*octal constant*	*(base 8)*

Q may be used as an octal radix to avoid confusion between figure zero and the letter 'O'. The omission of a radix indicator causes an assembler to use the default radix which is usually decimal, although it may be possible to change the default radix by including a RADIX pseudo-op at the start of the source code. Hexadecimal constants must begin with a numeric character to avoid confusion with labels, which means that if the constant starts with any of the hexadecimal codes A to F, a leading zero must be added. The following are all examples of the use of numeric constants:

1234   1234D   1011B   1234H   0A9FH   34720   1265Q

String constants

String constants are formed by enclosing ASCII characters within single apostrophe (') characters. The value of a character then becomes its corresponding ASCII code. The string length is mostly restricted to one or two characters, in which case the string becomes an 8 or 16 bit value. The exception to this is where the string constant is used with DEFB or DEFM pseudo-ops. The following are examples of the use of string constants:

LD A, 'A'	which represents	LD A,41H
LD HL, 'AB'	which represents	LD HL,4142H

Reserved words

There are several character sequences which are reserved by an assembler for its own use. In general, all Z80 mnemonics, register names and assembler directives are reserved by the assembler and may not be used by the programmer as labels.

Arithmetic and logic operators

The operands described may be combined in normal algebraic notation using any combination of properly formed operands, operators and expressions. The following are examples of arithmetic and logical operators supported by most assemblers:

$a + b$	unsigned arithmetic sum of a and b
$a - b$	unsigned arithmetic difference between a and b
$a*b$	unsigned magnitude multiplication of a and b
a/b	unsigned division of a by b
a MOD b	remainder after a/b
a SHL b	a shifted to the left b places
a SHR b	a shifted to the right b places
NOT b	one's complement of b
a EQ b	true if $a=b$, false otherwise
a LT b	true if $a<b$, false otherwise
a GT b	true if $a>b$, false otherwise
a GE b	true if $a \geqslant b$, false otherwise
a AND b	bit-by-bit logical AND of a and b
a OR b	bit-by-bit logical OR of a and b
a XOR b	bit-by-bit logical EX-OR of a and b

In each case, a and b represent simple operands (labels, numeric constants, one or two character strings). The following are examples of the use of these operators:

Expression	Which represents
LD A,3+4	LD A,7
LD A,0CH-4	LD A,8
LD A,3*4	LD A,0CH
LD A,9/5	LD A,1
LD A,9 MOD 5	LD A,4
LD A,5 SHL 3	LD A,28H
LD A,8 SHR 3	LD A,1
LD A,NOT 2	LD A,0FDH
LD A,5 AND 6	LD A,4
LD A,5 OR 6	LD A,7
LD A,5 XOR 6	LD A,3

More complex expressions may be formed by using combinations of these operators. All calculations are performed at assembly time as 16 bit unsigned operations, but the expression must evaluate to a number appropriate for its intended use.

Precedence of operators

Operators are applied in expressions in the following order:
  (i)   * / MOD SHL SHR   (*highest precedence*)
 (ii)   + −
(iii)   EQ LT LE GT GE NE
(iv)   NOT
 (v)   AND
(vi)   OR XOR   (*lowest precedence*)

Operators listed in the same line (e.g. *, /,MOD etc) have equal precedence and are applied from left to right as they are encountered. Therefore the expression:

a * b + c   equals (a * b) + c
a + b * c   equals a + (b * c)

Comments

This is an optional field which is reserved for the addition of comments which are intended to help follow the logical processes taking place in a program. Comments should not simply repeat the instruction, but should indicate why certain instructions have been included.

For example, if the source code contains the instruction LD B,5 then the comment 'load register B with 5' is virtually worthless, since this is obvious from the instruction. A more worthwhile comment would be 'print 5 characters' or 'count 5 pulses' since comments of this type give the reason for loading register B with 5.

The comment field is always preceded by a semi-colon (;) and all information between the semi-colon and the end of the line is ignored by the assembler. Some assemblers also allow the use of an asterisk (*) to precede the comment field.

Assembler directives

Assembler directives (or pseudo-ops) are instructions to an assembler and are used to set labels to specified values during assembly, specify starting addresses in the program, define storage areas, perform conditional assembly or control the format of the print file. Different assemblers support various directives, but the following are typical:

ORG	*set the program or data origin*
END	*end program*
EQU	*numeric 'equate'*
IF	*begin conditional assembly*
ELSE	*alternative to the previous IF*
ENDIF	*end of conditional assembly*
DEFB	*define data bytes*
DEFW	*define data words*
DEFM	*define text message*
DEFS	*define space (for data storage)*
INCLUDE	*read data from file specified*

ORG directive

An ORG directive is used to define the origin or starting address for a program or data area, and it takes the form:

label: ORG *expression*

where 'label' is an optional program identifier, and 'expression' is a 16 bit expression consisting of operands that must be defined before the ORG statement. In effect, an ORG directive presets the assembler location counter, and machine code generation starts at the address specified in the expression. A program may contain any number of ORG statements, but the programmer must ensure that overlapping does not occur, since no checks are normally made by an assembler. Most programs for CP/M begin with an ORG statement of the form:

ORG 100H

which causes the program to begin at the start of the TPA. If a label is given to an ORG statement, the label assumes the value of the ORG expression.

END directive

An END statement is optional in some assemblers and mandatory in others, but if present it must be the last statement since all subsequent statements are ignored by an assembler. Two forms used for the END directive are:

label: END
label: END *expression*

where 'label' is optional. In the first case, the assembly process is terminated and the default starting address is taken as 0000. In the second case the expression is evaluated, and this becomes the program starting address. Most assembly language programs end with the statement:

END 100H

which results in a starting address for the program of 100H which is the base address of the TPA.

EQU directive

The EQU (equate) directive is used to associate labels with particular numeric values. For example, a memory location may be used to store the result of a calculation. In this case the EQU directive may be used to associate the label 'RESULT' with the memory address where the result will be stored. In all subsequent references to this address the label 'RESULT' may be used in place of its actual hexadecimal value. The form of this directive is as follows:

label   EQU *expression*

where the label must be present and must not label any other statement, i.e. labels may not be redefined within a program with the EQU directive (some assemblers support a SET directive for this purpose). The assembler evaluates the expression, and assigns the resulting value to the label. As an aid to following a program, the name used for a label usually relates to its purpose within that program. Examples of the EQU directive are as follows:

TOTAL EQU 0C80H *assign the value 0C80H to the label TOTAL,*

FINAL EQU TOTAL *additionally, assign the value already assigned to TOTAL to the label FINAL, and*

DISP EQU TOTAL + 10 *assign a value to DISP which is 10 (decimal) more than the value already assigned to TOTAL.*

IF, ELSE and ENDIF directives

The IF, ELSE and ENDIF directives define a range of assembly language statements which may be included or excluded from the assembly process, depending upon the condition associated with the IF directive. This is known as 'conditional assembly', and the form of this directive is:

IF *expression*
statement #1
statement #2
....
statement #n
ENDIF

Some assemblers use COND and ENDC rather than IF and ENDIF. When an IF statement is encountered in an assembly language program, the expression which follows IF is evaluated by the assembler. If the expression evaluates to a non-zero value, statements *#1* to *#n* are assembled. If the expression evaluates to zero, the statements are not assembled, although they may still be listed.

Conditional assembly is often used to write a single program which may be required to operate under a number of different environments. By selecting only certain segments for a particular assembly, programs may be customised for particular environments. The following example shows how conditional assembly may be used to write a single program which may be assembled for two different types of I/O device:

```
                ;******* SELECT PIO OR PIA *******
FFFF=           TRUE    EQU  0FFFFH
FFFF=           PIA     EQU  TRUE
E81C=           PIAA    EQU  0E81CH
E81E=           PIAB    EQU  0E81EH
0004=           PIOA    EQU  4
0005=           PIOB    EQU  5

                ORG     100H
```

```
                        ;******* CONFIG 6820 PIA *******
                        IF    PIA
0100 AF                 XOR   A               ;clear Acc
0101 32 1D E8           LD    (PIAA+1),A      ;select port A DDR
0104 32 1F E8           LD    (PIAB+1),A      ;select port B DDR
0107 3E FF              LD    A,0FFH          ;port A direction word
0109 32 1C E8           LD    (PIAA),A        ;port A all outputs
010C 3E 6F              LD    A,01101111B     ;port B direction word
010E 32 1E E8           LD    (PIAB),A        ;port B, b4&b7 inputs
0111 3E 04              LD    A,4             ;set CTRL/DATA bit
0113 32 1D E8           LD    (PIAA+1),A      ;select data reg A
0116 32 1F E8           LD    (PIAB+1),A      ;select data reg B
                        ENDIF

                        ;******* CONFIG Z80 PIO *******
                        IF    NOT PIA
                        LD    A,0CFH          ;mode 3 control word
                        OUT   (PIOA+2),A      ;select mode 3 for A
                        XOR   A               ;clear Acc
                        OUT   (PIOA+2),A      ;port A all outputs
                        LD    A,0CFH          ;mode 3 control word
                        OUT   (PIOB+2),A      ;select mode 3 for B
                        LD    A,10010000B     ;port B direction word
                        OUT   (PIOB+2),A      ;port B, b4&b7 inputs
                        ENDIF
```

It can be seen in this example that, because PIA equates TRUE, code is generated for this device only and not for the PIO.

The ELSE directive may be used as an alternative to a second IF directive where a choice of two actions is available, but must occur between IF and ENDIF statements. The form used is as follows:

IF *expression*
statement #1
statement #2
. . . .
statement #n
ELSE
statement #n + 1
statement #n + 2
. . . .
statement #m
ENDIF

If the expression evaluates to a non-zero (true) value, then statements *#1* to #n are assembled, but statements #n + 1 to #m are skipped. If the expression evaluates to a zero (false) value, then statements #1 to #n are skipped, but statements #n + 1 to #m are assembled. The use of the ELSE directives may be studied using the following example:

```
FFFF=           TRUE    EQU  0FFFH       ;define TRUE
0000=           FALSE   EQU  NOT TRUE    ;define FALSE
0000=           SERIAL  EQU  FALSE       ;use parallel output
0004=           PIO     EQU  4           ;base address of PIO
0008=           SIO     EQU  8           ;base address of SIO
                        IF   SERIAL      ;use serial port
                PORT    EQU  SIO         ;serial output port
                        ELSE
0004=           PORT    EQU  PIO         ;parallel output port
                        ENDIF
0000  03 04             OUT  (PORT),A    ;output a character
0002                    END
```

In this example, conditional assembly is used to give the user the option of specifying serial or parallel output. The label PORT which is used in the output statement is equated to either PIO or SIO, where PIO is offered as the parallel alternative when SERIAL equates FALSE.

DEFB directive

The DEFB (define byte) directive is used when the programmer wishes to store constants directly into defined storage areas as single bytes. For example, a programmer may wish to create a look-up table at the end of a program which performs a code conversion process.

The form of the DEFB directive is as follows:

label: DEFB *e1,e2,e3,.........,en*

where *e1* to *en* are constants or expressions that evaluate to 8-bit numbers or single ASCII characters in quotes. Examples of the use of the DEFB directive are:

DATA: DEFB   0,1,2,15,20H,0FH,0CAH
MSSGE: DEFB   'X',CR,LF,0 (CR and LF previously equated)
            DEFB   'AB' SHR 8, 'CD' and 7FH

DEFW directive

The DEFW (define word) directive is similar to the DEFB directive except that double length (16 bit) words of storage are used. This may be used by a programmer to store addresses directly in a program, for example for the creation of a table of interrupt vectors.

The form of the DEFB directive is as follows:

label: DEFW *e1,e2,e3,.........,en*

where *e1* to *en* are constants or expressions that evaluate to 16-bit numbers or ASCII strings up to two characters in length. The least significant byte of an expression is stored first in memory, followed by the most significant byte at the next higher address, i.e. low order first as is normal for the Z80 microprocessor.

This facility is particularly suitable where addresses are to be stored in memory, since the correct order is automatically maintained. Examples of the use of the DEFW directive are as follows:

VECTR: DEFW 0FC8H,VECTR+6,$-NEXT,255+255
         DEFW 'A',3,'XY',3 SHL 8 OR 5

DEFM directive

The DEFM (define message) directive allows text to be inserted directly into memory as equivalent ASCII codes. This is useful where a program must generate text strings as part of its normal operation e.g. print error messages on a VDU screen. The use of the DEFM directive avoids having to look up ASCII codes for messages, and also allows the position of text within a program to be readily identified.

The form of the DEFM directive is as follows:

label: DEFM '*text message*'

where the text message may be any sequence of characters, usually with some limit imposed regarding its length.

DEFS directive

The DEFS (define space) directive is used to reserve space in memory, e.g. for the stack, or for system workspace, and takes the following form:

label: DEFS *expression*

Some assemblers allow the DEFS directive to be followed by a constant which then causes the assembler to generate code to fill the reserved space with the selected constant. The assembler continues to create subsequent code at the first address after the area reserved by the DEFS statement. The effect of the DEFS statement is the same as defining a new origin with an ORG directive, e.g.

label   EQU $
          ORG $+*expression*

INCLUDE directive

By using the INCLUDE directive, a previously written source code file can be inserted in the file currently being worked on, at the point where the INCLUDE directive is used. This facility is useful for including library programs, e.g. subroutines, without the need to retype. The format for the INCLUDE directive is as follows:

INCLUDE *filename*

where the file *filename*.ZSM must exist on the currently logged drive (or must be preceded by a reference to the currently logged drive, although this form tends to restrict its use).

At assembly time, the included file will be expanded and assembled as though it formed part of the original file.

Errors

Except for very short and simple programs, it is unlikely that a program will function as intended at the first attempt. In common with all other languages, assembly language may contain two types of error, and these are:

(i) syntax errors which are errors in the grammar or format of assembly language statements which make it impossible for the assembler program to interpret them and hence generate code, and

(ii) logical errors which do not prevent correct assembly of the program, but which cause the resultant object code to perform in an entirely different manner from that intended.

Error messages

Two distinct groups of error messages may be generated by an assembler during the assembly process, and these are:

(i) errors in the source code which are caused by incorrect use of the assembly language, or important omissions, and

(ii) terminal errors which are caused by the inability to read from or write files to the disk.

The method used to report errors in the source code may vary with different assemblers, but frequently an error code is printed against each offending line. The error code is intended to indicate the type of error wherever possible, thus enabling the programmer to locate its exact source. The following codes are examples of those that may be encountered in practice:

C   Comma error: *an expression was encountered in which the delimiting comma was missing, e.g. JP NZ LOOP instead of JP NZ,LOOP,*

E   Expression error: *an expression has been used which is ill-formed and which the assembler cannot evaluate,*

P   Phase error: *a label was found which did not have the same value on two separate passes through the program,*

R   Register error: *the register specified is incompatible with the instruction selected,*

S   Syntax error: *miscellaneous error in the format of a statement which prevents the assembler from processing the statement, and*

U   Undefined symbol: *a label has been used as an operand, but it has not been defined elsewhere in the program.*

Error messages which are generated due to problems concerned with the disk system are usually more explicit, and the following examples indicate the types of error message which may be expected:

NO SOURCE FILE: *the file specified for assembly cannot be found on the disk,*

NO DIRECTORY SPACE: *the disk directory is full (although there may still be space on the disk); erase unwanted files e.g. BAK files and retry,*

SOURCE FILE READ ERROR: *the assembler cannot read the specified source file; possible corruption of data on the disk,*

OUTPUT FILE WRITE ERROR: *the assembler cannot write to disk properly, possibly due to a full disk, and*

CANNOT CLOSE FILE: *the output file cannot be closed, perhaps due to the disk being 'write protected'.*

Assembly language documentation

An assembly language program should be well documented so that it is easy to follow the logical processes used in the program. This enables software to be subsequently maintained i.e. updated, debugged, installed in different environments or otherwise modified. Without such documentation, it is unlikely that even the original programmer would be able to readily identify the function of each section of program. This requires that all labels and symbolic addresses should, within limits set by the assembler, indicate their function in the program. Programs should also be partitioned into individual modules wherever possible, and comments should be liberally added at all stages.

The following program was written as an example of poor documentation.

```
        ORG 100H
L1:     LD E,0                      L3:     INC HL
        LD D,L5-1                           INC BC
        LD HL,L4                            DEC D
        LD BC,L4+1                          JP NZ,L2
L2:     LD A,(BC)                           LD A,E
        CP (HL)                             OR A
        JP NC,L3                            JP NZ,L1
        PUSH AF                             JP 0
        LD A,(HL)                   L4:     DEFB 93H,12H,75H,25H,62H,10H,37H,64H,29H
        LD (BC),A                   L5:     EQU $-L4
        POP AF                              DEFS 256-L5
        INC E                               END 100H
```

The program is difficult to follow, since:
(i) there is no indication as to its purpose, its source, and the environment in which it runs,
(ii) there are no comments to indicate what process is being carried out at each stage in the program,
(iii) the labels used give no indication of their purpose, and
(iv) the program has little or no partitioning into identifiable sections.

To illustrate these problems, it is left to the reader to determine the function of the program and thus experience the problems that poor documentation causes.

Assembly language examples

These assembly language subroutines are included to demonstrate some of the assembler facilities described in this chapter, and to show how programs may be enhanced by proper documentation.

(i) Multiplication

Most 8-bit microprocessors (unlike 16-bit microprocessors) have no instruction which allows them to perform ordinary arithmetical multiplication. Therefore it is necessary to write a short routine to perform this task. This routine performs multiplication between two 8-bit numbers using a standard 'shift and add' method.

```
                              ;****************************************
                              ;Subroutine to perform 8-bit unsigned
                              ;multiplication of H and L registers
                              ;using shift and add algorithm
                              ;16-bit product is returned in HL pair
                              ;All other registers are preserved
                              ;****************************************
                              ;
0100                          ORG     100H
                              ;
                              ;###### preserve registers ######
                              ;
0100 C5        MULT:   PUSH    BC      ;BC and DE registers are
0101 D5                PUSH    DE      ;corrupted by routine
                              ;
                              ;###### initialise registers ######
                              ;
0102 5D                LD      E,L     ;transfer multiplicand to E
0103 2E00              LD      L,0     ;product low byte = 0
0105 55                LD      D,L     ;multiplicand high byte = 0
0106 0608              LD      B,8     ;8 shifts and adds
```

Assemblers

```
                        ;
                        ;###### main multiplication loop ######
                        ;
0108 29         SHIFT:  ADD     HL,HL   ;shift HL left into C flag, if
0109 3001               JR      NC,ADD0 ;C=0, partial product is zero,
010B 19                 ADD     HL,DE   ;C=1, add multiplicand
010C 10FA       ADD0:   DJNZ    SHIFT   ;multiplication complete?
                        ;
                        ;###### restore registers ######
                        ;
010E D1                 POP     DE      ;recover previous contents
010F C1                 POP     BC      ;of BC and DE registers
0110 C9                 RET             ;go back to main program


010C ADD0    0100 MULT    0108 SHIFT

No errors
```

(ii) Division

Most 8-bit microprocessors are also unable to perform division, therefore a routine must be written for this purpose. This routine performs 8-bit by 8-bit division using a 'shift and subtract' or 'restoring' method.

```
                        ;****************************************
                        ;Subroutine to perform 8-bit unsigned
                        ;division of H and L registers
                        ;using shift and subtract algorithm
                        ;
                        ;Entry: divisor in H, dividend in L
                        ;Exit: quotient in L, remainder in H
                        ;
                        ;All other registers are preserved
                        ;****************************************
                        ;
0100                    ORG     100H    ;start of TPA
                        ;
                        ;###### preserve registers ######
                        ;
0100 F5         DIVIDE: PUSH    AF      ;preserve AF,BC & DE
0101 C5                 PUSH    BC      ;registers which are
0102 D5                 PUSH    DE      ;corrupted by this routine
                        ;
```

```
                            ;###### initialise registers ######
                            ;
     0103 54                LD    D,H       ;transfer divisor to E
     0104 2600              LD    H,0       ;clear H and E
     0106 5C                LD    E,H       ;registers
     0107 0608              LD    B,8       ;8 shifts and subtracts
                            ;
                            ;###### main division loop ######
                            ;
     0109 29       SHIFT:   ADD   HL,HL     ;shift HL left, and
     010A ED52              SBC   HL,DE     ;try to divide by D
     010C 3001              JR    NC,NOADD  ;it goes, so skip restore
     010E 19                ADD   HL,DE     ;D too big, so restore
     010F 17       NOADD:   RLA             ;record result in A
     0110 10F7     ADD0:    DJNZ  SHIFT     ;division completed?
     0112 2F                CPL             ;result complemented
     0113 6F                LD    L,A       ;and put into L
                            ;
                            ;###### restore registers ######
                            ;
     0114 D1                POP   DE        ;recover previous contents
     0115 C1                POP   BC        ;of BC and DE
     0116 F1                POP   AF        ;and AF registers
     0117 C9                RET             ;go back to main program


     0110 ADD0    0100 DIVIDE   010F NOADD   0109 SHIFT

     No errors
```

(iii) **Code conversion, BCD to 7-segment** *(facing page)*

When driving 7-segment display devices, it is necessary to convert from the normally available BCD results into equivalent segment codes. Since the logical relationships between BCD and 7-segment codes are quite complex, this routine uses a 'look-up table' method of conversion. Conditional assembly is included so that the routine may be used for either common anode or common cathode types of display device.

(iv) **Code conversion, binary to BCD** *(page 64)*

It is often simpler to perform calculations in pure binary when using a microprocessor. For example, the multiplication and division routines included in this chapter could be made to work with BCD numbers but this

```
                              ;***********************************
                              ;BCD to 7-segment subroutine for
                              ;common anode or common cathode
                              ;types of display
                              ;
                              ;Entry: BCD data in A
                              ;Exit:  segments code in A
                              ;***********************************
                              ;
        0100                          ORG  100H          ;start of TPA
                              ;
        FFFF =                 TRUE   EQU  0FFFFH        ;conditional equate
        0000 =                 COMAN  EQU  NOT TRUE      ;select com cathode
                              ;
        0100 E5                SEG7:  PUSH HL            ;preserve main HL
        0101 210801                   LD   HL,TABLE      ;base of code table
        0104 85                       ADD  A,L           ;segment index
        0105 7E                       LD   A,(HL)        ;get seg code
                              ;
                              ;assemble for common anode if C/ANODE true
                              ;
                                      COND COMAN         ;
                                      CPL                ;invert seg code
                                      ENDC
                              ;
        0106 E1                       POP  HL            ;restore main HL
        0107 C9                       RET                ;back to main prog
                              ;
                              ;look-up table of common cathode codes
                              ;
        0108 3F065B4F          TABLE: DEFB 3FH,6,5BH,4FH,66H  ;0,1,2,3,4
        010D 6D7D077F                 DEFB 6DH,7DH,7,7FH,67H  ;5,6,7,8,9


        0000 COMAN    0100 SEG7    0108 TABLE    FFFF TRUE

        No errors
```

would undoubtedly introduce complications, since the programmer would then find it necessary to ensure that illegal combinations were not generated. However, BCD results are required for display in most cases, therefore this routine may be used to perform the necessary conversion between 8-bit pure binary and BCD.

A 'double and add' method of conversion is used which enables a very simple conversion program to be implemented.

```
                        ;****************************************
                        ;Subroutine to perform binary to BCD
                        ;conversion using the 'double and add
                        ;method
                        ;
                        ;Entry: binary number in A
                        ;Exit:  BCD equivalent in HL
                        ;
                        ;All other registers are preserved
                        ;****************************************
                        ;
        0100            ORG     100H       ;start of TPA
                        ;
                        ;###### preserve registers ######
                        ;
0100 F5      BIDEC:     PUSH    AF         ;preserve AF & BC
0101 C5                 PUSH    BC         ;registers
                        ;
                        ;###### initialise registers ######
                        ;
0102 0608               LD      B,8        ;process 8-bit number
0104 4F                 LD      C,A        ;held in register C
0105 AF                 XOR     A          ;clear working reg
                        ;
                        ;###### main conversion loop ######
                        ;
0106 CB11    SHIFT:     RL      C          ;bit by bit into C flag
0108 8F                 ADC     A,A        ;double A and add carry
0109 27                 DAA                ;convert to valid BCD
010A CB14               RL      H          ;update hundreds in H
010C 10F8               DJNZ    SHIFT      ;repeat for all 8 bits
010E 6F                 LD      L,A        ;units and tens into L
                        ;
                        ;###### restore registers ######
                        ;
010F C1                 POP     BC         ;recover previous contents
0110 F1                 POP     AF         ;of AF and BC registers
0111 C9                 RET                ;go back to main program


0100 BIDEC    0106 SHIFT

No errors
```

(v) **Data sort routine**

There are occasions when a routine is required to sort data into numerical order. Several different algorithms are available for this purpose depending upon the rate at which the data must be sorted. This routine uses a 'bubble sort' algorithm which is not particularly fast in operation, but is simple in concept.

Starting at the bottom of a list, each byte of data is compared in magnitude with the next byte in the list, exchanging bytes if necessary to maintain the correct ascending (or descending) order. After one complete pass through the list, the largest (or smallest) value will have filtered, or 'bubbled' to the top of the list. This process is then repeated as many times as necessary until all data is in the correct order. The routine is arranged such that any data block to a maximum size of 256 bytes may be sorted by passing appropriate parameters in registers B and HL.

```
                        ;******************************
                        ;Subroutine to sort up to 256 bytes
                        ;of data into ascending numerical
                        ;order
                        ;
                        ;Entry: start of data table in HL
                        ;       length of table in B
                        ;Exit:  all registers preserved
                        ;
                        ;******************************
                        ;
0100                    ORG     100H        ;start of TPA
                        ;
                ;###### save registers ######
                        ;
0100 F5                 PUSH    AF          ;preserve
0101 C5                 PUSH    BC          ;register values from
0102 D5                 PUSH    DE          ;main program
0103 DDE5               PUSH    IX
                        ;
                ;###### initialise registers and exchange flag ######
                        ;
0105 0E00       SORT:   LD      C,0         ;clear exchange flag
0107 E5                 PUSH    HL          ;transfer table start
0108 DDE1               POP     IX          ;address to IX
                        ;
                ;##### compare two consecutive values in table ######
                        ;
010A DD5E00     NEXT:   LD      E,(IX+0)    ;get element (n)
010D DD7E01             LD      A,(IX+1)    ;get element (n+1)
0110 BB                 CP      E           ;see which is larger
0111 3008               JR      NC,NOEXCH   ;leave if in order
```

```
                ;
                ;###### byte exchange routine,exchanges numbers ######
                ;
0113 DD7301             LD      (IX+1),E        ;reverse the order
0116 DD7700             LD      (IX+0),A        ;of (n) and (n+1)
0119 CBC1               SET     0,C             ;set exchange flag
                ;
                ;###### loop control to check for end of pass ######
                ;
011B DD23       NOEXCH: INC     IX              ;move up the list
011D 10EB               DJNZ    NEXT            ;end of list?
                ;
                ;###### check for complete list sorted ######
                ;
011F CB41               BIT     0,C             ;finished sorting?
0121 20E2               JR      NZ,SORT         ;keep going if not
                ;
                ;###### restore registers and return ######
                ;
0123 DDE1               POP     IX              ;restore main program
0125 D1                 POP     DE              ;values in registers
0126 C1                 POP     BC              ;
0127 F1                 POP     AF              ;
0128 C9                 RET                     ;go back to main prog
                ;

010A NEXT    011B NOEXCH   0105 SORT

No errors
```

(vi) **Print hex characters** *(pages 67–68)*

This subroutine serves to convert the contents of a 16-bit register into 4 ASCII characters and print these on a new line of the console display. It makes use of two CP/M BDOS calls which are accessed via the primary entry point at address 0005H, 'console output' (function 02) and 'print string' (function 09).

Problems

1. Describe the advantages of using an assembler rather than programming directly in hexadecimal codes.
2. (a) Explain the term *'pseudo-op'*,
   (b) List *four* pseudo-ops used in Z80 assembly language, and describe the purpose of each of them.
3. Explain the term *forward reference*, and hence demonstrate why a 'two-pass' assembler is normally used.

```
                        ;*****************************************
                        ;Subroutine to print the contents of
                        ;a 16-bit register as 4 hex digits
                        ;
                        ;Entry: number in HL
                        ;Exit:  registers corrupted
                        ;
                        ;*****************************************
                        ;
0100                            ORG     100H            ;start of TPA
0005 =                  BDOS    EQU     5               ;BDOS entry point
0002 =                  WCHR    EQU     2               ;BDOS write
0009 =                  PSTR    EQU     9               ;BDOS string print
000D =                  CR      EQU     13              ;carriage return
000A =                  LF      EQU     10              ;line feed
                        ;
                        ;###### select a new line ######
0100 112D01             P4HEX:  LD      DE,NEWLN        ;CR/LF string
0103 0E09                       LD      C,PSTR          ;print string fn
0105 E5                         PUSH    HL              ;BDOS corrupts it!
0106 CD0500                     CALL    BDOS            ;start of new line
0109 E1                         POP     HL              ;put it right again

                        ;###### print 4 characters in HL ######

010A 7C                         LD      A,H             ;print high byte
010B CD0F01                     CALL    P2HEX
010E 7D                         LD      A,L             ;print low byte

                        ;###### print 2 characters in A ######

010F F5                 P2HEX:  PUSH    AF              ;save lower digit
0110 CB3F                       SRL     A               ;shift upper 4
0112 CB3F                       SRL     A               ;bits into
0114 CB3F                       SRL     A               ;position for
0116 CB3F                       SRL     A               ;printing
0118 CD1E01                     CALL    P1HEX           ;convert & print
011B F1                         POP     AF              ;get lower digit
011C E60F                       AND     0FH             ;mask off upper

                        ;###### convert to ASCII and print ######

011E C690               P1HEX:  ADD     A,90H           ;if A-F, decimal
0120 27                         DAA                     ;adj. sets C-flg
0121 CE40                       ADC     A,'@'           ;if A-F, adjust
0123 27                         DAA                     ;& C-flg adds 7
                                ;
```

```
                        ;###### print character ######

0124 5F                 LD      E,A             ;put in passing reg
0125 0E02               LD      C,WCHR          ;select BDOS fn
0127 E5                 PUSH    HL              ;BDOS corrupts!
0128 CD0500             CALL    BDOS            ;print it
012B E1                 POP     HL              ;back right again
012C C9                 RET                     ;go to calling prog

                        ;###### cr/lf string ######

012D 0D0A24    NEWLN:   DEFB    CR,LF,'$'       ;$=string terminator


0005 BDOS     000D CR      000A LF      012D NEWLN    011E P1HEX
010F P2HEX    0100 P4HEX   0009 PSTR    0002 WCHR

No errors
```

4. State the advantages of using 'labels' and 'symbolic addresses' in assembly language programs rather than hexadecimal codes.
5. With reference to the following assembly language program, identify:
   (i)   two pseudo-ops,
   (ii) two labels,
   (iii) two symbolic addresses, and
   (iv) two forward references.

```
        START   EQU     100H
        BUFF    EQU     START+256
        COUNT   EQU     BUFF+BUFLEN
        BUFLEN  EQU     80H
        ;
        ORG     START
        ;
        LD      A,(COUNT)       ;read byte counter
        OR      A               ;flags!
        JR      NZ,CHECK        ;null count?
        LD      A,BUFLEN        ;if so, set to max
        LD      (COUNT),A       ;otherwise leave
CHECK:  LD      B,A             ;B=search counter
        LD      HL,BUFF         ;buffer pointer
NEXT:   LD      A,(HL)          ;get character
        CP      '$'             ;look for terminator
        JR      Z,EXIT          ;exit when found
        INC     HL              ;bump pointer
        JR      NEXT            ;and try again
EXIT:   RET
        END
```

6. With reference to the following program segment, determine the values loaded into the A, B, C, D and E registers:

```
START   EQU     0100H
BUFF    EQU     START+256
COUNT   EQU     BUFF+80
CONST   EQU     58H
;
        ORG     START
;
        LD      A,(BUFF+2)
        LD      B,CONST SHR 2
        LD      C,CONST AND 15
        LD      D,CONST MOD 5
        LD      E,START-CONST*2
```

7. A microcomputer with a 2 MHz clock has an audio alarm connected to bit 0 of an output port located at I/O address 04.

   Write a program at assembly language level, using appropriate labels and symbolic addresses, to drive the alarm with a 1 kHz signal for a period of 2 seconds. The program should include comments which show how the correct time periods are obtained.

8. (a) Explain what is meant by the term 'conditional assembly'.
   (b) A microprocessor based system may be fitted with one of the following types of numerical display:
      (i) A common anode 7-segment device, or
      (ii) a dot matrix device which uses ASCII codes.

   Write an assembly language segment to show how conditional assembly may be used to produce a program which can be used for either type of device.

5 Macros

Introduction

A macro is a block of source code which is generated by a single reference, and which is subsequently expanded during assembly with a 'macro-assembler'.

Two commonly used forms of macro are:
 (i) in-line macros, and
(ii) stored macros

In-line macros simplify the generation of repetitive source code, e.g. a sequence of PUSH instructions, by allowing a programmer to specify both the number of times an instruction is to be repeated and the parameters that will be used for each repetition. This single reference is expanded during assembly so that the instruction is repeated as defined in the macro.

Stored macros are previously defined blocks of source code which are associated with a particular macro name. A programmer may reference an in-line macro at any point in the source code by specifying the macro name and parameters to be used during the expansion.

In order to make effective use of macros, a macro assembler is required which supports the necessary pseudo-ops for processing both in-line and stored macros, e.g. Microsoft's M80.

Macro pseudo-ops

Special pseudo-ops similar to the following are required in order to make use of macros:

 (i) In-line macros:
- REPT — *repeat*
- IRP — *indefinite repeat*
- IRPC — *indefinite repeat character*

(ii) Stored macros:
- MACRO — *macro definition*
- ENDM — *macro termination*
- EXITM — *exit before completion of expansion*

(iii) Labels:
- LOCAL — *symbols unique to a macro block*

(iv) Special operators:
- & — *concatenate text or symbols*
- ;; — *comment not saved in expansion*
- ! — *next character is a literal*
- % — *convert symbol to current radix*

In-line macros (repeat group)

In-line macros are used as a means of avoiding undue repetition when writing program source code. They are written into a program at the point where they are to be used (rather than being called), and cause controlled repetition of statements within the macro, thus automatically generating repetitive code, e.g. construction of data tables. For this reason, the pseudo-ops used for in-line macros are known as the 'repeat group'. Typical pseudo-ops are REPT (repeat), IRPC (indefinite repeat character) and IRP (indefinite repeat), each of which cause a macro-assembler to re-read parts of the source code under the control of a counter or list of substitutions.

REPT pseudo-op

The REPT or 'repeat' pseudo-op allows assembly language statements within a macro to be repeated a number of times, determined by the value of a parameter which is supplied by the programmer. A macro is formed using REPT in the following manner:

label: REPT *expression*
     statement #1
     statement #2
     ....
     statement #n
     ENDM

where '*label*' is optional. The expression following REPT is evaluated as a 16-bit count which is used to determine the number of times that the assembler is to process statements *#1* to *#n*. The following macro shows how REPT may be used to automatically generate a table of constants in a program.

```
        ;*******************************
        ;Macro 1
        ;macro to generate the table of
        ;constants 01 to 0AH
        ;*******************************
        ;
CONST   ASET    0           ;1st value = 0+1
        REPT    10          ;times to repeat
CONST   ASET    CONST+1     ;redefine CONST
        DEFB    CONST
        ENDM                ;macro end
        END                 ;program end
```

When a program which includes this macro is assembled, the following code is generated:

```
            MACRO-80 3.43   27-Jul-81       PAGE   1


                                        ;************************************
                                        ;Macro 1
                                        ;macro to generate the table of
                                        ;constants 01 to 0AH
                                        ;************************************
                                        ;
    0000                        CONST   ASET    0           ;1st value = 0+1
                                        REPT    10          ;times to repeat
                                CONST   ASET    CONST+1     ;redefine CONST
                                        DEFB    CONST
                                        ENDM                ;macro end
    0000'   01              +           DEFB    CONST
    0001'   02              +           DEFB    CONST
    0002'   03              +           DEFB    CONST
    0003'   04              +           DEFB    CONST
    0004'   05              +           DEFB    CONST
    0005'   06              +           DEFB    CONST
    0006'   07              +           DEFB    CONST
    0007'   08              +           DEFB    CONST
    0008'   09              +           DEFB    CONST
    0009'   0A              +           DEFB    CONST
                                        END                 ;program end


            MACRO-80 3.43   27-Jul-81       PAGE   S


Macros:

Symbols:
000A    CONST



No Fatal error(s)
```

In this example, a value of 0 is initially assigned to the label CONST, and the repeat counter is set to 10. Each time that the process is repeated, an ASET directive is used to assign a new value to CONST, 1 greater than its previous value. The current value of CONST is assigned to the DEFB statement, and this process is repeated for a total of 10 times to generate the data table shown. Macro lines which do not generate code are not listed in the repetition, while lines that do generate code are listed with a '+' sign to indicate that they result from a macro expansion.

IRPC pseudo-op

The IRPC (indefinite repeat character) pseudo-op is similar to REPT, except that the number of repeats is determined by a character list rather than a repeat counter. The format for using IRPC is as follows:

label: IRPC *identifier,character-list*
        statement #1
        statement #2
        ....
        statement #n
        ENDM

where '*label*' is optional, and any valid assembler name may be used for *identifier*. The '*character-list*' is a character string that is terminated with an acceptable delimiter, e.g. space, comment etc, and the IRPC pseudo-op causes the assembler to read the statement sequence once for each character in the character list. On each repetition, a character is taken from the character list and is assigned to the controlling identifier, starting with the first, and ending with the last character in the list. The following example shows how the IRPC facility operates:

```
;********************************
;Macro 2
;IRPC macro to clear all Z80
;8-bit registers
;********************************
;
XOR     A               ;clear A
IRPC    REG,BCDEHL      ;regs to clear
LD      REG,A
ENDM                    ;end of macro
END                     ;prog end
```

In this example, the statement LD REG,A is read six times, once for each character in the list BCDEHL. On the first iteration, character B is assigned to identifier REG. On the last iteration, character L is assigned to the controlling identifier. This creates a sequence of instructions which load registers B,C,D,E,H and L in turn, from register A. Note that the XOR A instruction must not be included within the IRPC loop, otherwise this instruction would also be coded six times. After assembly, the following code is produced:

```
                    MACRO-80 3.43   27-Jul-81      PAGE    1


                                                  ;********************************
                                                  ;Macro 2
                                                  ;IRPC macro to clear all Z80
                                                  ;8-bit registers
                                                  ;********************************
                                                  ;
            0000'   AF                            XOR     A               ;clear A
                                                  IRPC    REG,BCDEHL      ;regs to clear
                                                  LD      REG,A
                                                  ENDM                    ;end of macro
            0001'   47              +             LD      B,A
            0002'   4F              +             LD      C,A
            0003'   57              +             LD      D,A
            0004'   5F              +             LD      E,A
            0005'   67              +             LD      H,A
            0006'   6F              +             LD      L,A
                                                  END                     ;prog end

                    MACRO-80 3.43   27-Jul-81      PAGE    S
```

Macros:

Symbols:

No Fatal error(s)

IRP pseudo-op

The IRP (indefinite repeat) pseudo-op functions in a similar manner to IRPC, except that the controlling identifier may consist of multiple characters. The format for using IRP is as follows:

label: IRP *identifier, <cs1,cs2,cs3, ..., csn>*
        statement #1
        statement #2
        ....
        statement #n
        ENDM

where '*label*' is optional, and '*identifier*' is used as for IRPC. As an example of the use of the IRP pseudo-op, consider the following routine which is used to construct part of a 'jump' table for a CP/M BIOS program. The full jump table may be created by adding extra character lists.

```
        ;*******************************
        ;Macro 3
        ;IRP macro to create a BIOS
        ;jump table
        ;*******************************
        ;
        IRP     BIOS,<COLD,WARM,CONST,CONIN,CONOUT>
        JP      BIOS
        ENDM
        ;
COLD:   DEFS    20H     ;code for cold boot
WARM:   DEFS    20H     ;code for warm boot
CONST:  DEFS    20H     ;code for console status
CONIN:  DEFS    20H     ;code for console input
CONOUT: DEFS    20H     ;code for console output
        END
```

The instruction JP BIOS assembles as JP COLD, JP WARM etc until all character lists have been used. After assembly, the following code is produced:

MACRO-80 3.43   27-Jul-81   PAGE   1

```
                        ;*******************************
                        ;Macro 3
                        ;IRP macro to create a BIOS
                        ;jump table
                        ;*******************************
                        ;
                        IRP     BIOS,<COLD,WARM,CONST,CONIN,CONOUT>
```

```
                                        JP      BIOS
                                        ENDM
        0000'   C3 000F'        +       JP      COLD
        0003'   C3 002F'        +       JP      WARM
        0006'   C3 004F'        +       JP      CONST
        0009'   C3 006F'        +       JP      CONIN
        000C'   C3 008F'        +       JP      CONOUT
                                        ;
        000F'                   COLD:   DEFS    20H     ;code for cold boot
        002F'                   WARM:   DEFS    20H     ;code for warm boot
        004F'                   CONST:  DEFS    20H     ;code for console status
        006F'                   CONIN:  DEFS    20H     ;code for console input
        008F'                   CONOUT: DEFS    20H     ;code for console output
                                        END

            MACRO-80 3,43    27-Jul-81          PAGE    S
```

Macros:

Symbols:
```
000F'   COLD            006F'   CONIN           008F'   CONOUT
004F'   CONST           002F'   WARM
```

No Fatal error(s)

Stored macros

A 'stored macro' facility allows a programmer to associate a sequence of assembly language statements with a name which may be included at selected places throughout an assembly language source program. At first it might be thought that stored macros are similar to subroutines, but this is not the case. Macros simply provide a means of performing textual manipulation of assembly language statements at assembly time, thus effectively allowing large blocks of code to be generated with the minimum of effort on the part of a programmer. A source code statement need only contain a macro name with the addition of a few optional parameters to generate whole new blocks of code. However, using stored macros not only reduces program writing time, but also allows a programmer to simplify program control structures, devise extra instruction mnemonics and to develop languages appropriate for specific applications. A stored macro is formed by enclosing assembly language statements within MACRO and ENDM pseudo-ops in the following manner:

macname   MACRO *d1,d2,d3, ... ,dn*
              statement #1
              statement #2
              . . . .
              . . . .
              statement #n
              ENDM

where 'macname' is a label which is unique to one particular macro, *d1* to *dn* constitute a (possibly empty) list of 'dummy' parameters, and statements *#1* to *#n* are assembly language statements which form the body of a macro. Dummy parameters are used as place holders and are replaced by actual parameters on a one-for-one basis when the macro is called. Statements within the macro body may include properly formatted assembly language statements or groups, including nested in-line or stored macros. All macros must be properly terminated with an ENDM statement.

Calling a stored macro

A macro that is formed using MACRO–ENDM pseudo-ops is not assembled when encountered in a program, but is stored for subsequent use. When required, a stored macro may be 'called' for processing by a statement having the following format:

label: macname *a1,a2,a3, ... ,an*

where '*label*' is optional, and 'macname' has previously been used to identify a stored macro. Parameters to be passed to the macro are identified by sequences of characters *a1* to *an*. Upon recognition of macname, the assembler pairs off each dummy parameter in the MACRO heading (*d1* to *dn*) with the actual parameters specified in the macro call (*a1* to *an*), *d1* with *a1*, *d2* with *a2* etc until the list is exhausted. After each dummy parameter has been assigned to an actual parameter, the assembler re-reads and processes the macro body, using actual parameters in each statement. The following examples show the use of stored macros.

Saving and restoring register status

When using subroutines, it is often necessary to save the contents of registers before entering a subroutine, and restore the contents upon returning. The stack is often used for saving register contents, and the following two macros show how this task may be simplified. The SAVE macro has no parameters and is used to push register pairs AF, BC, DE and HL onto the stack. The RESTORE macro performs the reverse operation. Once these macros have been defined, the programmer may use SAVE and RESTORE as though they were normal Z80 instructions, as shown in the following program segment:

```
;************************************
;Macro 4
;subroutine calls using SAVE and
;RESTORE macros to preserve status
;************************************
;
        .Z80
        ASEG
        ORG     100H
PRINT   EQU     0F080H
;
;###### stored macro defn, ######
;
SAVE    MACRO           ;save contents of
        PUSH    AF      ;;Z80 registers
        PUSH    BC
        PUSH    DE
        PUSH    HL
        ENDM
;
RESTORE MACRO           ;restore contents
        POP     HL      ;;of Z80 registers
        POP     DE
        POP     BC
        POP     AF
        ENDM
;
;       ;###### main prog start ######
;
;use of above stored macros to
;preserve register status when
;calling a subroutine
;
        SAVE
        CALL    PRINT
        RESTORE
        END
```

Assembling this program causes the following code to be generated:

```
                    MACRO-80 3.43    27-Jul-81    PAGE    1


                                    ;************************************
                                    ;Macro 4
                                    ;subroutine calls using SAVE and
                                    ;RESTORE macros to preserve status
                                    ;************************************
                                    ;
                                            .Z80
    0000'                                   ASEG
                                            ORG     100H
    F080                        PRINT       EQU     0F080H
                                    ;
                                    ;###### stored macro defn, ######
                                    ;
                                    SAVE    MACRO           ;save contents of
                                            PUSH    AF      ;;Z80 registers
                                            PUSH    BC
                                            PUSH    DE
                                            PUSH    HL
                                            ENDM
                                    ;
```

```
                                RESTORE MACRO           ;restore contents
                                        POP     HL      ;;of Z80 registers
                                        POP     DE
                                        POP     BC
                                        POP     AF
                                        ENDM
                                        ;
                                        ;###### main prog start ######
                                        ;
                                        ;use of above stored macros to
                                        ;preserve register status when
                                        ;calling a subroutine
                                        ;
                                        SAVE
0100    F5              +               PUSH    AF
0101    C5              +               PUSH    BC
0102    D5              +               PUSH    DE
0103    E5              +               PUSH    HL
0104    CD F080                         CALL    PRINT
                                        RESTORE
0107    E1              +               POP     HL
0108    D1              +               POP     DE
0109    C1              +               POP     BC
010A    F1              +               POP     AF
                                        END

           MACRO-80 3.43   27-Jul-81    PAGE    S
```

Macros:
RESTORE   SAVE

Symbols:
F080   PRINT

No Fatal error(s)

Saving specific registers

Often it is unnecessary to save all working registers when calling subroutines. In these cases a macro may be written which allows a programmer to specify which registers are to be saved, i.e. register names are used as parameters for the macro. SAVE and RESTORE macros written in this manner are as follows:

```
;*******************************
;Macro 5
;subroutine calls using SAVE
;and RESTORE to preserve
;selected register pairs                    RESTORE MACRO   R1,R2,R3    ;restore regs
;*******************************                    POP     R1
;                                                   POP     R2
        .Z80                                        POP     R3
        ASEG                                        ENDM
        ORG     100H                        ;
PRINT   EQU     0F080H                      ;###### main program ######
        ;                                   ;
        ;###### stored macro defn, ######   ;use of above stored macros
        ;                                   ;to preserve register status
SAVE    MACRO   S1,S2,S3    ;save regs      ;when calling a subroutine
        PUSH    S1                          ;
        PUSH    S2                          SAVE    AF,HL,BC
        PUSH    S3                          CALL    PRINT
        ENDM                                RESTORE BC,HL,AF
        ;                                   END
```

After assembly, the following code is generated:

```
                        MACRO-80 3.43   27-Jul-81    PAGE   1


                                            ;*******************************
                                            ;Macro 5
                                            ;subroutine calls using SAVE
                                            ;and RESTORE to preserve
                                            ;selected register pairs
                                            ;*******************************
                                            ;
                                                    .Z80
            0000'                                   ASEG
                                                    ORG     100H
            F080                            PRINT   EQU     0F080H
                                            ;
                                            ;###### stored macro defn, ######
                                            ;
                                            SAVE    MACRO   S1,S2,S3    ;save regs
                                                    PUSH    S1
                                                    PUSH    S2
                                                    PUSH    S3
                                                    ENDM
                                            ;
```

```
                                RESTORE MACRO   R1,R2,R3    ;restore regs
                                        POP     R1
                                        POP     R2
                                        POP     R3
                                        ENDM
                                ;
                                ;###### main program ######
                                ;
                                ;use of above stored macros
                                ;to preserve register status
                                ;when calling a subroutine
                                ;
                                        SAVE    AF,HL,BC
    0100    F5              +           PUSH    AF
    0101    E5              +           PUSH    HL
    0102    C5              +           PUSH    BC
    0103    CD F080                     CALL    PRINT
                                        RESTORE BC,HL,AF
    0106    C1              +           POP     BC
    0107    E1              +           POP     HL
    0108    F1              +           POP     AF
                                        END

            MACRO-80 3.43   27-Jul-81           PAGE    S


Macros:
RESTORE         SAVE

Symbols:
F080    PRINT



No Fatal error(s)
```

Exchanging registers

The Z80 instruction set provides only one instruction to exchange the contents of register pairs (EX DE,HL), but frequently a programmer may wish to exchange the contents of other register pairs. This is possible, of course, by using available instructions to manipulate register contents, but a neater solution may be to add extra exchange instructions to the instruction set by writing a special macro. The following macro has been written for this purpose:

```
;******************************
;Macro 6
;sample program showing the               POP     R1
;use of EXCH to exchange                  POP     R2
;selected register pairs                  ENDM
;******************************           ;
;                                         ;###### main program ######
        .Z80                              ;
        ASEG                              ;use of above stored macros
        ORG     100H                      ;to create a full EXCH
        ;                                 ;instruction
        ;###### stored macro defn ######  ;
        ;                                 EXCH    BC,DE
EXCH    MACRO   R1,R2                     EXCH    IX,BC
        PUSH    R1                        EXCH    HL,BC
        PUSH    R2                        END
```

In this example, stack operations are used to store and retrieve register pairs. The order in which the specified registers are retrieved from the stack, however, is arranged to be opposite to that in which they were stored, thus resulting in an exchange of data between registers. After assembly, the following code is generated:

```
        MACRO-80 3.43    27-Jul-81         PAGE    1


                                           ;******************************
                                           ;Macro 6
                                           ;sample program showing the
                                           ;use of EXCH to exchange
                                           ;selected register pairs
                                           ;******************************
                                           ;
                                           .Z80
                                           ASEG
                     0000'                  ORG     100H
                                           ;
                                           ;###### stored macro defn ######
                                           ;
                                   EXCH    MACRO   R1,R2
                                           PUSH    R1
                                           PUSH    R2
                                           POP     R1
                                           POP     R2
                                           ENDM
                                           ;
```

```
                                        ;###### main program ######
                                        ;
                                        ;use of above stored macros
                                        ;to create a full EXCH
                                        ;instruction
                                        ;
                                        EXCH    BC,DE
        0100    C5              +       PUSH    BC
        0101    D5              +       PUSH    DE
        0102    C1              +       POP     BC
        0103    D1              +       POP     DE
                                        EXCH    IX,BC
        0104    DD E5           +       PUSH    IX
        0106    C5              +       PUSH    BC
        0107    DD E1           +       POP     IX
        0109    C1              +       POP     BC
                                        EXCH    HL,BC
        010A    E5              +       PUSH    HL
        010B    C5              +       PUSH    BC
        010C    E1              +       POP     HL
        010D    C1              +       POP     BC
                                        END


                MACRO-80 3.43  27-Jul-81         PAGE    S


        Macros:
        EXCH

        Symbols:


        No Fatal error(s)
```

ENDM and EXITM pseudo-ops

All macros or repeat blocks must end with an ENDM (end macro) statement which signifies that this is the point in the source code where macro expansion ceases. Without this statement, an assembler would have no way of knowing where a macro ends. Sometimes it is necessary to abort the expansion of a macro before an ENDM statement is encountered, for example, when a macro contains a section of conditional assembly. In such cases an EXITM (exit macro) statement must be used to terminate the macro. Under these circumstances it may be found that a conditional IF is left without a balancing ENDIF statement, therefore an EXITM statement performs the dual function of terminating an unmatched IF and terminating the macro. The format of an EXITM statement is as follows:

macname: MACRO
          statement #1
          ....
label: EXITM
          ....
          statement #n
          ENDM

where '*label*' is optional. The following example shows how an EXITM pseudo-op may be used to restrict the maximum number of repetitions which may occur when an REPT loop is used. When macro FILL is called, the user specifies parameters, CONST and LEN. CONST defines a data byte which is to be stored in LEN consecutive locations in memory. The macro accepts any value for LEN, but if a value greater than 8 is specified, the macro aborts after eight data bytes have been stored. Two call statements are shown, one with LEN less than 8 so that all data bytes are generated, and a second in which LEN is made greater than 8 so that the aborting action of EXITM may be studied.

```
;**********************************
;Macro 7
;macro to fill data block with
;user specified data constant
;and block length to a maximum
;of 8 bytes
;**********************************
;
        .Z80
        ASEG
        ORG     100H
        ;                                                   ENDM                    ;terminate macro
FILL    MACRO   CONST,LEN    ;define variables              ;
TOT     ASET    0            ;zero loop count               ;###### less than 8 ######
        REPT    LEN          ;repeats demanded              ;
        DEFB    CONST        ;;store constant               FILL    55H,4           ;4 data bytes
TOT     ASET    TOT+1        ;check for                     ;
        IFE     TOT-8        ;over limit                    ;###### more than 8 ######
        EXITM                ;if so,leave here              ;
        ENDIF                ;end conditional               FILL    20H,12          ;12 data bytes
        ENDM                 ;terminate repeat              END
```

After assembly, the following code is generated:

```
                MACRO-80 3.43   27-Jul-81      PAGE   1


                                                ;*******************************
                                                ;Macro 7
                                                ;macro to fill data block with
                                                ;user specified data constant
                                                ;and block length to a maximum
                                                ;of 8 bytes
                                                ;*******************************
                                                ;
                                                .Z80
                0000'                           ASEG
                                                ORG     100H
                                                ;
                                        FILL    MACRO   CONST,LEN       ;define variables
                                        TOT     ASET    0               ;zero loop count
                                                REPT    LEN             ;repeats demanded
                                                DEFB    CONST           ;;store constant
                                        TOT     ASET    TOT+1           ;check for
                                                IFE     TOT-8           ;over limit
                                                EXITM                   ;if so, leave here
                                                ENDIF                   ;end conditional
                                                ENDM                    ;terminate repeat
                                                ENDM                    ;terminate macro
                                                ;
                                                ;###### less than 8 ######
                                                ;
                                                FILL    55H,4           ;4 data bytes
                0100    55              +       DEFB    55H
                0101    55              +       DEFB    55H
                0102    55              +       DEFB    55H
                0103    55              +       DEFB    55H
                                                ;
                                                ;###### more than 8 ######
                                                ;
                                                FILL    20H,12          ;12 data bytes
                0104    20              +       DEFB    20H
                0105    20              +       DEFB    20H
                0106    20              +       DEFB    20H
                0107    20              +       DEFB    20H
                0108    20              +       DEFB    20H
                0109    20              +       DEFB    20H
                010A    20              +       DEFB    20H
                010B    20              + .     DEFB    20H
                                                END
```

```
                    MACRO-80 3.43   27-Jul-81      PAGE    S


                Macros:
                FILL

                Symbols:
                0008    TOT




                No Fatal error(s)
```

LOCAL pseudo-op

A macro may contain labels for jumps or data references, therefore it is important to avoid multiple-definition of labels on successive expansions of a macro, i.e. each label must be changed in some way for each expansion. This may be achieved by the use of a LOCAL statement which takes the following form:

       macro-heading
label: LOCAL *d1,d2,d3, ..., dn*
       . . . .
       ENDM

where '*label*' is optional, '*macro-heading*' is one of the REPT, IRPC, IRP or MACRO formats, and *d1* to *dn* form a list of local labels used within the macro. The LOCAL statement must appear in the macro itself, and should follow the macro header. Upon encountering a LOCAL statement, the assembler creates a symbol of the form:

..nnnn

for each of the local labels in the list. Symbols created by the assembler are in the range ..0001 to ..FFFF, and are assigned in ascending order to each local label as they are encountered, therefore a programmer should avoid using such labels for other purposes to avoid the possibility of conflicts. Each time that a macro is expanded, a complete new set of labels is created, as shown by the following example:

```
              ;**********************************
              ;Macro 8
              ;macro to print message with short
              ;delay between each character,
              ;uses BDOS function 2, and
              ;demonstrates use of 'LOCAL'
```

```
        ;************************************
        ;
        .Z80
        ASEG
        ORG     100H
BDDS    EQU     5          ;BDOS entry point
WCHR    EQU     2          ;write character
        ;
DELAY   MACRO              ;fixed time delay
        LOCAL   DLY1,DLY2
        LD      B,0        ;;256 outer loop
DLY1:   LD      C,128      ;;inner loop
DLY2:   DEC     C          ;;128,127,...etc
        JP      NZ,DLY2    ;;loop on C
        DEC     B          ;;256,255,...etc
        JP      NZ,DLY1    ;;loop on B
        ENDM
        ;
        ;###### print characters ######
        ;
        IRPC    CHAR,TEST  ;print T E S T
        LD      E,'&CHAR'  ;;load character
        LD      C,WCHR     ;;select write
        CALL    BDDS       ;;print character
        DELAY              ;;wait
        ENDM
        END
```

After assembly, the following code is generated:

```
MACRO-80 3.43   27-Jul-81      PAGE   1


                                ;************************************
                                ;Macro 8
                                ;macro to print message with short
                                ;delay between each character,
                                ;uses BDOS function 2, and
                                ;demonstrates use of 'LOCAL'
                                ;************************************
                                ;
                                .Z80
              0000'             ASEG
                                ORG     100H
```

88 *Microprocessor based systems*

```
        0005                            BDOS    EQU     5               ;BDOS entry point
        0002                            WCHR    EQU     2               ;write character
                                                ;
                                        DELAY   MACRO                   ;fixed time delay
                                                LOCAL   DLY1,DLY2
                                                LD      B,0             ;;256 outer loop
                                        DLY1:   LD      C,128           ;;inner loop
                                        DLY2:   DEC     C               ;;128,127,...etc
                                                JP      NZ,DLY2         ;;loop on C
                                                DEC     B               ;;256,255,...etc
                                                JP      NZ,DLY1         ;;loop on B
                                                ENDM
                                                ;
                                                ;###### print characters ######
                                                ;
                                                IRPC    CHAR,TEST       ;print T E S T
                                                LD      E,'&CHAR'       ;;load character
                                                LD      C,WCHR          ;;select write
                                                CALL    BDOS            ;;print character
                                                DELAY                   ;;wait
                                                ENDM
0100    1E 54                   +                LD      E,'T'
0102    0E 02                   +                LD      C,WCHR
0104    CD 0005                 +                CALL    BDOS
0107    06 00                   +                LD      B,0
0109    0E 80                   +       ..0000:  LD      C,128
010B    0D                      +       ..0001:  DEC     C
010C    C2 010B                 +                JP      NZ,..0001
010F    05                      +                DEC     B
0110    C2 0109                 +                JP      NZ,..0000
0113    1E 45                   +                LD      E,'E'
0115    0E 02                   +                LD      C,WCHR
0117    CD 0005                 +                CALL    BDOS
011A    06 00                   +                LD      B,0
011C    0E 80                   +       ..0002:  LD      C,128
011E    0D                      +       ..0003:  DEC     C
011F    C2 011E                 +                JP      NZ,..0003
0122    05                      +                DEC     B
0123    C2 011C                 +                JP      NZ,..0002
0126    1E 53                   +                LD      E,'S'
0128    0E 02                   +                LD      C,WCHR
012A    CD 0005                 +                CALL    BDOS
012D    06 00                   +                LD      B,0
012F    0E 80                   +       ..0004:  LD      C,128
0131    0D                      +       ..0005:  DEC     C
```

```
                MACRO-80 3.43    27-Jul-81      PAGE    1-1


        0132    C2 0131         +               JP      NZ,,.0005
        0135    05              +               DEC     B
        0136    C2 012F         +               JP      NZ,,.0004
        0139    1E 54           +               LD      E,'T'
        013B    0E 02           +               LD      C,WCHR
        013D    CD 0005         +               CALL    BDOS
        0140    06 00           +               LD      B,0
        0142    0E 80           +       ,,0006: LD      C,128
        0144    0D              +       ,,0007: DEC     C
        0145    C2 0144         +               JP      NZ,,.0007
        0148    05              +               DEC     B
        0149    C2 0142         +               JP      NZ,,.0006
                                                END


                MACRO-80 3.43    27-Jul-81      PAGE    S


Macros:
DELAY

Symbols:
0109    ,,0000          010B    ,,0001          011C    ,,0002
011E    ,,0003          012F    ,,0004          0131    ,,0005
0142    ,,0006          0144    ,,0007          0005    BDOS
0002    WCHR


No Fatal error(s)
```

MACLIB statement

A MACLIB statement is used to insert source code from another assembly language source file into the current source code file during assembly. This means that often-used sequences of statements may be kept in a macro library file which may be included in each newly-written program without the need to retype them. In this respect, the MACLIB statement is similar to the INCLUDE statement already described in Chapter 4. The default file type is .MAC for M80, and the file specified in the MACLIB statement is assumed to exist on the default drive.

Road intersection – Traffic light sequence

This example shows how a set of macros may be developed to simplify the writing of sequencing programs. The sequencing of traffic lights at a road junction is considered, although the principles involved are applicable to almost any similar type of problem. Two sets of lights are to be controlled, one set for the north-south direction and a second set for the east-west direction. The use of macros for this application allows an engineer to concentrate on writing programs in terms of traffic flow problems rather than worrying about detailed operation of the microprocessor.

Hardware interface

A simple interface circuit which may be connected to the parallel I/O port of a development system is shown in Fig. 5.1.

LEDs are used to simulate lights at the junction, and a counter/timer circuit is added to enable a 24 hour clock to be set up which varies the light sequence according to the time of day. In this implementation, however, the clock rate has been increased to permit testing of a system to be completed within a reasonable time period. A push-button switch is included in the circuit which may be used for a variety of different purposes, e.g. to simulate a vehicle sensor or to provide for manual operation of the lights.

Software

A special control language may be developed for traffic control systems by using routines from a macro library called XROAD.MAC. This library contains the following macros:

SETLIGHT

This macro is used to control the state of the lights in either direction at the intersection. The format for using this macro is:

SETLIGHT DIR,COLOUR

where DIR is the direction selected which may be either NS (north-south) or EW (east-west). COLOUR controls which lights are on in the selected direction, and valid colours for this parameter are:

OFF	——	*all lights off*
RED	——	*red light on*
AMBER	——	*amber light on*
GREEN	——	*green light on*

Combinations of colours may be selected by using the '+' arithmetic operator, e.g. RED+AMBER means red and amber on at the same time. Valid statements for the SETLIGHT macro are:

SETLIGHT NS,RED
SETLIGHT EW,AMBER
SETLIGHT NS,RED+AMBER

Fig. 5.1 *Traffic light interface*

WAIT

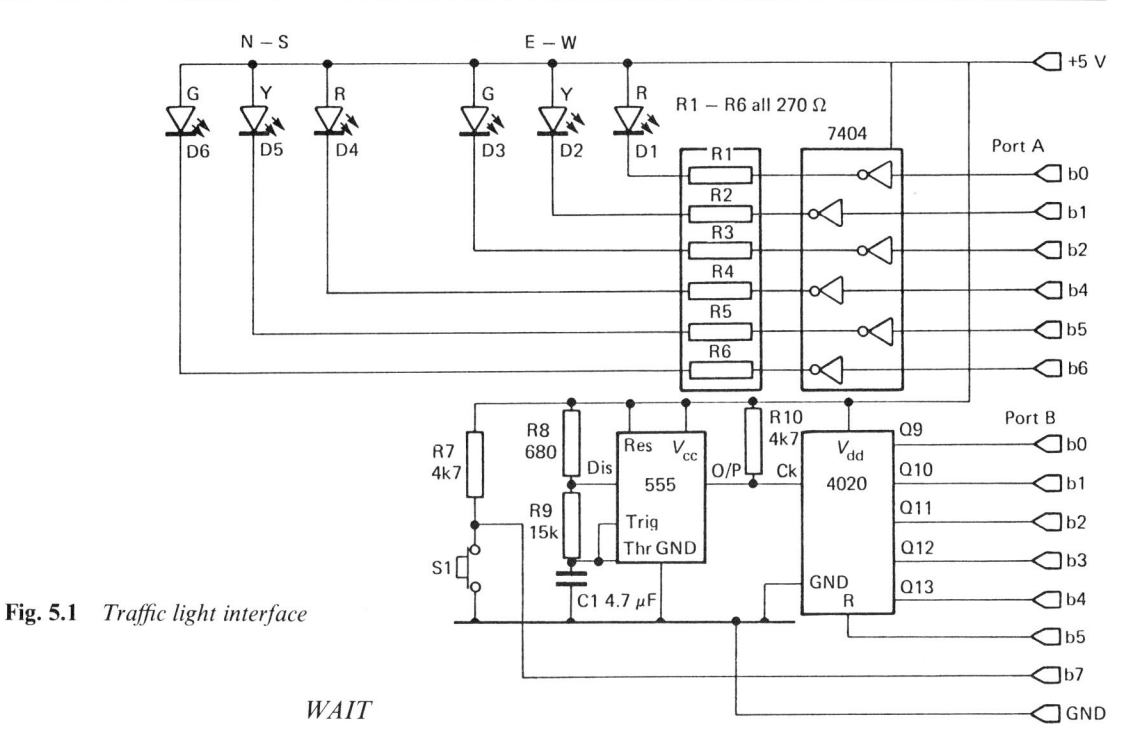

This macro provides the basic timing for the 'ON' and 'OFF' periods of the lights. The format for using this macro is:

WAIT SECONDS

where SECONDS is the approximate time period in seconds which may be expressed in any acceptable assembler form. The time period specified should not exceed 255 seconds. Valid statements are:

WAIT 1 *one second period*
WAIT 5 *five second period*

CLOCK

This macro is used to read the hour timer on the interface board, and hence determine whether the lights follow a normal day time sequence or any other selectable sequence. The format for using this macro is:

CLOCK LOW,HIGH,IFTRUE

where LOW and HIGH are the times in hours (0 to 23) during which an alternative sequence may be selected. IFTRUE enables the user to include the label for a routine which may be called if the clock indicates a time between the hours set by the LOW and HIGH parameters. Valid statements are:

CLOCK 2,5,NIGHT
CLOCK 9,18,DAY

The user must ensure that matching labels are used elsewhere in the program.

CONFIG

This macro enables the programmer to generate the necessary configuring sequence for a selected PIO or PIA. In this example a 6820 PIA is used as the I/O device, and it is located in the address range $E81C_{16}$ to $E81F_{16}$. The format for using this macro is:

CONFIG PORT,MODE

where PORT may be either PORTA or PORTB, and MODE may be either INPUT, OUTPUT or a hex value which defines the I/O configuration when using a mixture of inputs or outputs on any selected port. Valid statements are:

CONFIG PORTA,OUTPUT
CONFIG PORTB,0FH

GOTO

This macro simply redefines the Z80 mnemonic for jump (JP) as GOTO, and is used to enable a programmer to direct the program to continue processing at a different point. The format for using this macro is:

GOTO LABEL

where LABEL may be any label within the user's program that acts as the destination for the GOTO instruction.

Macro library listing

The following program listing is for the basic macro library XROAD.MAC.

```
;***********************************
;MACRO LIBRARY FOR ROAD JUNCTION
;***********************************
;
;###### input/output ports for light and clock ######
;
        PORTA   EQU     0E81CH  ;parallel port address
        PORTB   EQU     PORTA+2 ;
        OUTPUT  EQU     0FFH
        INPUT   EQU     0
        LIGHT   EQU     PORTA   ;traffic light control
        CLOCK   EQU     PORTB   ;24 hour clock
;
;
```

```
;###### bit positions for traffic light control ######
;
NSBITS  EQU     4               ;north-south bits
EWBITS  EQU     0               ;east-west bits
;
;
;###### constants for light control ######
;
OFF     EQU     0               ;light off
RED     EQU     1               ;red light on
AMBER   EQU     2               ;amber light on
GREEN   EQU     4               ;green light on
;
;
;###### macro to control each set of lights ######
;
TLIGHT  MACRO   DIR,STATE
;;      select "COLOUR" and "DIR" (direction)
COLOUR  ASET    STATE
        LD      A,(LIGHT)               ;;read port
        LD      B,240 SHR DIR&BITS      ;;prepare mask
        AND     B                       ;;mask nibble
        LD      B,A                     ;;save unchanged bits
        LD      A,COLOUR SHL DIR&BITS   ;;readied
        OR      B                       ;;combine nibbles
        LD      (LIGHT),A               ;;change lights
        ENDM
;
;
;###### macro to set cycle times ######
;
WAIT    MACRO   SECONDS         ;;assume 2MHz clock
;;      basic timing for lights in "SECONDS"
        LOCAL   DLY1,DLY2       ;;loop entry points
        LD      HL,1000*SECONDS ;;basic loop control
DLY1:   LD      B,142           ;;142*7*3,5 = 1ms
DLY2:   DEC     B               ;;142,141,...etc
        JP      NZ,DLY2         ;;loop on B
        DEC     HL              ;;1000,999,...etc
        LD      A,H             ;;make Z=1
        OR      L               ;;when HL=0
        JP      NZ,DLY1         ;;loop on HL
        ENDM
;
;
```

```
;###### macro to determine time of day ######
;
CLOCK   MACRO   LOW,HIGH,IFTRUE
;;      check for real-time clock between
;;      limits set by "LOW" and "HIGH"
;;      continue at "IFTRUE" when within
;;      these (inclusive) limits
        LOCAL   IFFALSE         ;;alternate to true
        LD      A,(PORTB)       ;;read clock
        AND     00011111B       ;;mask out clock
        CP      10              ;;greater than 09:00??
        JR      C,VALID ;;if so, then leave alone
        ADD     A,6             ;;otherwise correct it
        OR      A               ;;clear carry flag
        DAA                     ;;remove invalid BCD code
VALID:  CP      24              ;;past midnight??
        JR      C,TODAY ;;if not, check limits
        START                   ;;otherwise restart clock
;
TODAY:  CP      HIGH            ;;too late??
        JR      NC,IFFALSE
        CP      LOW             ;;or too early??
        JR      NC,IFTRUE       ;;
IFFALSE:
        ENDM
;
;
;###### macro to redefine "JP" as "GOTO" ######
;
GOTO    MACRO   GOLABEL
;;      continue execution at "GOLABEL"
        JP      GOLABEL
        ENDM
;
;
;###### macro to configure i/o port device ######
;
CONFIG  MACRO   PORT,MODE
;;      configure 6820 PIA as input or output
        XOR     A       ;;clear A
        LD      (PORT+1),A      ;;select DDR
        LD      A,MODE
        LD      (PORT),A        ;;load DDR
        LD      A,4     ;;set control bit 2
        LD      (PORT+1),A      ;;select I/O
        ENDM
;
;
```

```
;###### macro to reset clock counter ######
;
START   MACRO
;;      reset real time clock to 00hrs
        LD      A,20H           ;;pulse high
        LD      (PORTB),A       ;;reset it
        XOR     A               ;;pulse low
        LD      (PORTB),A       ;;count hrs
        ENDM
```

Sample application programs

(i) A program is required which will cause the lights to behave in the following manner:

NS continuously on GREEN
EW flashing AMBER

The source code required for this sequence is as follows:

```
;*******************************
;Traffic light sequence Road1
;*******************************
;
        .Z80                    ;assemble for Z80
        ASEG                    ;absolute location
        ORG     100H
        .XLIST                  ;suppress XROAD listing
        MACLIB  XROAD           ;library of routines
        .LIST                   ;continue listing here
        CONFIG  PORTA,OUTPUT
        CONFIG  PORTB,20H
        TLIGHT  NS,GREEN
FLASH:  TLIGHT  EW,AMBER
        WAIT    1
        TLIGHT  EW,OFF
        WAIT    1
        GOTO    FLASH
        END
```

To the reader meeting such a program for the first time, this may seem to be a radical departure from conventional Z80 assembly language. In fact, each line of program appears to be more like a high level language statement. It may come as a surprise, therefore, to learn that this program must be assembled to produce the equivalent object code. This may be carried out using a Z80 macro assembler e.g. Microsoft™ M80. Comments have been included to explain the less obvious commands, but the remainder of the program is largely self-documenting. The following code is generated after assembly by M80:

```
                  MACRO-80 3.43    27-Jul-81       PAGE    1


                                         ;*******************************
                                         ;Traffic light sequence Road1
                                         ;*******************************
                                         ;
                                         .Z80                    ;assemble for Z80
                  0000'                   ASEG                   ;absolute location
                                          ORG     100H
                                          .LIST                  ;continue listing here
                                          CONFIG  PORTA,OUTPUT
 0100   AF            +                   XOR     A
 0101   32 E81D       +                   LD      (PORTA+1),A
 0104   3E FF         +                   LD      A,OUTPUT
 0106   32 E81C       +                   LD      (PORTA),A
 0109   3E 04         +                   LD      A,4
 010B   32 E81D       +                   LD      (PORTA+1),A
                                          CONFIG  PORTB,20H
 010E   AF            +                   XOR     A
 010F   32 E81F       +                   LD      (PORTB+1),A
 0112   3E 20         +                   LD      A,20H
 0114   32 E81E       +                   LD      (PORTB),A
 0117   3E 04         +                   LD      A,4
 0119   32 E81F       +                   LD      (PORTB+1),A
                                          TLIGHT  NS,GREEN
 011C   3A E81C       +                   LD      A,(LIGHT)
 011F   06 0F         +                   LD      B,240 SHR NS&BITS
 0121   A0            +                   AND     B
 0122   47            +                   LD      B,A
 0123   3E 40         +                   LD      A,COLOUR SHL NS&BITS
 0125   B0            +                   OR      B
 0126   32 E81C       +                   LD      (LIGHT),A
 0129                           FLASH:    TLIGHT  EW,AMBER
 0129   3A E81C       +                   LD      A,(LIGHT)
 012C   06 F0         +                   LD      B,240 SHR EW&BITS
 012E   A0            +                   AND     B
 012F   47            +                   LD      B,A
 0130   3E 02         +                   LD      A,COLOUR SHL EW&BITS
 0132   B0            +                   OR      B
 0133   32 E81C       +                   LD      (LIGHT),A
                                          WAIT    1
 0136   21 03E8       +                   LD      HL,1000*1
 0139   06 8E         +      ..0000:      LD      B,142
 013B   05            +      ..0001:      DEC     B
 013C   C2 013B       +                   JP      NZ,..0001
 013F   2B            +                   DEC     HL
```

```
0140   7C              +           LD      A,H
0141   B5              +           OR      L
0142   C2 0139         +           JP      NZ,,.0000
                                   TLIGHT  EW,OFF
0145   3A E81C         +           LD      A,(LIGHT)
0148   06 F0           +           LD      B,240 SHR EW&BITS
014A   A0              +           AND     B
014B   47              +           LD      B,A
014C   3E 00           +           LD      A,COLOUR SHL EW&BITS
014E   B0              +           OR      B
014F   32 E81C         +           LD      (LIGHT),A
                                   WAIT    1
```

          MACRO-80 3.43   27-Jul-81   PAGE   1-1

```
0152   21 03E8         +           LD      HL,1000*1
0155   06 8E           +   ,,0002: LD      B,142
0157   05              +   ,,0003: DEC     B
0158   C2 0157         +           JP      NZ,,.0003
015B   2B              +           DEC     HL
015C   7C              +           LD      A,H
015D   B5              +           OR      L
015E   C2 0155         +           JP      NZ,,.0002
                                   GOTO    FLASH
0161   C3 0129         +           JP      FLASH
                                   END
```

          MACRO-80 3.43   27-Jul-81   PAGE   S

Macros:
CLOCK   CONFIG   GOTO   START   TLIGHT
WAIT

Symbols:
0139   ,,0000   013B   ,,0001   0155   ,,0002
0157   ,,0003   0002   AMBER   E81E   CLOCK
0000   COLOUR   0000   EWBITS   0129   FLASH
0004   GREEN   0000   INPUT   E81C   LIGHT
0004   NSBITS   0000   OFF   00FF   OUTPUT
E81C   PORTA   E81E   PORTB   0001   RED

No Fatal error(s)

The remaining examples are shown at source code level only. Readers with access to a microcomputer and appropriate macro assembler may choose to assemble these programs in order to study the resulting object code.

(ii) A program is required which causes the lights in the NS direction to cycle through a normal traffic light sequence, i.e. R,R + A,G,A,R... etc. The EW lights remain off.

```
;*******************************
;Traffic light sequence Road2
;*******************************
;
        .Z80                    ;assemble for Z80
        ASEG                    ;absolute location
        ORG     100H
        .XLIST                  ;suppress XROAD listing
        MACLIB  XROAD           ;library of routines
        .LIST                   ;continue listing here
        CONFIG  PORTA,OUTPUT
        CONFIG  PORTB,20H
CYCLE:  TLIGHT  EW,OFF
        TLIGHT  NS,RED
        WAIT    5
        TLIGHT  NS,RED+AMBER
        WAIT    1
        TLIGHT  NS,GREEN
        WAIT    5
        TLIGHT  NS,AMBER
        WAIT    1
        GOTO    CYCLE
        END
```

(iii) A program is required similar to example (ii), but which also causes the EW lights to cycle through the normal sequence in correct relationship with the NS lights.

```
;*******************************
;Traffic light sequence Road3
;*******************************
;
        .Z80                    ;assemble for Z80
        ASEG                    ;absolute location
        ORG     100H
        .XLIST                  ;suppress XROAD listing
        MACLIB  XROAD           ;library of routines
        .LIST                   ;continue listing here
        CONFIG  PORTA,OUTPUT
        CONFIG  PORTB,20H
        TLIGHT  NS,RED
```

Macros

```
CYCLE:  TLIGHT  EW,GREEN
        WAIT    5
        TLIGHT  EW,AMBER
        WAIT    1
        TLIGHT  EW,RED
        TLIGHT  NS,RED+AMBER
        WAIT    1
        TLIGHT  NS,GREEN
        WAIT    5
        TLIGHT  NS,AMBER
        WAIT    1
        TLIGHT  NS,RED
        TLIGHT  EW,RED+AMBER
        WAIT    1
        GOTO    CYCLE
        END
```

(iv) A program is required which causes the lights to cycle through the sequence described in (iii) during the hours 06:00 to 12:00, but to flash amber in both directions at all other times.

```
;********************************
;Traffic light sequence Road4
;********************************
;
        .Z80                    ;assemble for Z80
        ASEG                    ;absolute location
        ORG     100H
        .XLIST                  ;suppress XROAD listing
        MACLIB  XROAD           ;library of routines
        .LIST                   ;continue listing here
        CONFIG  PORTA,OUTPUT
        CONFIG  PORTB,20H
        START                   ;set clock to 00:00hrs
AM?:    CLOCK   6,12,NORMAL     ;what time is it?
        TLIGHT  EW,AMBER        ;if not morning, then
        TLIGHT  NS,AMBER        ;flash amber
        WAIT    1
        TLIGHT  EW,OFF
        TLIGHT  NS,OFF
        WAIT    1
        GOTO    AM?             ;check time again
NORMAL: TLIGHT  NS,RED
CYCLE:  TLIGHT  EW,GREEN
        WAIT    5
        TLIGHT  EW,AMBER
        WAIT    1
```

```
                TLIGHT  EW,RED
                TLIGHT  NS,RED+AMBER
                WAIT    1
                TLIGHT  NS,GREEN
                WAIT    5
                TLIGHT  NS,AMBER
                WAIT    1
                TLIGHT  NS,RED
                TLIGHT  EW,RED+AMBER
                WAIT    1           ;one cycle finished
                GOTO    AM?         ;check time again
                END
```

Problems

1. Describe the main purposes for which macros are used in an assembly language program.
2. With the aid of simple examples, describe the difference between 'stored' and 'in-line' macros.
3. Describe the operation of the following macro:

```
                            ;
                    POKE    MACRO   ADDR,DATA
                            LD      HL,ADDR
                            LD      (HL),DATA
                            ENDM
                            ;
                            ;
                            POKE    256,20
    0000'  21 0100    +     LD      HL,256
    0003'  36 14      +     LD      (HL),20
                            ;
                            END
```

4. Explain why it may be necessary to define certain labels used in stored macros as 'local'.
5. Write macros to create the following instructions for a Z80 microprocessor:
    (i)   MULT r,n—multiply the contents of register 'r' by a constant 'n',
    (ii) DIV r,n—divide the contents of register 'r' by a constant 'n',
    (iii) SHR r,n—shift the contents of register 'r' to the right 'n' places, and
    (iv) SHL r,n—shift the contents of register 'r' to the left 'n' places
    (in all cases 'r' is assumed to be an 8-bit register, and 'n' cannot exceed 255)
6. A weighing system is required to display readings in either Imperial (lb) or Metric (kg). Using macros devised in Q5, write short programs to convert:
    (i) lb to kg, and
    (ii) kg to lb.
    (only integer results are required, readings are to be left in hexadecimal form and are assumed to be within a suitable range for the macros)

6 Linking and Loading

Introduction

It is often convenient to divide software development into a number of smaller modules which may be created by different programmers, or which may be obtained from a fully debugged library of software routines.

Software development in this manner gives shorter development times, and leads to greater flexibility. At some stage, however, the separately developed modules must be combined to form the final program. The process that is used to combine these modules is known as 'linking'.

Linking source code

This is not linking in the generally accepted sense, but serves to demonstrate some of the problems associated with the linking process. If all modules are written in the same source code, e.g. Z80 assembly language, then separate modules may simply be combined with the aid of a text editor. Addresses are then allocated by a subsequent assembly process.

As an example of this technique, consider the following two Z80 source code modules:

```
;***********************************                    ;***********************************
;MODULE A                                                ;MODULE B
;move 32 bytes from BUFF1 to BUFF2                       ;Time delay routine
;adding odd parity bit during                            ;***********************************
;transfer                                                ;
;***********************************                            LD      HL,(DPARM)      ;get delay parameter
;                                                        DLY1:   LD      B,128           ;inner loop count
        LD      B,32            ;move 32 bytes           DLY2:   DEC     B               ;128,127,126 ......
        LD      HL,BUFF1        ;input buffer pointer            JP      NZ,DLY2         ;....0?
        LD      DE,BUFF2        ;output buffer pointer           DEC     HL              ;count down outer
TRANS:  LD      A,(HL)          ;get byte from buffer            LD      A,H             ;test for HL=0
        AND     01111111B       ;zero parity bit                 OR      L               ;by setting Z-flag
        JP      PO,ODDPAR       ;correct parity                  JP      NZ,DLY1         ;loop again if not 0
        OR      10000000B       ;if not, set parity bit          ;
ODDPAR: LD      (DE),A          ;send to output buffer   DPARM:  DEFS    2               ;outer loop parameter
        INC     HL              ;move input pointer
        INC     DE              ;move output pointer
        DEC     B               ;decr. byte counter
        JP      NZ,TRANS        ;moved all 32?
        ;
BUFF1:  DEFS    32              ;input buffer space
BUFF2:  DEFS    32              ;output buffer space
```

At this stage, it can be seen that addresses in neither module are fixed.

The allocation of absolute (actual) addresses in either module requires the addition of a suitable 'ORG' statement, and takes place during assembly.

Since addresses do not become fixed until after assembly, it follows that a program could be created by joining source code modules together, in any order, as a text editing process prior to assembly.

For example, joining these two modules in the order *Module A + Module B* and adding an ORG 100H statement gives the following PRN listing after assembly:

```
0100                    ORG     100H
                        ;
                        ;*********************************
                        ;MODULE A
                        ;move 32 bytes from BUFF1 to BUFF2
                        ;adding odd parity bit during
                        ;transfer
                        ;*********************************
                        ;
0100 0620               LD      B,32            ;move 32 bytes
0102 212801             LD      HL,BUFF1        ;input buffer pointer
0105 114801             LD      DE,BUFF2        ;output buffer pointer
0108 7E         TRANS:  LD      A,(HL)          ;get byte from buffer
0109 E67F               AND     01111111B       ;zero parity bit
010B E21001             JP      PO,ODDPAR       ;correct parity?
010E F680               OR      10000000B       ;if not, set parity bit
0110 12         ODDPAR: LD      (DE),A          ;send to output buffer
0111 23                 INC     HL              ;move input pointer
0112 13                 INC     DE              ;move output pointer
0113 05                 DEC     B               ;decr. byte counter
0114 C20801             JP      NZ,TRANS        ;moved all 32?
                        ;
                        ;*********************************
                        ;MODULE B
                        ;Time delay routine
                        ;*********************************
                        ;
0117 2A2601             LD      HL,(DPARM)      ;get delay parameter
011A 0680       DLY1:   LD      B,128           ;inner loop count
011C 05         DLY2:   DEC     B               ;128,127,126 ......
011D C21C01             JP      NZ,DLY2         ;....0?
0120 2B                 DEC     HL              ;count down outer
0121 7C                 LD      A,H             ;test for HL=0
0122 B5                 OR      L               ;by setting Z-flag
0123 C21A01             JP      NZ,DLY1         ;loop again if not 0
                        ;
```

Linking and loading 103

```
          0126           DPARM:  DEFS    2           ;outer loop parameter
          0128           BUFF1:  DEFS    32          ;input buffer space
          0148           BUFF2:  DEFS    32          ;output buffer space


    0128 BUFF1    0148 BUFF2    011A DLY1    011C DLY2    0126 DPARM
    0110 ODDPAR   0108 TRANS

    No errors
```

Note that it is necessary to move BUFF1 and BUFF2 to the end of the program so that the program code for Module B follows on from the end of Module A.

After assembly, it can be seen that the addresses assigned to each label are as follows:

BUFF1 = 0128   DPARM = 0126
BUFF2 = 0148   ODDPAR = 0110
DLY1 = 011A   TRANS = 0108
DLY2 = 011C

If the text editor is then used to join the two modules in the reverse order (Module B + Module A), the following PRN listing is obtained after assembly:

```
     0100                        ORG     100H
                                 ;
                                 ;***********************************
                                 ;MODULE B
                                 ;Time delay routine
                                 ;***********************************
                                 ;
     0100 2A6601                 LD      HL,(DPARM)   ;get delay parameter
     0103 0680         DLY1:     LD      B,128        ;inner loop count
     0105 05           DLY2:     DEC     B            ;128,127,126 ......
     0106 C20501                 JP      NZ,DLY2      ;....0?
     0109 2B                     DEC     HL           ;count down outer
     010A 7C                     LD      A,H          ;test for HL=0
     010B B5                     OR      L            ;by setting Z-flag
     010C C20301                 JP      NZ,DLY1      ;loop again if not 0
                                 ;
                                 ;***********************************
                                 ;MODULE A
                                 ;move 32 bytes from BUFF1 to BUFF2
                                 ;adding odd parity bit during
                                 ;transfer
                                 ;***********************************
                                 ;
```

```
010F 0620                LD      B,32            ;move 32 bytes
0111 212601              LD      HL,BUFF1        ;input buffer pointer
0114 114601              LD      DE,BUFF2        ;output buffer pointer
0117 7E         TRANS:   LD      A,(HL)          ;get byte from buffer
0118 E67F                AND     01111111B       ;zero parity bit
011A E21F01              JP      PO,ODDPAR       ;correct parity?
011D F680                OR      10000000B       ;if not, set parity bit
011F 12         ODDPAR:  LD      (DE),A          ;send to output buffer
0120 23                  INC     HL              ;move input pointer
0121 13                  INC     DE              ;move output pointer
0122 05                  DEC     B               ;decr, byte counter
0123 C21701              JP      NZ,TRANS        ;moved all 32?
                         ;
0126            BUFF1:   DEFS    32              ;input buffer space
0146            BUFF2:   DEFS    32              ;output buffer space
0166            DPARM:   DEFS    2               ;outer loop parameter
```

```
0126 BUFF1   0146 BUFF2   0103 DLY1   0105 DLY2   0166 DPARM
011F ODDPAR  0117 TRANS
```

No errors

Note that, in this example, it is necessary to move DPARM to the end of the program so that code for Module A follows on from the code for Module B.

After assembling the modules in reverse order, it can be seen that all addresses are different, and the following addresses are now assigned to the labels:

BUFF1 = 0126   DPARM = 0166
BUFF2 = 0146   ODDPAR = 011F
DLY1 = 0103   TRANS = 0117
DLY2 = 0105

Linking object code

The method just described for linking together source modules is satisfactory, provided that all modules have the same type of source code.

This may not always be the case, however, since in practice some modules may be produced using Z80 assembly language, whilst other modules may be produced using a variety of high level languages.

Provided that all source modules can be assembled or compiled into compatible object code, i.e. Z80 machine code, then it is possible to link them together to form a complete program. This is a more difficult process, however, since it entails determining which addresses within each object code module must be changed, and then making the necessary alterations.

A study of the .PRN listings for the previous examples illustrates the problems involved in linking object code modules. Therefore this is a process best carried out automatically using an appropriate linking program.

To enable a linker program to function correctly, an assembler (or high level language compiler) is required which is able to recognise and tag addresses in a module which are position dependent. Object code modules that are arranged so that addresses can be fixed by a linking process are known as 'relocatable' modules or .REL files.

M80 relocating assembler

M80 is an assembler produced by Microsoft which is capable of creating relocatable code. It is a very flexible assembler which is capable of assembling either Z80 or 8080 mnemonics, and which accepts a wide variety of the most commonly encountered pseudo-ops.

If Module A in the previous example is assembled using M80, the way in which it identifies addresses that depend upon the module position can be seen using the following PRN listing:

```
MACRO-80 3.43   27-Jul-81        PAGE   1


                                 ;********************************
                                 ;MODULE A
                                 ;move 32 bytes from BUFF1 to BUFF2
                                 ;adding odd parity bit during
                                 ;transfer
                                 ;********************************
                                 ;
0000'   06 20                    LD      B,32            ;move 32 bytes
0002'   21 0017'                 LD      HL,BUFF1        ;input buffer pointer
0005'   11 0037'                 LD      DE,BUFF2        ;output buffer pointer
0008'   7E              TRANS:   LD      A,(HL)          ;get byte from buffer
0009'   E6 7F                    AND     01111111B       ;zero parity bit
000B'   E2 0010'                 JP      PO,ODDPAR       ;correct parity?
000E'   F6 80                    OR      10000000B       ;if not, set parity bit
0010'   12              ODDPAR:  LD      (DE),A          ;send to output buffer
0011'   23                       INC     HL              ;move input pointer
0012'   13                       INC     DE              ;move output pointer
0013'   05                       DEC     B               ;decr. byte counter
0014'   C2 0008'                 JP      NZ,TRANS        ;moved all 32?
                                 ;
0017'                   BUFF1:   DEFS    32              ;input buffer space
0037'                   BUFF2:   DEFS    32              ;output buffer space
                                 ;
                                 END
```

```
                    MACRO-80 3.43    27-Jul-81          PAGE    S


         Macros:

         Symbols:
         0017'   BUFF1           0037'   BUFF2           0010'   ODDPAR
         0008'   TRANS
```

No Fatal error(s)

All addresses marked ' are addresses that are determined by a subsequent linking process, and they are all relative to the starting address of the module.

For example, if the first address of the module is 0100H, then all marked addresses within this module must have 0100H added to them during linking.

The first address of a module is determined by its position within the program and is evaluated during linking.

M80 command line

M80 may be brought into operation by entering one of the following commands:

(i) M80 [RETURN]
(ii) M80 *command line* [RETURN]

The first of these commands causes M80 to be loaded into the TPA and prompt for a command line by displaying an asterisk (*), which then allows a number of different modules to be assembled without the need to repeatedly reload M80.

The second form includes the command line when M80 is invoked, and a return to CP/M occurs at the end of the assembly process.

A command line consists of the following four fields:

object,list = source/switch

of which the source file reference (= *source*) is obligatory. The source file is assumed to have a .MAC extension, but if this is not the case, a filetype must be specified in the command line.

Acceptable formats for the command line are as follows:

(i) M80 = source   *assemble the source file, saving the result as a relocatable object file (.REL) with the same name as the source file,*

(ii) M80 , = source   *assemble the source file reporting any errors, but suppress all output files,*

(iii) M80 ,list = source   *assemble the source file, saving the result (as a relocatable object file (.REL) with the same name as the source file, and a list (.PRN) file with the name specified in the command line, and*

(iv) M80 object,list = source   *assemble the source file, saving the result as .REL and .PRN files with the names specified by 'object' and 'list'.*

Switches

Additional commands may be added at the end of a command line to 'switch on' certain assembler functions which control the manner in which assembly takes place. These additional commands, known as 'switches', consist of letters preceded by a back slash (/) mark.

A brief summary of the switches available with M80 is as follows:

/O   *use octal for the list file,*
/H   *use hexadecimal for the list file (default state),*
/R   *generate object (.REL) file with the same name as the source,*
/L   *generate list (.PRN) file with the same name as the source,*
/C   *generate special list file (.CRF) for use with the cross reference facility Microsoft CREF,*
/Z   *assemble for Z80 codes,*
/I   *assemble for 8080 codes,*
/P   *allocate extra 256 bytes of stack space for each /P (use when stack overflow error is reported),*
/M   *initialise data blocks defined by DEFS with zeros, and*
/X   *suppress listing of false conditionals.*

M80 file format

The list file (.PRN) format may be determined by studying the examples given in this chapter. However, certain indicators associated with addresses, data and labels may be noticed whose meanings are perhaps not obvious. These are:

'   *code relative,*
"   *data relative,*
!   *common relative,*
blank   *absolute,*
*   *external,*
I   *public symbol,*
U   *undefined symbol, and*
C   *common block name.*

M80 assembler directives

Since many M80 assembler directives (pseudo-ops) are identical to those already described in Chapter 4, this chapter concentrates on the additional directives that are provided to support relocation and linking of modules.

For complete details of all M80 directives, the reader is advised to consult the Microsoft M80 reference manual.

.Z80 directive

When included at the start of a source file, this directive causes the assembler to assemble Z80 mnemonics rather than 8080 mnemonics (there is a complementary .8080 directive).

The default condition is for 8080 assembly, therefore this directive must precede any Z80 programs, unless a /Z switch is used in the command line at assembly time.

ASEG directive

The ASEG directive takes the form:

label: ASEG

which instructs the assembler to use the absolute location (actual address) counter until otherwise directed. The physical location of code following ASEG is determined at assembly time by the absolute location counter which defaults to 0000, but which may be changed to a different value by means of an ORG statement. Program code which follows an ASEG directive is not relocatable.

Example of the use of ASEG in a program

The following code illustrates the effect of an ASEG directive:

```
MACRO-80 3.43   27-Jul-81        PAGE    1


                                 ;********************************
                                 ;Memory fill routine
                                 ;fills memory block with a
                                 ;defined constant
                                 ;non-relocatable
                                 ;********************************
                                 ;
                                 .Z80                ;Z80 codes
        0000'                    ASEG                ;actual addressess
                                 ORG     100H        ;start of TPA
                                 ;
        0000             BOOT    EQU     0           ;warm boot entry
```

```
0000                            CONST   EQU     0               ;constant to fill
0080                            COUNT   EQU     128             ;size of block
                                                                ;(max 256 = 0)
0100    06 80                           LD      B,COUNT         ;byte counter
0102    21 010D                         LD      HL,BUFF         ;buffer pointer
0105    36 00           FILL:           LD      (HL),CONST      ;store constant
0107    23                              INC     HL              ;move pointer
0108    10 FB                           DJNZ    FILL            ;end of block?
010A    C3 0000                         JP      BOOT            ;return to CP/M
                                        ;
010D                            BUFF:   DEFS    COUNT           ;start of block

                                        ;
018D                            $END:   END


        MACRO-80 3.43   27-Jul-81       PAGE    S


Macros:

Symbols:
018D    $END            0000    BOOT            010D    BUFF
0000    CONST           0080    COUNT           0105    FILL


No Fatal error(s)
```

CSEG directive

The CSEG directive takes the form:

label: CSEG

and instructs the assembler to use the code location counter until otherwise directed. This is the default condition, and is normally used to specify relocatable code which may subsequently be loaded into ROM. Code which follows the first CSEG directive in a program normally starts with a code relative address of 0, unless changed by a previous ORG statement. Note that an ORG statement following the CSEG directive never sets an absolute address, but merely specifies a displacement from the last used code relative address. All absolute addresses are determined at linking time, a default starting address of 0100H normally being used unless otherwise changed by switches in the linker command line. Subsequent CSEG directives cause code generation to continue from the last used code relative address.

Example of the use of CSEG in a program

The following relocatable program module shows the use of CSEG. In this case an ORG statement is included which would cause program code to start at actual address 0200H.

```
           MACRO-80 3.43   27-Jul-81      PAGE   1


                                  ;*********************************
                                  ;Memory fill routine
                                  ;fills memory block with a
                                  ;defined constant
                                  ;relocatable
                                  ;*********************************
                                  ;
                                          .Z80                    ;Z80 codes
      0000'                               CSEG                    ;relative  addresses
                                          ORG     100H            ;start of TPA
                                  ;
      0000                        BOOT    EQU     0               ;warm boot entry
      0000                        CONST   EQU     0               ;constant to fill
      0080                        COUNT   EQU     128             ;size of block
                                                                  ;(max 256 = 0)
      0100'  06 80                        LD      B,COUNT         ;byte counter
      0102'  21 010D'                     LD      HL,BUFF         ;buffer pointer
      0105'  36 00                 FILL:  LD      (HL),CONST      ;store constant
      0107'  23                           INC     HL              ;move pointer
      0108'  10 FB                        DJNZ    FILL            ;end of block?
      010A'  C3 0000                      JP      BOOT            ;return to CP/M
                                  ;
      010D'                        BUFF:  DEFS    COUNT           ;start of block

                                  ;
      018D'                        $END:  END


           MACRO-80 3.43   27-Jul-81      PAGE   S



Macros:

Symbols:
018D'   $END              0000    BOOT            010D'   BUFF
0000    CONST             0080    COUNT           0105'   FILL

No Fatal error(s)
```

DSEG directive

The DSEG directive takes the form:

label: DSEG

and instructs the assembler to use the data location counter until otherwise directed.

The reason for using separate location counters for code and data may not be obvious, but it is connected with the fact that many program modules have buffers, data tables or text following the program code. This causes no problem when considering the module in isolation, but once linked to other modules, data sandwiched between segments of code would prevent the final linked program from operating correctly. Therefore program data is usually preceded by a DSEG directive to separate it from program code.

Code which follows the first DSEG directive in a program normally starts with a data relative address of 0, unless changed by a previous ORG statement. As with CSEG, an ORG statement following the DSEG directive does not set an absolute address, but specifies a displacement from the last used data relative address. All absolute addresses are determined at linking time, a default starting address of 0100H normally being used unless otherwise changed by a data origin switch in the linker command line.

Subsequent DSEG directives cause code generation to continue from the last used data relative address.

Example of the use of DSEG in a program

The following relocatable program module shows how the use of CSEG and DSEG allows code and data in a program to be freely intermixed.

```
MACRO-80 3.43   27-Jul-81        PAGE    1

                                 ;*****************************
                                 ;Routine to display ASCII
                                 ;equivalent of character
                                 ;entered at keyboard
                                 ;*****************************
                                 ;
                                 .Z80                ;Z80 codes
0000                    BOOT     EQU     0           ;warm boot
0005                    BDOS     EQU     5           ;BDOS entry point
000D                    CR       EQU     13          ;carriage return
000A                    LF       EQU     10          ;line feed
0009                    PSTR     EQU     9           ;BDOS string print
0001                    RDCHR    EQU     1           ;BDOS console input
0002                    WCHAR    EQU     2           ;BDOS console output
                                 ;
```

```
0000'                            CSEG                        ;program code
0000'   11 0000"                 LD      DE,TEXT1            ;pointer TEXT1
0003'   0E 09                    LD      C,PSTR              ;display message
0005'   CD 0005                  CALL    BDOS                ;
                                 ;
0008'                            DSEG                        ;data
0000"   49 6E 70 75      TEXT1:  DEFM    "Input character ..... ","$"
0004"   74 20 63 68
0008"   61 72 61 63
000C"   74 65 72 20
0010"   2E 2E 2E 2E
0014"   2E 20 24
                                 ;
0017"                            CSEG                        ;program code
0008'   0E 01                    LD      C,RDCHR             ;read keyboard
000A'   CD 0005                  CALL    BDOS                ;input
000D'   32 0017"                 LD      (BUFF),A            ;store character
                                 ;
0010'                            DSEG                        ;data
0017"                    BUFF:   DEFS    1                   ;character buffer
                                 ;
0018"                            CSEG                        ;program code
0010'   11 0018"                 LD      DE,TEXT2            ;pointer TEXT2
0013'   0E 09                    LD      C,PSTR              ;display message
0015'   CD 0005                  CALL    BDOS                ;
                                 ;
0018'                            DSEG                        ;data
0018"   0D 0A 41 53      TEXT2:  DEFM    CR,LF,"ASCII code is ...... $"
001C"   43 49 49 20
0020"   63 6F 64 65
0024"   20 69 73 20
0028"   2E 2E 2E 2E
002C"   2E 2E 20 24
                                 ;
0030"                            CSEG                        ;program code
0018'   3A 0017"                 LD      A,(BUFF)            ;get ASCII code
001B'   CB 3F                    SRL     A                   ;move LH digit
001D'   CB 3F                    SRL     A                   ;into position
001F'   CB 3F                    SRL     A                   ;for display
0021'   CB 3F                    SRL     A                   ;
0023'   CD 0031'                 CALL    P1HEX               ;convert and display
```

```
              MACRO-80 3.43   27-Jul-81      PAGE    1-1


        0026'   3A 0017"              LD      A,(BUFF)        ;recover ASCII code
        0029'   E6 0F                 AND     0FH             ;mask out RH digit
        002B'   CD 0031'              CALL    P1HEX           ;convert and display
                                      ;
        002E'   C3 0000               JP      BOOT            ;return to CP/M
                                      ;
        0031'   C6 90         P1HEX:  ADD     A,90H           ;0-9, C-flag = 0
        0033'   27                    DAA                     ;A-F, C-flag = 1
        0034'   CE 40                 ADC     A,40H           ;0-9 = 30 to 39
        0036'   27                    DAA                     ;A-F = 41 to 46
        0037'   5F                    LD      E,A             ;BDOS passing reg.
        0038'   0E 02                 LD      C,WCHAR         ;display character
        003A'   CD 0005               CALL    BDOS            ;on screen
        003D'   C9                    RET
                                      ;
                                      END


              MACRO-80 3.43   27-Jul-81      PAGE    S


Macros:

Symbols:
0005    BDOS            0000    BOOT            0017"   BUFF
000D    CR              000A    LF              0031'   P1HEX
0009    PSTR            0001    RDCHR           0000"   TEXT1
0018"   TEXT2           0002    WCHAR

No Fatal error(s)
```

The linking process separates code relative and data relative sections of this program, and places all of the data segments, in correct order, following the code segments, or as otherwise directed.

Unfortunately it is not possible to obtain a list file of the final linked program, but the effect of linking may be seen by disassembling the resultant .COM file using ZSID debugger.

Note the position of the text strings in relation to the program code.

```
0100  LD    DE,013E ,TEXT1   ----------------------------
0103  LD    C,09                  Print TEXT1
0105  CALL  0005 ,BDOS
0108  LD    C,01             ----------------------------
010A  CALL  0005 ,BDOS            Read keyboard
010D  LD    (0155 ,BUFF),A
0110  LD    DE,0156 ,TEXT2   ----------------------------
0113  LD    C,09                  Print TEXT2
0115  CALL  0005 ,BDOS
0118  LD    A,(0155 ,BUFF)   ----------------------------
011B  SRL   A                     Convert and display
011D  SRL   A
011F  SRL   A
0121  SRL   A
0123  CALL  0131 ,P1HEX
0126  LD    A,(0155 ,BUFF)
0129  AND   0F
012B  CALL  0131 ,P1HEX      ----------------------------
012E  JP    0000 ,BOOT            Reboot
P1HEX:
0131  ADD   A,90             ----------------------------
0133  DAA                         Hex to ASCII
0134  ADC   A,40
0136  DAA
0137  LD    E,A
0138  LD    C,02
013A  CALL  0005 ,BDOS
013D  RET                    ----------------------------
TEXT1:
013E  LD    C,C                   ASCII text
013F  LD    L,(HL)
0140  LD    (HL),B                Input character .....
      ..............
      ............

0151  LD    L,2E
0153  JR    NZ,24            ----------------------------
BUFF:
0155  NOP                         Character buffer
TEXT2:
0156  DEC   C                ----------------------------
0157  LD    A,(BC)
0158  LD    B,C                   ASCII text
      ..............
      ............               ASCII code is ......
```

```
0167  LD   L,2E
0169  LD   L,2E
016B  LD   L,20
016D  INC  H    ----------------------------------------


013E:  49 6E                              ASCII text dump
        I  n
0140:  70 75 74 20 63 68 61 72 61 63 74 65 72 20 2E 2E
        p  u  t     c  h  a  r  a  c  t  e  r     .  .
0150:  2E 2E 2E 20 24 00 0D 0A 41 53 43 49 49 20 63 6F
        .  .  .     $  .  .  .  A  S  C  I  I     c  o
0160:  64 65 20 69 73 20 2E 2E 2E 2E 2E 2E 20 24 1A 1A
        d  e     i  s     .  .  .  .  .  .     $  .  .
0170:  1A 1A 1A 1A 1A 1A 1A 1A 1A 1A 1A 1A 1A 1A 1A 1A
        .  .  .  .  .  .  .  .  .  .  .  .  .  .  .  .
```

COMMON directive

This directive has the following format:

COMMON/*block name*/

and statements which follow are assembled to a common area of memory under the associated *block name*.

This directive is required when programs are constructed from modules, each of which must refer to a common block of memory.

For example, consider a program in which three program modules KEYIN, DISPLAY and FLUSH operate on a common buffer. The KEYIN module reads eight keyboard entries and stores them in a buffer. The DISPLAY routine reads this buffer and displays each character on the VDU screen, whilst FLUSH clears the buffer by filling it with ASCII space characters.

Allocating buffer space in each of these modules with a DSEG directive would create three separate buffers, which is clearly unacceptable. The use of a COMMON directive avoids this problem, since it allocates buffers KBUFF, PBUFF and BUFF in each of the three modules to the same common BUFFER area once the linking process has been executed.

Example showing the use of the COMMON directive

The following example shows how COMMON is used to allow these three separate modules to share a common area of buffer memory:

Module 1 – Keyboard read routine

```
                MACRO-80 3.43   27-Jul-81        PAGE    1


                                        ;********************************
                                        ;MODULE 1
                                        ;Keyboard read routine
                                        ;gets 8 characters from
                                        ;the console input (KEYIN)
                                        ;********************************
                                        ;
                                        .Z80                ;Z80 codes
        0000'                           CSEG                ;relocatable code
                                        ;
        0005                    BDOS    EQU     5           ;BDOS entry point
        0001                    RDCHR   EQU     1           ;BDOS console input
                                        ;
        0000'   21 0000!                LD      HL,KBUFF    ;keyboard buffer
        0003'   06 08                   LD      B,8         ;read 8 key presses
        0005'   0E 01                   LD      C,RDCHR     ;console input code
        0007'   C5              KEYIN:  PUSH    BC          ;save status, BDOS
        0008'   E5                      PUSH    HL          ;corrupts these
        0009'   CD 0005                 CALL    BDOS        ;get key code
        000C'   E1                      POP     HL          ;put back as they
        000D'   C1                      POP     BC          ;were
        000E'   77                      LD      (HL),A      ;fill buffer
        000F'   23                      INC     HL          ;move buffer pointer
        0010'   10 F5                   DJNZ    KEYIN       ;get all 8
                                        ;
                                        COMMON/BUFFER/
        0000!                   KBUFF:  DEFS    9,32        ;keyboard buffer
                                        ;                   ;fill with ASCII space
                                        END


                MACRO-80 3.43   27-Jul-81        PAGE    S



Macros:

Symbols:
0005    BDOS            0009C   BUFFER          0000!   KBUFF
0007'   KEYIN           0001    RDCHR


No Fatal error(s)
```

Module 2 – Display routine

```
            MACRO-80 3.43    27-Jul-81       PAGE   1


                                             ;********************************
                                             ;MODULE 2
                                             ;Print buffer routine
                                             ;prints 8 characters in
                                             ;keyboard buffer (DISPLAY)
                                             ;********************************
                                             ;
                                             .Z80                ;Z80 codes
     0000'                                   CSEG                ;relocatable code
                                             ;
     0005                        BDOS        EQU    5            ;BDOS entry point
     000D                        CR          EQU    13           ;carriage return
     000A                        LF          EQU    10           ;line feed
     0009                        PSTR        EQU    9            ;BDOS string print
     0009                        TAB         EQU    9            ;ASCII tab
     0002                        WCHR        EQU    2            ;BDOS write char
                                             ;
     0000'  1E 09                             LD     E,TAB        ;tab character
     0002'  0E 02                             LD     C,WCHR       ;write function
     0004'  CD 0005                           CALL   BDOS         ;write tab
                                             ;
     0007'  11 0000!                          LD     DE,PBUFF     ;print buffer
     000A'  0E 09                             LD     C,PSTR       ;console input code
     000C'  CD 0005                           CALL   BDOS         ;get key code
                                             ;
                                             COMMON/BUFFER/
     0000!                        PBUFF:     DEFS   8            ;print buffer
     0008!  24                               DEFB   '$'          ;string terminator
                                             ;
                                             END


            MACRO-80 3.43    27-Jul-81       PAGE   S

Macros:

Symbols:
0005    BDOS           0009C   BUFFER          000D    CR
000A    LF             0000!   PBUFF           0009    PSTR
0009    TAB            0002    WCHR

No Fatal error(s)
```

Module 3 – Clear buffer

```
              MACRO-80 3.43   27-Jul-81      PAGE   1


                                        ;******************************
                                        ;MODULE 3
                                        ;Clear old data from buffer
                                        ;and fill with ASCII space
                                        ;character (20H)  (FLUSH)
                                        ;******************************
                                        ;
                                        .Z80                    ;Z80 codes
         0000'                          CSEG                    ;relocatable codes
                                        ;
         0020                   SPACE   EQU     32              ;ASCII space
                                        ;
         0000'  21 0000!                LD      HL,BUFF         ;buffer pointer
         0003'  06 08                   LD      B,8             ;buffer size
         0005'  36 20           CLEAR:  LD      (HL),SPACE      ;clear it
         0006'  2B                      INC     HL              ;
         0007'  10 FB                   DJNZ    CLEAR           ;all cleared?
                                        ;
                                        COMMON/BUFFER/
         0000!                  BUFF:   DEFS    8               ;common buffer
                                        ;
                                        END


              MACRO-80 3.43   27-Jul-81      PAGE   S



Macros:

Symbols:
0000!   BUFF            0008C   BUFFER          0005'   CLEAR



No Fatal error(s)
```

Module 4 – Reboot system

```
                MACRO-80 3.43   27-Jul-81       PAGE   1


                                                ;******************************
                                                ;MODULE 4
                                                ;Return to CP/M
                                                ;(warm boot)     (BOOT)
                                                ;******************************
                                                ;
                                                .Z80
        0000'                                   CSEG
                                                ;
        0000                            BOOT    EQU     0
                                                ;
        0000'   C3 0000                         JP      BOOT
                                                END


                MACRO-80 3.43   27-Jul-81       PAGE   S


Macros:

Symbols:
0000    BOOT


No Fatal error(s)
```

These modules may be linked together using Digital Research's LINK program, using a command line with the following format:

LINK ECHO = KEYIN,DISPLAY,FLUSH,BOOT [RETURN]

This command generates a file called ECHO.COM which gets eight characters from the keyboard, prints these characters, clears the keyboard buffer then returns to CP/M. Unfortunately ECHO.COM cannot be listed directly, but disassembling with ZSID debugger produces the following listing in which the effect of the COMMON directive can be clearly seen.

Disassembled ECHO.COM program

```
0100  LD    HL,012E ,BUFFER  --------------------
0103  LD    B,08                Module 1 (KEVIN)
0105  LD    C,01
0107  PUSH  BC
0108  PUSH  HL
0109  CALL  0005
010C  POP   HL
010D  POP   BC
010E  LD    (HL),A
010F  INC   HL
0110  DJNZ  F5              --------------------
0112  LD    E,09                Module 2 (DISPLAY)
0114  LD    C,02
0116  CALL  0005
0119  LD    DE,012E ,BUFFER
011C  LD    C,09
011E  CALL  0005            --------------------
0121  LD    HL,012E ,BUFFER     Module 3 (FLUSH)
0124  LD    B,08
0126  LD    (HL),20
0128  INC   HL
0129  DJNZ  FB              --------------------
012B  JP    0000                Module 4 (BOOT)
BUFFER:                     --------------------
012E  JR    NZ,20
0130  JR    NZ,20               Common Buffer
0132  JR    NZ,20
0134  JR    NZ,20           --------------------
```

EXTERNAL directive

This directive has the following format:

EXTRN *label1,label2,....,labelN*

All labels in the list following EXTRN are defined as external, i.e. defined in a different module. Labels defined within the current module must not be included in this list, otherwise a 'multiple definition' error occurs.

This directive is required when constructing programs in modular form, since it frequently becomes necessary to reference labels which do not exist within the module currently being assembled. Such references would produce 'undefined label' errors when using assemblers which generate absolute code, but with relocating assemblers, the EXTRN directive may be used to suppress reporting of these particular errors. All external references are resolved during the linking process.

PUBLIC directive

This directive has the following format:

PUBLIC *label1,label2,....,labelN*

All labels in the list following this directive are defined as 'public', i.e. they may be referred to by statements within this and other modules, and are used to resolve external references during linking. All labels in the list must be defined within the current module.

Example of the use of EXTERNAL and PUBLIC in a program

The two modules shown below and on pages 122 and 123 are to be linked to form a subroutine which gets a number from the keyboard and checks whether it is valid, i.e. 0 to 9. If the number is not valid, an appropriate error message is generated.

The print routine is created as a general purpose module which has its entry point 'PRINT' declared as 'public', and the calling routine references this label as an 'external'. The reverse situation applies to the label BDOS.

Module 1 – Keyboard read

```
MACRO-80 3.43   27-Jul-81           PAGE   1

                                    ;**************************************
                                    ;Subroutine to get single digit numeric
                                    ;from keyboard
                                    ;Return with number in A and C-flag set
                                    ;if valid, otherwise clear C-flag
                                    ;and report error
                                    ;**************************************
                                    ;
                                    .Z80                ;Z80 codes
0005                        BDOS    EQU     5           ;BDOS entry point
000D                        CR      EQU     13          ;carriage return
000A                        LF      EQU     10          ;line feed
0001                        RDCHR   EQU     1           ;BDOS console input
                                    ;
                                    PUBLIC  BDOS
                                    EXTRN   PRINT
                                    ;
0000'                               CSEG                ;program code
0000'   0E 01                       LD      C,RDCHR     ;get character from
0002'   CD 0005                     CALL    BDOS        ;keyboard
0005'   FE 30                       CP      '0'         ;less than zero?
0007'   38 03                       JR      C,ERRM      ;if so, error
0009'   FE 3A                       CP      ':'         ;greater than 9?
```

```
000B'   D8                              RET     C           ;must be valid!
000C'   11 0000"            ERRM:       LD      DE,TEXT1    ;pointer TEXT1
000F'   CD 0000*                        CALL    PRINT       ;
0012'   AF                              XOR     A           ;clear C-flag
0013'   C9                              RET
                                        ;
0014'                                   DSEG
0000"   0D 0A 45 72         TEXT1:      DEFM    CR,LF,"Error ---- try again!",CR,LF,"$"
0004"   72 6F 72 20
0008"   2D 2D 2D 2D
000C"   20 74 72 79
0010"   20 61 67 61
0014"   69 6E 21 0D
0018"   0A 24
                                        ;
                                        END
```

```
            MACRO-80 3.43   27-Jul-81       PAGE    S


Macros:

Symbols:
  0005I   BDOS          000D    CR          000C'   ERRM
  000A    LF            0010*   PRINT       0001    RDCHR
  0000"   TEXT1


No Fatal error(s)
```

Linking loaders

Most linkers programs such as Microsoft's L80 or Digital Research's LINK are actually linking loaders which perform the dual functions of linking and loading.

Loading is a process which physically places a file into memory and replaces the relative addresses which were assigned by the assembler with absolute addresses.

Linking is a process which assigns absolute addresses to those parts of one loaded module which reference instructions or data in another loaded module, i.e. the assigned address links the two modules.

These two processes combine to generate a machine executable (.COM) file from one or more relocatable (.REL) files. The code contained in .REL files cannot be executed without first being subjected to this linking and loading process.

Module 2 – Print routine

```
            MACRO-80 3.43   27-Jul-81        PAGE    1


                                        ;***********************************
                                        ;Subroutine to display text string
                                        ;Enter with DE pointing to start of
                                        ;text string
                                        ;***********************************
                                        ;
                                        .Z80                    ;Z80 codes
  0009                         PSTR     EQU     9               ;BDOS print string
                                        ;
                                        PUBLIC  PRINT
                                        EXTRN   BDOS

                                        ;
  0000'                                 CSEG                    ;program code
  0000'    0E 09              PRINT:    LD      C,PSTR          ;display message
  0002'    CD 0000*                     CALL    BDOS            ;
  0005'    C9                           RET
                                        ;
                                        END


            MACRO-80 3.43   27-Jul-81        PAGE    S

Macros:

Symbols:
0003*    BDOS           0000I'  PRINT            0009    PSTR



No Fatal error(s)
```

LINK linker/loader

The Digital Research LINK program may be used to combine or link relocatable object code modules produced by RMAC (8080), M80 (8080 or Z80), or any high level languages (e.g. BASCOM, F80) which are capable of generating REL files in Microsoft format.

A LINK command line takes the following form:

LINK *filename1,filename2,....,filenameN*

where filename1 to filenameN are the object files to be linked. If file types are not specified, .REL files are assumed.

For example, two modules MOD1.REL and MOD2.REL are linked by entering the following command:

LINK MOD1,MOD2

After completing linking, the following information is listed at the console output:
 (i) the symbol table,
 (ii) any unresolved symbols,
 (iii) the memory map, and
 (iv) the use factor.

For example, when Module 1 and Module 2 in the previous example are linked, the following information is listed:

```
LINK 1,31

BDOS      0005    PRINT    0114  (----------- symbol table
          (----------------------------------- unresolved symbols (none)
ABSOLUTE       0000              |
CODE SIZE      001A (0100-0119)  |
DATA SIZE      001A (011A-0133)  |(----------- memory map
COMMON SIZE    0000              |
USE FACTOR     00   (----------------------- use factor
```

Output files created

Two output files are normally created by the linking process, *filename1*.COM and *filename1*.SYM, where '*filename1*' is the first file listed in the command line. If a different filename is required for the linked modules rather than assigning the .COM file to the first filename in the list, a command line of the following type may be used:

LINK *newfilename=filename1,filename2,......,filenameN*

For example, the command line:

LINK ECHO=KEYIN,DISPLAY,FLUSH,BOOT

creates the file ECHO.COM which consists of modules KEYIN, DISPLAY, FLUSH and BOOT linked together in that order. The file ECHO.SYM, which contains a symbol table for the linked program, is also generated.

Switches

Most linkers also support a number of optional 'switches' which control the manner in which linking takes place. These switches should not be confused with the switches used with an assembler, they are quite different.

LINK supports a number of switches which must be enclosed in square brackets, separated by commas, immediately following one or more of the filenames in the command line. For example:

LINK *KEYIN*[L2000],*DISPLAY,FLUSH,BOOT* [NL,GSTART]

A summary of the switches used with LINK is as follows:

[A] *provide additional space for the symbol table,*
[D] *origin for DATA and COMMON segments,*
[G] *program start label (LINK inserts jump to this label),*
[L] *load address (base address of COM file – usually 0100H),*
[NL] *suppress listing of symbol table at console,*
[NR] *suppress generation of SYM file,*
[OC] *generate COM file (default condition),*
[P] *program origin (defaults to load address),*
[Q] *list and record run-time library ?nnnn symbols,*
[S] *search preceding library file, link reference modules only, and*
[$] *control source and destination devices.*

Other switches are provided for more specialised applications, e.g., when using MP/M or special languages. For details of these and full information on the switches listed, the reader is advised to consult a Digital Research LINK reference manual.

Error messages

When errors are detected in the command line, LINK echoes the command line up to the point where the error occurs to indicate to the user the source of the error.

The following types of error messages may be displayed:

CANNOT CLOSE:	*output file cannot be closed— disk write protected?*
COMMON ERROR:	*undefined COMMON block selected,*
DIRECTORY FULL:	*no directory space for output files,*
DISK READ ERROR:	*cannot read file properly,*
DISK WRITE ERROR:	*cannot write file—disk full?,*
FIRST COMMON NOT LARGEST:	*subsequent COMMON larger than the first COMMON declared,*
INSUFFICIENT MEMORY:	*not enough room for LINKs buffers,*
INVALID REL FILE:	*REL file incorrect format,*
MAIN MODULE ERROR:	*second main module encountered,*

MEMORY OVERFLOW:	*not enough room to complete linking,*
MULTIPLE DEFINITION:	*symbol defined in more than one module,*
NO FILE:	*cannot find file specified,*
OVERLAPPING SEGMENTS:	*loading into segment already in use,*
UNDEFINED START SYMBOL:	*G switch symbol non-existent,*
UNDEFINED SYMBOLS:	*symbols referenced but not defined, and*
UNRECOGNISED ITEM:	*unfamiliar bit pattern—ignored.*

Loading

In general, the .HEX object code produced by an assembler cannot be executed as a program, since it is usually still in ASCII form.

For example, consider an instruction such as LD A,5 which represents the object code 3E 05. This code is stored in a .HEX file as the following sequence of ASCII codes:

Object code ⎯⎯» 3 E 0 5
ASCII codes ⎯⎯» 33 45 30 35

While this format simplifies the transfer of data files, it is obvious that if it is presented to a Z80 microprocessor, it will not perform the intended operation.

A program is required which can operate on a .HEX file and convert the ASCII encoded instructions into their pure binary equivalents. Such a program is called a 'loader', and the binary codes that it generates are stored as a machine-executable (.COM) file.

Some assemblers, e.g. Z80ASM, and most linkers contain loader modules which enable them to generate .COM files directly.

Debugging programs such as ZSID also contain loader routines, since it is necessary to convert the ASCII instruction codes of a .HEX file into binary instructions before debugging can take place. It is therefore possible to create a machine-executable file by writing this 'memory image' back onto disk with a .COM file extension. This may be achieved using the 'W' (Write) command of the debugger if one is available. If such a command is not available, then it is possible to save the memory image by returning to CP/M, and then executing an appropriate 'save' command (see Chapter 2).

If CP/M 3.0 is being used, SAVE is not available as a built-in command, since a warm boot causes this operating system to overwrite the lower end of the TPA with its CCP, thus making any attempt to save data in these locations a pointless exercise. Instead, it is necessary to execute the program SAVE.COM prior to calling up the debugger program. This then intercepts the return to CP/M and prompts the user for a filename and memory limits before performing the actual save, the warm boot being delayed until after completion of the save operation.

Using a debugging program to create a .COM file may seem a little complicated, but in most cases it is not necessary, since loader programs are available specially for this purpose, e.g. LOAD.COM for CP/M 2.2 or HEXCOM.COM for CP/M 3.0.

The LOAD command reads a file (*ufn*) which is assumed to contain HEX format machine code, and produces a memory image file which may be subsequently executed.

For example, assuming the file FILL.HEX is available, FILL.COM may be created by means of the following command line:

LOAD FILL   (or HEXCOM.FILL)

Note that it is only necessary to specify the filename in the command line, the file extension .HEX being assumed.

Upon completion of the loading operation, a message similar to the following is displayed:

HEXCOM VERS: 3.00

FIRST ADDRESS 0100
LAST ADDRESS 010C
BYTES READ 000D
RECORDS WRITTEN 01

LOAD/HEXCOM error messages

Typical error messages associated with LOAD or HEXCOM are as follows:

DISK READ ERROR:	*cannot read file properly*
LOAD ADDRESS LESS THAN 100:	*program origin less than 0100H*
DISK WRITE ERROR:	*disk full?*
LOAD ADDRESS ERROR:	*cannot load at this address*
INVALID HEX DIGIT:	*non-hex value found in .HEX file*
CHECKSUM ERROR:	*checksum not*
CANNOT OPEN SOURCE FILE:	*hex file not on specified drive*
DIRECTORY FULL:	*no space for .COM file entry*
CANNOT CLOSE FILE:	*disk write protected?*

Relocatable file library manager

It is good programming practice to construct programs by linking together a series of .REL modules. Therefore a programmer may wish to store frequently used modules as a library file which can be searched at linking time for routines referenced by any of the .REL files being linked. The linker program can then extract the appropriate routine from the library.

A library manager program can be used to create such a library, and to maintain it by allowing modules to be appended, replaced, selected or deleted. Both Microsoft (LIB80) and Digital Research (LIB) provide library managers for managing object modules in Microsoft .REL format, although the commands, particularly the switches, are not compatible.

LIB library manager

Assuming that a library called '*libname.REL*' is being created or modified using modules '*mod1.REL, mod2.REL*' etc, command lines of the following type may be used:

(i)   LIB libname = mod1,mod2,...., modN   ——— *construct a library using modules mod1, mod2 etc*

(ii) LIB libname = libname < mod1 = >   ——— *delete mod1 from the library*

(iii) LIB libname = libname < mod1 = mod5 >   ——— *replace mod1 in the library with mod5*

(iv) LIB libname = libname,mod4   ——— *append mod4 to library*

(v)   LIB newlib = libname(mod1,mod4)   ——— *select modules mod1 and mod4 from library to construct a new library*

Combinations of these commands may be used, for example:

LIB IOLIB = IOLIB < INIT = > ,CONFIG

This command line deletes the file INIT.REL from library IOLIB.REL and appends the file CONFIG.REL.

LIB options

Certain options are available when using LIB. Options are selected by adding a letter (enclosed in square brackets) to the preceding filename. The following options are available:

(i)   [I]   *(INDEX option) create an indexed library file (.IRL) which enables the linker to perform a much faster search. This facility can only be used in conjunction with Digital Research's LINK.COM,*

(ii) [M] *(MODULE option) display names of modules in the selected library,*

(iii) [P]   *(PUBLIC option) display names of modules and public variables contained within selected library, and*

(iv) [D] *(DUMP option) display the contents of .REL files in ASCII, generating displays similar to this sample:*

```
LIB 1,1

program name KEYIN
define common size BUFFER A0009
define data size A0000
```

```
        define program size P0012
        set program counter P0000
         P0000  21
        select common block BUFFER
         P0001  C0000 06 08 0E 01 C5 E5 CD 05 00 E1 C1 77 23
         P0010  10 F5
        set program counter C0000
         C0000  20 20 20 20 20 20 20 20 20
        end program A0000

        program name FILL
        define data size A0000
        set program counter A0100
         A0100  06 80 21 0D 01 36 00 23 10 FB C3 00 00
        set program counter A018D
        end program A0000
```

Cross-referencing of symbols

A cross-referencing facility is designed to provide a special cross-reference list file which shows the usage of all symbols within an assembly language program, and record where they occur. Although this is not an essential facility, it can simplify the tracing of large programs during debugging or maintenance operations. It may also be used to locate redundant labels and routines after program modifications. Examples of cross-reference utilities are Microsoft's CREF and Digital Research's XREF.

XREF cross-reference facility

This facility requires a list file (.PRN), and a symbol file (.SYM) for the program for which a cross-reference is required.
The command line has the following format:
 (i) XREF *filename*, or
 (ii) XREF *filename* $P

The first of these commands generates a cross-reference file (.XRF) from the .PRN and .SYM files, whilst the second form sends cross-referencing data to the list device (printer).

The .XRF listing on pages 130–131 shows how XREF appends line numbers and a cross-reference table to a typical .PRN file.

Problems

1. (a) Describe the main difference between files created by relocatable and non-relocatable assemblers.
   (b) Name the processes which must be used to convert files produced by a relocatable assembler into machine-executable object code files.

130 *Microprocessor based systems*

```
1                               ;********************************
2                               ;Routine to display ASCII
3                               ;equivalent of character
4                               ;entered at keyboard
5                               ;********************************
6                               ;
7    0100                ORG     100H
8                               ;
9    0000 =      BOOT    EQU    0            ;warm boot
10   0005 =      BDOS    EQU    5            ;BDOS entry point
11   000D =      CR      EQU    13           ;carriage return
12   000A =      LF      EQU    10           ;line feed
13   0009 =      PSTR    EQU    9            ;BDOS string print
14   0001 =      RDCHR   EQU    1            ;BDOS console input
15   0002 =      WCHAR   EQU    2            ;BDOS console output
16                               ;
17   0100 113F01         LD     DE,TEXT1     ;pointer TEXT1
18   0103 0E09           LD     C,PSTR       ;display message
19   0105 CD0500         CALL   BDOS         ;
20                               ;
21   0108 0E01           LD     C,RDCHR      ;read keyboard
22   010A CD0500         CALL   BDOS         ;input
23   010D 323E01         LD     (BUFF),A     ;store character
24                               ;
25   0110 115301         LD     DE,TEXT2     ;pointer TEXT2
26   0113 0E09           LD     C,PSTR       ;display message
27   0115 CD0500         CALL   BDOS         ;
28                               ;
29   0118 3A3E01         LD     A,(BUFF)     ;get ASCII code
30   011B CB3F           SRL    A            ;move LH digit
31   011D CB3F           SRL    A            ;into position
32   011F CB3F           SRL    A            ;for display
33   0121 CB3F           SRL    A            ;
34   0123 CD3101         CALL   P1HEX        ;convert and display
35   0126 3A3E01         LD     A,(BUFF)     ;recover ASCII code
36   0129 E60F           AND    0FH          ;mask out RH digit
37   012B CD3101         CALL   P1HEX        ;convert and display
38                               ;
39   012E C30000         JP     BOOT         ;return to CP/M
40                               ;
41   0131 C690   P1HEX:  ADD    A,90H        ;0-9, C-flag = 0
42   0133 27             DAA                 ;A-F, C-flag = 1
43   0134 CE40           ADC    A,40H        ;0-9 = 30 to 39
44   0136 27             DAA                 ;A-F = 41 to 46
45   0137 5F             LD     E,A          ;BDOS passing reg.
46   0138 0E02           LD     C,WCHAR      ;display character
47   013A CD0500         CALL   BDOS         ;on screen
```

Linking and loading 131

```
48   013D C9                  RET
49                             ;
50   013E            BUFF:    DEFS    1                    ;character buffer
51                             ;
52   013F 496E7075  TEXT1:   DEFM    'Input character,,,,$'
53   0153 0D0A      TEXT2:   DEFB    CR,LF
54   0155 41534349           DEFM    'ASCII code is ,,,,,$'
55                             ;
56   0000                    END
57
58
59   0005 BDOS      0000 BOOT     013E BUFF      000D CR       000A LF
60   0131 P1HEX     0009 PSTR     0001 RDCHR     013F TEXT1    0153 TEXT2
61   0002 WCHAR
62
63   No errors
```

```
BDOS      0005    10#    19    22    27    47
BOOT      0000     9#    39    59#
BUFF      013E    23     29    35    50#    59
CR        000D    11#    53    59
LF        000A    12#    53    59
P1HEX     0131    34     37    41#
PSTR      0009    13#    18    26    60#
RDCHR     0001    14#    21    60
TEXT1     013F    17     52#   60
TEXT2     0153    25     53#   60
WCHAR     0002    15#    46
```

2. (a) In an assembly language program, what is:
   (i) a public symbol, and
   (ii) an external symbol?
   (b) With the aid of a simple example, demonstrate the necessity for using PUBLIC and EXTRN directives (pseudo-ops) in program modules.
3. Identify the changes that must be made to the following object code when the program is moved to a new location in memory.

```
0004 =                PORT    EQU     4
                       ;                              010D C20501            JP      NZ,SEND
0100 1E08             LD      E,8                    0110 C30000            JP      0
0102 211301           LD      HL,TABLE               0113          TABLE:   DEFS    8
0105 7E      SEND:    LD      A,(HL)                                        ;
0106 D304             OUT     (PORT),A               011B 0680    WAIT:    LD      B,80H
0108 23               INC     HL                     011D 05      DLY:     DEC     B
0109 CD1B01           CALL    WAIT                   011E C21D01            JP      NZ,DLY
010C 1D               DEC     E                      0121 C9                RET
```

4. (a) Describe the function of CSEG and DSEG directives (pseudo-ops) in an assembly language program.
   (b) In the following program module, show where CSEG and DSEG directives should be used if the module is to be effectively linked to other modules.

```
                PORT    EQU     4
        ;
        ;configure PIO
        ;
                LD      B,5
                LD      HL,CTRLB
        CONFIG: LD      A,(HL)
                OUT     (PORT+2),A
                INC     HL
                DJNZ    CONFIG
        ;
        CTRLB:  DEFB    0CFH,29H,20H,0B7H,0D6H
        ;
        ;interrupt vector
        ;
                LD      A,0DH
                LD      I,A
                LD      HL,0D25H
                LD      (INTVEC),HL
        ;
        INTVEC: DEFS    2
        ;
        ;read port
        ;
                IN      A,(PORT)
                LD      (IOBYTE),A
        ;
        IOBYTE: DEFS    1
        ;
        ;
        ;
                END
```

5. (a) State the function of a loader program.
   (b) If a loader program operates upon the file SAMPLE.HEX, name the additional file created, and describe how this file differs from the original file.

7 Debuggers

Introduction

Once a program has been correctly assembled, it is necessary to test it for correct functioning, i.e. dynamic testing. The fact that a program assembles without errors is no indication that it is free from logical errors. Such logical errors which prevent a program from operating correctly are known as 'bugs', and the process of detecting and eliminating them is known as 'debugging'.

Debugging programs

Special programs are required which allow dynamic testing of programs under controlled conditions, and these are called 'debugging programs' or 'debuggers'. A debugging program actually consists of a number of independent test routines, each selectable from within a command loop by a single command letter followed by parameters. This arrangement is shown in Fig. 7.1.

Certain routines must be available in a debugging program, but others are desirable rather than being essential. Typically routines may be included to perform the following operations:

  (i) inspection/alteration of the contents of specified memory locations
 (ii) inspection/alteration of the contents of specified registers
(iii) dumping blocks of memory on the display device in tabular form
 (iv) executing a program in real time from a specified address
  (v) single instruction execution or 'single stepping'
 (vi) setting 'break-points' so that a program may be halted once a specified instruction address is encountered
(vii) performing a software trace so that the sequence of instructions leading up to a selected event may be studied
(viii) moving blocks of data from one area of memory to another
 (ix) filling blocks of memory with a selected constant
  (x) performing 'in-line' assembly
 (xi) listing programs as disassembled mnemonics

CP/M is usually supplied with a debugger for the 8080 microprocessor such as DDT (Dynamic Debugging Tool) or SID (Symbolic Instruction Debugger), but for most Z80 programs neither of these is particularly

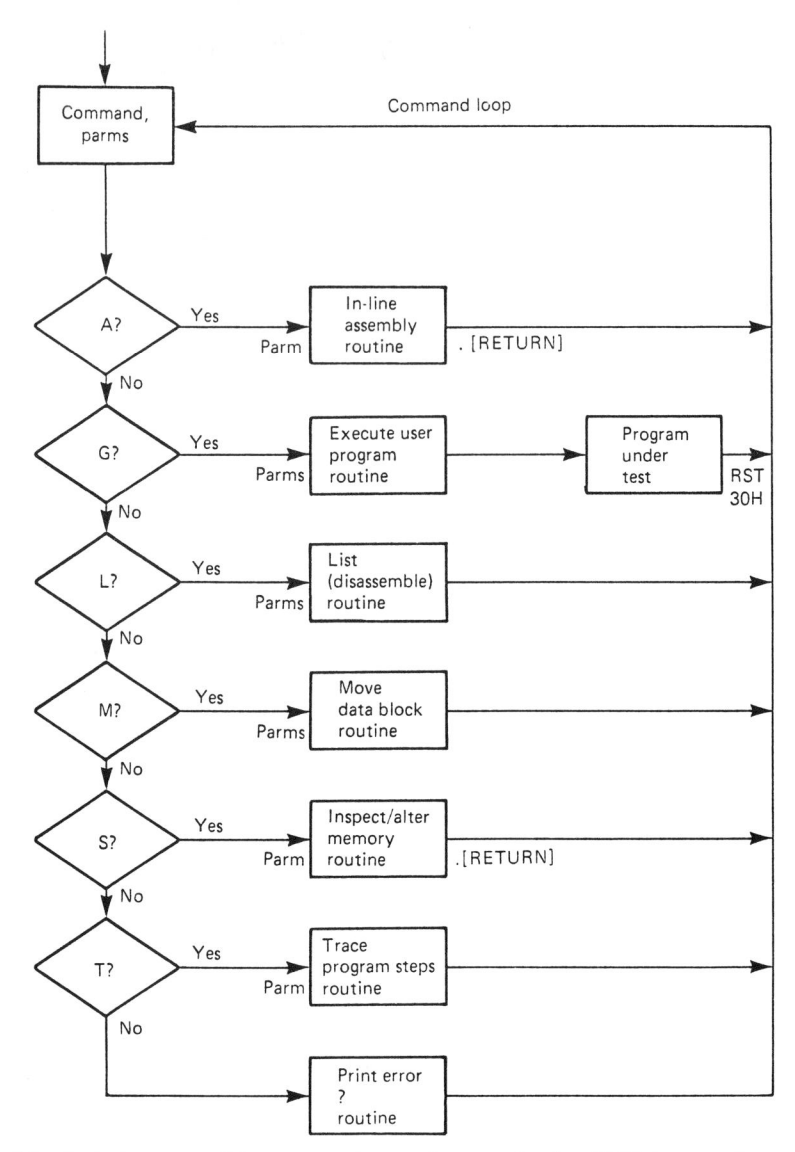

Fig. 7.1 *Debugger command loop*

suitable. It is just possible to use them where only the 8080 instruction subset of the Z80 has been used for writing a program, and the states of registers unique to the Z80 do not need to be considered.

A number of Z80 debuggers are available to run under CP/M, and in fact, Digital Research have produced a version of SID specifically for the Z80 called ZSID (Z80 Symbolic Instruction Debugger). This chapter concentrates on the use of ZSID because its commands are compatible with many other debugging programs. It is not intended, however, to cover all aspects of ZSID. For full information, the reader is advised to study the reference manuals, normally supplied with the software at the time of purchase.

Loading ZSID

The ZSID debugger may be brought into operation by entering a command line having one of the following forms:

ZSID [RETURN]
ZSID filename.HEX [RETURN]
ZSID filename.COM [RETURN]

The first form of this command simply loads the debugger program into the TPA. The second and third forms of command additionally load specified files into the TPA for debugging, and are also equivalent to entering the following sequence of commands:

ZSID [RETURN]
I filename.HEX [RETURN]   (or filename.COM)
R [RETURN]

where the I and R commands are used to select and load a file once ZSID is in operation. Other file types may be loaded into the TPA, e.g. text files, but there are few advantages in doing this.

Once loaded into the TPA, ZSID relocates itself to the top of memory, overwriting the CCP in CP/M 2.2 systems, so that maximum memory space is available for programs being debugged. This relocation process automatically takes into account the actual amount of memory available, thus making it independent of any specific CP/M configuration. The memory map with ZSID loaded is shown in Fig. 7.2.

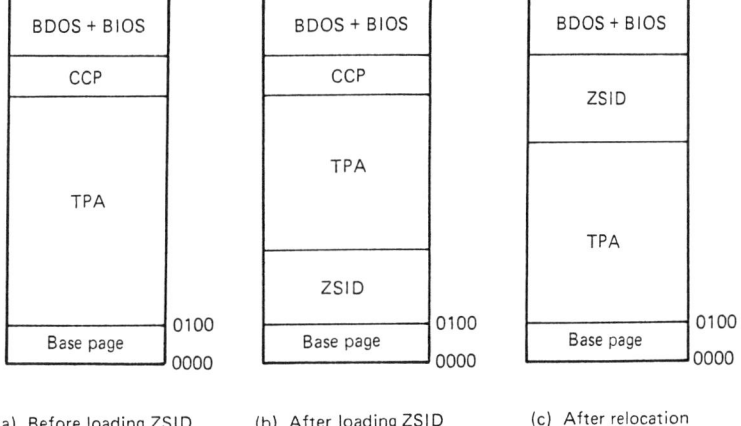

Fig. 7.2 *Location of ZSID in memory*

(a) Before loading ZSID
(b) After loading ZSID
(c) After relocation

Once loaded, ZSID prints a sign-on message similar to the following:

ZSID VERS 1.4

The character '#' is then printed as a prompt to indicate that the debugging program is waiting for an input command from the keyboard. Commands are executed once the 'RETURN' or 'NEWLINE' key is pressed, indicated in the remainder of this chapter as [RETURN].

Leaving ZSID

At any point during the debugging process, a return to CP/M may be effected by responding to the # prompt with one of the following commands:

[CTRL]–C
G0   (*execute from address 0*)

Either of these commands causes CP/M to execute a 'warm boot' sequence.

ZSID commands

The following basic commands are available with ZSID, and are typical of the commands that may be expected in most debugging programs. They may be entered at any time when the # prompt is being displayed.

A	*enter assembly language mnemonics and operands*
D	*dump a block of memory in hex and ASCII*
F	*fill memory with a constant*
G	*execute program (with optional breakpoints)*
I	*set up input file control block*
L	*disassemble (list) memory*
M	*move data from one location to another*
R	*read file specified by I command into memory*
S	*inspect/alter memory locations*
T	*trace program execution*
U	*untrace (trace without intermediate step displays)*
W	*write specified memory block to disk*
X	*inspect/alter MPU state (registers and flags)*

Input data and addresses are normally considered as hexadecimal, although decimal inputs may be used if preceded by a hash symbol (#), and ASCII inputs may be used if preceded by a quote symbol ("). Additionally, provided that an appropriate symbol table has been loaded, symbolic data and addresses may be used in commands.

If control is handed over to the user's program using the G command, a return to ZSID may be effected by executing one of the RST instructions (typically RST 30H, since RST 38H may be used for the console interrupt system). Therefore, for debugging purposes only, programs normally terminate with an RST 30H instruction.

A (*Assemble*) command

This command allows in-line assembly to be used to write code directly into memory. Such a facility is very useful for making small alterations to a program or for devising short routines for subsequent incorporation into a larger program.

The forms of this command are:

(i) As
(ii) A
(iii) −A

where 's' is a numeric or symbolic address.

The first of these forms allows in-line assembly to start at an address defined by 's'. For example:

```
A100 [RETURN]              start assembly at 0100H
0100 LD C,8 [RETURN]       load register C with 8
0102 DEC C [RETURN]        decrement register C
0103 JR NZ,102 [RETURN]    jump to 0102 until C=0
0105 RST 30 [RETURN]       return to ZSID
0107 [RETURN]              leave 'A' command
```

The second form is similar except that, since no starting address is supplied, assembly continues from the last used address.

The third form of the command removes the assembler/disassembler module from the system to give extra memory space for debugging of large programs.

D (*Dump*) memory command

This command allows blocks of memory to be displayed in both hex and ASCII using either byte or word format. Such a facility is useful for identifying certain blocks of data within a program, particularly blocks of text.

The forms of this command are:

(i)   Ds   or   DWs
(ii) Ds,f   or   DWs,f
(iii) D   or   DW
(iv) D,f   or   DW,f

where 's' (start) and 'f' (finish) are numeric or symbolic addresses. Where start or finish addresses are not specified, default values are adopted automatically. The 'W' form of the command displays words (16-bit) rather than bytes (8-bits). Examples are shown on page 138.

Note how the word format reverses the low and high byte, so that any addresses which are stored in memory in the usual 'low order first' format may be read more easily.

(i) *Byte format*

```
#D100 [RETURN]
0100: 01 F9 21 C3 A0 01 43 4F 50 59 52 49 47 48 54 20
      . . ! . . . C  O  P  Y  R  I  G  H  T
0110: 28 43 29 20 31 39 37 37 2C 20 44 49 47 49 54 41
      (  C  )     1  9  7  7  ,     D  I  G  I  T  A
0120: 4C 20 52 45 53 45 41 52 43 48 20 20 20 20 20 5A
      L     R  E  S  E  A  R  C  H                 Z
0130: 53 49 44 20 56 45 52 53 20 31 2E 34 24 31 00 02
      S  I  D     V  E  R  S     1  .  4  $  1  .  .
0140: C5 C5 11 2F 01 0E 09 CD 05 00 C1 21 07 00 7E 3D
      .  .  .  /  .  .  .  .  .  .  .  !  .  .  ~  =
0150: 90 57 1E 00 D5 21 00 02 78 B1 CA 65 01 0B 7E 12
      .  W  .  .  .  !  .  .  x  .  .  e  .  .  ~  .
```

(ii) *Word format*

```
#DW100 [RETURN]
0100: F901 C321 01A0 4F43 5950 4952 4847 2054
      . . ! . . . C O  P Y  R I  G H  T
0110: 4328 2029 3931 3737 202C 4944 4947 4154
      ( C  )    1 9  7 7  ,    D I  G I  T A
0120: 204C 4552 4553 5241 4843 2020 2020 5A20
        L  R E  S E  A R  C H            Z
0130: 4953 2044 4556 5352 3120 342E 3124 0200
      S I  D    V E  R S  1    4 .  1 $  . .
0140: C5C5 2F11 0E01 CD09 0005 21C1 0007 3D7E
      . .  . /  . .  . .  . .  . !  . .  = ~
0150: 5790 001E 21D5 0200 B178 65CA 0B01 127E
      . W  . .  ! .  . .  . x  e .  . .  . ~
```

F (*Fill*) command

This command may be used to initialise a block of memory with a constant. For example, 0FFH may be used where a partially written block is copied into EPROM, or 1AH (end of file marker) may be used when the data block is to be subsequently written to disk.

The form of this command is:

Fs,f,c

where 's' (start of block), 'f' (end of block) and 'c' (constant) are in numeric or symbolic form.

For example:

F100,1FF,1A [RETURN]

which fills memory locations 0100H to 01FFH with the constant 1AH.

G (*Go*) command

This command passes control to the program under test which then executes in real time from the address specified.

The formats for this command are:

(i) G or −G
(ii) Gp or −Gp
(iii) G,a or −G,a
(iv) Gp,a or −Gp,a
(v) G,a,b or −G,a,b
(vi) Gp,a,b or −Gp,a,b

where 'p' (initial value of program counter), 'a' (first breakpoint address), and 'b' (second breakpoint address) are in numeric or symbolic form, except for the −G forms when the symbolic features are disabled.

For example:

G100,120 [RETURN]

which causes the program to execute from address 0100H up to a temporary breakpoint at address 0120H.

I (*Input*) command

This command allows data to be entered into the default file control block, starting at address 005CH, as though it had formed part of the original command line. This allows successive files to be specified for debugging without having to repeatedly reload the debugging program.

The format for this command is:

I *filename*.typ

For example:

IMYFILE.HEX [RETURN]

which causes the file control block at 005CH to be initialised with the following data:

```
0050: 01 00 00 00 00 00 00 61 6B 73 3A 00 00 4D 59 46
               , , , , , , a k s : , , M Y F
0060: 49 4C 45 20 20 48 45 58 00 00 00 00 00 20 20 20
      I  L  E        H  E  X  , , , , ,
0070: 20 20 20 20 20 20 20 20 00 00 00 00 00 73 00 50
                             , , , , , s , P
```

If a symbol table is available, the file control block for this may also be initialised at the same time by using a command line with the following format:

IMYFILE.HEX MYFILE.SYM

L (*List*) command

This command may be used to disassemble the contents of a specified block of memory into assembly language mnemonics, thus making it much easier to follow a given section of code during the debugging process.

The formats for this command are:

(i) L   or   −L
(ii) Ls   or   −Ls
(iii) Ls,f   or   −Ls,f

where 's' (start) and 'f' (finish) are numeric or symbolic, except for −L forms when the symbolic features are disabled.

The first form of this command lists half a screen (approximately 12 or 13 lines) of disassembled code from the currently stored address. This is frequently used as a means of continuing a listing once started.

The second and third forms of the command cause disassembly to take place from a specified starting address, or between specified addresses.

The following examples show the appearance of the listing with and without the inclusion of symbols:

```
#1100,130 [RETURN]                #1100,130 [RETURN]
    0100  PUSH AF                 SORT:
    0101  PUSH BC                     0100  PUSH AF
    0102  PUSH DE                     0101  PUSH BC
    0103  PUSH IX                     0102  PUSH DE
    0105  LD   C,00                   0103  PUSH IX
    0107  PUSH HL                     0105  LD   C,00
    0108  POP  IX                     0107  PUSH HL
    010A  LD   E,(IX+00H)             0108  POP  IX
    010D  LD   A,(IX+01H)         NEXT:
    0110  CP   E                      010A  LD   E,(IX+00H)
    0111  JR   NC,08                  010D  LD   A,(IX+01H)
    0113  LD   (IX+01H),E             0110  CP   E
    0116  LD   (IX+00H),A             0111  JR   NC,08
    0119  SET  0,C                    0113  LD   (IX+01H),E
    011B  INC  IX                     0116  LD   (IX+00H),A
    011D  DJNZ EB                     0119  SET  0,C
    011F  BIT  0,C                    011B  INC  IX
    0121  JR   NZ,E2                  011D  DJNZ EB
    0123  POP  IX                     011F  BIT  0,C
    0125  POP  DE                     0121  JR   NZ,E2
    0123  POP  IX                 LIST:
                                      0123  POP  IX
                                      0125  POP  DE
```

M (*Move*) command

This command allows specified blocks of data to be moved from one area of memory to another, thus enabling program code to be rearranged. This may be necessary, for example, when inserting or deleting instructions during debugging. The format for this command is:

Ms,f,d

where 's' and 'f' indicate the start and finish addresses of the block to be moved, and 'd' (destination) is the new starting address for the block.

For example:

M100,1FF,200 [RETURN]

moves data located between addresses 0100H and 01FFH to a new location starting at address 0200H.

Often this is not an 'intelligent' move, which means that the implication of overlapping of source and destination must be studied carefully. In such circumstances it is often better to perform the move in two stages, first moving the data block to a completely different area, and then moving it back to its final location.

P (*Pass counter*) command

This command is used to initialise 'pass points' and 'pass counts' in a program under test. Pass points are permanent break points which are not automatically cleared during program execution. A pass counter may be set so that the program passes the pass point a controlled number of times before the break occurs. The formats for this command are:

(i) Pp   or   −Pp
(ii) Pp,c
(iii) P   or   −P

where 'p' (pass point) is a numeric or symbolic passpoint address, and 'c' is the pass count.

The first form of this command either sets (P) or clears (−P) a pass point at address 'p' with a default count of 1.

The second form of the command sets a pass point at address 'p' with a pass count of 'c'.

The third form of the command either lists (P) all pass points, or clears (−P) all pass points.

Each time that an active pass point is encountered, information is displayed with the following format:

06 PASS 0100 .SORT
↑ ↑ ↑
pass count   pass address   symbol

Command forms '−G' and '−U' are available to suppress intermediate steps, so that only the final (pass 1) display appears.

142 *Microprocessor based systems*

R *(Read)* command

This command is used to read the file previously defined by an 'I' command, from disk into the TPA, in preparation for a debug run.
   The formats for this command are:
(i) R
(ii) Rb
where 'b' is an optional bias to be added to each address in the program as it is loaded. The addition of a bias allows programs with an ORG less than 0100H to be loaded without overwriting system parameters in the base page 0000–00FFH. Often programs destined for ROMs in Z80 systems have a starting address of 0000, in which case a bias of 0100H would be used.

S *(Set)* command

This command is used to inspect and optionally alter the contents of selected memory locations.
   The formats for this command are:
(i) Ss   *(8-bit data entry)*
(ii) SWs   *(16-bit data entry)*
where 's' is the starting address (numeric or symbolic) for inspection and alteration of memory. Each entry consists of numeric, ASCII or symbolic data, terminated with a return. Entering a return without data leaves the memory contents unaltered, and entering invalid data (.) exits from the 'S' command.
   The following examples illustrate the use of the 'S' command:

(i) *Alter/inspect consecutive locations, byte format*

```
#S100 [RETURN]                    #S100 [RETURN]
0100 F5 [RETURN]                  0100 F5 [RETURN]
0101 C5 01 [RETURN]               0101 01 [RETURN]
0102 D5 02 [RETURN]               0102 02 [RETURN]
0103 DD 03 [RETURN]               0103 03 [RETURN]
0104 E5 ,[RETURN]                 0104 E5 ,[RETURN]
#                                 #
      Alter                             Inspect
```

(ii) *Alter/inspect consecutive locations, word format*

```
#sw100 [RETURN]                   #sw100 [RETURN]
0100 C5F5 [RETURN]                0100 C5F5 [RETURN]
0102 DDD5 0102 [RETURN]           0102 0102 [RETURN]
0104 0EE5 0304 [RETURN]           0104 0304 [RETURN]
0106 E500 0506 [RETURN]           0106 0506 [RETURN]
0108 E1DD , [RETURN]              0108 E1DD , [RETURN]
#                                 #
      Alter                             Inspect
```

(iii) *Alter/inspect consecutive bytes using symbolic values*

```
#S,NEXT [RETURN]                    #S,NEXT [RETURN]
010A 04 =LIST [RETURN]              010A DD [RETURN]
010B 5E "A [RETURN]                 010B 41 [RETURN]
010C 00 #12 [RETURN]                010C 0C [RETURN]
010D DD 6+3 [RETURN]                010D 09 [RETURN]
010E 7E "STRING [RETURN]            010E 53 [RETURN]
0114 73 , [RETURN]                  010F 54 [RETURN]
#                                   0110 52 [RETURN]
      Alter                         0111 49 [RETURN]
                                    0112 4E [RETURN]
                                    0113 47 [RETURN]
                                    0114 73 , [RETURN]
                                    #
                                          Inspect
```

(iv) *Alter/inspect consecutive words using symbolic values*

```
#SW,NEXT [RETURN]                   #S,NEXT [RETURN]
010A 41DD ,LIST [RETURN]            010A 0123 [RETURN]
010C 090C "AB [RETURN]              010C 4241 [RETURN]
010E 5453 #512 [RETURN]             010E 0200 [RETURN]
0110 4952 0148 [RETURN]             0110 0148 [RETURN]
0112 474E , [RETURN]                0112 474E , [RETURN]
#                                   #
      Alter                               Inspect
```

T *(Trace)* command

This command allows selected program steps (1 to 65535) to be executed with register contents displayed after each step, thus enabling the effect of each instruction in a program to be studied.

The formats for this command are as follows:

(i) T
(ii) Tn

The first form of this command (T) displays the current state of the Z80 registers, then executes the next instructions of the program. The register display has the following format:

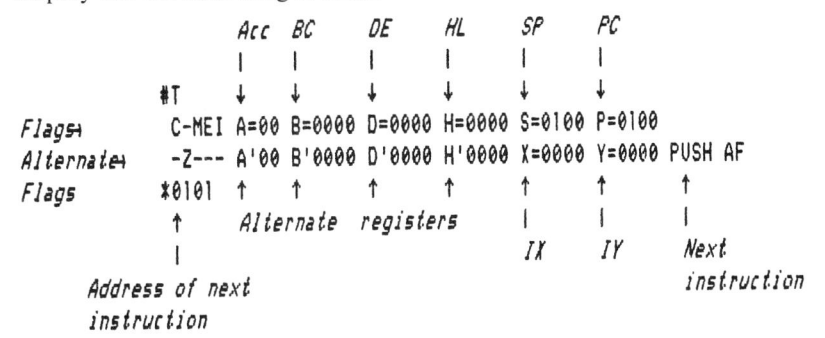

```
                    Acc   BC    DE    HL    SP    PC
                     |    |     |     |     |     |
              #T     ↓    ↓     ↓     ↓     ↓     ↓
Flags→       C-MEI  A=00 B=0000 D=0000 H=0000 S=0100 P=0100
Alternate→   -Z---  A'00 B'0000 D'0000 H'0000 X=0000 Y=0000 PUSH AF
Flags        *0101   ↑    ↑     ↑     ↑     ↑     ↑       ↑
              ↑         Alternate  registers    |     |       |
              |                                 IX    IY      Next
         Address of next                                      instruction
         instruction
```

The second form of this command (Tn) displays the current state of the Z80 registers, then executes the program for 'n' steps, displaying the state of the Z80 after each step, so that changes in the register contents may be monitored as the program runs. For example, consider the following short program segment:

```
0100   XOR   A
0101   LD    B,05
0103   LD    HL,0230
0106   SUB   B
0107   RST   30
```

Tracing the five steps of this program results in the following type of display:

```
#t5
----- A=00 B=0000 D=0000 H=0000 S=0100 P=0100
----- A'00 B'0000 D'0000 H'0000 X=0000 Y=0000 XOR  A
-Z-E- A=00 B=0000 D=0000 H=0000 S=0100 P=0101
----- A'00 B'0000 D'0000 H'0000 X=0000 Y=0000 LD   B,05
-Z-E- A=00 B=0500 D=0000 H=0000 S=0100 P=0103
----- A'00 B'0000 D'0000 H'0000 X=0000 Y=0000 LD   HL,0230
-Z-E- A=00 B=0500 D=0000 H=0230 S=0100 P=0106
----- A'00 B'0000 D'0000 H'0000 X=0000 Y=0000 SUB  B
C-M-I A=FB B=0500 D=0000 H=0230 S=0100 P=0107
----- A'00 B'0000 D'0000 H'0000 X=0000 Y=0000 RST  30
*0108
```

Due to the time taken to monitor and display the state of the Z80 after each step, the program runs much slower than normal (approximately 500 times slower).

U *(Untrace)* command

Sometimes during debugging, the program must be run under fully monitored conditions so that it may be stopped at any point. For this purpose a 'U' command may be used which operates in a similar manner to the 'T' command except that intermediate register displays are not provided.

X *(eXamine)* command

This command may be used to examine and optionally alter the Z80 registers or flags.

The formats for this command are as follows:
  (i) X   *(display all registers/flags)*
  (ii) Xr or Xr' *(inspect/alter selected register)*
  (iii) Xf or Xf' *(inspect/alter selected flag)*

The display of all registers and flags is achieved by the following command:

```
#X [RETURN]
----- A=00 B=0000 D=0000 H=0000 S=00F8 P=0105
----- A'00 B'0000 D'0000 H'0000 X=0000 Y=0000 LD   C,00
#
```

The contents of a selected register, e.g. the Program Counter, may be inspected and optionally altered by means of the following command:

#XP [RETURN]
P =0 0 0 0   1 0 0   [RETURN]
#

The state of a selected flag, e.g. the C-flag, may be inspected and optionally altered by means of the following command:

#XC [RETURN]
C =0   1   [RETURN]
#

Sample debug run

A program has been written to sort numbers into ascending numerical order, and after removal of all syntactical errors, the following PRN listing was obtained. This program, however, contains a number of logical errors, and the following debug run shows how these errors are detected and rectified.

Initial program

```
              ;*******************************
              ;BUBBLE SORT PROGRAM
              ;sorts up to 256 bytes of data into
              ;ascending numerical order
              ;*******************************
              ;
              ;
              ;
0100                    ORG   100H          ;start of CP/M tpa
              ;
              ;initialise registers and exchange flag
              ;
0100 1E00     SORT:     LD    E,0           ;clear exchange flag
0102 1616     NEXT:     LD    D,LEN-1       ;length of table to sort
0104 212201             LD    HL,LIST       ;start of table
0107 012301             LD    BC,LIST+1     ;pointer to next value
              ;
```

```
                        ;compare two consecutive values in the table
                        ;
010A 0A                 LD      A,(BC)          ;get first value
010B 96                 SUB     (HL)            ;compare with previous
010C DA1501             JP      C,NOEXCH        ;leave if in order
                        ;
                        ;byte exchange routine, exchanges number
                        ;pointed to by BC with that pointed to by HL
                        ;
010F F5                 PUSH    AF              ;preserve second on list
0110 77                 LD      (HL),A          ;get first on list
0111 02                 LD      (BC),A          ;change its position
0112 F1                 POP     AF              ;recover second on list
0113 77                 LD      (HL),A          ;complete exchange
0114 1C                 INC     E               ;mark up exchange
                        ;
                        ;loop control determines end of one complete pass
                        ;
0115 23         NOEXCH: INC     HL              ;move pointers
0116 03                 INC     BC              ;up the list
0117 15                 DEC     D               ;check if at end of list
0118 C20201             JP      NZ,NEXT         ;continue if not
                        ;
                        ;check for sorting finished
                        ;
011B 7B                 LD      A,E             ;exchange flag to A
011C C20001             JP      NZ,SORT         ;check for sort complete
011F C30000     DONE:   JP      0               ;return to CP/M
                        ;
                        ;list of numbers to sort (maximum 256)
                        ;
0122 931275     LIST:   DEFB    12H,93H,75H     ;sample list to sort
0125 256210             DEFB    25H,62H,10H     ;for debug run
0128 376429             DEFB    37H,64H,29H
012B C4DF07             DEFB    0C4H,0DFH,7
012E 0009023F           DEFB    0,9,2,3FH,5
0133 FACD01             DEFB    0FAH,0CDH,1
0136 88AC06             DEFB    88H,0ACH,06

0017 =          LEN     EQU     $-LIST          ;length of list to sort
0139                    DEFS    256-LEN         ;space for up to 256


011F DONE       0017 LEN        0122 LIST       0102 NEXT       0115 NOEXCH
0100 SORT



No errors
```

Debug sequence

Load ZSID and the program to be debugged into the TPA by typing the following command line:

```
A>ZSID SORT.HEX [RETURN]
```

Shortly afterwards, a message similar to the following should appear:

```
ZSID VERS 1.4
NEXT  PC   END
0139 0000 CBFF
```

Examine registers before the debug run:

```
#X [RETURN]
 ----- A=00 B=0000 D=0000 H=0000 S=0100 P=0000
 ----- A'00 B'0000 D'0000 H'0000 X=0000 Y=0000 JP   FC03
```

Set the program counter to the starting address of the program:

```
#XP [RETURN]
P=0000 100 [RETURN]
```

Look at the registers again

```
#X [RETURN]
 ----- A=00 B=0000 D=0000 H=0000 S=0100 P=0100
 ----- A'00 B'0000 D'0000 H'0000 X=0000 Y=0000 LD   E,00
```

Disassemble the code loaded into the TPA and check this against the PRN listing to make sure that SORT.HEX was loaded:

```
#L100 [RETURN]                    #L [RETURN]
  0100  LD    E,00                  0113  LD    (HL),A
  0102  LD    D,16                  0114  INC   E
  0104  LD    HL,0122               0115  INC   HL
  0107  LD    BC,0123               0116  INC   BC
  010A  LD    A,(BC)                0117  DEC   D
  010B  SUB   (HL)                  0118  JP    NZ,0102
  010C  JP    C,0115                011B  LD    A,E
  010F  PUSH  AF                    011C  JP    NZ,0100
  0110  LD    (HL),A                011F  JP    0000
  0111  LD    (BC),A                0122  LD    (DE),A
  0112  POP   AF                    0123  SUB   E
```

Change the JP 0000 instruction to RST 30 so that a return to ZSID occurs if the instruction at address 011F is ever executed:

```
#A11F [RETURN]
011F  RST 30 [RETURN]
0120  [RETURN]       (leave assembly mode)
```

Check address 011F to check that the RST 30 instruction has been correctly inserted:

```
#L118 [RETURN]
    0118  JP    NZ,0102
    011B  LD    A,E
    011C  JP    NZ,0100
    011F  RST   30H
    0120  NOP
    0121  NOP
    0122  LD    (DE),A
    0123  SUB   E
    0124  LD    (HL),L
    0125  DEC   H
    0126  LD    H,D
```

Look at the registers again:

```
#X [RETURN]
 ----- A=00 B=0000 D=0000 H=0000 S=0100 P=0100
 ----- A'00 B'0000 D'0000 H'0000 X=0000 Y=0000 LD  E,00
```

Trace program for one step (execute first instruction):

```
#T [RETURN]
 ----- A=00 B=0000 D=0000 H=0000 S=0100 P=0100
 ----- A'00 B'0000 D'0000 H'0000 X=0000 Y=0000 LD  E,00
*0102
```

Trace program for three more steps:

```
#T3 [RETURN]
 ----- A=00 B=0000 D=0000 H=0000 S=0100 P=0102
 ----- A'00 B'0000 D'0000 H'0000 X=0000 Y=0000 LD  D,16
 ----- A=00 B=0000 D=1600 H=0000 S=0100 P=0104
 ----- A'00 B'0000 D'0000 H'0000 X=0000 Y=0000 LD  HL,0122
 ----- A=00 B=0000 D=1600 H=0122 S=0100 P=0107
 ----- A'00 B'0000 D'0000 H'0000 X=0000 Y=0000 LD  BC,0123
*010A
```

Trace program for three more steps:

```
#T3 [RETURN]
 ----- A=00 B=0123 D=1600 H=0122 S=0100 P=010A
 ----- A'00 B'0000 D'0000 H'0000 X=0000 Y=0000 LD  A,(BC)
 ----- A=93 B=0123 D=1600 H=0122 S=0100 P=010B
 ----- A'00 B'0000 D'0000 H'0000 X=0000 Y=0000 SUB (HL)=12
 --M-- A=81 B=0123 D=1600 H=0122 S=0100 P=010C
 ----- A'00 B'0000 D'0000 H'0000 X=0000 Y=0000 JP  C,0115
*010F
```

The SUB (HL) instruction has corrupted the accumulator. Change this to a CP (HL) instruction:

```
#A10B [RETURN]
010B  CP (HL) [RETURN]
010C  [RETURN]
```

Check address 010B to check that the CP (HL) instruction has been correctly inserted:

```
#L100 [RETURN]
   0100  LD    E,00
   0102  LD    D,16
   0104  LD    HL,0122
   0107  LD    BC,0123
   010A  LD    A,(BC)
   010B  CP    (HL)
   010C  JP    C,0115
   010F  PUSH  AF
   0110  LD    (HL),A
   0111  LD    (BC),A
   0112  POP   AF
```

Reset program counter to the start of the program:

```
#XP [RETURN]
P=010F 100 [RETURN]
```

Untrace program for six steps (trace without listing register contents for the intermediate steps):

```
#U6 [RETURN]
  --M-- A=81 B=0123 D=1600 H=0122 S=0100 P=0100
  ----- A'00 B'0000 D'0000 H'0000 X=0000 Y=0000 LD   E,00
*010C
```

Trace four more steps:

```
#T4 [RETURN]
  --M-- A=93 B=0123 D=1600 H=0122 S=0100 P=010C
  ----- A'00 B'0000 D'0000 H'0000 X=0000 Y=0000 JP   C,0115
  --M-- A=93 B=0123 D=1600 H=0122 S=0100 P=010F
  ----- A'00 B'0000 D'0000 H'0000 X=0000 Y=0000 PUSH AF
  --M-- A=93 B=0123 D=1600 H=0122 S=00FE P=0110
  ----- A'00 B'0000 D'0000 H'0000 X=0000 Y=0000 LD   (HL),A
  --M-- A=93 B=0123 D=1600 H=0122 S=00FE P=0111
  ----- A'00 B'0000 D'0000 H'0000 X=0000 Y=0000 LD   (BC),A
*0112
```

The value of A has not changed due to the wrong instruction being used at 0110. It should have been LD A,(HL) instead of LD (HL),A so change this instruction:

```
#A110 [RETURN]
0110 LD A,(HL) [RETURN]
0111      [RETURN]
```

Check address 0110 to check that the LD A,(HL) instruction has been correctly inserted:

```
#L10C [RETURN]
  010C  JP   C,0115
  010F  PUSH AF
  0110  LD   A,(HL)
  0111  LD   (BC),A
  0112  POP  AF
  0113  LD   (HL),A
  0114  INC  E
  0115  INC  HL
  0116  INC  BC
  0117  DEC  D
  0118  JP   NZ,0102
```

Restore starting values to the program counter and stack pointer:

```
#XP [RETURN]
P=0112 100 [RETURN]
#XS [RETURN]
S=00FE 100 [RETURN]
```

Inspect current state of the MPU:

```
#X [RETURN]
  --M-- A=93 B=0123 D=1600 H=0122 S=0100 P=0100
  ----- A'00 B'0000 D'0000 H'0000 X=0000 Y=0000 LD   E,00
```

Untrace eight steps of the program:

```
#U8 [RETURN]
  --M-- A=93 B=0123 D=1600 H=0122 S=0100 P=0100
  ----- A'00 B'0000 D'0000 H'0000 X=0000 Y=0000 LD   E,00
#0110
```

Trace two steps:

```
#T2 [RETURN]
  -Z--- A=93 B=0123 D=1600 H=0122 S=00FE P=0110
  ----- A'00 B'0000 D'0000 H'0000 X=0000 Y=0000 LD   A,(HL)
  -Z--- A=93 B=0123 D=1600 H=0122 S=00FE P=0111
  ----- A'00 B'0000 D'0000 H'0000 X=0000 Y=0000 LD   (BC),A
#0112
```

Debuggers

The contents of the accumulator are still unchanged, therefore use the S command to inspect the data table at address 0122:

```
#S122 [RETURN]
0122 93 [RETURN]
0123 93 [RETURN]
0124 75 , [RETURN]
```

A previous bug has corrupted the data table, therefore use the 'S' command to restore the correct values:

```
#S122 [RETURN]
0122 93 12 [RETURN]
0123 93 , [RETURN]
```

Restore starting values to the program counter and stack pointer:

```
#XP [RETURN]
P=0112 100 [RETURN]
#XS [RETURN]
S=00FE 100 [RETURN]
```

Untrace eight steps of the program:

```
#U8 [RETURN]
  -Z--- A=93 B=0123 D=1600 H=0122 S=0100 P=0100
  ----- A'00 B'0000 D'0000 H'0000 X=0000 Y=0000 LD   E,00
*0110
```

Trace two more steps:

```
#T2 [RETURN]
  --M-- A=93 B=0123 D=1600 H=0122 S=00FE P=0110
  ----- A'00 B'0000 D'0000 H'0000 X=0000 Y=0000 LD   A,(HL)
  --M-- A=12 B=0123 D=1600 H=0122 S=00FE P=0111
  ----- A'00 B'0000 D'0000 H'0000 X=0000 Y=0000 LD   (BC),A
*0112
```

Trace seven more steps:

```
#T7 [RETURN]
  --M-- A=12 B=0123 D=1600 H=0122 S=00FE P=0112
  ----- A'00 B'0000 D'0000 H'0000 X=0000 Y=0000 POP  AF
  --M-- A=93 B=0123 D=1600 H=0122 S=0100 P=0113
  ----- A'00 B'0000 D'0000 H'0000 X=0000 Y=0000 LD   (HL),A
  --M-- A=93 B=0123 D=1600 H=0122 S=0100 P=0114
  ----- A'00 B'0000 D'0000 H'0000 X=0000 Y=0000 INC  E
  ----- A=93 B=0123 D=1601 H=0122 S=0100 P=0115
  ----- A'00 B'0000 D'0000 H'0000 X=0000 Y=0000 INC  HL
  ----- A=93 B=0123 D=1601 H=0123 S=0100 P=0116
  ----- A'00 B'0000 D'0000 H'0000 X=0000 Y=0000 INC  BC
```

```
----- A=93 B=0124 D=1601 H=0123 S=0100 P=0117
----- A'00 B'0000 D'0000 H'0000 X=0000 Y=0000 DEC  D
----- A=93 B=0124 D=1501 H=0123 S=0100 P=0118
----- A'00 B'0000 D'0000 H'0000 X=0000 Y=0000 JP   NZ,0102
#0102
```

Trace one more program step to check the behaviour of the jump instruction:

```
#T [RETURN]
----- A=93 B=0124 D=1501 H=0123 S=0100 P=0102
----- A'00 B'0000 D'0000 H'0000 X=0000 Y=0000 LD   D,16
#0104
```

This causes a jump to the wrong address, inspection of the PRN listing reveals that the label NEXT is in the wrong place, therefore patch in the correct jump for now:

```
#A118 [RETURN]
0118  JP NZ,10A [RETURN]
011B  [RETURN]
```

Reset program counter to start of program:

```
#XP [RETURN]
P=0104 100 [RETURN]
```

Untrace ten program steps (the exchange routine will be by-passed this time since data in 0122H and 0123H have already been exchanged):

```
#UA [RETURN]
 ----- A=93 B=0124 D=1601 H=0123 S=0100 P=0100
 ----- A'00 B'0000 D'0000 H'0000 X=0000 Y=0000 LD   E,00
#0118
```

Trace two more steps:

```
#T2 [RETURN]
C---- A=12 B=0124 D=1500 H=0123 S=0100 P=0118
----- A'00 B'0000 D'0000 H'0000 X=0000 Y=0000 JP   NZ,010A
C---- A=12 B=0124 D=1500 H=0123 S=0100 P=010A
----- A'00 B'0000 D'0000 H'0000 X=0000 Y=0000 LD   A,(BC)
#010B
```

The program seems to function correctly for one pass, therefore, for a complete test, run the program in real time with a break point set at address 011CH:

```
#G100,11C [RETURN]

#011C
```

Inspect the registers:

```
#X [RETURN]
-Z--- A=12 B=0139 D=0012 H=0138 S=0100 P=011C
----- A'00 B'0000 D'0000 H'0000 X=0000 Y=0000 JP   NZ,0100
```

The Z flag is set, despite the value in A being non-zero. Inspection of the PRN listing shows that this error is caused because the LD A,E instruction used at address 011B does not set any flags. Therefore we must make room for a flag-setting instruction.

Move code from address 011C to free memory at address 0140:

```
#M11C,12B,140 [RETURN]
```

Move code back to start at address 011D:

```
#M140,14F,11D [RETURN]
```

Inspect memory to check that the move operation has been correctly executed:

```
#S11B [RETURN]
011B 7B [RETURN]
011C C2 [RETURN]
011D C2 [RETURN]
011E 00 [RETURN]
011F 01 [RETURN]
0120 F7 , [RETURN]
```

Patch in an OR A instruction to set flags after the LD A,E instruction:

```
#A11C [RETURN]
011C  OR A [RETURN]
011D  [RETURN]
```

Inspect memory to check that the correct code has been inserted:

```
#S11B [RETURN]
011B 7B [RETURN]
011C B7 [RETURN]
011D C2 [RETURN]
011E 00 , [RETURN]
```

Adjust memory pointers now that the data table has been relocated one place further up in memory:

```
#S105 [RETURN]
0105 22 23 [RETURN]
0106 01 [RETURN]
0107 01 [RETURN]
0108 23 24 [RETURN]
0109 01 , [RETURN]
```

Run the program in real time with a breakpoint set at address 011D:

```
#G100,11D [RETURN]

*011D
```

Examine the registers:

```
#X [RETURN]
 ---E- A=0F B=013A D=000F H=0139 S=0100 P=011D
 ----- A'00 B'0000 D'0000 H'0000 X=0000 Y=0000 JP   NZ,0100
```

Everything looks OK, so run the program from the start in real time:

```
#G100

*0120
```

Inspect registers at end of program:

```
#X [RETURN]
 -Z-E- A=00 B=013A D=0000 H=0139 S=0100 P=0120
 ----- A'00 B'0000 D'0000 H'0000 X=0000 Y=0000 RST  30H
```

Looks OK, so display memory contents to check for correct sorting:

```
#D123 [RETURN]
0123: FA DF CD C4 AC 93 88 75 64 62 3F 37 31
        . . . . . . . u d b ? 7 1
0130: 29 25 12 09 07 06 05 02 01 00 2E 34 24 31 00 02
      ) % . . . . . . . . . 4 $ 1 . .
0140: C2 00 01 F7 00 00 93 75 25 62 12 37 64 29 C4 DF
      . . . . . . . u % b . 7 d ) . .
0150: 90 57 1E 00 D5 21 00 02 78 B1 CA 65 01 0B 7E 12
      . W . . . ! . . x . . e . . ~ .
0160: 13 23 C3 58 01 D1 C1 E5 62 78 B1 CA 87 01 0B 7B
      . # . X . . . . b x . . . . . {
0170: E6 07 C2 7A 01 E3 7E 23 E3 6F 7D 17 6F D2 83 01
      . . . z . . ~ # . o } . o . . .
```

The program has sorted the data into descending order. Inspection of the PRN listing shows that the JP C, NOEXCH instruction at address 010C should be a JP NC,NOEXCH instruction. Patch in the correct instruction for now:

```
#A10C [RETURN]
010C JP NC,115 [RETURN]
010F [RETURN]
```

Try again in real time:

```
#G100 [RETURN]

*0120
```

Display memory contents again:

```
#D123 [RETURN]
0123: 00 01 02 05 06 07 09 12 25 29 31 37 3F
        . . . . . . . . % ) 1 7 ?
0130: 62 64 75 88 93 AC C4 CD DF FA 2E 34 24 31 00 02
      b  d  u  .  .  .  .  .  .  .  .  4  $  1  .  .
0140: C2 00 01 F7 00 00 93 75 25 62 12 37 64 29 C4 DF
      .  .  .  .  .  .  .  u  %  b  .  7  d  )  .  .
0150: 90 57 1E 00 D5 21 00 02 78 B1 CA 65 01 0B 7E 12
      .  W  .  .  .  !  .  .  x  .  .  e  .  .  ~  .
0160: 13 23 C3 58 01 D1 C1 E5 62 78 B1 CA 87 01 0B 7B
      .  #  .  X  .  .  .  .  b  x  .  .  .  .  .  {
0170: E6 07 C2 7A 01 E3 7E 23 E3 6F 7D 17 6F D2 83 01
      .  .  .  z  .  .  ~  #  .  o  }  .  o  .  .  .
```

The source code must now be corrected to incorporate the changes which were discovered necessary during this debug run.

Final debugged program

```
            ;****************************************
            ;BUBBLE SORT PROGRAM
            ;sorts up to 256 bytes of data into
            ;ascending numerical order
            ;****************************************
            ;
            ;
            ;
0100                    ORG     100H            ;start of CP/M tpa
            ;
            ;initialise registers and exchange flag
            ;
0100 1E00   SORT:       LD      E,0             ;clear exchange flag
0102 1616               LD      D,LEN-1         ;length of table to sort
0104 212301             LD      HL,LIST         ;start of table
0107 012401             LD      BC,LIST+1       ;pointer to next value
            ;
            ;compare two consecutive values in the table
            ;
010A 0A     NEXT:       LD      A,(BC)          ;get first value
010B BE                 CP      (HL)            ;compare with previous
010C D21501             JP      NC,NOEXCH       ;leave if in order
            ;
```

```
                        ;byte exchange routine, exchanges number
                        ;pointed to by BC with that pointed to by HL
                        ;
010F F5                 PUSH AF          ;preserve second on list
0110 7E                 LD   A,(HL)      ;get first on list
0111 02                 LD   (BC),A      ;change its position
0112 F1                 POP  AF          ;recover second on list
0113 77                 LD   (HL),A      ;complete exchange
0114 1C                 INC  E           ;mark up exchange
                        ;
                        ;loop control determines end of one complete pass
                        ;
0115 23      NOEXCH:    INC  HL          ;move pointers
0116 03                 INC  BC          ;up the list
0117 15                 DEC  D           ;check if at end of list
0118 C20A01             JP   NZ,NEXT     ;continue if not
                        ;
                        ;check for sorting finished
                        ;
011B 7B                 LD   A,E         ;exchange flag to A
011C B7                 OR   A           ;set flags
011D C20001             JP   NZ,SORT     ;check for sort complete
0120 C30000  DONE:      JP   0           ;return to CP/M
                        ;
                        ;list of numbers to sort (maximum 256)
                        ;
0123 931275  LIST:      DEFB 93H,12H,75H ;sample list to sort
0126 256210             DEFB 25H,62H,10H ;for debug run
0129 376429             DEFB 37H,64H,29H
012C C4DF07             DEFB 0C4H,0DFH,7
012F 0009023F           DEFB 0,9,2,3FH,5
0134 FACD01             DEFB 0FAH,0CDH,1
0137 88AC06             DEFB 88H,0ACH,06

0017 =       LEN        EQU  $-LIST      ;length of list to sort
013A                    DEFS 256-LEN     ;space for up to 256


0120 DONE    0017 LEN   0123 LIST   010A NEXT   0115 NOEXCH
0100 SORT


No errors
```

Symbol tables

Use can be made of the symbolic facilities of ZSID provided that the source code is assembled with an assembler which generates a sorted symbol table in the form of a SYM file.

The symbol file for the SORT program, used as a debugging example in this chapter, contains the following information:

```
0120 DONE     0017 LEN     0123 LIST     010A NEXT     0115 NOEXCH
0100 SORT
```

A hex dump of this SORT.SYM file reveals that it is simply an ASCII text file which contains addresses and associated labels.

```
0100: 30 31 32 30 20 44 4F 4E 45 09 30 30 31 37 20 4C
       0  1  2  0     D  O  N  E     0  0  1  7     L
0110: 45 4E 09 30 31 32 33 20 4C 49 53 54 09 30 31 30
       E  N     0  1  2  3     L  I  S  T     0  1  0
0120: 41 20 4E 45 58 54 09 30 31 31 35 20 4E 4F 45 58
       A     N  E  X  T     0  1  1  5     N  O  E  X
0130: 43 48 0D 0A 30 31 30 30 20 53 4F 52 54 0D 0A 1A
       C  H  .  .  0  1  0  0     S  O  R  T  .  .  .
0140: 1A 1A 1A 1A 1A 1A 1A 1A 1A 1A 1A 1A 1A 1A 1A 1A
        .  .  .  .  .  .  .  .  .  .  .  .  .  .  .  .
```

Therefore, if the assembler used does not create a SYM file, a suitable file may be generated by either editing the sorted symbol table at the end of the PRN file, or by creating a SYM file of the type shown using data obtained from the PRN listing. The latter method, although tedious, may be the only option if an assembler is used which does not generate a sorted symbol listing. Tabs should be used between each entry rather than spaces.

Utility programs

Utilities are programs which operate in conjunction with a debugger program to provide enhanced facilities.

Two utility programs are available for use with ZSID which allow histograms and software traces to be produced so that program execution may be more closely analysed. These utilities are HIST.UTL and TRACE.UTL.

Histogram utility

This utility program collects data, between user defined limits, concerning the relative frequency of execution of each instruction. The collected data is displayed in the form of a suitably scaled bar chart or histogram, which enables a programmer to identify those sections of a program that are executed most frequently. A study of these sections of code may reveal that improvements are possible which help to reduce the overall execution time of the program.

Sample histogram using HIST.UTL

Load ZSID and HIST.UTL into the TPA:

```
ZSID HIST.UTL [ENTER]

ZSID VERS 1.4
TYPE HISTOGRAM BOUNDS 100,200[ENTER]
.INITIAL = C821
.COLLECT = C824
.DISPLAY = C827
```

Load the SORT program with symbols into the TPA:

```
#ISORT.HEX SORT.SYM [ENTER]
#R [ENTER]

SYMBOLS
NEXT  PC   END
0600  0100 C7D4
```

Set a permanent breakpoint at DONE so that the program does not return to CP/M when it executes to this address:

```
#P,DONE [ENTER]
```

Set a 'pass point' at SORT and a 'pass count' of six:

```
#P,SORT,6 [ENTER]
```

Run the program, passing the SORT label six times to allow the program to attain steady operating conditions:

```
#G [ENTER]

06 PASS 0100 ,SORT
 ----- A=00 B=0000 D=0000 H=0000 S=0100 P=0100
 ----- A'00 B'0000 D'0000 H'0000 X=0000 Y=0000 LD   E,00
05 PASS 0100 ,SORT
 ----- A=13 B=013A D=0013 H=0139 S=0100 P=0100
 ----- A'00 B'0000 D'0000 H'0000 X=0000 Y=0000 LD   E,00
04 PASS 0100 ,SORT
 ---E- A=11 B=013A D=0011 H=0139 S=0100 P=0100
 ----- A'00 B'0000 D'0000 H'0000 X=0000 Y=0000 LD   E,00
03 PASS 0100 ,SORT
 ----- A=0D B=013A D=000D H=0139 S=0100 P=0100
 ----- A'00 B'0000 D'0000 H'0000 X=0000 Y=0000 LD   E,00
02 PASS 0100 ,SORT
 ---E- A=0C B=013A D=000C H=0139 S=0100 P=0100
 ----- A'00 B'0000 D'0000 H'0000 X=0000 Y=0000 LD   E,00
01 PASS 0100 ,SORT
 ----- A=0B B=013A D=000B H=0139 S=0100 P=0100
 ----- A'00 B'0000 D'0000 H'0000 X=0000 Y=0000 LD   E,00
*0102
```

Remove the pass point at SORT, and run the program under monitored conditions for 0FFF steps to collect data for the histogram:

```
#UFFF,,COLLECT [ENTER]
  ----- A=0B B=013A D=0000 H=0139 S=0100 P=0102
  ----- A'00 B'0000 D'0000 H'0000 X=0000 Y=0000 LD   D,16
01 PASS 0100 ,SORT
  ----- A=08 B=013A D=0008 H=0139 S=0100 P=0100
  ----- A'00 B'0000 D'0000 H'0000 X=0000 Y=0000 LD   E,00
*0102
```

Display the collected data in the form of a histogram:

```
#C,DISPLAY [ENTER]

HISTOGRAM:
ADDR       RELATIVE FREQUENCY, LARGEST VALUE = 004A
0100 *
0104 *
0108 ***********************
010C ***************
0110 ****************
0114 *****************************************
0118 ***********
011C *
 ....
0200 *
```

The most frequently executed instructions are around addresses 0108 and 0114, therefore see what code is being executed at these addresses:

```
#L107 [ENTER]
    0107 LD    BC,0124         + see if code can be improved
    010A LD    A,(BC)
    010B CP    (HL)
    010C JP    NC,0115 ,NOEXCH
    010F PUSH  AF
    0110 LD    A,(HL)
    0111 LD    (BC),A
    0112 POP   AF
    0113 LD    (HL),A
    0114 INC   E               + see if code can be improved
NOEXCH:
    0115 INC   HL
    0116 INC   BC
#G0
```

Trace utility

This utility program collects instruction addresses leading up to a user selectable break address in a program under execution. These addresses and their corresponding instructions may then be displayed as a back-trace so that the programmer is presented with information concerning the execution of a program which might otherwise be difficult to obtain.

Sample trace run using TRACE.UTL

Load ZSID and TRACE.UTL into the TPA:

```
ZSID TRACE.UTL [RETURN]

ZSID VERS 1.4
INITIAL = C921
COLLECT = C924
DISPLAY = C927
READY FOR SYMBOLIC BACKTRACE
```

Load SORT.HEX and SORT.SYM into the TPA ready for a trace run:

```
#ISORT.HEX SORT.SYM [RETURN]
#R

SYMBOLS
NEXT  PC   END
0600  0100 C8D4
```

Set a permanent breakpoint at DONE so that the program does not return to CP/M when it executes to this address:-

```
#P,DONE [RETURN]
```

Set a 'pass point' at NOEXCH and a 'pass count' of four, so that the program passes four times through NOEXCH before stopping:

```
#P,NOEXCH,4 [RETURN]
```

Collect data, displaying the register contents each time the program executes the pass point instruction:

```
#UFFF,,COLLECT [RETURN]
 ----- A=00 B=0000 D=0000 H=0000 S=0100 P=0100
 ----- A'00 B'0000 D'0000 H'0000 X=0000 Y=0000 LD   E,00
04 PASS 0115 ,NOEXCH
 C---- A=12 B=0124 D=1601 H=0123 S=0100 P=0115
 ----- A'00 B'0000 D'0000 H'0000 X=0000 Y=0000 INC  HL
03 PASS 0115 ,NOEXCH
 C---- A=75 B=0125 D=1502 H=0124 S=0100 P=0115
 ----- A'00 B'0000 D'0000 H'0000 X=0000 Y=0000 INC  HL
02 PASS 0115 ,NOEXCH
 C---- A=25 B=0126 D=1403 H=0125 S=0100 P=0115
 ----- A'00 B'0000 D'0000 H'0000 X=0000 Y=0000 INC  HL
01 PASS 0115 ,NOEXCH
 C---- A=62 B=0127 D=1304 H=0126 S=0100 P=0115
 ----- A'00 B'0000 D'0000 H'0000 X=0000 Y=0000 INC  HL
*0116
```

Display the trace data:

```
#C,DISPLAY [RETURN]
BACKTRACE:
NOEXCH:
   0115  INC   HL              (most recently executed instruction)
   0114  INC   E
   0113  LD    (HL),A
   0112  POP   AF
   0111  LD    (BC),A
   0110  LD    A,(HL)
   010F  PUSH  AF
   010C  JP    NC,0115 ,NOEXCH
   010B  CP    (HL)
NEXT:
   010A  LD    A,(BC)
   0118  JP    NZ,010A ,NEXT
   0117  DEC   D
   0116  INC   BC
NOEXCH:
   0115  INC   HL
   0114  INC   E
   0113  LD    (HL),A
   0112  POP   AF
   0111  LD    (BC),A
   0110  LD    A,(HL)
   010F  PUSH  AF
   010C  JP    NC,0115 ,NOEXCH
   010B  CP    (HL)
NEXT:
   010A  LD    A,(BC)
   0118  JP    NZ,010A ,NEXT
   0117  DEC   D
   0116  INC   BC
NOEXCH:
   0115  INC   HL
   0114  INC   E
   0113  LD    (HL),A
   0112  POP   AF
   0111  LD    (BC),A
   0110  LD    A,(HL)
   010F  PUSH  AF
   010C  JP    NC,0115 ,NOEXCH
   010B  CP    (HL)
NEXT:
   010A  LD    A,(BC)
```

```
        0118    JP      NZ,010A ,NEXT
        0117    DEC     D
        0116    INC     BC
NOEXCH:
        0115    INC     HL
        0114    INC     E
        0113    LD      (HL),A
        0112    POP     AF
        0111    LD      (BC),A
        0110    LD      A,(HL)
        010F    PUSH    AF
        010C    JP      NC,0115 ,NOEXCH
        010B    CP      (HL)
NEXT:
        010A    LD      A,(BC)
        0107    LD      BC,0124
        0104    LD      HL,0123 ,LIST
        0102    LD      D,16
SORT:
        0100    LD      E,00            (least recently executed instruction)
#G0
```

Problems

1. List six commands which would be expected in a debugger for Z80 machine code programs, and describe the purpose of each of these.
2. (a) Describe how tracing (single-stepping) a program may be used as an aid to locating software bugs.
   (b) Explain why this form of testing does not fully test the software, particularly with respect to real-time performance.
3. The following section of program is intended to unpack two hex digits in the accumulator and store them in consecutive memory locations:

```
        0100                    ORG     100H
                                ;
        0100    210002          LD      HL,200H ;data store pointer
        0103    F5              PUSH    AF      ;free A for use
        0104    0F              RRCA            ;shift higher 4 bits
        0105    0F              RRCA            ;into lower 4 bit
        0106    0F              RRCA            ;position
        0107    0F              RRCA
        0108    77              LD      (HL),A  ;and store it
        0109    23              INC     HL      ;bump pointer
        010A    F1              POP     AF      ;recover packed data
```

```
010B E60F            AND     0FH      ;mask off upper 4 bits
010D 77              LD      (HL),A   ;save in next
010E C9              RET              ;location
```

The program fails to function correctly, and when tested with an initial value of 35H in the accumulator, the following trace is obtained:

```
#t0b
 -Z-EI A=35 B=0000 D=0000 H=0201 S=0100 P=0100
 ----- A'00 B'0000 D'0000 H'0000 X=0000 Y=0000 LD   HL,0200
 -Z-EI A=35 B=0000 D=0000 H=0200 S=0100 P=0103
 ----- A'00 B'0000 D'0000 H'0000 X=0000 Y=0000 PUSH AF
 -Z-EI A=35 B=0000 D=0000 H=0200 S=00FE P=0104
 ----- A'00 B'0000 D'0000 H'0000 X=0000 Y=0000 RRCA
 CZ-E- A=9A B=0000 D=0000 H=0200 S=00FE P=0105
 ----- A'00 B'0000 D'0000 H'0000 X=0000 Y=0000 RRCA
 -Z-E- A=4D B=0000 D=0000 H=0200 S=00FE P=0106
 ----- A'00 B'0000 D'0000 H'0000 X=0000 Y=0000 RRCA
 CZ-E- A=A6 B=0000 D=0000 H=0200 S=00FE P=0107
 ----- A'00 B'0000 D'0000 H'0000 X=0000 Y=0000 RRCA
 -Z-E- A=53 B=0000 D=0000 H=0200 S=00FE P=0108
 ----- A'00 B'0000 D'0000 H'0000 X=0000 Y=0000 LD   (HL),A
 -Z-E- A=53 B=0000 D=0000 H=0200 S=00FE P=0109
 ----- A'00 B'0000 D'0000 H'0000 X=0000 Y=0000 INC  HL
 -Z-E- A=53 B=0000 D=0000 H=0201 S=00FE P=010A
 ----- A'00 B'0000 D'0000 H'0000 X=0000 Y=0000 POP  AF
 -Z-EI A=35 B=0000 D=0000 H=0201 S=0100 P=010B
 ----- A'00 B'0000 D'0000 H'0000 X=0000 Y=0000 AND  0F
 ---EI A=05 B=0000 D=0000 H=0201 S=0100 P=010D
 ----- A'00 B'0000 D'0000 H'0000 X=0000 Y=0000 LD   (HL),A
```

Suggest a reason for the program failing to perform as intended, and determine the action necessary to remedy this fault.

8 Hardware Design

Introduction

This chapter is concerned with the hardware design for small Z80 MPU based systems, and in particular concentrates on the microcontroller circuits. Basic I/O arrangements are considered, but the many different interface circuits which may be required for specific applications are considered to be outside the scope of this book, and are indeed the subject of many specialised books on interfacing.

The design of a Z80 microcontroller is a relatively simple task, particularly if Z80 support chips are specified, since these have Z80 MPU compatible control signals which make direct interconnections possible.

Basic circuits are given for each of the stages which may be required in a Z80 microcontroller circuit, and combinations of these circuits may be used to construct controllers for specific applications.

Design considerations

The system development design cycle was outlined in Chapter 1. It is now necessary to consider in more detail those elements of system development which relate specifically to hardware design, and these are:

(1) Speed of operation

The speed of operation depends upon the clocking speed of the Z80 and the efficiency of the program code. The maximum permitted clocking frequency depends upon the speed option selected, the Z80A being suitable for clock frequencies up to 4 MHz, whilst the Z80B extends this to 6 MHz. The final decision regarding choice of clock frequency depends upon each particular application, but there is little point in using an excessively high clock frequency if the application does not demand it. Sometimes other factors influence the frequency selected, for example, other timing signals for the system may be derived by dividing down this fundamental frequency.

The technical data relating to Z80 MPU based systems that is given on pages 167–238 is reproduced by permission and is copyright © 1988 Zilog (UK) Ltd. This material may not be reproduced without the written consent of Zilog (UK) Ltd.

If a high clocking frequency is required, the designer must ensure that all other components in the system, e.g. PIO, RAM or ROM, are also capable of operating at this frequency.

(ii) **I/O requirements**

In order to communicate effectively with its peripheral devices, a microprocessor based controller requires I/O facilities which fall into one of the following categories:

(a) parallel,
(b) serial, and
(c) interrupt

Parallel I/O may be provided by means of buffers and latches, but the greater flexibility of programmable devices such as the Z80 PIO may be preferred.

Serial I/O could be provided by using individual lines of a Z80 PIO provided that the designer is content to include the necessary software routines to operate a parallel I/O device in this manner. It is more likely, however, that a Z80 SIO would be selected for this purpose.

Interrupt systems may be implemented using standard Z80 support devices which are organised internally so that they may be 'daisy-chained' to provide multi-level priority interrupts. For less demanding systems, a designer may choose to implement interrupts using discrete TTL devices.

An initial study of the overall system should enable a designer to determine the number of I/O ports required, thus enabling suitable devices to be selected.

(iii) **ROM size**

Virtually all of the controller software is destined to reside in EPROM as firmware, therefore adequate provision for this must be made in the controller design. The software writer must initially estimate how much memory space will be required for the software routines and then confine the final program to this space.

Sometimes, for reasons such as cost, the size of available memory is strictly limited and in these cases the software writer is obliged to write very efficient code so that it fits into the available memory space.

Therefore determining the optimum size of ROM is obviously a matter which requires close co-operation between the software and hardware designers. For most small controllers, however, the size of ROM is unlikely to exceed 8K bytes.

(iv) **RAM size**

It is generally much easier to determine the size of RAM required for a given system. In fact, some systems may be designed without RAM, although the software writer should obviously be aware of this at the outset.

166 *Microprocessor based systems*

Most systems require just a small amount of **RAM** for stack operations and for storage of variable data. Nowadays few **RAM** devices are available with less than 1K bytes of storage, and much of this storage space is likely

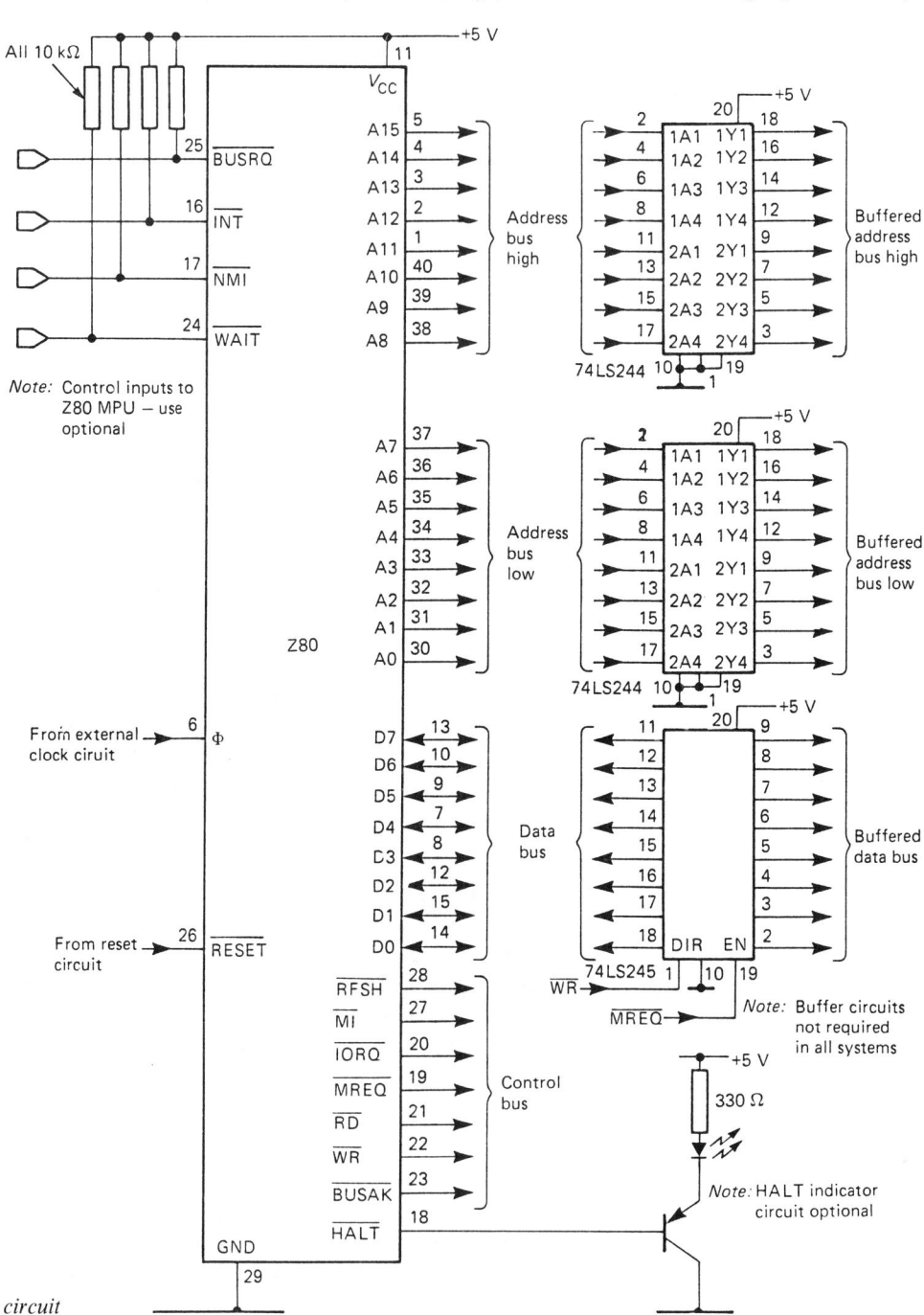

Fig. 8.1 *MPU kernel circuit*

to remain unused. This is one of the reasons why a designer may prefer to avoid using RAM altogether, and instead make use of the large number of registers provided within the Z80 MPU.

Data logging systems require a relatively large amount of RAM, but it is usually a simple task to estimate the exact amount required from the initial specification. For most small controllers, however, the size of RAM is unlikely to exceed 8K bytes.

(v) **Power supply requirements**

Two factors to consider in the design of a microprocessor based controller are supply potentials and current consumption.

NMOS and TTL devices operate on a 5 V supply, therefore if wide variations in supply potential are likely, e.g. battery powered equipment, consideration should be given to using CMOS devices which are more tolerant in this respect and are capable of operation over a range of supplies from 3 V to 18 V. CMOS devices also have the advantage that they have much lower current consumption.

Some devices may require negative potentials in addition to the normal (positive) supply, and in some cases this may preclude their use.

Consideration should also be given to retention of data in the event of power failure, which may require the inclusion of a battery back-up system.

(vi) **Physical considerations**

Initial hardware development will usually be carried out using breadboarding, wire wrap and other similar techniques which are designed to simplify the task of prototype construction.

Subsequent development involves the design of a suitable printed circuit board during which initial specifications such as board size, component layout and types of connector will have been taken into consideration. Frequently a design specification includes reference to standard board sizes, e.g. Eurocard, or standard bus arrangements, e.g. S100, STE.

Z80 MPU circuits

Fig. 8.1 shows the Z80 MPU kernel circuit. Figs 8.2 and 8.3 show the MPU clock circuits and reset circuits, respectively.

Z80 CPU technical data

The Z80-CPU is a third generation single chip microprocessor. The increased computational power results in higher system through-put and more efficient memory utilisation when compared to second generation microcomputers. In addition, the Z80 CPU is very easy to implement into a system because of its single voltage requirement plus all output signals are fully decoded and timed to control standard memory or peripheral circuits. The circuit is implemented using an N-channel, ion implanted, silicon gate MOS process.

Fig. 8.2 *MPU clock circuits*

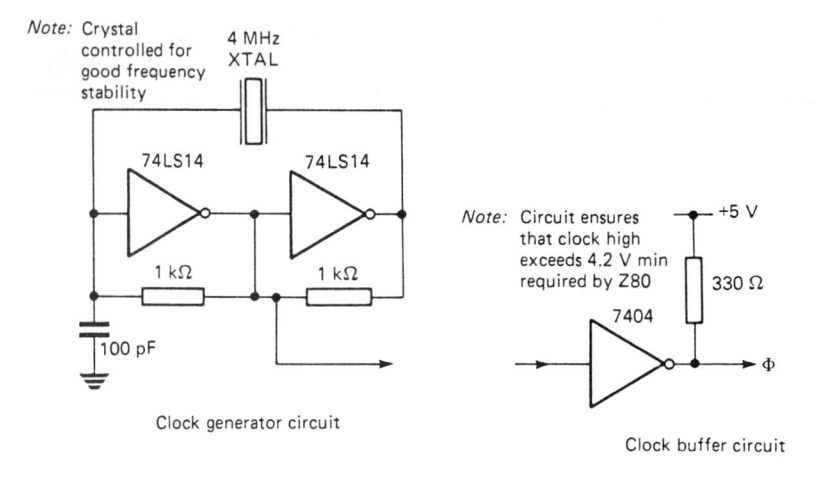

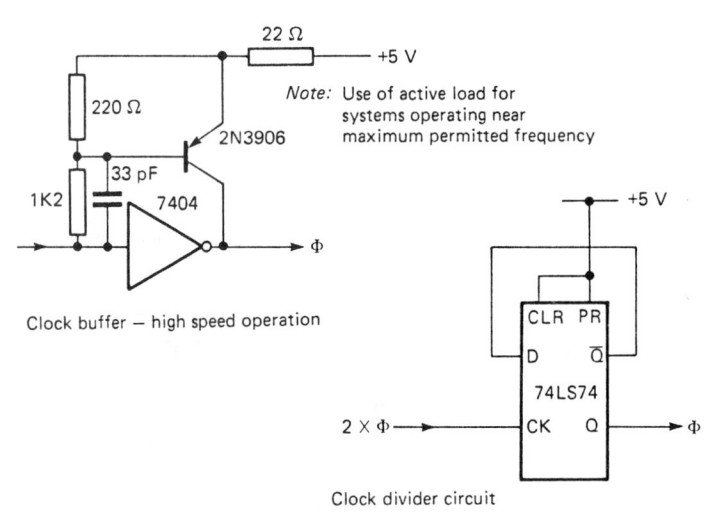

Note: Crystal controlled for good frequency stability

4 MHz XTAL

74LS14 74LS14

1 kΩ 1 kΩ

100 pF

Clock generator circuit

Note: Circuit ensures that clock high exceeds 4.2 V min required by Z80

+5 V
330 Ω
7404
Φ

Clock buffer circuit

22 Ω +5 V
220 Ω
2N3906
1K2 33 pF
7404
Φ

Note: Use of active load for systems operating near maximum permitted frequency

Clock buffer – high speed operation

+5 V
CLR PR
D   Q̄
74LS74
2 × Φ → CK Q → Φ

Clock divider circuit

Fig. 8.4 is a block diagram of the CPU, Fig. 8.5 details the internal register configuration which contains 208 bits of Read/Write memory that are accessible to the programmer. The registers include two sets of six general purpose registers that may be used individually as 8-bit registers or as 16-bit register pairs. There are also two sets of accumulator and flag registers. The programmer has access to either set of main or alternate registers through a group of exchange instructions. This alternate set allows foreground/background mode of operation or may be reserved for very fast Interrupt response. The CPU also contains a 16-bit stack pointer which permits simple implementation of multiple level interrupts, unlimited subroutine nesting and simplification of many types of data handling.

The two 16-bit index registers allow tabular data manipulation and easy implementation of relocatable code. The Refresh register provides for

Hardware design 169

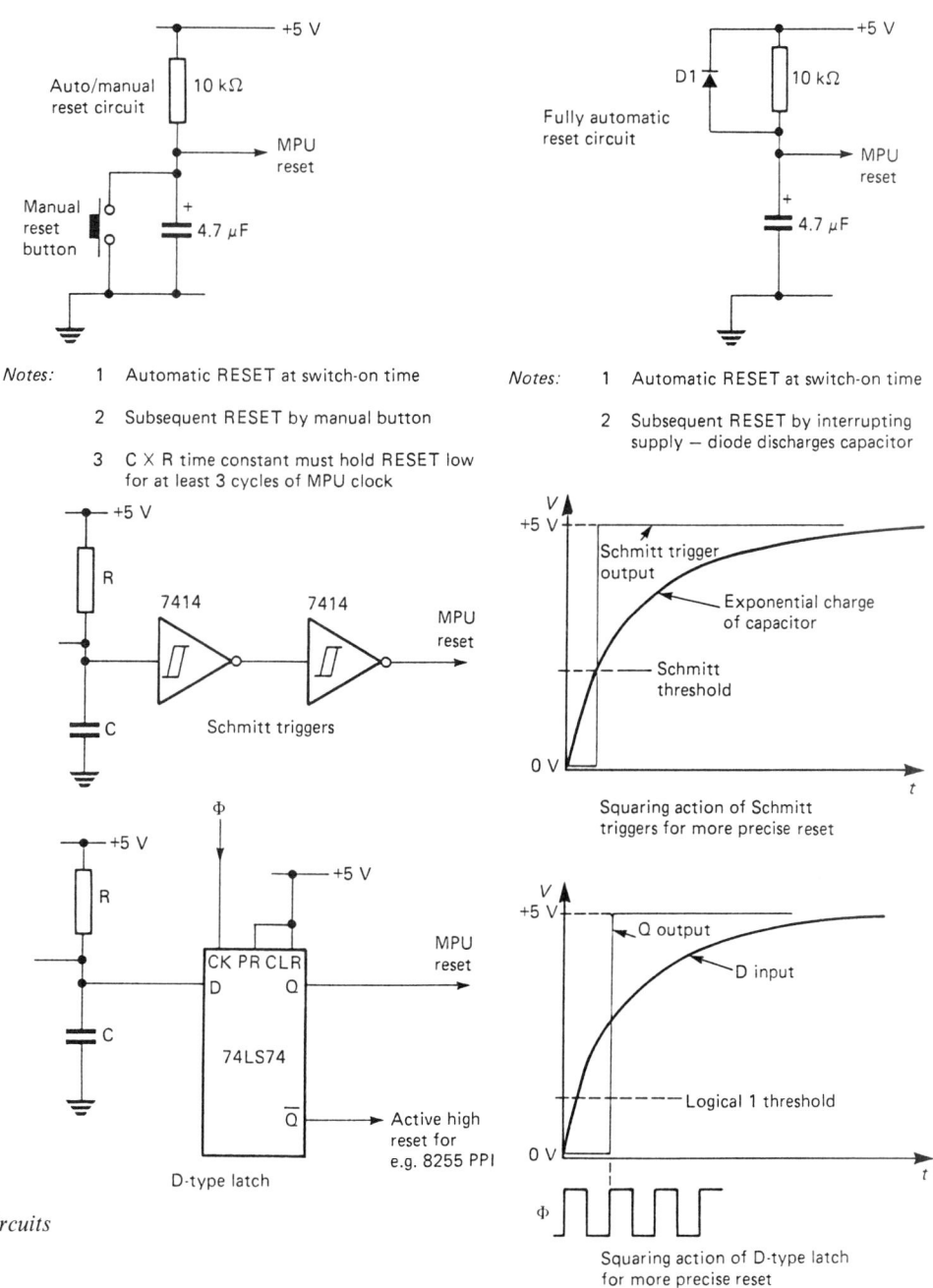

Fig. 8.3 *MPU reset circuits*

Auto/manual reset circuit
- 10 kΩ, +5 V
- Manual reset button
- 4.7 μF
- MPU reset

Notes:
1. Automatic RESET at switch-on time
2. Subsequent RESET by manual button
3. C × R time constant must hold RESET low for at least 3 cycles of MPU clock

Fully automatic reset circuit
- D1, 10 kΩ, +5 V
- 4.7 μF
- MPU reset

Notes:
1. Automatic RESET at switch-on time
2. Subsequent RESET by interrupting supply – diode discharges capacitor

Schmitt triggers (7414, 7414) → MPU reset

Squaring action of Schmitt triggers for more precise reset
- Schmitt trigger output
- Exponential charge of capacitor
- Schmitt threshold

D-type latch (74LS74) with CK, PR, CLR, D, Q, Q̄ → MPU reset; Q̄ → Active high reset for e.g. 8255 PPI

Squaring action of D-type latch for more precise reset
- Q output
- D input
- Logical 1 threshold
- Φ clock

automatic, totally transparent refresh of external dynamic memories. The I register is used in a powerful interrupt response mode to form the upper 8 bits of a pointer to an interrupt service address table, while the interrupting device supplies the lower 8 bits of the pointer. An indirect call is then made to this service address.

170 *Microprocessor based systems*

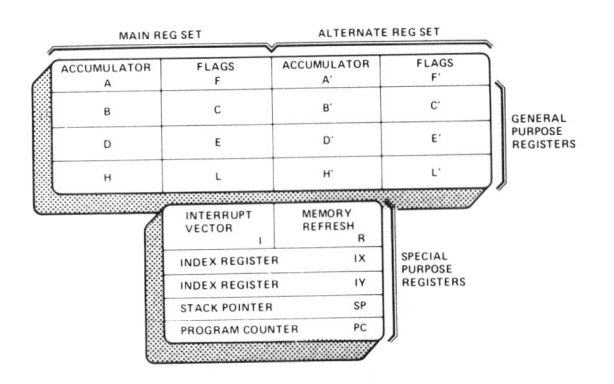

Fig. 8.4 *Z80 CPU block diagram*

Fig. 8.5 *Z80 CPU registers*

Fig. 8.6 *Z80 CPU pin configuration*

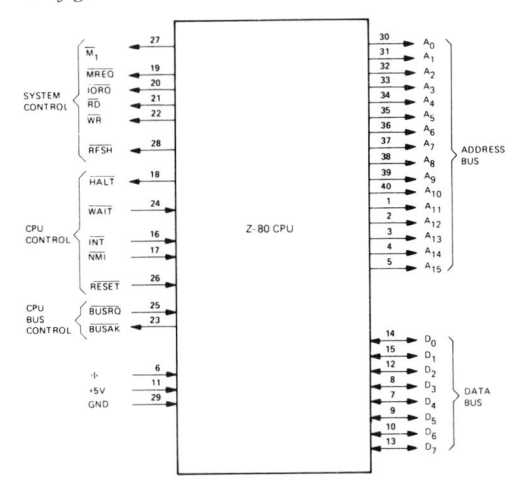

Pin Description–see Fig. 8.6

A_0–A_{15} (Address Bus) — Tri-state output, active high. A_0–A_{15} constitute a 16-bit address bus. The address bus provides the address for memory (up to 64K bytes) data exchanges and for I/O device data exchanges.

D_0–D_7 (Data Bus) — Tri-state input/output, active high. D_0–D_7 constitute an 8-bit bidirectional data bus. The data bus is used for data exchanges with memory and I/O devices.

$\overline{M_1}$ (Machine Cycle one) — Output, active low. $\overline{M_1}$ indicates that the current machine cycle is the OP code fetch cycle of an instruction execution.

$\overline{\text{MREQ}}$ (Memory Request)	Tri-state output, active low. The memory request signal indicates that the address bus holds a valid address for a memory read or memory write operation.
$\overline{\text{IORQ}}$ (Input/Output Request)	Tri-state output, active low. The $\overline{\text{IORQ}}$ signal indicates that the lower half of the address bus holds a valid I/O read or write operation. An $\overline{\text{IORQ}}$ signal is also generated when an interrupt is being acknowledged to indicate that an interrupt response vector can be placed on the data bus.
$\overline{\text{RD}}$ (Memory Read)	Tri-state output, active low. $\overline{\text{RD}}$ indicates that the CPU wants to read data from memory or an I/O device. The addressed I/O device or memory should use this signal to gate data onto the CPU data bus.
$\overline{\text{WR}}$ (Memory Write)	Tri-state output, active low. $\overline{\text{WR}}$ indicates that the CPU data bus holds valid data to be stored in the addressed memory or I/O device.
$\overline{\text{RFSH}}$ (Refresh)	Output, active low. $\overline{\text{RFSH}}$ indicates that the lower 7 bits of the address bus contain a refresh address for dynamic memories and the current $\overline{\text{MREQ}}$ signal should be used to do a refresh read to all dynamic memories.
$\overline{\text{HALT}}$ (Halt state)	Output, active low. $\overline{\text{HALT}}$ indicates that the CPU has executed a HALT software instruction and is awaiting either a non-maskable or a maskable interrupt (with the mask enabled) before operation can resume. While halted, the CPU executes NOP's to maintain memory refresh activity.
$\overline{\text{WAIT}}$ (Wait)	Input, active low. $\overline{\text{WAIT}}$ indicates to the Z-80 CPU that the addressed memory or I/O devices are not ready for a data transfer. The CPU continues to enter wait states for as long as this signal is active.
$\overline{\text{INT}}$ (Interrupt Request)	Input, active low. The Interrupt Request signal is generated by I/O devices. A request will be honoured at the end of the current instruction if the internal software controlled interrupt enable flip-flop (IFF) is enabled.
$\overline{\text{NMI}}$ (Non Maskable Interrupt)	Input, active low. The non-maskable interrupt request line has a higher priority than $\overline{\text{INT}}$ and is always recognised at the end of the current instruction, independent of the status of the interrupt enable flip-flop.

172 *Microprocessor based systems*

$\overline{\text{NMI}}$ automatically forces the Z-80 CPU to restart to location 0066_H.

$\overline{\text{RESET}}$ — Input, active low. $\overline{\text{RESET}}$ initialises the CPU as follows: reset interrupt enable flip-flop, clear PC and registers I and R and set interrupt to 8080A mode. During reset time, the address and data bus go to a high impedance state and all control output signals go to the inactive state.

$\overline{\text{BUSRQ}}$ (Bus Request) — Input, active low. The bus request signal has a higher priority than $\overline{\text{NMI}}$ and is always recognised at the end of the current machine cycle and is used to request the CPU address bus, data bus and tri-state output control signals to go to a high impedance state so that other devices can control these busses.

$\overline{\text{BUSAK}}$ (Bus Acknowledge) — Output, active low. Bus acknowledge is used to indicate to the requesting device that the CPU address bus, data bus and tri-state control bus signals have been set to their high impedance state and the external device can now control these signals.

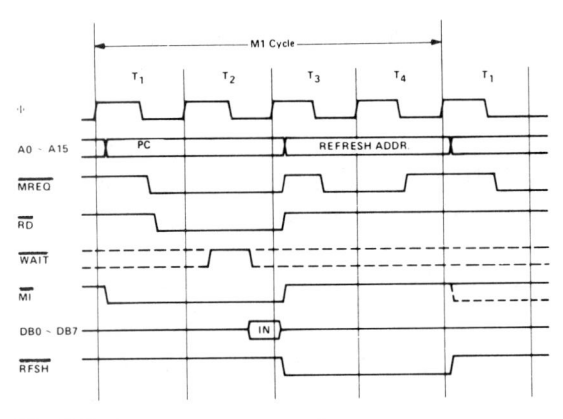

Fig. 8.7 *Instruction OP code fetch*

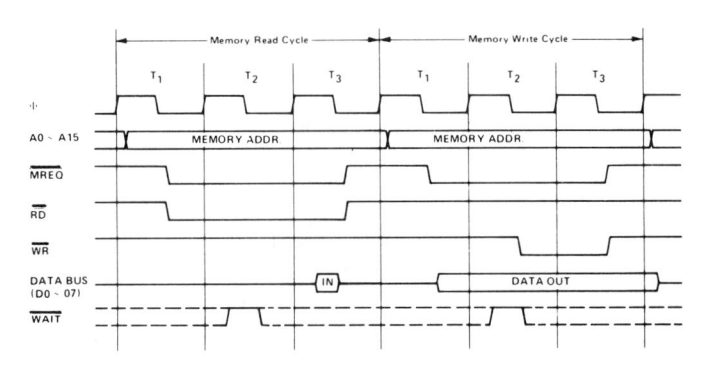

Fig. 8.8 *Memory read/write cycles*

Hardware design 173

Timing Waveforms

Instruction OP code fetch (Fig. 8.7)

The program counter content (PC) is placed on the address bus immediately at the start of the cycle. One half clock time later $\overline{\text{MREQ}}$ goes active. The falling edge of $\overline{\text{MREQ}}$ can be used directly as a chip enable to dynamic memories. $\overline{\text{RD}}$ when active indicates that the memory data should be enabled onto the CPU data bus. The CPU samples data with the rising edge of the clock state T_3. Clock states T_3 and T_4 of a fetch cycle are used to refresh dynamic memories while the CPU is internally decoding and executing the instruction. The refresh control signal $\overline{\text{RFSH}}$ indicates that a refresh read of all dynamic memories should be accomplished.

Memory read or write cycles (Fig. 8.8)

Illustrated in Fig. 8.8 is the timing of memory read or write cycles other than an OP code fetch (M_1 cycle). The $\overline{\text{MREQ}}$ and $\overline{\text{RD}}$ signals are used exactly as in the fetch cycle. In the case of a memory write cycle, the $\overline{\text{MREQ}}$ also becomes active when the address bus is stable so that it can be used directly as a chip enable for dynamic memories. The $\overline{\text{WR}}$ line is active when data on the data bus is stable so that it can be used directly as a R/W pulse to virtually any type of semiconductor memory.

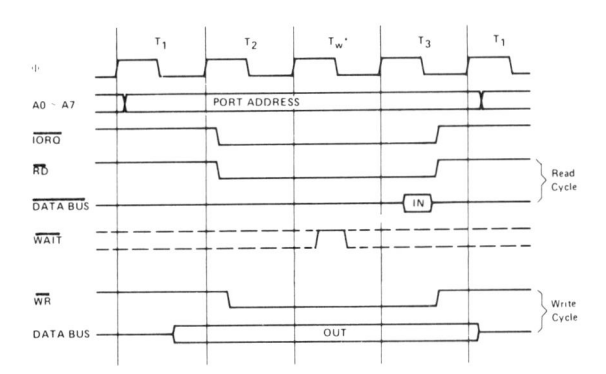

Fig. 8.9 *Input/output cycles*

Input or output cycles (Fig. 8.9)

Illustrated in Fig. 8.9 is the timing for an I/O read or I/O write operation. Notice that during I/O operations a single wait state is automatically inserted (Tw*). The reason for this is that during I/O operations this extra state allows sufficient time for an I/O port to decode its address and activate the $\overline{\text{WAIT}}$ line if a wait is required.

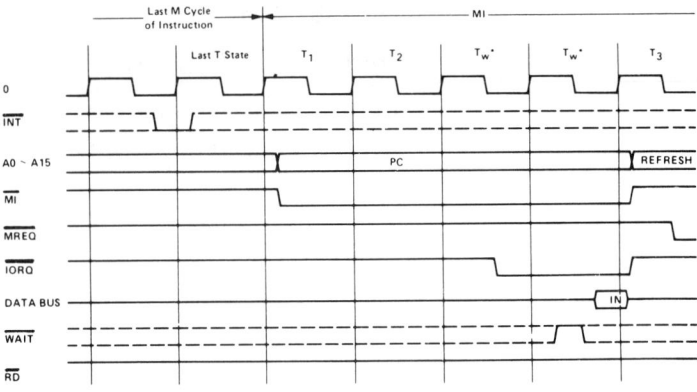

Fig. 8.10 *Interrupt request/acknowledge cycles*

Interrupt request/acknowledge cycle (Fig. 8.10)

The interrupt signal is sampled by the CPU with the rising edge of the last clock at the end of any instruction. When an interrupt is accepted, a special M_1 cycle is generated. During this M_1 cycle, the $\overline{IORQ}$ signal becomes active (instead of $\overline{MREQ}$) to indicate that the interrupting device can place an 8-bit vector on the data bus. Two wait states (Tw*) are automatically added to this cycle so that a ripple priority interrupt scheme, such as the one used in the Z80 peripheral controllers, can be easily implemented.

Z80 Instruction Set

Table 8.1 summarises the Z80 instruction set, showing the assembly language mnemonic and the symbolic operation performed by the instruction. A more detailed listing appears in the Z80 CPU technical manual. The instructions are divided into the following categories:

8-bit loads	Miscellaneous group
16-bit loads	Rotates and shifts
Exchanges	Bit, set, reset and test
Memory block moves	Input and output
Memory block searches	Jumps
8-bit arithmetic and logic	Calls
16-bit arithmetic	Restarts
General purpose accumulator and flag operations	Returns

Addressing modes implemented include combinations of the following:

Immediate	Indexed
Immediate extended	Register
Modified page zero	Implied
Relative	Register indirect
Extended	Bit

Table 8.1   Summary of the Z80 instruction set

	Mnemonic	**Symbolic Operation**	**Comments**
8-BIT LOADS	LD r, s	r ← s	s ≡ r, n, (HL), (IX + e), (IY + e)
	LD d, r	d ← r	d ≡ (HL), r (IX + e), (IY + e)
	LD d, n	d ← n	d ≡ (HL), (IX + e), (IY + e)
	LD A, s	A ← s	s ≡ (BC), (DE), (nn), I, R
	LD d, A	d ← A	d ≡ (BC), (DE), (nn), I, R
16-BIT LOADS	LD dd, nn	dd ← nn	dd ≡ BC, DE, HL, SP, IX, IY
	LD dd, (nn)	dd ← (nn)	dd ≡ BC, DE, HL, SP, IX, IY
	LD (nn), ss	(nn) ← ss	ss ≡ BC, DE, HL, SP, IX, IY
	LD SP, ss	SP ← ss	ss = HL, IX, IY
	PUSH ss	(SP-1) ← ss_H; (SP-2) ← ss_L	ss = BC, DE, HL, AF, IX, IY
	POP dd	dd_L ← (SP); dd_H ← (SP + 1)	dd = BC, DE, HL, AF, IX, IY
EXCHANGES	EX DE, HL	DE ↔ HL	
	EX AF, AF'	AF ↔ AF'	
	EXX	$\begin{pmatrix} BC & & BC' \\ DE & \leftrightarrow & DE' \\ HL & & HL' \end{pmatrix}$	
	EX (SP), ss	(SP) ↔ ss_L, (SP + 1) ↔ ss_H	ss ≡ HL, IX, IY
MEMORY BLOCK MOVES	LDI	(DE) ← (HL), DE ← DE + 1 HL ← HL + 1, BC ← BC − 1	
	LDIR	(DE) ← (HL), DE ← DE + 1 HL ← HL + 1, BC ← BC − 1 Repeat until BC = 0	
	LDD	(DE) ← (HL), DE ← DE − 1 HL ← HL − 1, BC ← BC − 1	
	LDDR	(DE) ← (HL), DE ← DE − 1 HL ← HL − 1, BC ← BC − 1 Repeat until BC = 0	

	Mnemonic	Symbolic Operation	Comments
MEMORY BLOCK SEARCHES	CPI	A − (HL), HL ← HL + 1 BC ← BC − 1	A − (HL) sets the flags only. A is not affected
	CPIR	A − (HL), HL ← HL + 1 BC ← BC − 1, Repeat until BC = 0 or A = (HL)	
	CPD	A − (HL), HL ← HL − 1 BC ← BC − 1	
	CPDR	A − (HL), HL ← HL − 1 BC ← BC − 1, Repeat until BC = 0 or A = (HL)	
8-BIT ALU	ADD s	A ← A + s	
	ADC s	A ← A + s + CY	CY is the carry flag
	SUB s	A ← A − s	
	SBC s	A ← A − s − CY	$s \equiv$ r, n, (HL)
	AND s	A ← A ∧ s	(IX + e), (IY + e)
	OR s	A ← A ∨ s	
	XOR s	A ← A ⊕ s	
	CP s	A − s	s = r, n, (HL) (IX + e), (IY + e)
	INC d	d ← d + 1	d = r, (HL) (IX + e), (IY + e)
	DEC d	d ← d − 1	
16-BIT ARITHMETIC	ADD HL, ss	HL ← HL + ss	$ss \equiv$ BC, DE HL, SP
	ADC HL, ss	HL ← HL + ss + CY	
	SBC HL, ss	HL ← HL − ss − CY	
	ADD IX, ss	IX ← IX + ss	$ss \equiv$ BC, DE, IX, SP
	ADD IY, ss	IY ← IY + ss	$ss \equiv$ BC, DE, IY, SP
	INC dd	dd ← dd + 1	$dd \equiv$ BC, DE, HL, SP, IX, IY
	DEC dd	dd ← dd − 1	$dd \equiv$ BC, DE, HL, SP, IX, IY
GP ACC. & FLAG	DAA	Converts A contents into packed BCD following add or subtract.	Operands must be in packed BCD format
	CPL	A ← $\overline{A}$	
	NEG	A ← 00 − A	
	CCF	CY ← $\overline{CY}$	
	SCF	CY ← 1	

Hardware design 177

	Mnemonic	Symbolic Operation	Comments
MISCELLANEOUS	NOP	No operation	
	HALT	Halt CPU	
	DI	Disable Interrupts	
	EI	Enable Interrupts	
	IM 0	Set interrupt mode 0	8080A mode
	IM 1	Set interrupt mode 1	Call to 0038_H
	IM 2	Set interrupt mode 2	Indirect Call
ROTATES AND SHIFTS	RLC s		
	RL s		
	RRC s		
	RR s		
	SLA s		$s \equiv r, (HL)$
	SRA s		$(IX + e), (IY + e)$
	SRL s		
	RLD		
	RRD		
BIT S, R, & T	BIT b, s	$Z \leftarrow \overline{s_b}$	Z is zero flag
	SET b, s	$s_b \leftarrow 1$	$s \equiv r, (HL)$
	RES b, s	$s_b \leftarrow 0$	$(IX + e), (IY + e)$
INPUT AND OUTPUT	IN A, (n)	$A \leftarrow (n)$	
	IN r, (C)	$r \leftarrow (C)$	Set flags
	INI	$(HL) \leftarrow (C), HL \leftarrow HL + 1$ $B \leftarrow B - 1$	
	INIR	$(HL) \leftarrow (C), HL \leftarrow HL + 1$ $B \leftarrow B - 1$ Repeat until $B = 0$	
	IND	$(HL) \leftarrow (C), HL \leftarrow HL - 1$ $B \leftarrow B - 1$	

	Mnemonic	Symbolic Operation	Comments
INPUT AND OUTPUT	INDR	$(HL) \leftarrow (C)$, $HL \leftarrow HL - 1$ $B \leftarrow B - 1$ Repeat until $B = 0$	
	OUT(n), A	$(n) \leftarrow A$	
	OUT(C), r	$(C) \leftarrow r$	
	OUTI	$(C) \leftarrow (HL)$, $HL \leftarrow HL + 1$ $B \leftarrow B - 1$	
	OTIR	$(C) \leftarrow (HL)$, $HL \leftarrow HL + 1$ $B \leftarrow B - 1$ Repeat until $B = 0$	
	OUTD	$(C) \leftarrow (HL)$, $HL \leftarrow HL - 1$ $B \leftarrow B - 1$	
	OTDR	$(C) \leftarrow (HL)$, $HL \leftarrow HL - 1$ $B \leftarrow B - 1$ Repeat until $B = 0$	
JUMPS	JP nn	$PC \leftarrow nn$	cc $\begin{cases} NZ & PO \\ Z & PE \\ NC & P \\ C & M \end{cases}$
	JP cc, nn	If condition cc is true $PC \leftarrow nn$, else continue	
	JR e	$PC \leftarrow PC + e$	
	JR kk, e	If condition kk is true $PC \leftarrow PC + e$, else continue	kk $\begin{cases} NZ & NC \\ Z & C \end{cases}$
	JP (ss)	$PC \leftarrow ss$	ss = HL, IX, IY
	DJNZ e	$B \leftarrow B - 1$, if $B = 0$ continue, else $PC \leftarrow PC + e$	
CALLS	CALL nn	$(SP - 1) \leftarrow PC_H$ $(SP - 2) \leftarrow PC_L$, $PC \leftarrow nn$	cc $\begin{cases} NZ & PO \\ Z & PE \\ NC & P \\ C & M \end{cases}$
	CALL cc, nn	If condition cc is false continue, else same as CALL nn	
RESTARTS	RST L	$(SP - 1) \leftarrow PC_H$ $(SP - 2) \leftarrow PC_L$, $PC_H \leftarrow 0$ $PC_L \leftarrow L$	
RETURNS	RET	$PC_L \leftarrow (SP)$, $PC_H \leftarrow (SP + 1)$	cc $\begin{cases} NZ & PO \\ Z & PE \\ NC & P \\ C & M \end{cases}$
	RET cc	If condition cc is false continue, else same as RET	
	RETI	Return from interrupt, same as RET	
	RETN	Return from non- maskable interrupt	

b ≡ a bit number in any 8-bit register or memory location
cc ≡ flag condition code
    NZ ≡ non zero
    Z ≡ zero
    NC ≡ non carry
    C ≡ carry
    PO ≡ parity odd or no over flow
    PE ≡ parity even or over flow
    P ≡ positive
    M ≡ negative (minus)
d ≡ any 8-bit destination register or memory location
dd ≡ any 16-bit destination register or memory location
e ≡ 8-bit signed 2's complement displacement used in relative jumps and indexed addressing
L ≡ 8 special call locations in page zero. In decimal notation these are 0, 8, 16, 24, 32, 40, 48 and 56
n ≡ any 8-bit binary number
nn ≡ any 16-bit binary number
r ≡ any 8-bit general purpose register (A, B, C, D, E, H, or L)
s ≡ any 8-bit source register or memory location
s_b ≡ a bit in a specific 8-bit register or memory location
ss ≡ any 16-bit source register or memory location
    subscript "L" ≡ the low order 8 bits of a 16-bit register
    subscript "H" ≡ the high order 8 bits of a 16-bit register
( ) ≡ the contents within the ( ) are to be used as a pointer to a memory location or I/O port number

8-bit registers areand R
16-bit register pairs are AF, BC, DE and HL
16-bit registers are SP, PC, IX and IY

Further data

Table 8.2 gives a.c. characteristics and Fig. 8.11 shows the a.c. timing diagram. D.C. characteristics, maximum ratings and capacitance are given in Tables 8.3–8.5.

180 *Microprocessor based systems*

Table 8.2 A.C. characteristics of the Z80 CPU
$T_A = 0°C$ to $70°C$, $V_{CC} = +5V \pm 5\%$, unless otherwise noted

Signal	Symbol	Parameter	Min	Max	Unit	Test Condition
	t_c	Clock period	0.25	[12]	μs	
Φ	$t_w(ΦH)$	Clock pulse width, clock high	110	[E]	ns	
	$t_w(ΦL)$	Clock pulse width, clock low	110	2000	ns	
	$t_{r,f}$	Clock rise and fall time		30	ns	
	$t_{D(AD)}$	Address output delay		110	ns	
	$t_{F(AD)}$	Delay to float		90	ns	
A_{0-15}	t_{acm}	Address stable prior to $\overline{MREQ}$ (Memory cycle)	[1]		ns	$C_L = 50$ pF
	t_{aci}	Address stable prior to $\overline{IORQ}$, $\overline{RD}$ or $\overline{WR}$ (I/O cycle)	[2]		ns	
	t_{ca}	Address stable from $\overline{RD}$ or $\overline{WR}$	[3]		ns	
	t_{caf}	Address stable from $\overline{RD}$ or $\overline{WR}$ during float	[4]		ns	
	$t_{D(D)}$	Data output delay		180	ns	
	$t_{F(D)}$	Delay to float during write cycle			ns	
	$t_{sΦ(D)}$	Data setup time to rising edge of clock during M1 cycle	35		ns	
D_{0-7}	$t_{s\overline{Φ}(D)}$	Data setup time to falling edge of clock during M2 to M5	50		ns	$C_L = 200$ pF

Hardware design 181

	t_{dcm}	Data stable prior to $\overline{\text{WR}}$ (Memory cycle)	[5]		ns	
	t_{dci}	Data stable prior to $\overline{\text{WR}}$ (I/O cycle)	[6]		ns	
	t_{cdf}	Data stable from $\overline{\text{WR}}$	[7]		ns	
	t_H	Any hold time for setup time		0	ns	
$\overline{\text{MREQ}}$	$t_{DL\overline{\Phi}(MR)}$	$\overline{\text{MREQ}}$ delay from falling edge of clock, $\overline{\text{MREQ}}$ low		75	ns	
	$t_{DH\Phi(MR)}$	$\overline{\text{MREQ}}$ delay from rising edge of clock, $\overline{\text{MREQ}}$ high		75	ns	
	$t_{DH\overline{\Phi}(MR)}$	$\overline{\text{MREQ}}$ delay from falling edge of clock, $\overline{\text{MREQ}}$ high		75	ns	$C_L = 50\,\text{pF}$
	$t_w(\overline{\text{MRL}})$	Pulse width, $\overline{\text{MREQ}}$ low	[8]		ns	
	$t_w(\overline{\text{MRH}})$	Pulse width, $\overline{\text{MREQ}}$ high	[9]		ns	
$\overline{\text{IORQ}}$	$t_{DL\Phi(IR)}$	$\overline{\text{IORQ}}$ delay from rising edge of clock, $\overline{\text{IORQ}}$ low		75	ns	
	$t_{DL\overline{\Phi}(IR)}$	$\overline{\text{IORQ}}$ delay from falling edge of clock, $\overline{\text{IORQ}}$ low		80	ns	
	$t_{DH\Phi(IR)}$	$\overline{\text{IORQ}}$ delay from rising edge of clock, $\overline{\text{IORQ}}$ high		80	ns	$C_L = 50\,\text{pF}$
	$t_{DH\overline{\Phi}(IR)}$	$\overline{\text{IORQ}}$ delay from falling edge of clock, $\overline{\text{IORQ}}$ high		80	ns	
$\overline{\text{RD}}$	$t_{DL\Phi(RD)}$	$\overline{\text{RD}}$ delay from rising edge of clock, $\overline{\text{RD}}$ low		75	ns	
	$t_{DL\overline{\Phi}(RD)}$	$\overline{\text{RD}}$ delay from falling edge of clock, $\overline{\text{RD}}$ low		95	ns	
	$t_{DH\Phi(RD)}$	$\overline{\text{RD}}$ delay from rising edge of clock, $\overline{\text{RD}}$ high		75	ns	$C_L = 50\,\text{pF}$
	$t_{DH\overline{\Phi}(RD)}$	$\overline{\text{RD}}$ delay from falling edge of clock, $\overline{\text{RD}}$ high		80	ns	

Signal	Symbol	Parameter	Min	Max	Unit	Test Condition
	$t_{DL\Phi(WR)}$	$\overline{WR}$ delay from rising edge of clock, $\overline{WR}$ low		60	ns	
$\overline{WR}$	$t_{DL\overline{\Phi}(WR)}$	$\overline{WR}$ delay from falling edge of clock, $\overline{WR}$ low		80	ns	$C_L = 50\,\text{pF}$
	$t_{DH\Phi(WR)}$	$\overline{WR}$ delay from falling edge of clock, $\overline{WR}$ high		80	ns	
	$t_{w(\overline{WRL})}$	Pulse width, $\overline{WR}$ low	[10]		ns	
$\overline{M1}$	$t_{DL(M1)}$	$\overline{M1}$ delay from rising edge of clock, M1 low		100	ns	$C_L = 30\,\text{pF}$
	$t_{DH(M1)}$	$\overline{M1}$ delay from rising edge of clock, $\overline{M1}$ high		100	ns	
$\overline{RFSH}$	$t_{DL(RF)}$	$\overline{RFSH}$ delay from rising edge of clock, $\overline{RFSH}$ low		130	ns	$C_L = 30\,\text{pF}$
	$t_{DH(RF)}$	$\overline{RFSH}$ delay from rising edge of clock, $\overline{RFSH}$ high		120	ns	
$\overline{WAIT}$	$t_{s(WT)}$	$\overline{WAIT}$ setup time to falling edge of clock	70		ns	
$\overline{HALT}$	$t_{D(HT)}$	$\overline{HALT}$ delay time from falling edge of clock		200	ns	$C_L = 50\,\text{pF}$
$\overline{INT}$	$t_{s(IT)}$	$\overline{INT}$ setup time to rising edge of clock	80		ns	
$\overline{NMI}$	$t_{w(NML)}$	Pulse width, $\overline{NMI}$ low	80		ns	
$\overline{BUSRQ}$	$t_{s(BQ)}$	$\overline{BUSRQ}$ setup time to rising edge of clock	50		ns	

BUSAK	$t_{DL(BA)}$	$\overline{\text{BUSAK}}$ delay from rising edge of clock, $\overline{\text{BUSAK}}$ low		100	ns
	$t_{DH(BA)}$	$\overline{\text{BUSAK}}$ delay from falling edge of clock, $\overline{\text{BUSAK}}$ high		100	ns
$\overline{\text{RESET}}$	$t_{s(RS)}$	$\overline{\text{RESET}}$ setup time to rising edge of clock	60		ns
	$t_{F(C)}$	Delay to float ($\overline{\text{MREQ}}$, $\overline{\text{IORQ}}$, $\overline{\text{RD}}$ and $\overline{\text{WR}}$)		80	ns
	t_{mr}	M1 stable prior to $\overline{\text{IORQ}}$ (Interrupt ack.)	[11]		ns

$C_L = 50$ pF

A. Data should be enabled onto the CPU data bus when $\overline{\text{RD}}$ is active. During interrupt acknowledge data should be enabled when $\overline{\text{M1}}$ and $\overline{\text{IORQ}}$ are both active.
B. All control signals are internally synchronised, so they may be totally asynchronous with respect to the clock.
C. The $\overline{\text{RESET}}$ signal must be active for a minimum of 3 clock cycles.
D. Output Delay vs. Loaded Capacitance
 $TA = 70°C$ $V_{CC} = +5V \pm 5\%$
 (1) $\Delta C_L = +100$ pF ($A_\phi - A_{15}$ and Control Signals), add 30 ns to timing shown.
E. Although static by design, testing guarantees $t_{w(\Phi H)}$ of 200 μs maximum.

[1] $t_{acm} = t_{w(\Phi H)} + t_f - 65$
[2] $t_{aci} = t_c - 70$
[3] $t_{ca} = t_{w(\Phi L)} + t_r - 30$
[4] $t_{caf} = t_{w(\Phi L)} + t_r - 45$
[5] $t_{dcm} = t_c - 140$
[6] $t_{dci} = t_{w(\Phi L)} + t_r - 140$
[7] $t_{cdf} = t_{w(\Phi L)} + t_r - 40$
[8] $t_{w(\overline{\text{MRL}})} = t_c - 30$
[9] $t_{w(\overline{\text{MRH}})} = t_{w(\Phi H)} + t_f - 20$
[10] $t_{w(WR)} = t_c - 30$
[11] $t_{mr} = 2t_c + t_{w(\Phi H)} + t_f - 65$
[12] $t_c = t_{w(\Phi H)} + t_{w(\Phi L)} + t_r + t_f$

Load circuit for Output

184 *Microprocessor based systems*

Table 8.3 D.C. characteristics of the Z80 CPU
$T_A = 0°C$ to $70°C$, $V_{CC} = 5V \pm 5\%$, unless otherwise specified

Symbol	Parameter	Min.	Typ.	Max.	Unit	Test Condition
V_{ILC}	Clock input low voltage	-0.3		0.45	V	
V_{IHC}	Clock input high voltage	$V_{CC} - 0.2$		V_{CC}	V	
V_{IL}	Input low voltage	-0.3		0.8	V	
V_{IH}	Input high voltage	2.0		V_{CC}	V	
V_{OL}	Output low voltage			0.4	V	$I_{OL} = 1.8\,mA$
V_{OH}	Output high voltage	2.4			V	$I_{OH} = -250\,\mu A$
I_{CC}	Power supply current		90	200	mA	$t_c = 400\,ns$
I_{LI}	Input leakage current			10	μA	$V_{IN} = 0$ to V_{CC}
I_{LOH}	Tri-state output leakage current in float			10	μA	$V_{OUT} = 2.4$ to V_{CC}
I_{LOL}	Tri-state output leakage current in float			-10	μA	$V_{OUT} = 0.4\,V$
I_{LD}	Data bus leakage current in input mode			± 10	μA	$0 \leqslant V_{IN} \leqslant V_{CC}$

Table 8.4 Absolute maximum ratings for the Z80 CPU

Temperature under bias	Specified operating range
Storage temperature	$-65°C$ to $+150°C$
Voltage on any pin with respect to ground	$-0.3\,V$ to $+7\,V$
Power dissipation	$1.5\,W$

Table 8.5 Capacitance data for the Z80 CPU
$T_A = 25°C$, $f = 1\,MHz$, unmeasured pins returned to ground

Symbol	Parameter	Max	Unit
C_Φ	Clock capacitance	35	pF
C_{IN}	Input capacitance	5	pF
C_{OUT}	Output capacitance	10	pF

Fig. 8.11 (facing page) A.C. timing diagram for the Z80 CPU Timing measurements are made at the following voltages, unless otherwise specified:

	'1'	'0'
Clock	4.2 V	0.8 V
Input	2.0 V	0.8 V
Output	2.0 V	0.8 V
Float	$\Delta V = \pm 0.5\,V$	

Hardware design 185

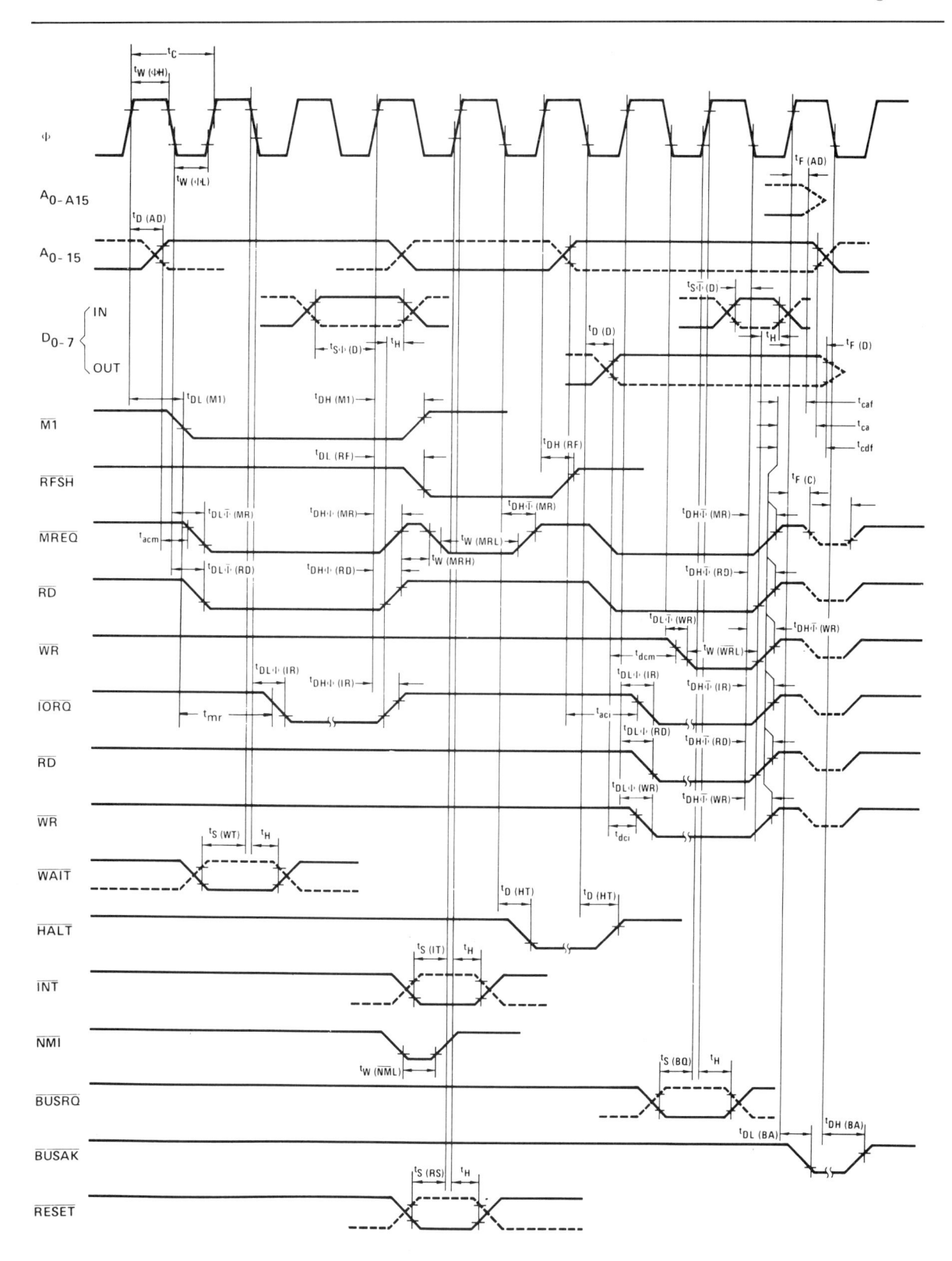

ROM/RAM

Figs. 8.12 and 8.13 show ROM/RAM connections to the Z80 MPU.

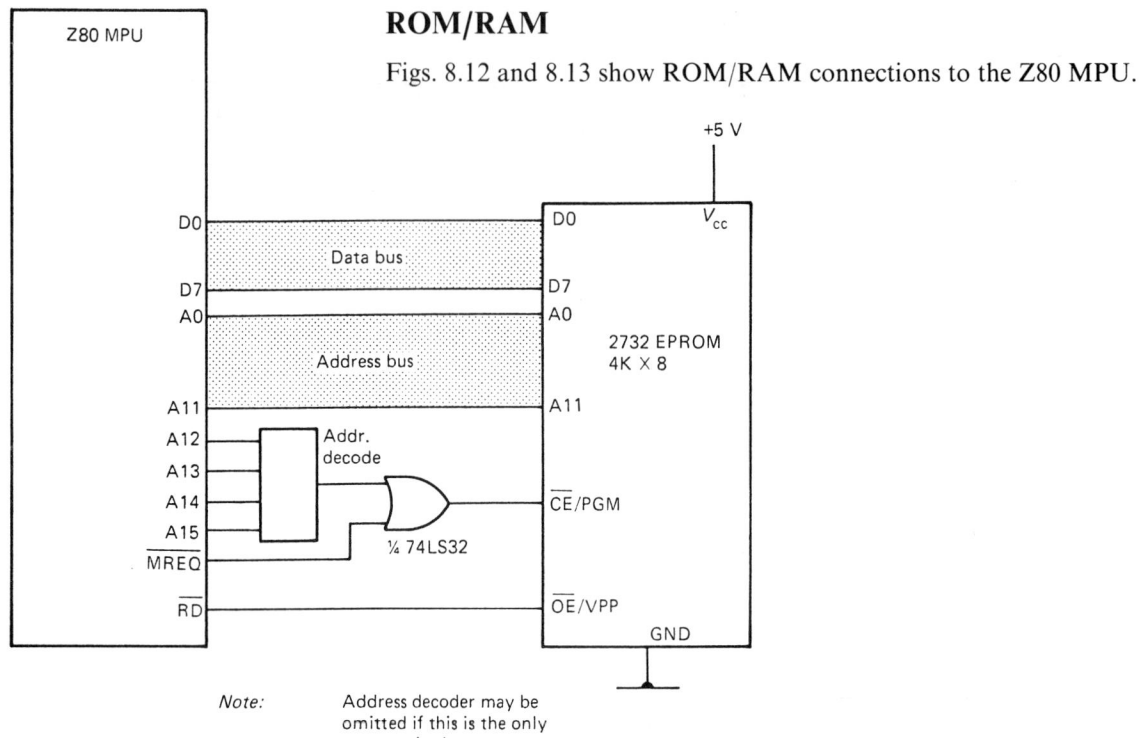

Note: Address decoder may be omitted if this is the only memory in the system

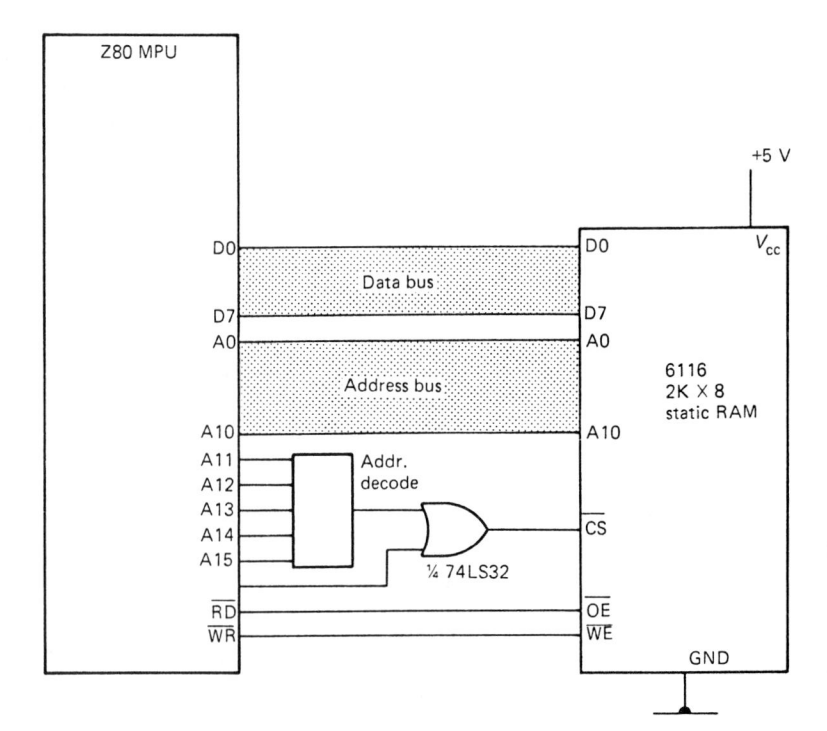

Fig. 8.13 *Connecting static RAM to a Z80 MPU*

Hardware design 187

Z80 PIO technical data

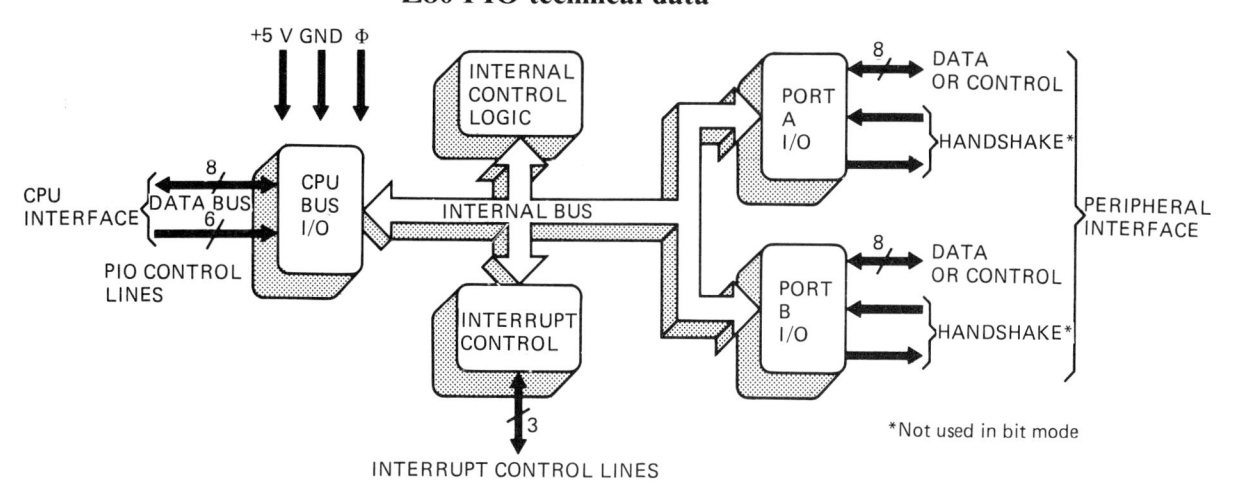

Fig. 8.14 *PIO block diagram*

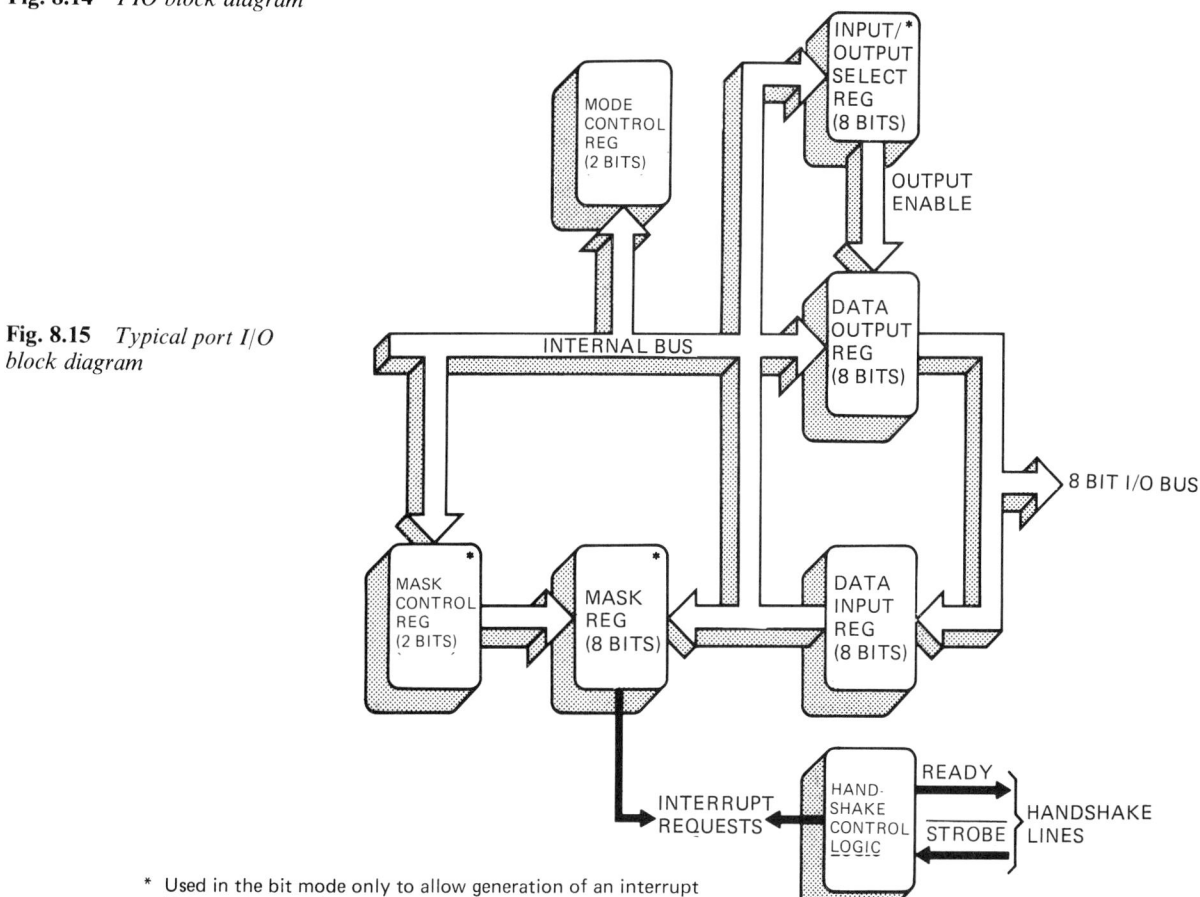

Fig. 8.15 *Typical port I/O block diagram*

* Used in the bit mode only to allow generation of an interrupt if the peripheral I/O pins go to the specified state.

*Not used in bit mode

The Z80 Parallel I/O (PIO) Interface Controller is a programmable, two port device which provides TTL compatible interfacing between peripheral devices and the Z80 CPU. The Z80 CPU configures the Z80 PIO to interface with standard peripheral devices such as tape punches, printers, keyboards, etc.

A block diagram of the Z80 PIO is shown in Fig. 8.14. The internal structure of the Z80 PIO consists of a Z80 CPU bus interface, internal control logic, Port A I/O logic, Port B I/O logic, and interrupt control logic. A typical application might use Port A as the data transfer channel and Port B for the status and control monitoring.

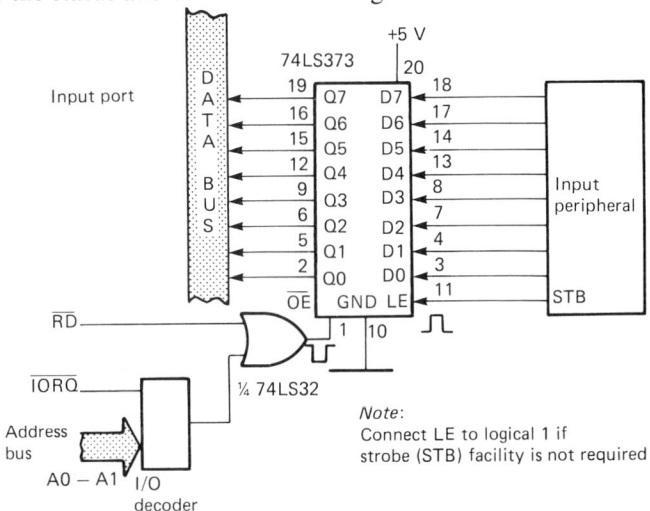

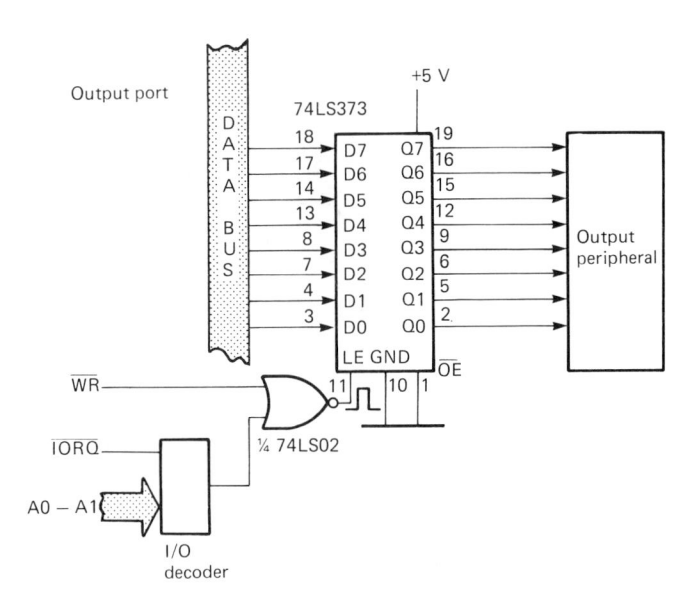

Fig. 8.16 *Simple I/O ports using 74LS373 buffer/latch*

Hardware design   189

The Port I/O logic is composed of 6 registers with 'handshake' control logic as shown in Fig. 8.15. The registers include an 8-bit input register, an 8-bit output register, a 2-bit mode control register, an 8-bit mask register, an 8-bit input/output select register, and a 2-bit mask control register. The last three registers are used only when the port has been programmed to operate in the bit mode.

Fig. 8.16 shows I/O ports using 74LS373 buffer/latch, and Fig. 8.17 shows how the Z80 PIO is connected to the Z80 MPU.

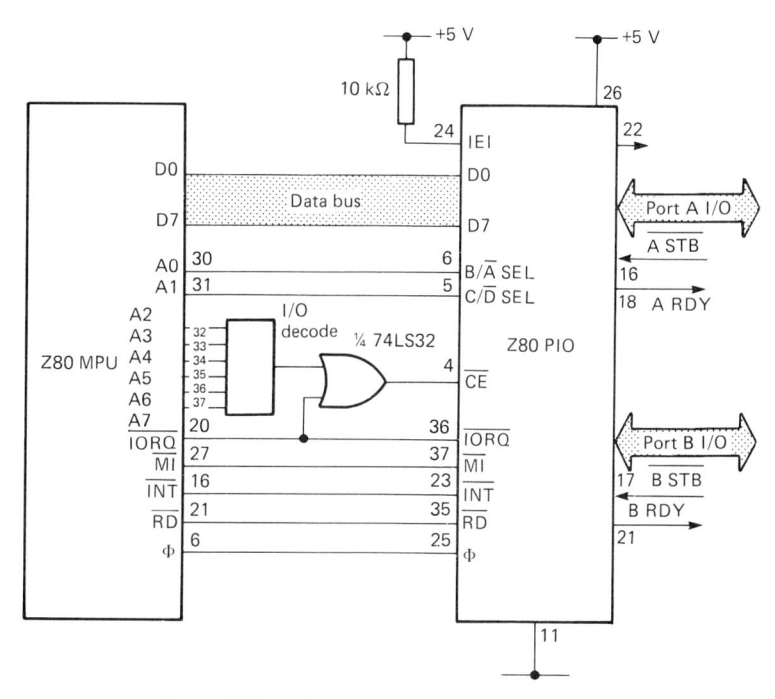

Note: I/O Decoder not necessary if this is the only I/O device

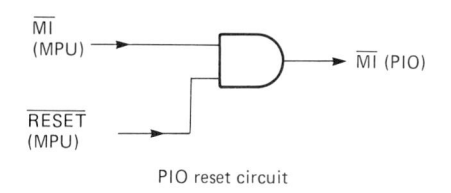

PIO reset circuit

Note: PIO has no RESET pin but resets from power down. PIO may be reset whilst in operation by pulling $\overline{MI}$ low when both $\overline{RD}$ and $\overline{IORQ}$ are high. Circuit shown allows this form of reset to operate

Fig. 8.17 *Connecting a Z80 PIO to a Z80 MPU*

Register description

Mode Control Register—2 bits, loaded by CPU to select the operating mode: byte output, byte input, byte bidirectional bus or bit mode.

Data Output Register—8 bits, permits data to be transferred from the CPU to the peripheral.

Data Input Register—8 bits, accepts data from the peripheral for transfer to the CPU.

Mask Control Register—2 bits, loaded by the CPU to specify the active state (high or low) of any peripheral device interface pins that are to be monitored and, if an interrupt should be generated when all unmasked pins are active (AND condition) or, when any unmasked pin is active (OR condition).

Mask Register—8 bits, loaded by the CPU to determine which peripheral device interface pins are to be monitored for the specified status condition.

Input/Output Select Register—8 bits, loaded by the CPU to allow any pin to be an output or an input during bit mode operation.

Pin description—see Fig. 8.18

D_7–D_0	Z80 CPU Data Bus (bidirectional, tristate)
B/A Sel	Port B or A Select (input, active high)
C/D Sel	Control or Data Select (input, active high)
$\overline{CE}$	Chip Enable (input, active low)
Φ	System Clock (input)
$\overline{M1}$	Machine Cycle One Signal from CPU (input, active low)
$\overline{IORQ}$	Input/Output Request from Z80 CPU (input, active low)
$\overline{RD}$	Read Cycle Status from the Z80 CPU (input, active low)
IEI	Interrupt Enable In (input, active high)
IEO	Interrupt Enable Out (output, active high). IEI and IEO form a daisy chain connection for priority interrupt control.
$\overline{INT}$	Interrupt Request (output, open drain, active low)
A_0–A_7	Port A Bus (bidirectional, tristate)
$\overline{A\ STB}$	Port A Strobe Pulse from Peripheral Device (input, active low)
A RDY	Register A Ready (output, active high)
B_0–B_7	Port B Bus (bidirectional, tristate)
$\overline{B\ STB}$	Port B Strobe Pulse from Peripheral Device (input, active low)
B RDY	Register B Ready (output, active high)

Fig. 8.18 *Z80 PIO pin description*

Fig. 8.19 *Output mode*

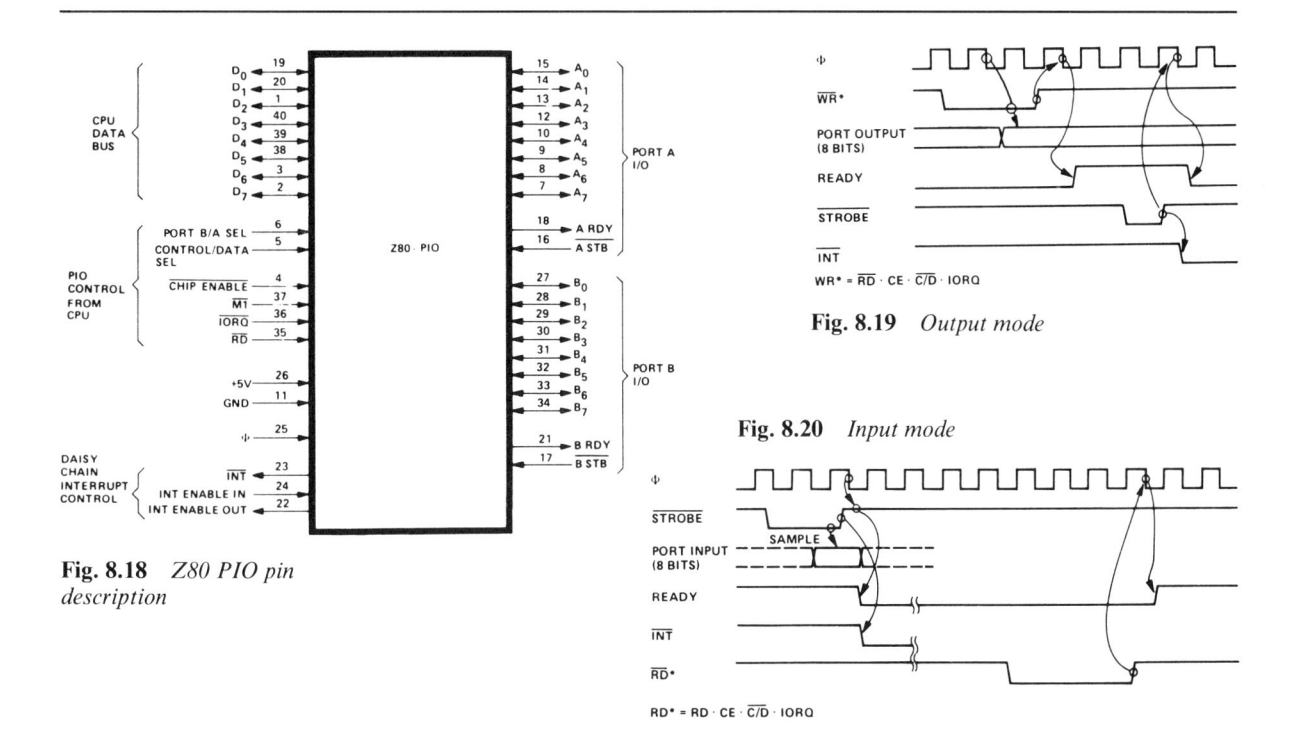

Fig. 8.20 *Input mode*

Timing waveforms

Output mode (Fig. 8.19)

An output cycle is always started by the execution of an output instruction by the CPU. The $\overline{WR}$ pulse from the CPU latches the data from the CPU data bus into the selected port's output register. The write pulse sets the ready flag after a low going edge of Φ, indicating data is available. Ready stays active until the positive edge of the strobe line is received indicating that data was taken by the peripheral. The positive edge of the strobe pulse generates an $\overline{INT}$ if the interrupt flip flop has been set and if this device has the highest priority.

Input mode (Fig. 8.20)

When $\overline{STROBE}$ goes low data is loaded into the selected port input register. The next rising edge of strobe activates $\overline{INT}$ if interrupt enable is set and this is the highest priority requesting device. The following falling edge of Φ resets Ready to an inactive state, indicating that the input register is full and cannot accept any more data until the CPU completes a read. When a read is complete the positive edge of $\overline{RD}$ will set Ready at the next low going transition of Φ. At this time new data can be loaded into the PIO.

Fig. 8.21 *Bidirectional mode*

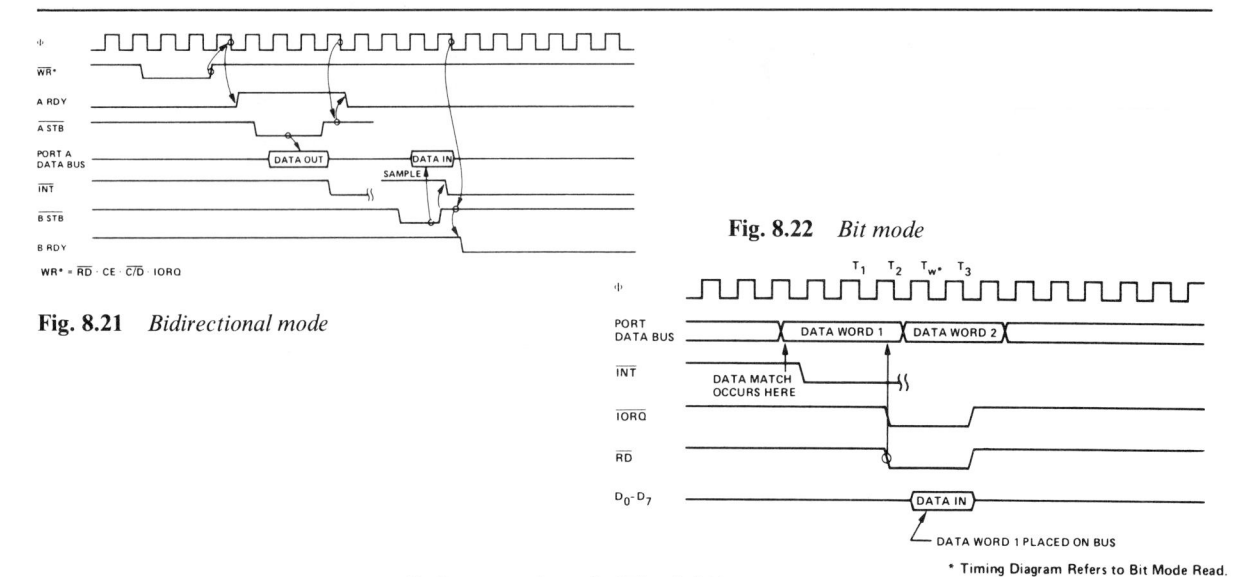

Fig. 8.22 *Bit mode*

Bidirectional mode (Fig. 8.21)

This is a combination of modes 0 and 1 using all four handshake lines and the 8 Port A I/O lines. Port B must be set to the Bit Mode. The Port A handshake lines are used for output control and the Port B lines are used for input control. Data is allowed out onto the Port A bus only when $\overline{\text{A STB}}$ is low. The rising edge of this strobe can be used to latch the data into the peripheral.

Bit mode (Fig. 8.22)

The bit mode does not utilise the handshake signals and a normal port write or port read can be executed at any time. When writing, the data will be latched into the output registers with the same timing as the output mode.

When reading the PIO, the data returned to the CPU will be composed of output register data from those port data lines assigned as outputs and input register data from those port data lines assigned as inputs. The input register will contain data which was present immediately prior to the falling edge of $\overline{\text{RD}}$. An interrupt will be generated if interrupts from the port are enabled and the data on the port data lines satisfy the logical equation defined by the 8-bit mask and 2-bit mask control registers.

Interrupt acknowledge (Fig. 8.23)

During $\overline{\text{MI}}$ time, peripheral controllers are inhibited from changing their interrupt enable status, permitting the $\overline{\text{INT}}$ Enable signal to ripple through the daisy chain. The peripheral with IEI high and IEO low during $\overline{\text{INTA}}$ will place a preprogrammed 8-bit interrupt vector on the data bus at this time. IEO is held low until a return from interrupt (RETI) instruction is executed by the CPU while IEI is high. The 2-byte RETI instruction is decoded internally by the PIO for this purpose.

Hardware design 193

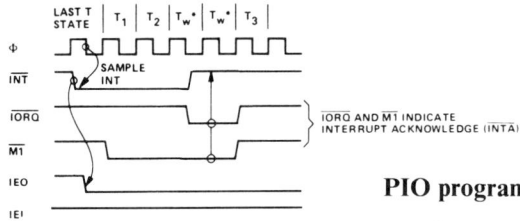

Fig. 8.23 *Interrupt acknowledge*

PIO programming

Load interrupt vector

The Z80 CPU requires an 8-bit interrupt vector to be supplied by the interrupting device. The CPU forms the address for the interrupt service routine of the port using this vector. During an interrupt acknowledge cycle the vector is placed on the Z80 data bus by the highest priority device requesting service at that time. The desired interrupt vector is loaded into the PIO by writing a control word to the desired port of the PIO with the following format.

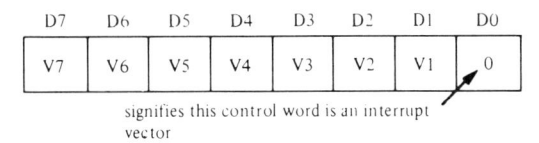

D7	D6	D5	D4	D3	D2	D1	D0
V7	V6	V5	V4	V3	V2	V1	0

D0 signifies this control word is an interrupt vector

Selecting an operating mode

When selecting an operating mode, the 2-bit mode control register is set to one of four values. These two bits are the most significant bits of the register, bits 7 and 6; bits 5 and 4 are not used while bits 3 through 0 are all set to 1111 to indicate "set mode.".

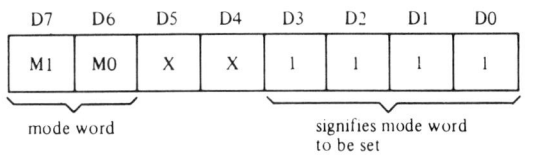

D7	D6	D5	D4	D3	D2	D1	D0
M1	M0	X	X	1	1	1	1

D7–D6: mode word
D3–D0: signifies mode word to be set

X = unused bit

Mode	M_1	M_0
Output	0	0
Input	0	1
Bidirectional	1	0
Bit	1	1

MODE 0 active indicates that data is to be written from the CPU to the peripheral.

MODE 1 active indicates that data is to be read from the peripheral to the CPU.

MODE 2 allows data to be written to or read from the peripheral device.
MODE 3 is intended for status and control applications. When selected, the next control word must set the I/O Register to indicate which lines are to be input and which lines are to be output.

$I/O = 1$ sets bit to input.
$I/O = 0$ sets bit to output.

D7	D6	D5	D4	D3	D2	D1	D0
I/O_7	I/O_6	I/O_5	I/O_4	I/O_3	I/O_2	I/O_1	I/O_0

Interrupt control

Bit 7 = 1	interrupt enable is set–allowing interrupt to be generated.
Bit 7 = 0	indicates the enable flag is reset and interrupts may not be generated.
Bits 6, 5, 4	are used in the bit mode interrupt operations; otherwise they are disregarded.
Bits 3, 2, 1, 0	signify that this command word is an interrupt control word.

D7	D6	D5	D4	D3	D2	D1	D0
Enable Interrupt	AND/OR	High/Low	Mask follows	0	1	1	1

used in Mode 3 only   signifies interrupt control word

If the 'mask follows' bit is high (D4 = 1), the next control word written to the port must be the mask.

D7	D6	D5	D4	D3	D2	D1	D0
MB_7	MB_6	MB_5	MB_4	MB_3	MB_2	MB_1	MB_0

Only those port lines whose mask bit is a 0 will be monitored for generating an interrupt.

The interrupt enable flip-flop of a port may be set or reset without modifying the rest of the interrupt control word by the following command.

D7	D6	D5	D4	D3	D2	D1	D0
Int Enable	X	X	X	0	0	1	1

Further data

Table 8.6 gives a.c. characteristics and Fig. 8.24 shows the a.c. timing diagram. D.C. characteristics, maximum ratings and capacitance are given in Tables 8.7, 8.8 and 8.9.

Table 8.6 A.C. Characteristics of the Z80 PIO
$T_A = 0°C$ to $70°C$, $V_{CC} = +5 V \pm 5\%$, unless otherwise noted

Signal	Symbol	Parameter	Min.	Max.	Unit	Comments
Φ	t_c	Clock period	0.4	[1]	μs	
	$t_{W(\Phi H)}$	Clock pulse width, clock high	180	2000	ns	
	$t_{W(\Phi L)}$	Clock pulse width, clock low	180	2000	ns	
	t_r, t_f	Clock rise and fall times		30	ns	
D_0–D_7	$t_{HW(D)}$	Data hold time during write cycle	0		ns	
	$t_{HR(D)}$	Data hold time from rising edge of $\overline{RD}$ during M1 cycle	0		ns	
	$t_{DR(D)}$	Data output delay during read cycle		430	ns	
	$t_{DI(D)}$	Data output delay during INTA		[2]		
	$t_{F(D)}$	Delay to floating bus during read cycle		160	ns	
	$t_{S(D)}$	Data setup time to rising edge of $\overline{IORQ}$ during write cycle	200		ns	
	$t_{S\Phi(D)}$	Data setup time to rising edge of clock during M1 cycle	50		ns	
A_0–A_7, B_0–B_7	$t_{H(PD)}$	Port data hold time from rising edge of $\overline{STROBE}$	0		ns	Mode 1
	$t_{S(PD)}$	Port data setup time to rising edge of $\overline{STROBE}$	260		ns	Mode 1
	$t_{DS(PD)}$	Port data output delay from falling edge of $\overline{STROBE}$		230	ns	Mode 2
	$t_{F(PD)}$	Delay to floating port data bus from rising edge of $\overline{STROBE}$	200		ns	Mode 2
	$t_{DI(PD)}$	Port data stable from rising edge of $\overline{IORQ}$ during write cycle		200	ns	Mode 0
B/A, C/D, $\overline{CE}$	$t_{H(CS)}$	Control signal hold time from rising edge of $\overline{IORQ}$	0		ns	
	$t_{S(CS)}$	Control signal setup time to falling edge of $\overline{IORQ}$	30		ns	
$\overline{A\ STB}$, $\overline{B\ STB}$	$t_{W(ST)}$	Pulse width, $\overline{STROBE}$	150		ns	Mode 0 or 1
			[3]		ns	Mode 2
$\overline{INT}$	$t_{D(IT)}$	$\overline{INT}$ delay time from rising edge of $\overline{STROBE}$		490	ns	Mode 0, 1, or 2
	$t_{D(IT3)}$	$\overline{INT}$ delay time from data match during Mode 3 operation		420	ns	Mode 3

196 *Microprocessor based systems*

Signal	Symbol	Parameter	Min.	Max.	Unit	Comments
IEI	$t_{S(IEI)}$	Setup time of IEI prior to $\overline{IORQ}$ during interrupt acknowledge	0		ns	
IEO	$t_{DL(IO)}$	IEO delay time from falling edge of IEI		210	ns	
	$t_{DH(IO)}$	IEO delay time from rising edge of $\overline{RD}$ during RETI		$1.5t_c + 500$	ns	
	$t_{DM(IEO)}$	Delay time from falling edge of $\overline{M1}$ to falling edge of IEO		310	ns	See [4] below
A RDY or B RDY	$t_{DH(RY)}$	READY response time from rising edge of $\overline{IORQ}$		$t_c + 460$	ns	
	$t_{DL(RY)}$	READY response time from rising edge of $\overline{STROBE}$		$t_c + 400$	ns	

[1] $t_c = t_{W(\Phi H)} + t_{W(\Phi L)} + t_r + t_f$
[2] 380 ns for $C_L = 100$ pF; 410 ns for $C_L = 200$ pF
[3] $t_{W(ST)} > t_{S(PD)}$
[4] $2.5t_c > (N - 2)t_{DL(IO)} + t_{DM(IEO)} + t_{S(IEI)} +$ TTL buffer delay, if any where N = number of PIO's in daisy chain.

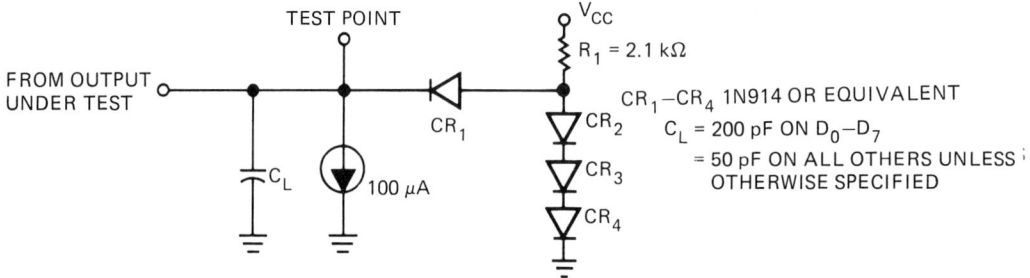

Output load circuit.

CR₁–CR₄ 1N914 OR EQUIVALENT
$C_L = 200$ pF ON D_0–D_7
 = 50 pF ON ALL OTHERS UNLESS OTHERWISE SPECIFIED
$R_1 = 2.1$ kΩ

Fig. 8.24 (facing page) *A.C. timing diagram for the Z80 PIO Timing measurements are made at the following voltages, unless otherwise specified:*

	'1'	'0'
Clock	4.2 V	0.8 V
Input	2.0 V	0.8 V
Output	2.0 V	0.8 V
Float	ΔV	$= \pm 0.5$ V

Hardware design 197

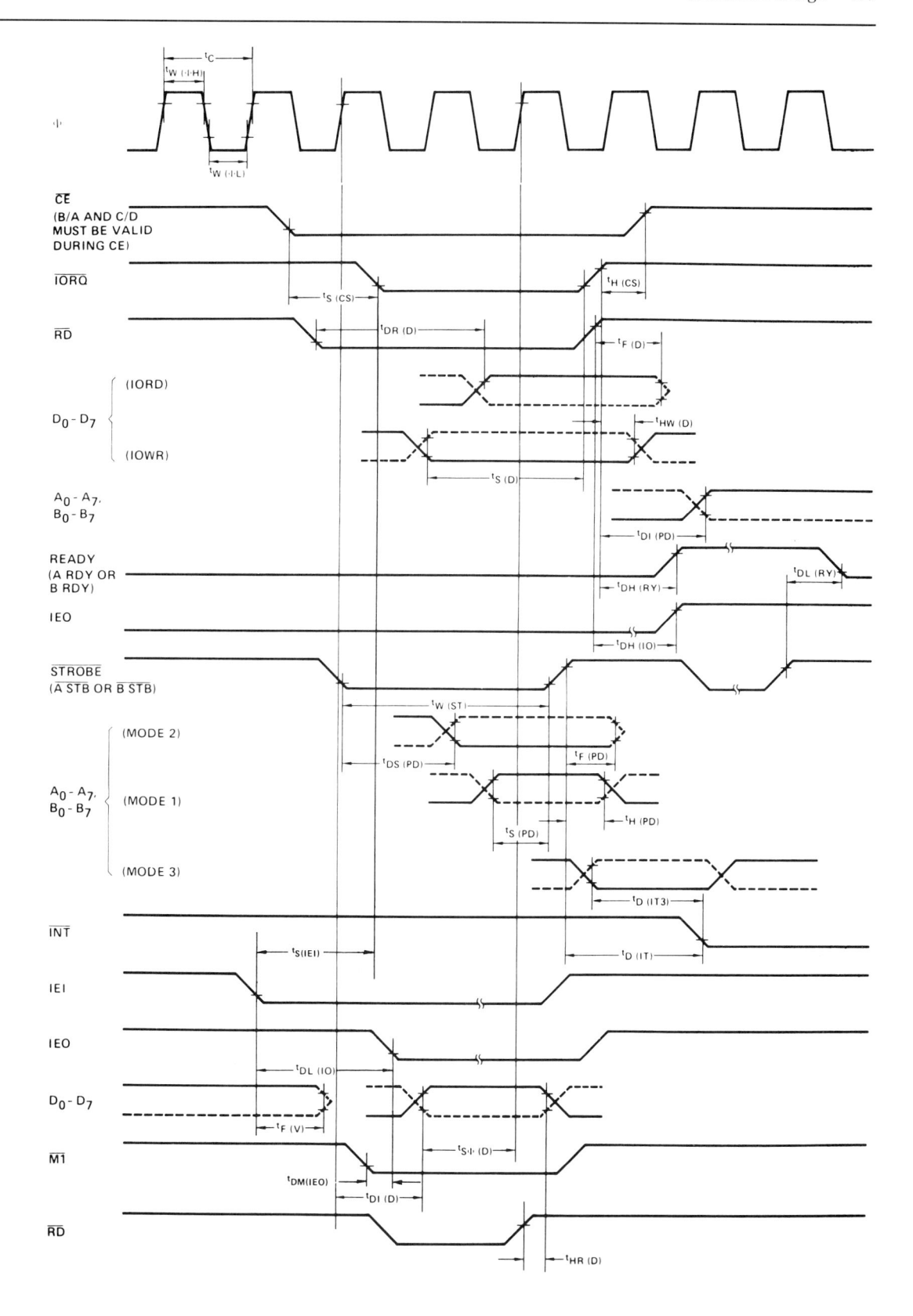

Table 8.7 D.C. Characteristics of the Z80 PIO
$T_A = 0°C$ to $70°C$, $V_{CC} = 5\,V \pm 5\%$ unless otherwise specified

Symbol	Parameter	Min.	Max.	Unit	Test Condition
V_{ILC}	Clock input low voltage	−0.3	0.45	V	
V_{IHC}	Clock input high voltage	$V_{CC} - 0.2$	V_{CC}	V	$I_{OL} = 1.8\,mA$
V_{IL}	Input low voltage	−0.3	0.8	V	$I_{OH} - 250\,\mu A$
					$T_C = 400\,ns$
V_{IH}	Input high voltage	2.0	V_{CC}	V	$V_{IN} = 0$ to V_{CC}
V_{OL}	Output low voltage		0.4	V	$V_{OUT} = 2.4$ to V_{CC}
V_{OH}	Output high voltage	2.4		V	$V_{OUT} = 0.4\,V$
					$0 \leqslant V_{IN} \leqslant V_{CC}$
I_{CC}	Power supply current		70	mA	
I_{LI}	Input leakage current		10	μA	
I_{LOH}	Tri-state output leakage current in float		10	μA	
I_{LOL}	Tri-state output leakage current in float		−10	μA	
I_{LD}	Data bus leakage current in input mode		±10	μA	$V_{OH} = 1.5\,V$
I_{OHD}	Darlington drive current	1.5		mA	$R_{EXT} = 390\,\Omega$ Port B Only

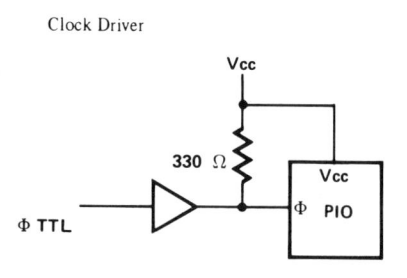

Clock Driver

An external pull-up resistor of 330 Ω will meet all A.C. and D.C. clock requirements.

Table 8.8 Absolute Maximum Ratings for the Z80 PIO

Temperature under bias	Specified operating range.
Storage temperature	−65°C to +150°C
Voltage on any pin with respect to ground	−0.3 V to +7 V
Power dissipation	0.6 W

Table 8.9 Capacitance data for the Z80 PIO
$T_A = 25°C$, $f = 1$ MHz

Symbol	Parameter	Max.	Unit	Test Condition
C_Φ	Clock capacitance	10	pF	Unmeasured pins Returned to ground
C_{IN}	Input capacitance	5	pF	
C_{OUT}	Output capacitance	10	pF	

Z80 SIO technical data

The Z80 SIO Serial Input/Output Controller is a dual-channel data communication interface. Its basic functions as a serial-to-parallel, parallel-to-serial converter/controller can be programmed by a CPU for a broad range of serial communication applications.

The device supports all common asynchronous and synchronous protocols, byte- or bit-oriented, and performs all of the functions traditionally done by UARTs, USARTs, and synchronous communication controllers combined, plus additional functions traditionally performed by the CPU. It does this on two fully-independent channels, with a sophisticated interrupt structure that allows fast transfers.

Full interfacing is provided for CPU or DMA control. In addition to data communication, the circuit can handle virtually all types of serial I/O with fast, or slow, peripheral devices. While designed primarily as a member of the Z80 family, its versatility makes it well suited to many other CPUs.

The Z80 SIO uses a single +5 V power supply and the standard Z80 family single-phase clock. The SIO/0, SIO/1, and SIO/2 are packaged in a 40-pin plastic DIP and the SIO/4 is packaged in a 44-pin PCC.

Fig. 8.25 shows how the Z80 SIO is connected to the Z80 MPU.

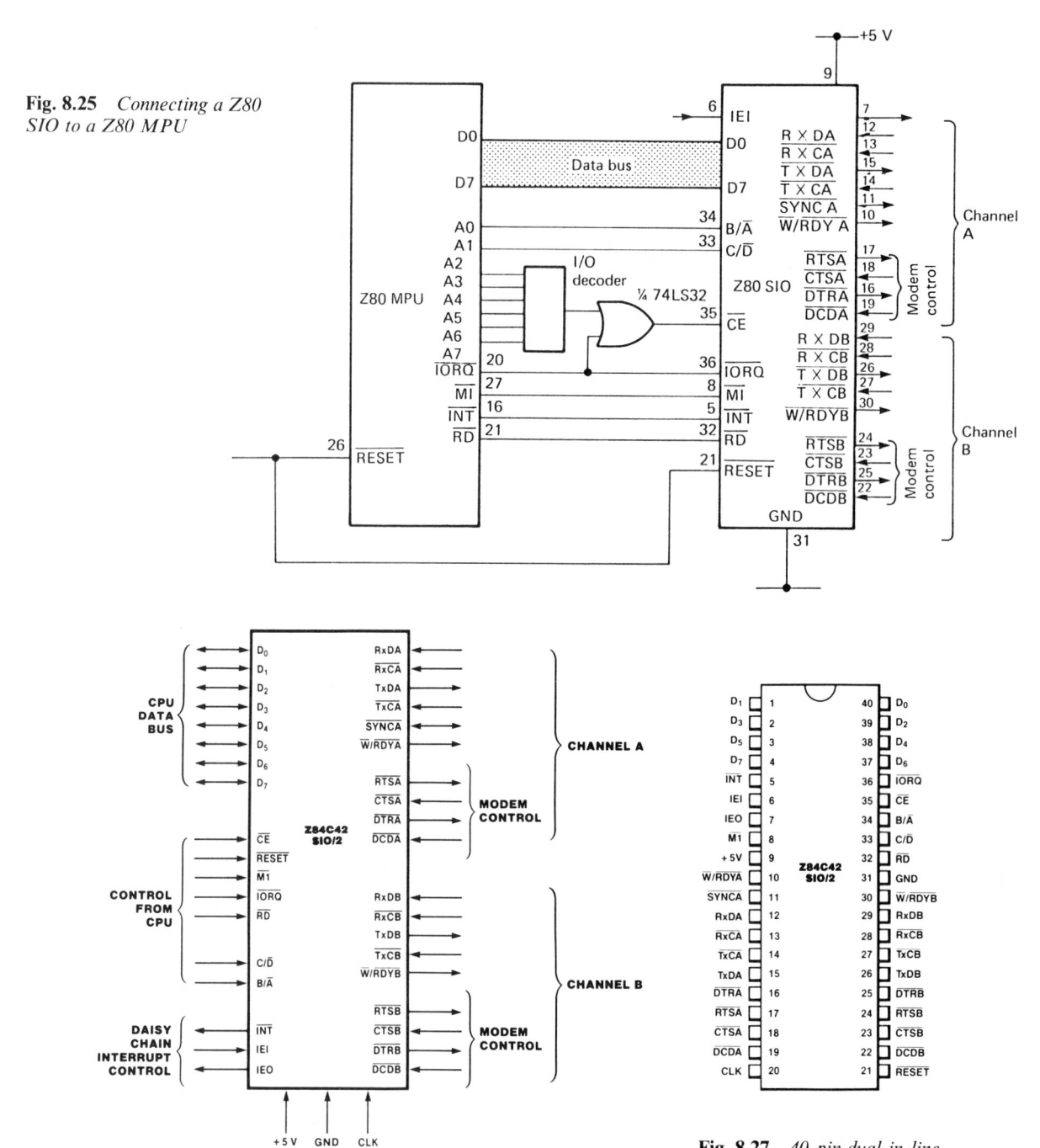

Fig. 8.25 *Connecting a Z80 SIO to a Z80 MPU*

Fig. 8.26 *Pin functions, Z80 SIO/2*

Fig. 8.27 *40-pin dual-in-line package (DIP) pin assignments, Z80 SIO/2*

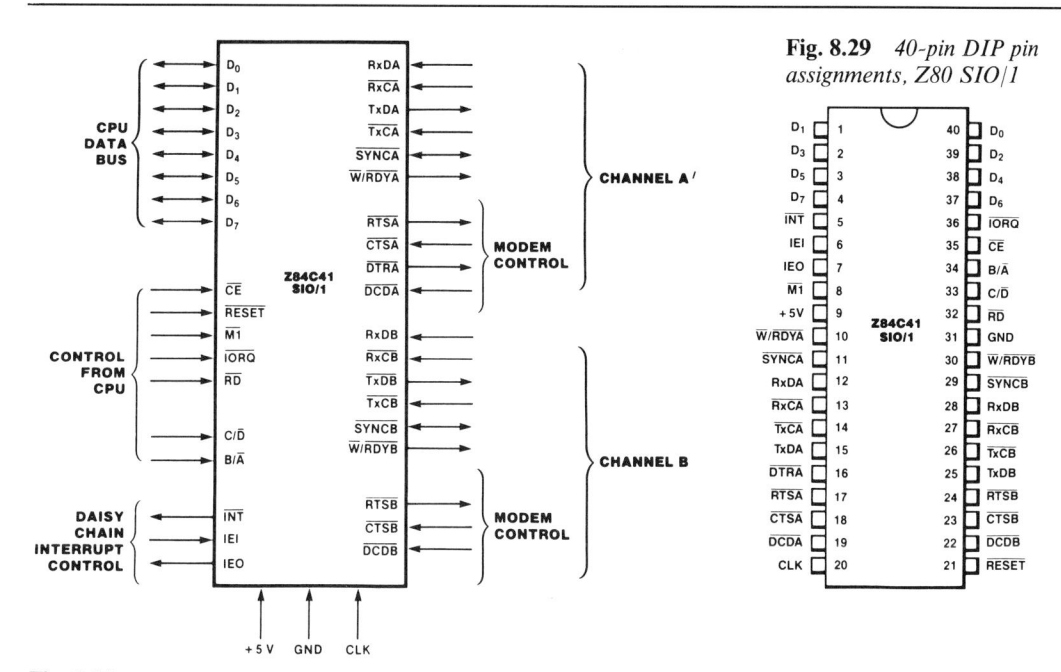

Hardware design 201

Fig. 8.28 *Pin functions, Z80 SIO/1*

Fig. 8.29 *40-pin DIP pin assignments, Z80 SIO/1*

Fig. 8.30 *Pin functions, Z80 SIO/0*

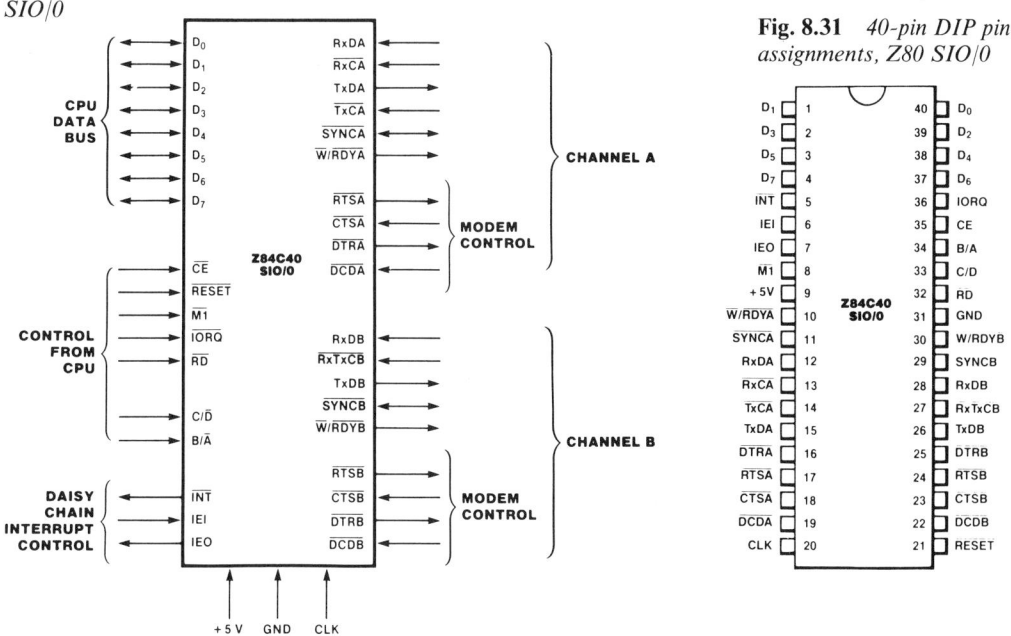

Fig. 8.31 *40-pin DIP pin assignments, Z80 SIO/0*

Pin description

Figs. 8.26 to 8.31 illustrate the three 40-pin configurations (bonding options) available in the Z80 SIO. The constraints of a 40-pin package make it impossible to bring out the Receive Clock ($\overline{RxC}$), Transmit Clock ($\overline{TxC}$), Data Terminal Ready ($\overline{DTR}$) and Sync ($\overline{SYNC}$) signals for both channels.

Therefore, either Channel B lacks a signal or two signals are bonded together:

Z80 SIO/2 lacks $\overline{\text{SYNCB}}$,

Z80 SIO/1 lacks $\overline{\text{DTRB}}$

Z80 SIO/O has all four signals, but $\overline{\text{TxCB}}$ and $\overline{\text{RxCB}}$ are bonded together.

The 44-pin package, the Z80 SIO/4, has all options (Fig. 8.32).

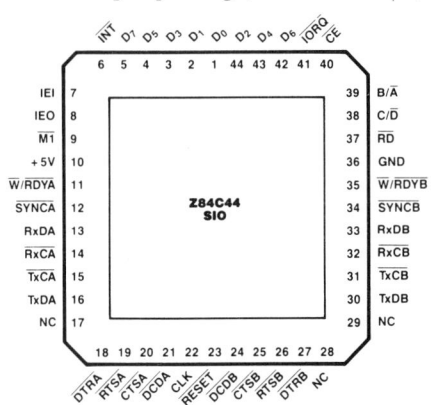

Fig. 8.32 *44-pin chip carrier, pin assignments*

The first bonding option above (SIO/2) is the preferred version for most applications. The pin descriptions are as follows:

$B/\overline{A}$. — *Channel A or B Select* (input, High selects Channel B). This input defines which channel is accessed during a data transfer between the CPU and the SIO. Address bit A_0 from the CPU is often used for the selection function.

$C/\overline{D}$. — *Control or Data Select* (input, High selects Control). This input defines the type of information transfer performed between the CPU and the SIO. A High at this input during a CPU write to the SIO causes the information on the data bus to be interpreted as a command for the channel selected by $B/\overline{A}$. A Low at $C/\overline{D}$ means that the information on the data bus is data. Address bit A_1 is often used for this function.

CE. — *Chip Enable* (Input, active Low). A Low level at this input enables the SIO to accept command or data input from the CPU during a write cycle, or to transmit data to the CPU during a read cycle.

CLK. — *System Clock* (input). The SIO uses the standard Z80 System Clock to synchronise internal signals. This is a single-phase clock.

CTSA, $\overline{\text{CTSB}}$.   *Clear To Send* (inputs, active Low). When programmed as Auto Enables, a Low on these inputs enables the respective transmitter. If not programmed as Auto Enables, these inputs may be programmed as general-purpose inputs. Both inputs are Schmitt-trigger buffered to accommodate slow-risetime signals. The SIO detects pulses on these inputs and interrupts the CPU on both logic level transitions. The Schmitt-trigger buffering does not guarantee a specified noise-level margin.

D_0-D_7.   *System Data Bus* (bidirectional, 3-state). The system data bus transfers data and commands between the CPU and the Z80 SIO. D_0 is the least significant bit.

$\overline{\text{DCDA}}$, $\overline{\text{DCDB}}$.   *Data Carrier Detect* (inputs, active Low). These pins function as receiver enables if the SIO is programmed for Auto Enables; otherwise they may be used as general-purpose input pins. Both pins are Schmitt-trigger buffered to accommodate slow-risetime signals. The SIO detects pulses on these pins and interrupts the CPU on both logic level transitions. Schmitt-trigger buffering does not guarantee a specific noise-level margin.

$\overline{\text{DTRA}}$, $\overline{\text{DTRB}}$.   *Data Terminal Ready* (outputs, active Low). These outputs follow the state programmed into the Z80 SIO. They can also be programmed as general-purpose outputs.

In the Z80 SIO/1 bonding option, $\overline{\text{DTRB}}$ is omitted.

IEI.   *Interrupt Enable In* (input, active High). This signal is used with IEO to form a priority daisy chain when there is more than one interrupt-driven device. A High on this line indicates that no other device of higher priority is being serviced by a CPU interrupt service routine.

IEO.   *Interrupt Enable Out* (output, active High). IEO is High only if IEI is High and the CPU is not servicing an interrupt from this SIO. Thus, this signal blocks lower priority devices from interrupting while a higher priority device is being serviced by its CPU interrupt service routine.

INT. *Interrupt Request* (output, open drain, active Low). When the SIO is requesting an interrupt, it pulls $\overline{\text{INT}}$ Low.

IORQ. *Input/Output Request* (input from CPU, active Low). $\overline{\text{IORQ}}$ is used in conjunction with B/A, C/D, $\overline{\text{CE}}$, and $\overline{\text{RD}}$ to transfer commands and data between the CPU and the SIO. When $\overline{\text{CE}}$, $\overline{\text{RD}}$, and $\overline{\text{IORQ}}$ are all active, the channel selected by B/A transfers data to the CPU (a read operation). When $\overline{\text{CE}}$ and $\overline{\text{IORQ}}$ are active, but $\overline{\text{RD}}$ is inactive, the channel selected by B/A is written to by the CPU with either data or control information as specified by C/$\overline{\text{D}}$. As mentioned previously, if $\overline{\text{IORQ}}$ and $\overline{\text{M1}}$ are active simultaneously, the CPU is acknowledging an interrupt and the SIO automatically places its interrupt vector on the CPU data bus if it is the highest priority device requesting an interrupt.

M1. *Machine Cycle One* (input from Z80 CPU, active Low). When $\overline{\text{M1}}$ is active and $\overline{\text{RD}}$ is also active, the Z80 CPU is fetching an instruction from memory; when $\overline{\text{M1}}$ is active while $\overline{\text{IORQ}}$ is active, the SIO accepts $\overline{\text{M1}}$ and $\overline{\text{IORQ}}$ as an interrupt acknowledge if the SIO is the highest priority device that has interrupted the Z80 CPU.

RxCA, RxCB. *Receiver Clocks* (inputs). Receive data is sampled on the rising edge of $\overline{\text{RxC}}$. The Receive Clocks may be 1, 16, 32, or 64 times the data rate in asynchronous modes. These clocks may be driven by the Z80 CTC Counter Timer Circuit for programmable baud rate generation. Both inputs are Schmitt-trigger buffered; no noise level margin is specified.

In the Z80 SIO/0 bonding option, $\overline{\text{RxCB}}$ is bonded together with $\overline{\text{TxCB}}$.

RD. *Read Cycle Status* (input from CPU, active Low). If $\overline{\text{RD}}$ is active, a memory or I/O read operation is in progress. $\overline{\text{RD}}$ is used with B/A, $\overline{\text{CE}}$, and $\overline{\text{IORQ}}$ to transfer data from the SIO to the CPU.

RxDA, RxDB.   *Receive Data* (inputs, active High). Serial data at TTL levels.

RESET.   *Reset* (input, active Low). A Low $\overline{\text{RESET}}$ disables both receivers and transmitters, forces TxDA and TxDB marking, forces the modem controls High, and disables all interrupts. The control registers must be rewritten after the SIO is reset and before data is transmitted or received.

$\overline{\text{RTSA}}$, $\overline{\text{RTSB}}$.   *Request To Send* (outputs, active Low). When the RTS bit in Write Register 5 (Fig. 8.39) is set, the $\overline{\text{RTS}}$ output goes Low. When the RTS bit is reset in the Asynchronous mode, the output goes High after the transmitter is empty. In Synchronous modes, the $\overline{\text{RTS}}$ pin strictly follows the state of the RTS bit. Both pins can be used as general-purpose outputs.

$\overline{\text{SYNCA}}$, $\overline{\text{SYNCB}}$.   *Synchronisation* (bidirectional, active Low). These pins can act either as inputs or outputs. In the asynchronous receive mode, they are inputs similar to $\overline{\text{CTS}}$ and $\overline{\text{DCD}}$. In this mode, the transitions on these lines affect the state of the Sync/Hunt status bits in Read Register 0 (Figure 8.38), but have no other function. In the External Sync mode, these lines also act as inputs. When external synchronisation is achieved, $\overline{\text{SYNC}}$ must be driven Low on the second rising edge of $\overline{\text{RxC}}$ after that rising edge of $\overline{\text{RxC}}$ on which the last bit of the sync character was received. In other words, after the sync pattern is detected, the external logic must wait for two full Receive Clock cycles to activate the $\overline{\text{SYNC}}$ input. Once $\overline{\text{SYNC}}$ is forced Low, it should be kept Low until the CPU informs the external synchronisation detect logic that synchronisation has been lost or a new message is about to start. Character assembly begins on the rising edge of $\overline{\text{RxC}}$ that immediately precedes the falling edge of $\overline{\text{SYNC}}$ in the External Sync mode.

In the internal synchronisation mode (Monosync and Bisync), these pins act as outputs that are active during the part of the receive clock ($\overline{\text{RxC}}$) cycle in which sync characters are recognised. The sync condition is not latched, so these outputs are active each time a sync pattern is recognised, regardless of character boundaries.

In the Z80 SIO/2 bonding option, $\overline{\text{SYNCB}}$ is omitted.

$\overline{\text{TxCA}}$, $\overline{\text{TxCB}}$. *Transmitter Clocks* (inputs). In asynchronous modes, the Transmitter Clocks may be 1, 16, 32, or 64 times the data rate; however, the clock multiplier must be the same for the transmitter and the receiver. The Transmit-Clock inputs are Schmitt-trigger buffered for relaxed rise- and fall-time requirements; no noise level margin is specified. Transmitter Clocks may be driven by the Z80 CTC Counter Timer Circuit for programmable baud rate generation.

In the Z80 SIO/0 bonding option, $\overline{\text{TxCB}}$ is bonded together with $\overline{\text{RxCB}}$.

TxDA, TxDB. *Transmit Data* (outputs, active High). Serial data at TTL levels. TxD changes from the falling edge of $\overline{\text{TxC}}$.

$\overline{\text{W/RDYA}}$, $\overline{\text{W/RDYB}}$. *Wait/Ready* (outputs, open drain when programmed for Wait function; driven High and Low when programmed for Ready function). These dual-purpose outputs may be programmed as Ready lines for a DMA controller or as Wait lines that synchronise the CPU to the SIO data rate. The reset state is open drain.

Functional description

The functional capabilities of the Z80 SIO can be described from two different points of view: as a data communications device, it transmits and receives serial data in a wide variety of data-communication protocols; as a Z80 family peripheral, it interacts with the Z80 CPU and other peripheral circuits, sharing the data, address and control buses, as well as being a part of the Z80 interrupt structure. As a peripheral to other microprocessors, the SIO offers valuable features such as non-vectored interrupts, polling, and simple handshake capability. Fig. 8.33 is a block diagram.

Fig. 8.34 illustrates the conventional devices that the SIO replaces.

Data communication capabilities

The SIO provides two independent full-duplex channels that can be programmed for use in any common asynchronous, or synchronous data-

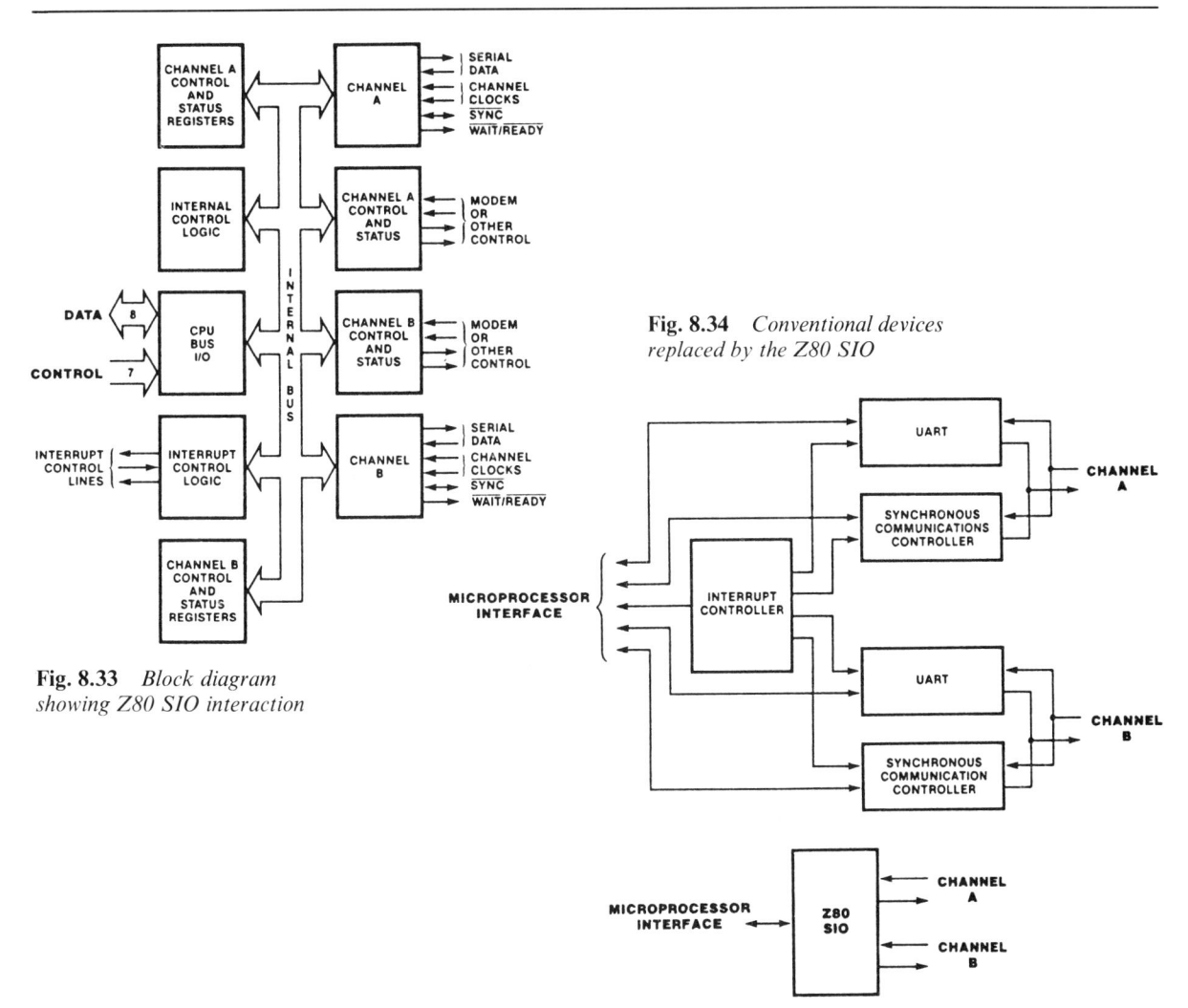

Fig. 8.33 *Block diagram showing Z80 SIO interaction*

Fig. 8.34 *Conventional devices replaced by the Z80 SIO*

communication protocol. Fig. 8.35a illustrates some of these protocols. The following is a short description of them. A more detailed explanation of these modes can be found in the *Z80 SIO Technical Manual* (03-3033-01).

(a) **Asynchronous modes.** Transmission and reception can be done independently on each channel with five to eight bits per character, plus optional even or odd parity. The transmitters can supply one, one-and-a-half, or two stop bits per character and can provide a break output at any time. The receiver break-detection logic interrupts the CPU both at the start and end of a received break. Reception is protected from spikes by a transient spike-rejection mechanism that checks the signal one-half a bit time after a Low level is detected on the receive data input (RxDA or RxDB in Fig. 8.30). If the Low does not persist, as in the case of a transient, the character assembly process is not started.

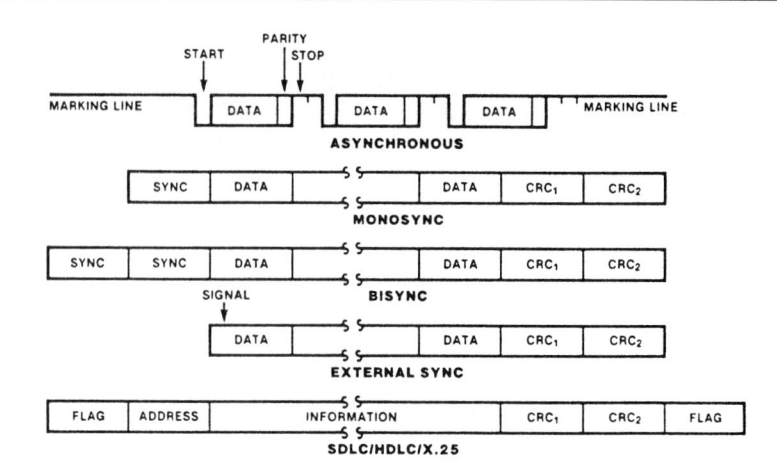

Fig. 8.35 *(a) Some Z80 SIO protocols*

(b) Six-bit SYNC character recognition

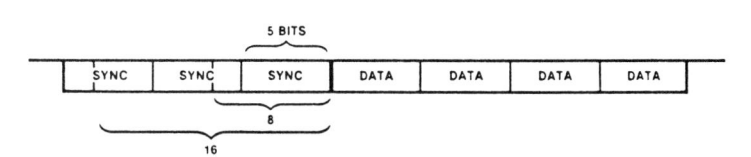

Framing errors and overrun errors are detected and buffered together with the partial character on which they occurred. Vectored interrupts allow fast servicing of error conditions using dedicated routines. Furthermore, a built-in checking process avoids interpreting a framing error as a new start bit: a framing error results in the addition of one-half a bit time to the point at which the search for the next start bit is begun.

The SIO does not require symmetric transmit and receive clock signals, a feature that allows it to be used with a Z80 CTC or many other clock sources. The transmitter and receiver can handle data at a rate of 1, 1/16, 1/32, or 1/64 of the clock rate supplied to the receive and transmit clock inputs.

In asynchronous modes, the $\overline{\text{SYNC}}$ pin may be programmed as an input that can be used for functions such as monitoring a ring indicator.

(b) **Synchronous modes.** The SIO supports both byte-oriented and bit-oriented synchronous communication.

Synchronous byte-oriented protocols can be handled in several modes that allow character synchronisation with an 8-bit sync character (Monosync), any 16-bit pattern (Bisync), or with an external sync signal. Leading sync characters can be removed without interrupting the CPU.

Five-, six-, or seven-bit sync characters are detected with 8- or 16-bit patterns in the SIO by overlapping the larger pattern across multiple incoming sync characters, as shown in Fig. 8.35b.

CRC checking for synchronous byte-oriented modes is delayed by one character time so the CPU may disable CRC checking on specific characters. This permits implementation of protocols such as IBM Bisync.

Both CRC-16 ($X^{16} + X^{15} + X^2 + 1$) and CCITT ($X^{16} + X^{12} + X^5 + 1$) error checking polynomials are supported. In all non-SDLC modes, the CRC generator is initialised to 0s; in SDLC modes, it is initialised to 1s. The SIO can be used for interfacing to peripherals such as hard-sectored floppy disks, but it cannot generate or check CRC for IBM-compatible soft-sectored disks. The SIO also provides a feature that automatically transmits CRC data when no other data is available for transmission. This allows very high-speed transmissions under DMA control with no need for CPU intervention at the end of a message. When there is no data or CRC to send in synchronous modes, the transmitter inserts 8- or 16-bit sync characters regardless of the programmed character length.

The SIO supports synchronous bit-oriented protocols such as SDLC and HDLC by performing automatic flag sending, zero insertion, and CRC generation. A special command can be used to abort a frame in transmission. At the end of a message the SIO automatically transmits the CRC and trailing flag when the transmit buffer becomes empty. If a transmit underrun occurs in the middle of a message, an external/status interrupt warns the CPU of this status change so that an abort may be issued. One to eight bits per character can be sent, which allows reception of a message with no prior information about the character structure in the information field of a frame.

The receiver automatically synchronises on the leading flag of a frame in SDLC or HDLC, and provides a synchronisation signal on the $\overline{\text{SYNC}}$ pin; an interrupt can also be programmed. The receiver can be programmed to search for frames addressed by a single byte to only a specified user-selected address or to a global broadcast address. In this mode, frames that do not match either the user-selected or broadcast address are ignored. The number of address bytes can be extended under software control. For transmitting data, an interrupt on the first received character or on every character can be selected. The receiver automatically deletes all zeros inserted by the transmitter during character assembly. It also calculates and automatically checks the CRC to validate frame transmission. At the end of transmission, the status of a received frame is available in the status registers.

The SIO can be conveniently used under DMA control to provide high-speed reception or transmission. In reception, for example, the SIO can interrupt the CPU when the first character of a message is received. The CPU then enables the DMA to transfer the message to memory. The SIO then issues an end-of-frame interrupt and the CPU can check the status of the received message. Thus, the CPU is freed for other service while the message is being received.

I/O Interface capabilities

The SIO offers the choice of polling, vectored or non-vectored interrupts and block-transfer modes to transfer data, status, and control information to, and from, the CPU. The block-transfer mode can also be implemented under DMA control.

(a) **Polling.** Two status registers are updated at appropriate times for each function being performed (for example, CRC error-status valid at the end of a message). When the CPU is operated in a polling fashion, one of the SIO's two status registers is used to indicate whether the SIO has some data or needs some data. Depending on the contents of this register, the CPU will either write data, read data, or just go on. Two bits in the register indicate that a data transfer is needed. In addition, error and other conditions are indicated. The second status register (special receive conditions) does not have to be read in a polling sequence, until a character has been received. All interrupt modes are disabled when operating the device in a polled environment.

(b) **Interrupts.** The SIO has an elaborate interrupt scheme to provide fast interrupt service in real-time applications. A control register and a status register in Channel B contain the interrupt vector. When programmed to do so, the SIO can modify three bits of the interrupt vector in the status register so that it points directly to one of eight interrupt service routines in memory, thereby servicing conditions in both channels and eliminating most of the needs for a status-analysis routine.

Transmit interrupts, receive interrupts, and external/status interrupts are the main source of interrupts. Each interrupt source is enabled under program control, with Channel A having a higher priority than Channel B, and with receive, transmit, and external/status interrupts prioritised in that order within each channel. When the transmit interrupt is enabled, the CPU is interrupted by the transmit buffer becoming empty. (This implies that the transmitter must have had a data character written into it so it can become empty.) The receiver can interrupt the CPU in one of two ways:

interrupt on first received character, or
interrupt on all received characters.

Interrupt-on-first-received-character is typically used with the block-transfer mode. Interrupt-on-all-received-characters has the option of modifying the interrupt vector in the event of a parity error. Both of these interrupt modes will also interrupt under special receive conditions on a character or message basis (end-of-frame interrupt in SDLC, for example). This means that the special-receive condition can cause an interrupt only if the interrupt-on-first-received-character or interrupt-on-all-received-characters mode is selected. In interrupt-on-first-received-character, an interrupt can occur from special-receive conditions (except parity error) after the first-received-character interrupt (example: receive-overrun interrupt).

The main function of the external/status interrupt is to monitor the signal transitions of the Clear To Send ($\overline{CTS}$), Data Carrier Detect ($\overline{DCD}$), and Synchronisation ($\overline{SYNC}$) pins (Figs 8.26–32). In addition, an external/status interrupt is also caused by a CRC-sending condition, or by the detec-

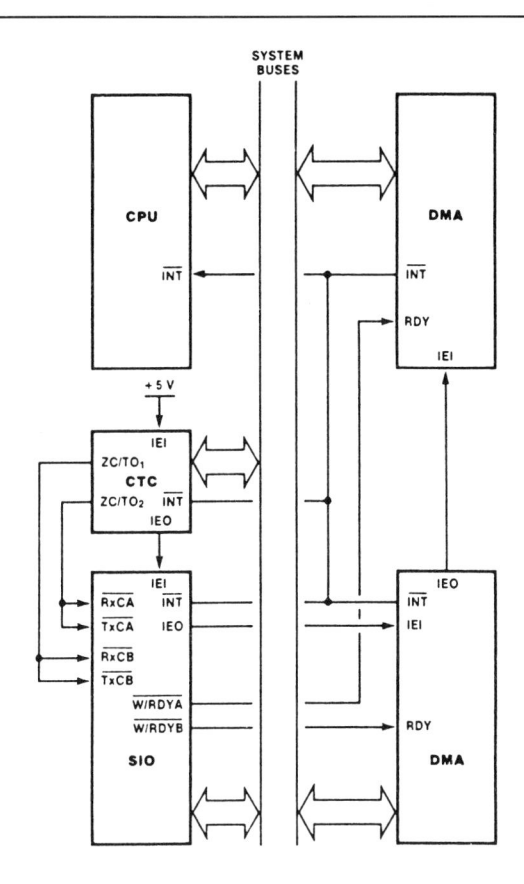

Fig. 8.36 *Typical Z80 environment*

tion of a break sequence (asynchronous mode) or abort sequence (SDLC mode) in the data stream. The interrupt caused by the break/abort sequence allows the SIO to interrupt when the break/abort sequence is detected or terminated. This feature facilitates the proper termination of the current message, correct initialisation of the next message, and the accurate timing of the break/abort condition in external logic.

In a Z80 CPU environment (Fig. 8.36), SIO interrupt vectoring is 'automatic': the SIO passes its internally-modifiable 8-bit vector to the CPU, which adds an additional 8-bits from its interrupt-vector (I) register to form the memory address of the interrupt-routine table. This table contains the address of the beginning of the interrupt routine itself. The process entails an indirect transfer of CPU control to the interrupt routine, so that the next instruction executed after an interrupt acknowledge by the CPU is the first instruction of the interrupt routine itself.

(c) **CPU/DMA block transfer.** The SIO's block-transfer mode accommodates both CPU block transfers and DMA controllers (Z80 DMA or other designs). The block-transfer mode uses the Wait/Ready output signal, which is selected with three bits in an internal control register. The Wait/Ready output signal can be programmed as a $\overline{\text{WAIT}}$ line in the CPU block-transfer mode or as a $\overline{\text{READY}}$ line in the DMA block-transfer mode.

To a DMA controller, the SIO $\overline{\text{READY}}$ output indicates that the SIO is ready to transfer data to, or from, memory. To the CPU, the $\overline{\text{WAIT}}$ output indicates that the SIO is not ready to transfer data, thereby requesting the CPU to extend the I/O cycle.

Internal structure

The internal structure of the device includes a Z80 CPU interface, internal control and interrupt logic, and two full-duplex channels. Each channel contains its own set of control and status (write and read) registers, and control and status logic that provides the interface to modems or other external devices.

The registers for each channel are designated as follows:

WR0-WR7—Write registers 0 through 7
RR0-RR2—Read registers 0 through 2

The register group includes five 8-bit control registers, two sync-character registers and two status registers. The interrupt vector is written into an additional 8-bit register (Write Register 2) in Channel B that may be read through another 8-bit register (Read Register 2) in Channel B. The bit assignment and functional grouping of each register is configured to simplify and organise the programming process. Table 8.10 lists the functions assigned to each read or write register.

Table 8.10   Register Functions

	Read Register Functions
RR0	Transmit/Receive buffer status, interrupt status and external status
RR1	Special Receive Condition status
RR2	Modified interrupt vector (Channel B only)

	Write Register Functions
WR0	Register pointers, CRC initialise, and initialisation commands for the various modes.
WR1	Transmit/Receive interrupt and data transfer mode definition.
WR2	Interrupt vector (Channel B only)
WR3	Receive parameters and control
WR4	Transmit/Receive miscellaneous parameters and modes
WR5	Transmit parameters and controls
WR6	Sync character or SDLC address field
WR7	Sync character or SDLC flag

Hardware design 213

The logic for both channels provides formats, synchronisation, and validation for data transferred to and from the channel interface. The modem control inputs, Clear To Send ($\overline{\text{CTS}}$) and Data Carrier Detect ($\overline{\text{DCD}}$), are monitored by the external control and status logic under program control. All external control-and-status-logic signals are general-purpose in nature and can be used for functions other than modem control.

Data path

The transmit and receive data path illustrated for Channel A in Fig. 8.37 is identical for both channels. The receiver has three 8-bit buffer registers in a FIFO arrangement, in addition to the 8-bit receive shift register. This scheme creates additional time for the CPU to service an interrupt at the beginning of a block of high-speed data. Incoming data is routed through one of several paths (data or CRC) depending on the selected mode and—in asynchronous modes—the character length.

Fig. 8.37 *Transmit and Receive data path (Channel 4)*

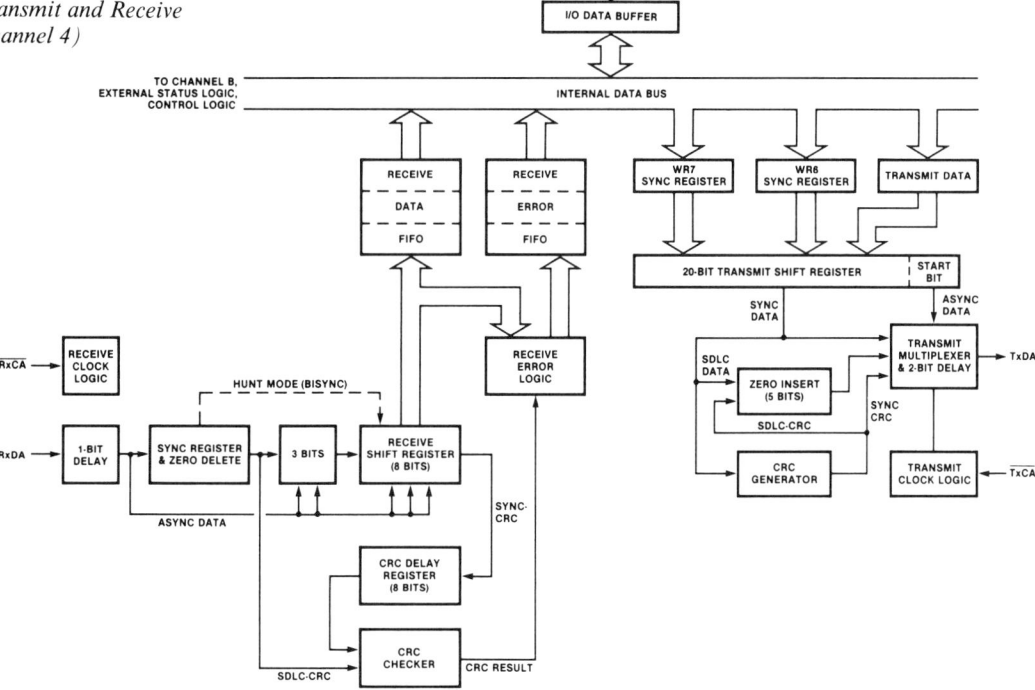

The transmitter has an 8-bit transmit data buffer register that is loaded from the internal data bus, and a 20-bit transmit shift register that can be loaded from the sync-character buffers or from the transmit data register. Depending on the operational mode, outgoing data is routed through one of four main paths before it is transmitted from the Transmit Data output (TxD).

Programming

The system program first issues a series of commands that initialise the basic mode of operation and then issues other commands that qualify conditions within the selected mode. For example, the asynchronous mode, character length, clock rate, number of stop bits, even or odd parity might be set first; then the interrupt mode; and finally, receiver or transmitter enable.

Both channels contain registers that must be programmed via the system program prior to operation. The channel-select input ($B/\overline{A}$) and the control/data ($C/\overline{D}$) are the command-structure addressing controls, and are normally controlled by the CPU address bus. Figs. 8.40 and 8.41 illustrate the timing relationships for programming the write registers and transferring data and status.

Read registers

The SIO contains three read registers for Channel B and two read registers for Channel A (RR0-RR2 in Fig. 8.38) that can be read to obtain the status information; RR2 contains the internally-modifiable interrupt vector and is only in the Channel B register set. The status information includes error conditions, interrupt vector, and standard communications-interface signals.

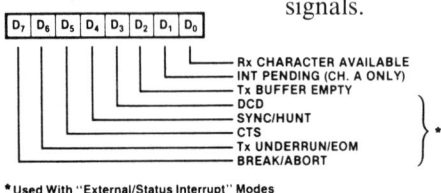

Fig. 8.38 *Read register bit functions*

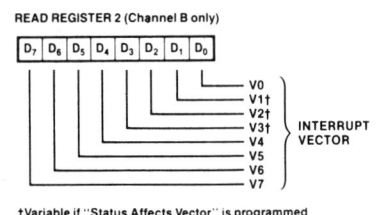

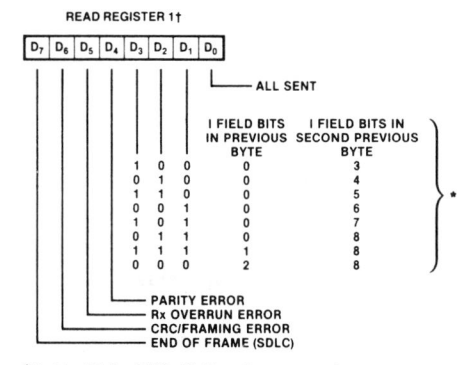

To read the contents of a selected read register other than RR0, the system program must first write the pointer byte to WR0 in exactly the same way as a write register operation. Then, by executing a read instruction, the contents of the addressed read register can be read by the CPU.

The status bits of RR0 and RR1 are carefully grouped to simplify status monitoring. For example, when the interrupt vector indicates that a Special Receive Condition interrupt has occurred, all the appropriate error bits can be read from a single register (RR1).

Hardware design 215

Write registers

Fig. 8.39 *Write register bit functions*

The SIO contains eight write registers for Channel B and seven write registers for Channel A (WR0–WR7 in Fig. 8.39) that are programmed separately to configure the functional personality of the channels; WR2 contains the interrupt vector for both channels and is only in the Channel B

WRITE REGISTER 0

| D7 | D6 | D5 | D4 | D3 | D2 | D1 | D0 |

```
            0  0  0  REGISTER 0
            0  0  1  REGISTER 1
            0  1  0  REGISTER 2
            0  1  1  REGISTER 3
            1  0  0  REGISTER 4
            1  0  1  REGISTER 5
            1  1  0  REGISTER 6
            1  1  1  REGISTER 7
0  0  0  NULL CODE
0  0  1  SEND ABORT (SDLC)
0  1  0  RESET EXT/STATUS INTERRUPTS
0  1  1  CHANNEL RESET
1  0  0  ENABLE INT ON NEXT Rx CHARACTER
1  0  1  RESET TxINT PENDING
1  1  0  ERROR RESET
1  1  1  RETURN FROM INT (CH-A ONLY)

0  0  NULL CODE
0  1  RESET Rx CRC CHECKER
1  0  RESET Tx CRC GENERATOR
1  1  RESET Tx UNDERRUN/EOM LATCH
```

WRITE REGISTER 1

| D7 | D6 | D5 | D4 | D3 | D2 | D1 | D0 |

```
                  EXT INT ENABLE
                  Tx INT ENABLE
                  STATUS AFFECTS VECTOR (CH. B ONLY)
0  0  Rx INT DISABLE
0  1  Rx INT ON FIRST CHARACTER
1  0  INT ON ALL Rx CHARACTERS (PARITY AFFECTS VECTOR)   } *
1  1  INT ON ALL Rx CHARACTERS (PARITY DOES NOT AFFECT VECTOR)
      WAIT/READY ON R/T
      WAIT/READY FUNCTION
      WAIT/READY ENABLE
```

*Or on special condition

WRITE REGISTER 2 (Channel B only)

| D7 | D6 | D5 | D4 | D3 | D2 | D1 | D0 |

V0, V1, V2, V3, V4, V5, V6, V7 — INTERRUPT VECTOR

WRITE REGISTER 3

| D7 | D6 | D5 | D4 | D3 | D2 | D1 | D0 |

```
               Rx ENABLE
               SYNC CHARACTER LOAD INHIBIT
               ADDRESS SEARCH MODE (SDLC)
               Rx CRC ENABLE
               ENTER HUNT PHASE
               AUTO ENABLES
0  0  Rx 5 BITS/CHARACTER
0  1  Rx 7 BITS/CHARACTER
1  0  Rx 6 BITS/CHARACTER
1  1  Rx 8 BITS/CHARACTER
```

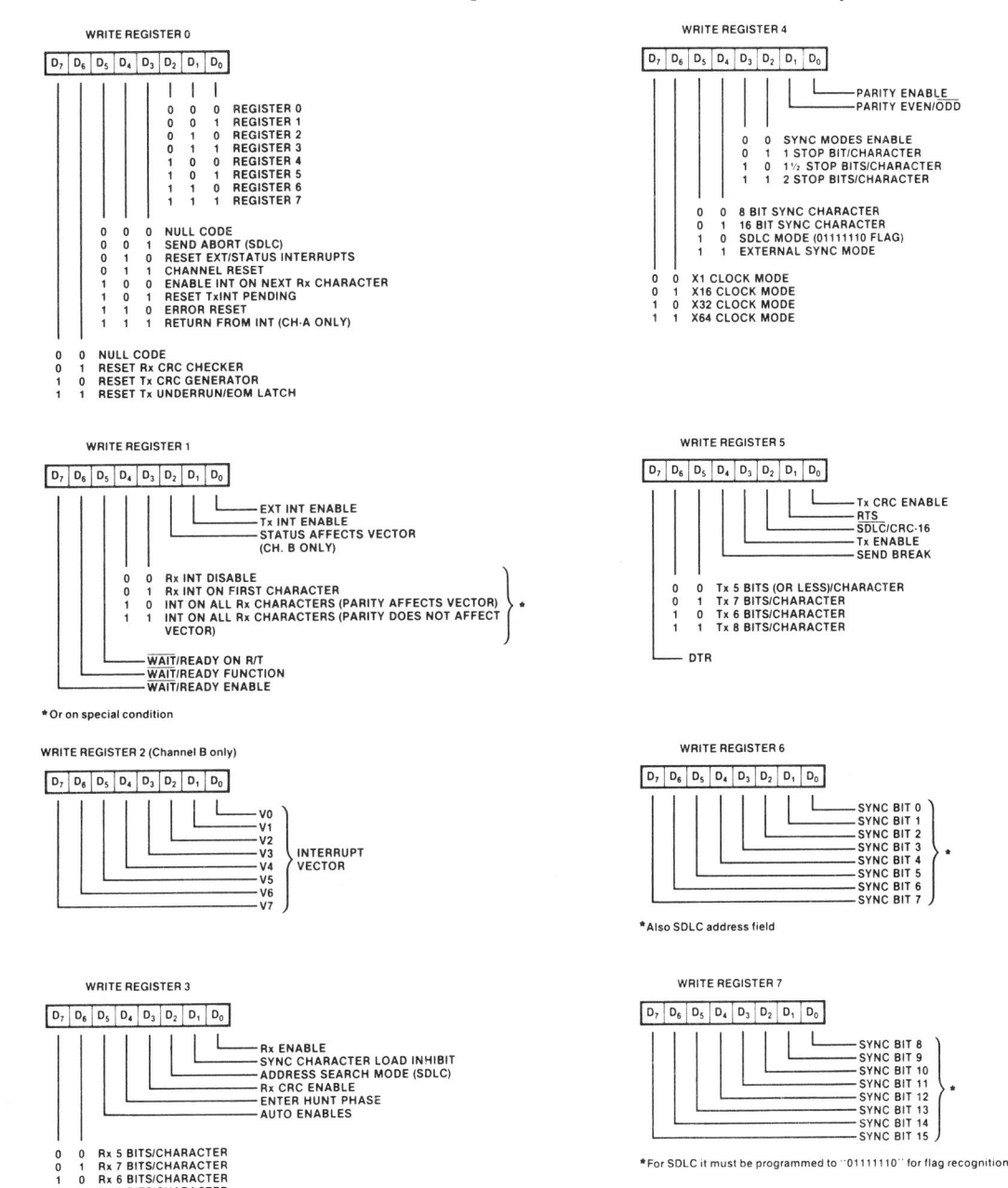

WRITE REGISTER 4

| D7 | D6 | D5 | D4 | D3 | D2 | D1 | D0 |

```
                  PARITY ENABLE
                  PARITY EVEN/ODD
0  0  SYNC MODES ENABLE
0  1  1 STOP BIT/CHARACTER
1  0  1½ STOP BITS/CHARACTER
1  1  2 STOP BITS/CHARACTER
0  0  8 BIT SYNC CHARACTER
0  1  16 BIT SYNC CHARACTER
1  0  SDLC MODE (01111110 FLAG)
1  1  EXTERNAL SYNC MODE
0  0  X1 CLOCK MODE
0  1  X16 CLOCK MODE
1  0  X32 CLOCK MODE
1  1  X64 CLOCK MODE
```

WRITE REGISTER 5

| D7 | D6 | D5 | D4 | D3 | D2 | D1 | D0 |

```
                  Tx CRC ENABLE
                  RTS
                  SDLC/CRC-16
                  Tx ENABLE
                  SEND BREAK
0  0  Tx 5 BITS (OR LESS)/CHARACTER
0  1  Tx 7 BITS/CHARACTER
1  0  Tx 6 BITS/CHARACTER
1  1  Tx 8 BITS/CHARACTER
      DTR
```

WRITE REGISTER 6

| D7 | D6 | D5 | D4 | D3 | D2 | D1 | D0 |

SYNC BIT 0, SYNC BIT 1, SYNC BIT 2, SYNC BIT 3, SYNC BIT 4, SYNC BIT 5, SYNC BIT 6, SYNC BIT 7 *

*Also SDLC address field

WRITE REGISTER 7

| D7 | D6 | D5 | D4 | D3 | D2 | D1 | D0 |

SYNC BIT 8, SYNC BIT 9, SYNC BIT 10, SYNC BIT 11, SYNC BIT 12, SYNC BIT 13, SYNC BIT 14, SYNC BIT 15 *

*For SDLC it must be programmed to "01111110" for flag recognition

register set. With the exception of WR0, programming the write registers requires two bytes. The first byte is to WR0 and contains three bits (D_0-D_2) that point to the selected register; the second byte is the actual control word that is written into the register to configure the SIO.

WR0 is a special case in that all of the basic commands can be written to it with a single byte. Reset (internal or external) initialises the pointer bits D_0-D_2 to point to WR0. This implies that a channel reset must not be combined with the pointing to any register.

Timing

The SIO must have the same clock as the CPU (same phase and frequency relationship, not necessarily the same driver).

Read cycle

The timing signals generated by a Z80 CPU input instruction to read a data or status byte from the SIO are illustrated in Fig. 8.40.

Write cycle

Fig. 8.41 illustrates the timing and data signals generated by a Z80 CPU output instruction to write a data or control byte into the SIO.

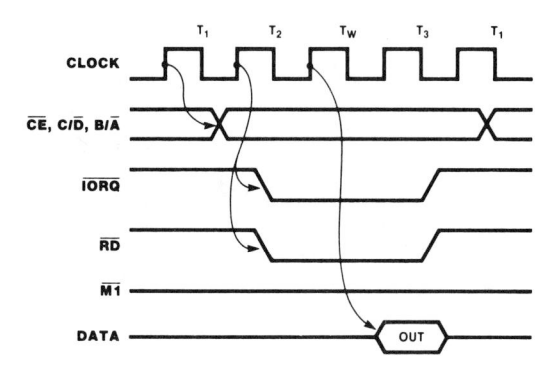

Fig. 8.40 *Read cycle*

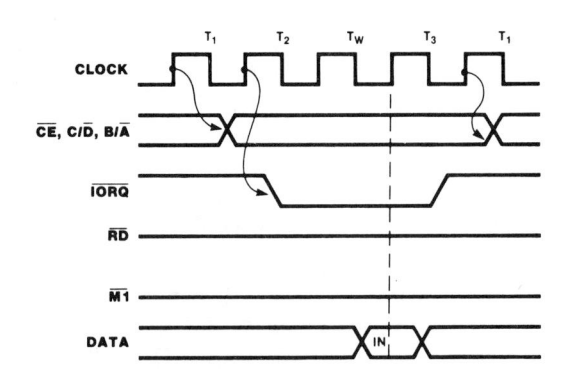

Fig. 8.41 *Write cycle*

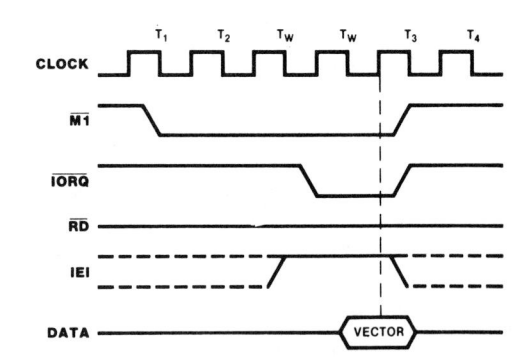

Fig. 8.42 *Interrupt acknowledge cycle*

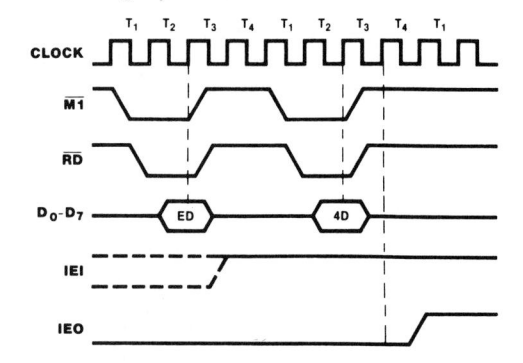

Fig. 8.43 *Return from interrupt cycle*

Interrupt-acknowledge cycle

After receiving an interrupt-request signal from an SIO ($\overline{\text{INT}}$ pulled Low), the Z80 CPU sends an interrupt-acknowledge sequence, $\overline{\text{M1}}$ Low and $\overline{\text{IORQ}}$ Low, a few cycles later (Fig. 8.42).

The SIO contains an internal daisy-chained interrupt structure for prioritising nested interrupts for the various functions of its two channels, and this structure can be used within an external user-defined daisy chain that prioritises several peripheral circuits.

The IEI of the highest-priority device is terminated High. A device that has an interrupt pending or under service forces its IEO Low. For devices with no interrupt pending or under service, IEO = IEI.

To ensure stable conditions in the daisy chain, all interrupt status signals are prevented from changing while $\overline{\text{M1}}$ is Low. When $\overline{\text{IORQ}}$ is Low, the highest priority interrupt requestor (the one with IEI High) places its interrupt vector on the data bus and sets its internal interrupt-under-service latch.

Return from interrupt cycle

Fig. 8.43 illustrates the return from interrupt cycle. Normally, the Z80 CPU issues a Return From Interrupt (RETI) instruction at the end of an interrupt service routine. RETI is a 2-byte opcode (ED-4D) that resets the interrupt-under-service latch in the SIO to terminate the interrupt that has just been processed. This is accomplished by manipulating the daisy chain in the following way.

The normal daisy-chain operation can be used to detect a pending interrupt; however, it cannot distinguish between an interrupt under service and a pending unacknowledged interrupt of a higher priority. Whenever ED is decoded, the daisy chain is modified by forcing High the IEO of any interrupt that has not yet been acknowledged. Thus the daisy chain identifies the device presently under service as the only one with an IEI High and an IEO Low. If the next opcode byte is 4D, the interrupt-under-service latch is reset.

The ripple time of the interrupt daisy chain (both the High-to-Low and the Low-to-High transitions) limits the number of devices that can be placed in the daisy chain. Ripple time can be improved with carry-look-ahead, or by extending the interrupt-acknowledge cycle. For further information about techniques for increasing the number of daisy-chained devices, refer to the *Z8400 Z80 CPU Product Specification* (00-2001-04).

Further data

Tables 8.11 and 8.12 give a.c. characteristics and Figs 8.44 and 8.45 show the a.c. timing diagrams. D.C. characteristics, maximum ratings and capacitance are given in Tables 8.13–8.15.

The characteristics given apply for the following test conditions, unless otherwise noted. All voltages are referenced to GND (0 V). Positive current flows into the referenced pin. Available operating temperature range is:

$$E = -40°C \text{ to } +85°C, +4.50\,\text{V} \leqslant V_{CC} \leqslant 5.50\,\text{V}.$$

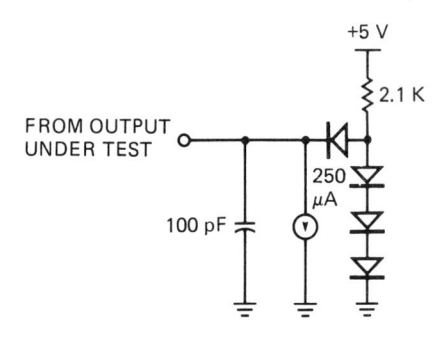

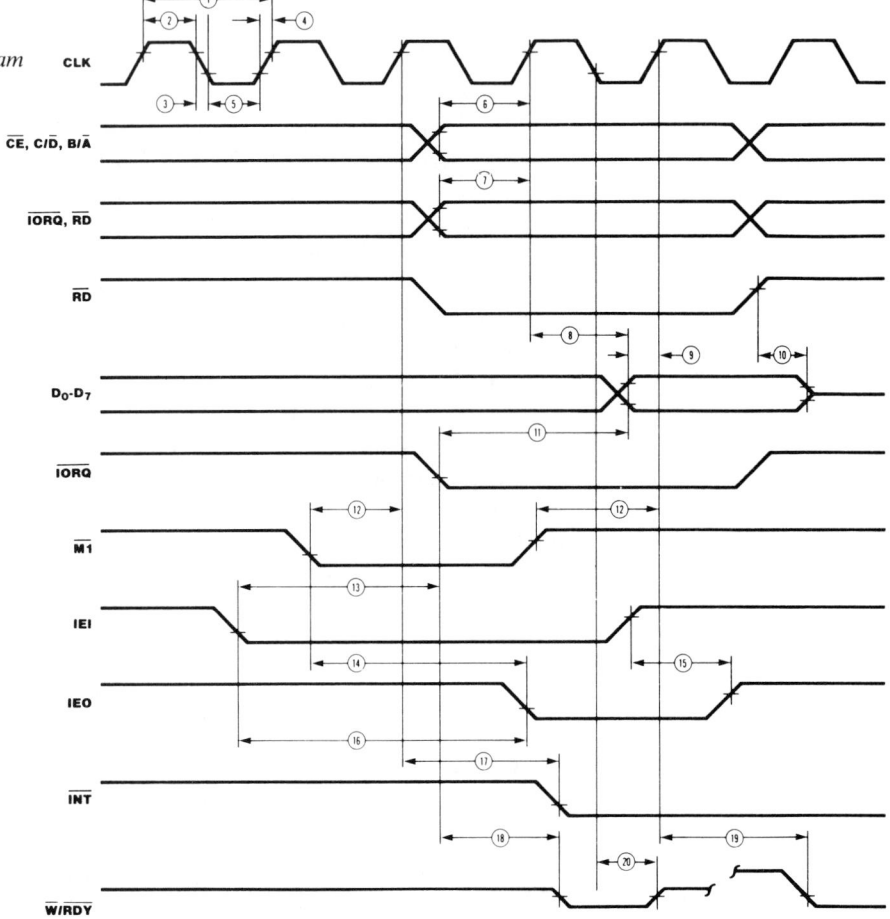

Fig. 8.44 *A.C. timing diagram for the Z80 SIO*

Table 8.11 A.C. Characteristics of the Z80 SIO

Number (Fig. 8.44)	Symbol	Parameter	Min (ns)	Max (ns)
1	TcC	Clock cycle time	250	
2	TwCh	Clock width (high)	105	
3	TfC	Clock fall time		30
4	TrC	Clock rise time		30
5	TwCl	Clock width (low)	105	
6	TsAD(C)	$\overline{CE}$, C/$\overline{D}$, B/$\overline{A}$ to Clock ↑ Setup Time	145	
7	TsCS(C)	$\overline{IORQ}$, $\overline{RD}$ to Clock ↑ Setup Time	115	
8	TdC(DO)	Clock ↑ to Data Out Delay		220
9	TsDl(C)	Data in to Clock ↑ Setup (Write or $\overline{M1}$ cycle)	50	
10	TdRD(DOz)	$\overline{RD}$ ↑ to Data Out Float Delay		110
11	TdlO(DOI)	$\overline{IORQ}$ ↓ Data Out Delay (INTACK cycle)		160
12	TsM1(C)	$\overline{M1}$ to Clock ↑ Setup Time	90	
13	TsIEI(IO)	IEI to $\overline{IORQ}$ ↓ Setup Time (INTACK cycle)	140	
14	TdM1(IEO)	$\overline{M1}$ ↓ to IEO ↓ Delay (interrupt before $\overline{M1}$)		190
15	TdIEI(IEOr)	IEI ↑ to IEO ↑ Delay (after ED decode)		160
16	TdIEI(IEOf)	IEI ↓ to IEO ↓ Delay		100
17	TdC(INT)	Clock ↑ to $\overline{INT}$ ↓ Delay		200
18	TdIO (W/RWf)	$\overline{IORQ}$ ↓ or $\overline{CE}$ ↓ to $\overline{W/RDY}$ ↓ Delay (Wait mode)		210
19	TdC(W/RR)	Clock ↑ to $\overline{W/RDY}$ ↓ Delay (Ready mode)		120
20	TdC(W/RWz)	Clock ↓ to $\overline{W/RDY}$ Float Delay (Wait mode)		130
21	Th	Any unspecified Hold when Setup is specified	0	

Table 8.12 A.C. Characteristics of the Z80 SIO (continued)

Number (Fig. 8.45)	Symbol	Parameter	Min	Max	Unit
1	TwPh	Pulse width (high)	200		ns
2	TwPl	Pulse width (low)	200		ns
3	TcTxC	$\overline{\text{TxC}}$ cycle time	400	∞	ns
4	TwTxCl	$\overline{\text{TxC}}$ width (low)	180	∞	ns
5	TwTxCh	$\overline{\text{TxC}}$ width (high)	180	∞	ns
6	TdTxC(TxD)	$\overline{\text{TxC}}\downarrow$ to TxD Delay		300	ns
7	TdTxC(W/RRf)	$\overline{\text{TxC}}\downarrow$ to $\overline{\text{W/RDY}}\downarrow$ Delay (Ready Mode)	5	9	System clock period*
8	TdTxC(INT)	$\overline{\text{TxC}}\downarrow$ to $\overline{\text{INT}}\downarrow$ Delay	5	9	System clock period
9	TcRxC	$\overline{\text{RxC}}$ cycle time	400	∞	ns
10	TwRxCl	$\overline{\text{RxC}}$ width (low)	180	∞	ns
11	TwRxCh	$\overline{\text{RxC}}$ width (high)	180	∞	ns
12	TsRxD(RxC)	RxD to $\overline{\text{RxC}}\uparrow$ Setup Time (x1 mode)	0		ns
13	ThRxD(RxC)	$\overline{\text{RxC}}\uparrow$ RxD Hold Time (x1 mode)	140		ns
14	TdRxC(W/RRf)	$\overline{\text{RxC}}\uparrow$ to $\overline{\text{W/RDY}}\downarrow$ Delay (Ready mode)	10	13	System clock period
15	TdRxC(INT)	$\overline{\text{RxC}}\uparrow$ to $\overline{\text{INT}}\downarrow$ Delay	10	13	System clock period
16	TdRxC(SYNC)	$\overline{\text{RxC}}\uparrow$ to $\overline{\text{SYNC}}\downarrow$ Delay (Output modes)	4	7	System clock period
17	TsSYNC(RxC)	$\overline{\text{SYNC}}\downarrow$ to $\overline{\text{RxC}}\uparrow$ Setup (External Sync modes)	−100		ns

* In all modes, the System Clock rate must be at least five times the maximum data rate. RESET must be active a minimum of one complete clock cycle.

Table 8.13 Absolute maximum ratings for the Z80 SIO

Voltages in V_{CC} with respect to V_{SS}	−0.3 V to +0.7 V
Voltages on all inputs with respect to V_{SS}	−0.3 V to V_{CC} + 0.3 V
Storage temperature	−65°C to 150°C

Hardware design 221

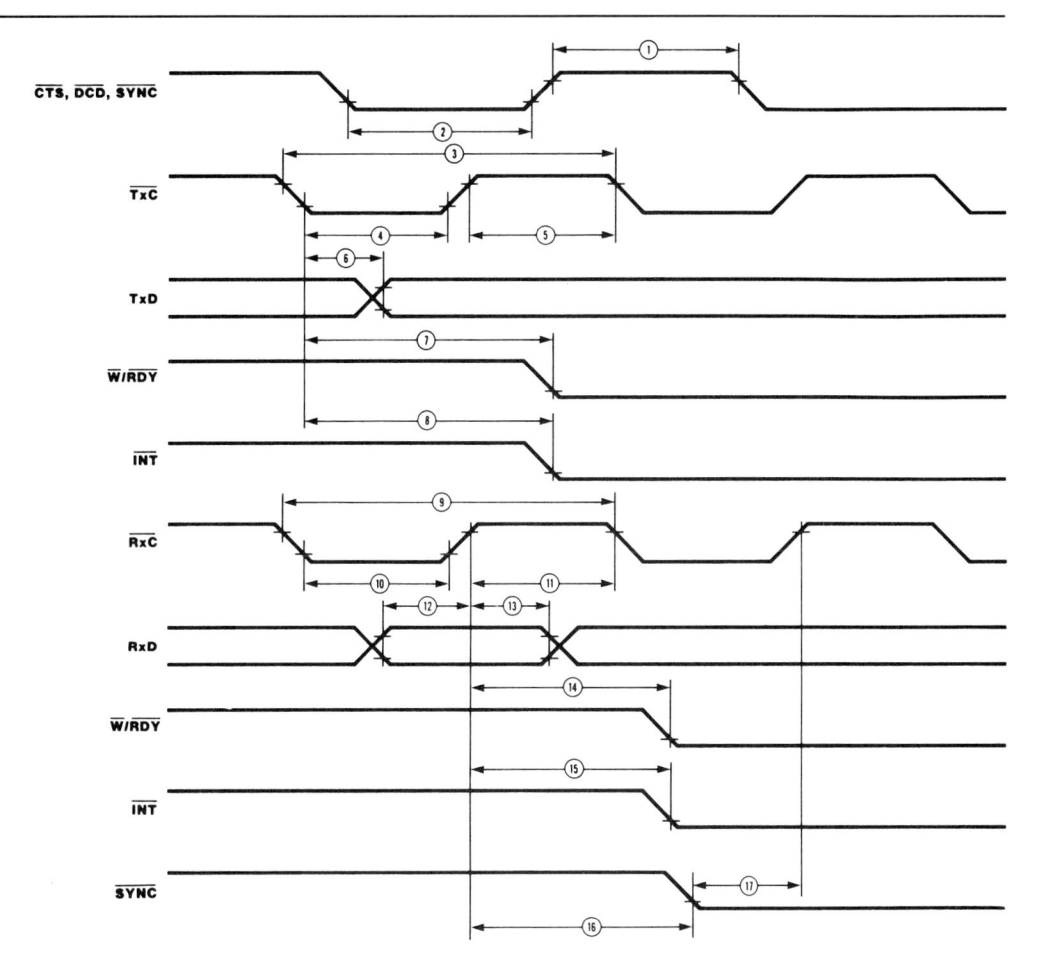

Fig. 8.45 A.C. timing diagram for the Z80 SIO *(continued)*

Table 8.14 Capacitance data for the Z80 SIO

Symbol	Parameter	Max
C	Clock capacitance	7 pF
C_{IN}	Input capacitance	5 pF
C_{OUT}	Output capacitance	10 pF

Over specified temperature range $f = 1$ MHz
Unmeasured pins returned to ground.

Table 8.15 D.C. characteristics of the Z80 SIO

Symbol	Parameter	Min	Max	Typ	Unit	Test Condition
V_{ILC}	Clock input low voltage	−0.3	+0.45		V	
V_{IHC}	Clock input high voltage	V_{CC} −0.6	V_{CC} +0.3		V	
V_{IL}	Input low voltage	−0.3	+0.8		V	
V_{IH}	Input high voltage	+2.2	V_{CC}		V	
V_{OL}	Output low voltage		+0.4		V	$I_{OL} = 2.0$ mA
V_{OH_1}	Output high voltage	+2.4			V	$I_{OH} = -1.6$ mA
V_{OH_2}	Output high voltage	V_{CC} −0.8			V	$I_{OH} = -250\,\mu A$
I_{LI}	Input leakage current		±10		μA	$V_{IN} = 0.4$ to V_{CC}
I_{LO}	3-state output leakage current in float		±10		μA	$V_{OUT} = 0.4$ to V_{CC}
$I_{L(SY)}$	SYNC pin leakage current		+10/−40		μA	$V_{IN} = 0.4$ to V_{CC}
I_{CC_1}	Power supply current		10	7	mA	$V_{CC} = 5$ V CLK = 4 MHz
I_{CC_2}	Standby supply current		10	0.5	μA	$V_{IH} = V_{CC} - 0.2$ V $V_{IL} = 0.2$ V $V_{CC} = 5$ V CLK = (0) $V_{IH} = V_{CC} - 0.2$ V $V_{IL} = 0.2$ V

Over specified temperature and voltage range.

Z80 CTC technical data

The Z80 CTC four-channel counter/timer can be programmed by system software for a broad range of counting and timing applications. The four independently programmable channels of the Z80 CTC satisfy common microcomputer system requirements for event counting, interrupt and interval timing, and general clock rate generation.

System design is simplified because the CTC connects directly to both the Z80 CPU and the Z80 SIO with no additional logic. In larger systems, address decoders and buffers may be required.

Fig. 8.46 shows how the Z80 CTC is connected to the Z80 MPU.

Programming the CTC is straightforward: each channel is programmed with two bytes; a third is necessary when interrupts are enabled. Once started, the CTC counts down, automatically reloads its time constant, and resumes counting. Software timing loops are completely eliminated. Interrupt processing is simplified because only one vector need be specified; the CTC internally generates a unique vector for each channel.

Hardware design 223

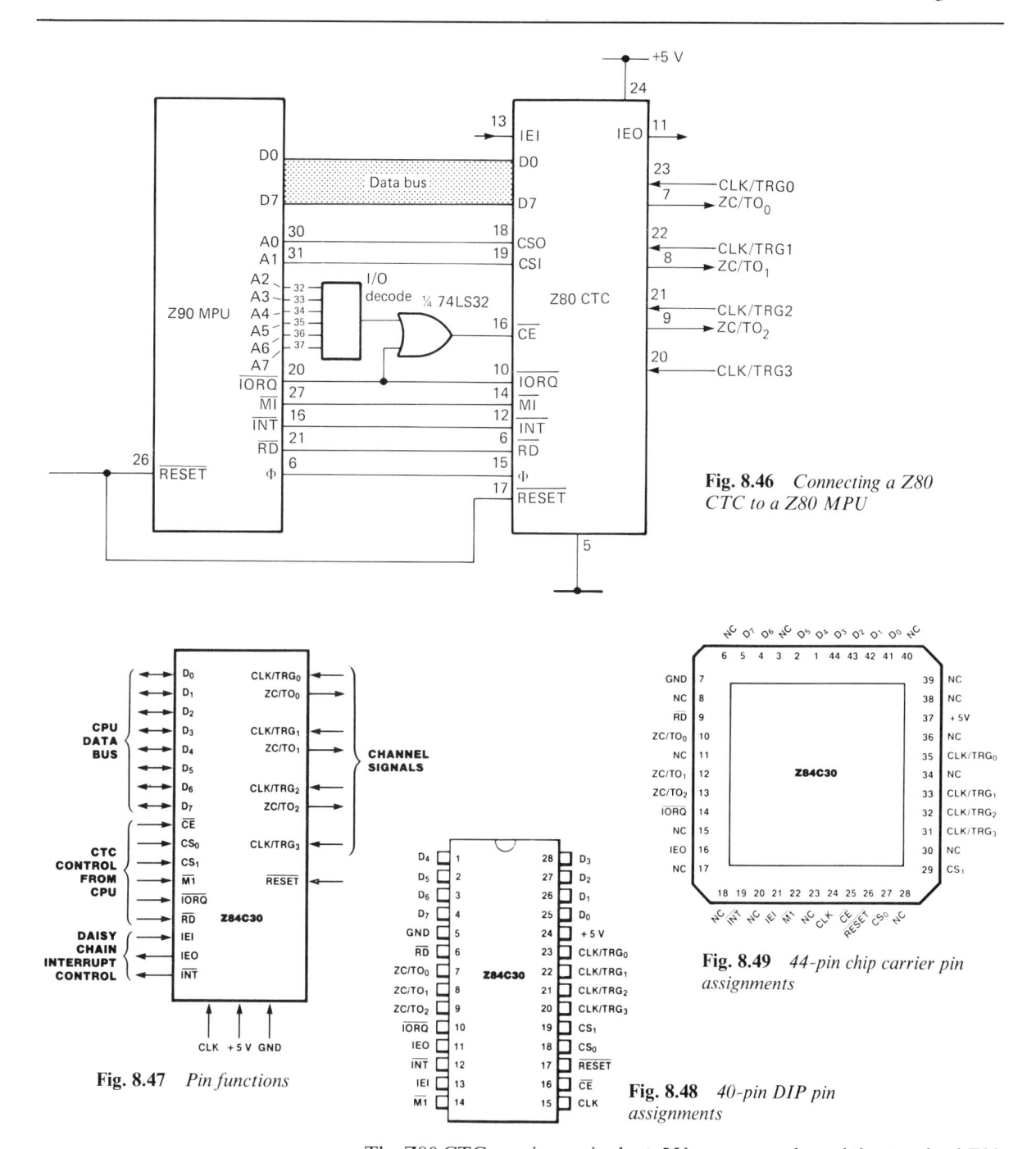

Fig. 8.46 *Connecting a Z80 CTC to a Z80 MPU*

Fig. 8.47 *Pin functions*

Fig. 8.48 *40-pin DIP pin assignments*

Fig. 8.49 *44-pin chip carrier pin assignments*

The Z80 CTC requires a single +5 V power supply and the standard Z80 single-phase system clock. It is fabricated with n-channel silicon-gate depletion-load technology, and packaged in 28-pin DIPs and a 44-pin plastic chip carrier (Figs. 8.48 and 8.49).

Functional description

The Z80 CTC has four independent counter/timer channels. Each channel is individually programmed with two words: a control word and a time-constant word. The control word selects the operating mode (counter or timer), enables or disables the channel interrupt, and selects certain other operating parameters. If the timing mode is selected, the control word also sets a prescaler, which divides the system clock by either 16 or 256. The time-constant word is a value from 1 to 256.

During operation, the individual counter channel counts down from the present time constant value. In counter mode operation the counter decrements on each of the CLK/TRG input pulses until zero count is reached. Each decrement is synchronised by the system clock. For counts greater than 256, more than one counter can be cascaded. At zero count, the down-counter is automatically reset with the time constant value.

The timer mode determines time intervals as small as $4\,\mu s$ (Z80A) or $6.4\,\mu s$ (Z80) without additional logic or software timing loops. Time intervals are generated by dividing the system clock with a prescaler that decrements a preset down-counter.

Thus, the time interval is an integral multiple of the clock period, the prescaler value (16 or 256), and the time constant that is preset in the down-counter. A timer is triggered automatically when its time constant value is programmed, or by an external CLK/TRG input.

Three channels have two outputs that occur at zero count. The first output is a zero-count/timeout pulse at the ZC/TO output. The fourth channel (Channel 3) does not have a ZC/TO output; interrupt request is the only output available from Channel 3.

The second output is Interrupt Request ($\overline{INT}$), which occurs if the channel has its interrupt enabled during programming. When the Z80 CPU acknowledges Interrupt Request, the Z80 CTC places an interrupt vector on the data bus.

The four channels of the Z80 CTC are fully prioritised and fit into four contiguous slots in a standard Z80 daisy-chain interrupt structure. Channel 0 is the highest priority and Channel 3 the lowest. Interrupts can be individually enabled (or disabled) for each of the four channels.

Internal structure

The CTC has four major elements, as shown in Fig. 8.50:
    CPU bus I/O
    Channel control logic
    Interrupt logic
    Counter/timer circuits

CPU bus I/O

The CPU bus I/O circuit decodes the address inputs, and interfaces the CPU data and control signals to the CTC for distribution on the internal bus.

Fig. 8.50 *Functional block diagram for the Z80 CTC*

Fig. 8.51 *Block diagram for the counter/timer circuits*

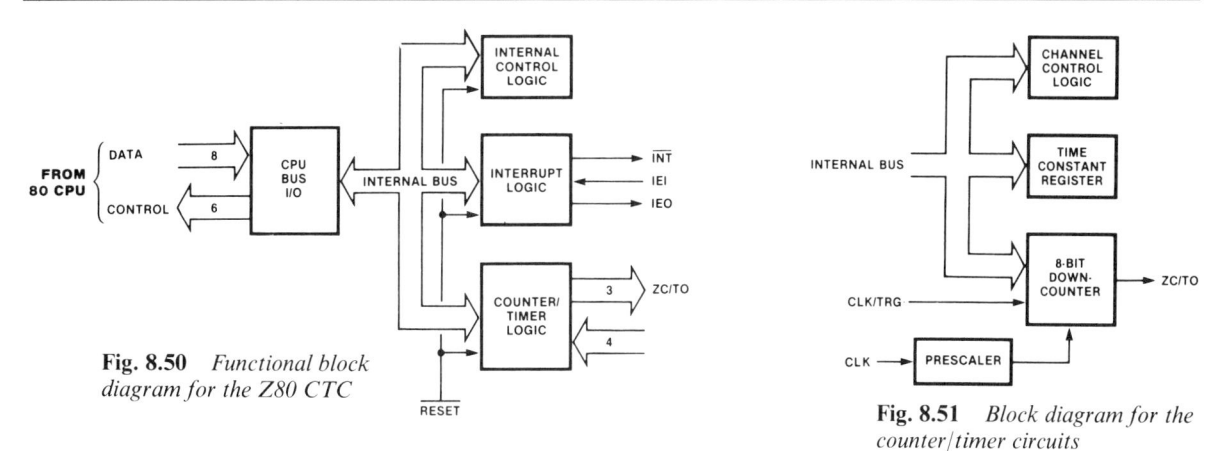

Internal control logic

The CTC internal control logic controls overall chip operating functions such as the chip enable, reset, and read/write logic.

Interrupt logic

The interrupt control logic ensures that the CTC interrupts interface properly with the Z80 CPU interrupt system. The logic controls the interrupt priority of the CTC as a function of the IEI signal. If IEI is High, the CTC has priority. During interrupt processing, the interrupt logic holds IEO Low, which inhibits the interrupt operation on lower priority devices. If the IEI input goes Low, priority is relinquished and the interrupt logic drives IEO Low.

If a channel is programmed to request an interrupt, the interrupt logic drives IEO Low at the zero count, and generates an $\overline{INT}$ signal to the Z80 CPU. When the Z80 CPU responds with interrupt acknowledge ($\overline{M1}$ and $\overline{IORQ}$), then the interrupt logic arbitrates the CTC internal priorities, and the interrupt control logic places a unique interrupt vector on the data bus.

If an interrupt is pending, the interrupt logic holds IEO Low. When the Z80 CPU issues a Return From Interrupt (RETI) instruction, each peripheral device decodes the first byte (ED_{16}). If the device has a pending interrupt, it raises IEO (High) for one $\overline{M1}$ cycle. This ensures that all lower priority devices can decode the entire RETI instruction and reset properly.

Counter/timer circuits

The CTC has four independent counter/timer circuits, each containing the logic shown in Figure 8.51.

Channel control logic

The channel control logic receives the 8-bit channel control word when the counter/timer channel is programmed. The channel control logic decodes the control word and sets the following operating conditions:

Interrupt enable (or disable)
Operating mode (timer or counter)
Timer mode prescaler factor (16 or 256)
Active slope for CLK/TRG input
Timer mode trigger (automatic or CLK/TRG input)
Time constant data word to follow
Software reset

Time constant register

When the counter/timer channel is programmed, the time constant register receives and stores an 8-bit time constant value, which can be anywhere from 1 to 256 (0 = 256). This constant is automatically loaded into the down-counter when the counter/timer channel is initialised, and subsequently after each zero count.

Prescaler

The prescaler, which is used only in timer mode, divides the system clock frequency by a factor of either 16 or 256. The prescaler output clocks the down-counter during timer operation. The effect of the prescaler on the down-counter is a multiplication of the system clock period by 16 or 256. The prescaler factor is programmed by bit 5 of the channel control word.

Down-counter

Prior to each count cycle, the down-counter is loaded with the time constant register contents. The counter is then decremented one of two ways, depending on operating mode:

by the prescaler output (timer mode), or
by the trigger pulses into the CLK/TRG input (counter mode).

Without disturbing the down-count, the Z80 CPU can read the count remaining at any time by performing an I/O read operation at the port address assigned to the CTC channel. When the down-counter reaches the zero count, the ZC/TO output generates a positive-going pulse. When the interrupt is enabled, zero count also triggers an interrupt request signal ($\overline{\text{INT}}$) from the interrupt logic.

Programming

Each Z80 CTC channel must be programmed prior to operation. Programming consists of writing two words to the I/O port that corresponds to the desired channel. The first word is a control word that selects the operating mode and other parameters; the second word is a time constant, which is a binary data word with a value from 1 to 256. A time constant word must be preceded by a channel control word.

After initialisation, channels may be reprogrammed at any time. If updated control and time constant words are written to a channel during the count operation, the count continues to zero before the new time constant is loaded into the counter.

If the interrupt on any Z80 CTC channel is enabled, the programming procedure should also include an interrupt vector. Only one vector is required for all four channels, because the interrupt logic automatically modifies the vector for the channel requesting service.

A control word is identified by a 1 in bit 0. A 1 in bit 2 indicates a time constant word is to follow. Interrupt vectors are always addressed to Channel 0, and identified by a 0 in bit 0.

Addressing

During programming, channels are addressed with the channel select pins CS_1 and CS_2. A 2-bit binary code selects the appropriate channel as follows:

Channel	CS_1	CS_0
0	0	0
1	0	1
2	1	0
3	1	1

Reset

The CTC has both hardware and software resets. The hardware reset terminates all down-counts and disables all CTC interrupts by resetting the interrupt bits in the control registers. In addition, the ZC/TO and Interrupt outputs go inactive. IEO reflects IEI, and D_0-D_7 go to the high-impedance state. All channels must be completely reprogrammed after a hardware reset.

The software reset is controlled by bit 1 in the channel control word. When a channel receives a software reset, it stops counting. When a software reset is used, the other bits in the control word also change the contents of the channel control register. After a software reset a new time constant word must be written to the same channel.

If the channel control word has both bits D_1 and D_2 set to 1, the addressed channel stops operating, pending a new time constant word. The channel is ready to resume after the new constant is programmed. In timer mode, if $D_3 = 0$, operation is triggered automatically when the time constant word is loaded.

Channel control word programming

The channel control word is shown in Fig. 8.52. It sets the modes and parameters described below.

Interrupt Enable. D_7 enables the interrupt, so that an interrupt output

228 *Microprocessor based systems*

```
            D7 D6 D5 D4 D3 D2 D1 D0
```

INTERRUPT
1 ENABLES INTERRUPT
0 DISABLES INTERRUPT

MODE
0 SELECTS TIMER MODE
1 SELECTS COUNTER MODE

PRESCALER VALUE*
1 = VALUE OF 256
0 = VALUE OF 16

CLK/TRG EDGE SELECTION
0 SELECTS FALLING EDGE
1 SELECTS RISING EDGE

CONTROL OR VECTOR
0 = VECTOR
1 = CONTROL WORD

RESET
0 = CONTINUED OPERATION
1 = SOFTWARE RESET

TIME CONSTANT
0 = NO TIME CONSTANT FOLLOWS
1 = TIME CONSTANT FOLLOWS

TIMER TRIGGER*
0 = AUTOMATIC TRIGGER WHEN TIME CONSTANT IS LOADED
1 = CLK/TRG PULSE STARTS TIMER

*TIMER MODE ONLY

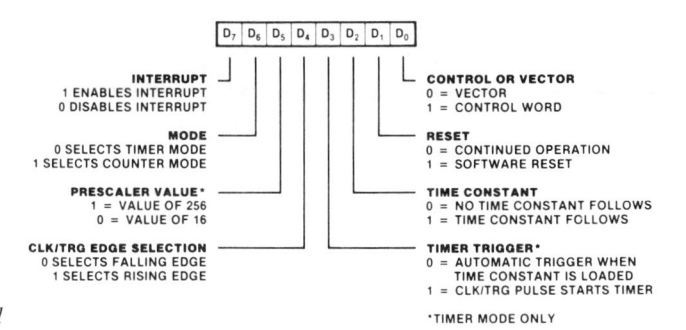

Fig. 8.52 *Channel control word*

(INT) is generated at zero count. Interrupts may be programmed in either mode and may be enabled or disabled at any time.

Mode. D_6 selects either timer or counter operating mode.

Prescaler Factor. (*Timer Mode Only*). D_5 selects factor—either 16 or 256.

Clock/Trigger Edge Selector. D_4 selects the active edge or slope of the CLK/TRG input pulses. Note that reprogramming the CLK/TRG slope during operation is equivalent to issuing an active edge. If the trigger slope is changed by a control word update while a channel is pending operation in timer mode, the result is the same as a CLK/TRG pulse and the timer starts. Similarly, if the channel is in counter mode, the counter decrements.

Timer Trigger (*Timer Mode Only*). D_3 selects the trigger mode for timer operation. When D_3 is reset to 0, the timer is triggered automatically. The time constant word is programmed during an I/O write operation, which takes one machine cycle. At the end of the write operation there is a setup delay of one clock period. The timer starts automatically (decrements) on the rising edge of the second clock pulse (T_2) of the machine cycle following the write operation. Once started, the timer runs continuously. At zero count the timer reloads automatically and continues counting without interruption or delay, until stopped by a reset.

When D_3 is set to 1, the timer is triggered externally through the CLK/TRG input. The time constant word is programmed during an I/O write operation, which takes one machine cycle. The timer is ready for operation on the rising edge of the second clock pulse (T_2) of the following machine cycle. Note that the first timer decrement follows the active edge of the CLK/TRG pulse by a delay time of one clock cycle if a minimum setup time to the rising edge of clock is met. If this minimum is not met, the delay is extended by another clock period. Consequently, for immediate triggering, the CLK/TRG input must precede T_2 by one clock cycle plus its minimum setup time. If the minimum time is not met, the timer will start on the third clock cycle (T_3).

Once started, the timer operates continuously, without interruption or delay, until stopped by a reset.

Time Constant. A 1 in D_2 indicates that the next word addressed to the selected channel is a time constant data word for the time constant register. The time constant word may be written at any time.

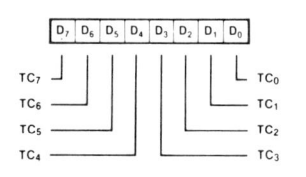

A 0 in D_2 indicates no time constant word is to follow. This is ordinarily used when the channel is already in operation and the new channel control word is an update. A channel will not operate without a time constant value. The only way to write a time constant value is to write a control word with D_2 set.

Software Reset. Setting D_1 to 1 causes a software reset, which is described in the Reset section.

Control Word. Setting D_0 to 0 identifies the word as a control word.

Time constant programming

Before a channel can start counting it must receive a time constant word from the CPU. During programming or reprogramming, a channel control word in which bit 2 is set must precede the time constant word to indicate that the next word is a time constant. The time constant word can be any value from 1 to 256 (Figure 8.53). Note that 00_{16} is interpreted as 256.

In timer mode, the time interval is controlled by three factors:

The system clock period (CLK)
The prescaler factor (P), which multiplies the interval by either 16 or 256
The time constant (T), which is programmed into the time constant register

Fig. 8.53 *Time constant word*

Consequently, the time interval is the product of $CLK \times P \times T$. The minimum timer resolution is $16 \times CLK$ ($4\,\mu s$ with a 4 MHz clock). The maximum timer interval is $256 \times CLK \times 256$ (16.4 ms with a 4 MHz clock). For longer intervals timers may be cascaded.

Interrupt vector programming

If the Z80 CTC has one or more interrupts enabled, it can supply interrupt vectors to the Z80 CPU. To do so, the Z80 CTC must be pre-programmed

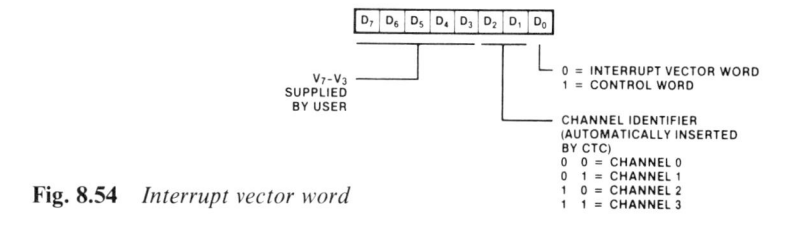

Fig. 8.54 *Interrupt vector word*

with the most-significant five bits of the interrupt vector. Programming consists of writing a vector word to the I/O port corresponding to the Z80 CTC Channel 0. Note that D_0 of the vector word is always zero, to distinguish the vector from a channel control word. D_1 and D_2 are not used in programming the vector word. These bits are supplied by the interrupt logic to identify the channel requesting interrupt service with a unique interrupt vector (Fig. 8.54). Channel 0 has the highest priority.

Pin description

$\overline{\text{CE}}$.   *Chip Enable* (input, active Low). When enabled the CTC accepts control words, interrupt vectors, or time constant data words from the data bus during an I/O write cycle; or transmits the contents of the downcounter to the CPU during an I/O read cycle. In most applications this signal is decoded from the eight least significant bits of the address bus for any of the four I/O port addresses that are mapped to the four counter-timer channels.

CLK.   *System Clock* (input). Standard single-phase Z80 system clock.

CLK/TRG$_0$– CLK/TRG$_3$.   *External Clock/Timer Trigger* (input, user-selectable active High or Low). Four pins corresponding to the four Z80 CTC channels. In counter mode, every active edge on this pin decrements the downcounter. In timer mode, an active edge starts the timer.

CS$_0$–CS$_1$.   *Channel Select* (inputs active High). Two-bit binary address code selects one of the four CTC channels for an I/O write or read (usually connected to A$_0$ and A$_1$).

D$_0$–D$_7$.   *System Data Bus* (bidirectional, 3-state). Transfers all data and commands between the Z80 CPU and the Z80 CTC.

IEI.   *Interrupt Enable In* (input, active High). A High indicates that no other interrupting devices of higher priority in the daisy chain are being serviced by the Z80 CPU.

IEO.   *Interrupt Enable Out* (output, active High). High only if IEI is High and the Z80 CPU is not servicing an interrupt from any Z80 CTC channel. IEO blocks lower priority devices from interrupting while a higher priority interrupting device is being serviced.

$\overline{\text{INT}}$.   *Interrupt Request* (output, open drain, active Low). Low when any Z80 CTC channel that has been programmed to enable interrupts as a zero-count condition in its downcounter.

$\overline{\text{IORQ}}$.   *Input/Output Request* (input from CPU, active Low). Used with $\overline{\text{CE}}$ and $\overline{\text{RD}}$ to transfer data and channel control words between the Z80 CPU and the Z80 CTC. During a write cycle, $\overline{\text{IORQ}}$ and $\overline{\text{CE}}$ are active and $\overline{\text{RD}}$ inactive. The Z80 CTC does not receive a specific write signal; rather, it internally generates its own from the inverse of an active $\overline{\text{RD}}$ signal. In a read cycle, $\overline{\text{IORQ}}$, $\overline{\text{CE}}$, and $\overline{\text{RD}}$ are active; the contents of the downcounter are read by the Z80 CPU. If $\overline{\text{IORQ}}$ and $\overline{\text{M1}}$ are both true, the CPU is acknowledging an interrupt request, and the highest priority interrupting channel places its interrupt vector on the Z80 data bus.

M1. *Machine Cycle One* (input from CPU, active Low). When $\overline{M1}$ and $\overline{IORQ}$ are active, the Z80 CPU is acknowledging an interrupt. The Z80 CTC then places an interrupt vector on the data bus if it has highest priority, and if a channel has requested an interrupt ($\overline{INT}$).

$\overline{RD}$. *Read Cycle Status* (input, active Low). Used in conjunction with $\overline{IORQ}$ and $\overline{CE}$ to transfer data and channel control words between the Z80 CPU and the Z80 CTC.

$\overline{RESET}$. *Reset* (input, active Low). Terminates all down-counts and disables all interrupts by resetting the interrupt bits in all control registers; the ZC/TO and the interrupt outputs go inactive; IEO reflects IEI; D_0–D_7 go to the high-impedance state.

ZC/TO$_0$– *Zero Count/Timeout* (output, active High). Three ZC/TO
ZC/TO$_2$. pins corresponding to Z80 CTC channels 2 through 0 (Channel 3 has no ZC/TO pin). In both counter and timer modes the output is an active High pulse when the down-counter decrements to zero.

Timing

Read cycle timing

Fig. 8.55 shows read cycle timing. This cycle reads the contents of a down-counter without disturbing the count. During clock cycle T_2, the Z80 CPU initiates a read cycle by driving the following inputs Low: $\overline{RD}$, $\overline{IORQ}$, and $\overline{CE}$. A 2-bit binary code at inputs CS_1 and CS_0 selects the channel to be read. $\overline{M1}$ must be High to distinguish this cycle from an interrupt acknowledge.

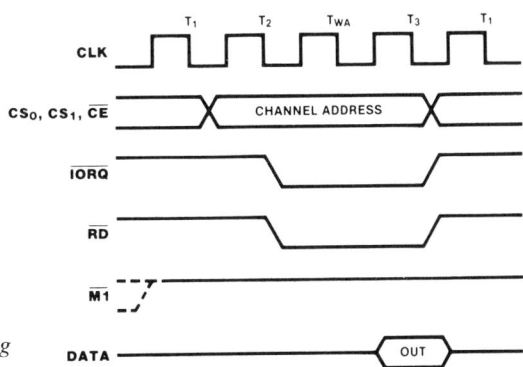

Fig. 8.55 *Read cycle timing*

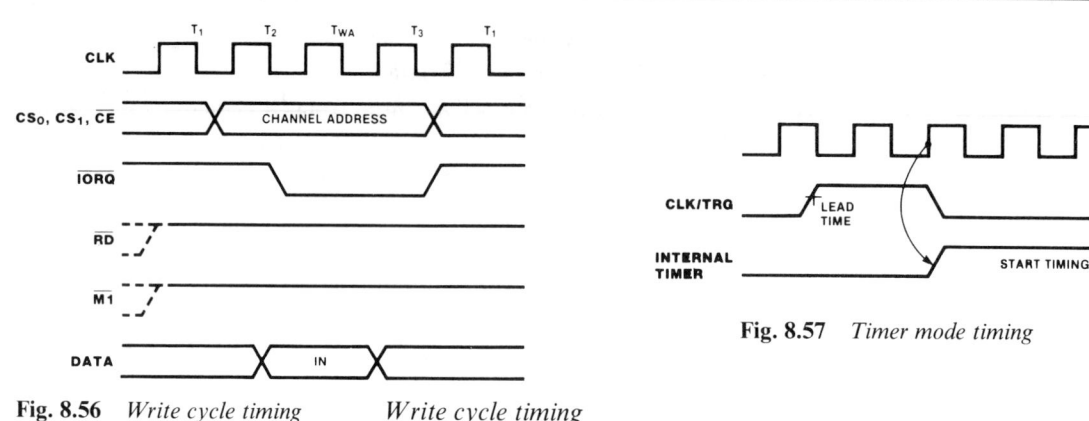

Fig. 8.56 *Write cycle timing*

Fig. 8.57 *Timer mode timing*

Write cycle timing

Fig. 8.56 shows write cycle timing for loading control, time constant, or vector words.

The CTC does not have a write signal input, so it generates one internally when the read ($\overline{\text{RD}}$) input is High during T_1. During T_2 $\overline{\text{IORQ}}$ and $\overline{\text{CE}}$ inputs are Low. $\overline{\text{M1}}$ must be High to distinguish a write cycle from an interrupt acknowledge. A 2-bit binary code at inputs CS_1 and CS_0 selects the channel to be addressed, and the word being written is placed on the Z80 data bus. The data word is latched into the appropriate register with the rising edge of clock cycle T_3.

Timer operation

In the timer mode, a CLK/TRG pulse input starts the timer (Fig. 8.57) on the second succeeding rising edge of CLK. The trigger pulse is asynchronous, and it must have a minimum width. A minimum lead time (210 ns) is required between the active edge of the CLK/TRG and the next rising edge of CLK to enable the prescaler on the following clock edge. If the CLK/TRG edge occurs closer than this, the initiation of the timer function is delayed one clock cycle. This corresponds to the start-up timing discussed in the programming section. The timer can also be started automatically if so programmed by the channel control word.

Counter operation

In the counter mode, the CLK/TRG pulse input decrements the down-counter. The trigger is asynchronous, but the count is synchronised with CLK. For the decrement to occur on the next rising edge of CLK, the trigger edge must precede CLK by a minimum lead time as shown in Fig. 8.58. If the lead time is less than specified, the count is delayed by one clock cycle. The trigger pulse must have a minimum width, and the trigger period must be at least twice the clock period. If the trigger repetition rate is faster than 1/3 the clock frequency, then TsCTR(Cs), AC Characteristics Specification 26, must be met.

The ZC/TO output occurs immediately after zero count, and follows the rising CLK edge.

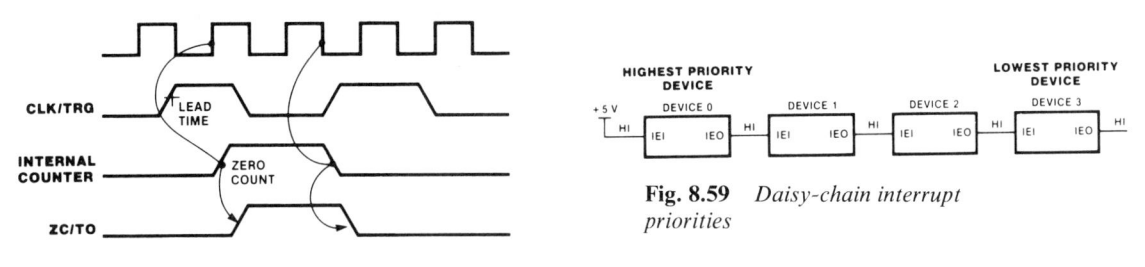

Fig. 8.58 *Counter mode timing*

Fig. 8.59 *Daisy-chain interrupt priorities*

Interrupt operation

The Z80 CTC follows the Z80 system interrupt protocol for nested priority interrupts and return from interrupt, wherein the interrupt priority of a peripheral is determined by its location in a daisy chain. Two lines—IEI and IEO—in the CTC connect it to the system daisy chain. The device closest to the +5 V supply has the highest priority (Fig. 8.59). For additional information on the Z80 interrupt structure, refer to the *Z80 CPU Product Specification* and the *Z80 CPU Technical Manual*.

Within the Z80 CTC, interrupt priority is predetermined by channel number: Channel 0 has the highest priority, and Channel 3 the lowest. If a device or channel is being serviced with an interrupt routine, it cannot be interrupted by a device or channel with lower priority until service is complete. Higher priority devices or channels may interrupt the servicing of lower priority devices or channels.

A Z80 CTC channel may be programmed to request an interrupt every time its downcounter reaches zero. Note that the CPU must be programmed for interrupt mode 2. Some time after the interrupt request, the CPU sends an interrupt acknowledge. The CTC interrupt control logic determines the highest priority channel that is requesting an interrupt. Then, if the CTC IEI input is High (indicating that it has priority within the system daisy chain) it places an 8-bit interrupt vector on the system data bus. The high-order five bits of this vector were written to the CTC during the programming process; the next two bits are provided by the CTC interrupt control logic as a binary code that identifies the highest priority channel requesting an interrupt; the low-order bit is always zero.

Interrupt acknowledge timing

Figure 8.60 shows interrupt acknowledge timing. After an interrupt request, the Z80 CPU sends an interrupt acknowledge ($\overline{M1}$ and $\overline{IORQ}$). All channels are inhibited from changing their interrupt request status when $\overline{M1}$ is active—about two clock cycles earlier than $\overline{IORQ}$. $\overline{RD}$ is High to distinguish this cycle from an instruction fetch.

The CTC interrupt logic determines the highest priority channel requesting an interrupt. If the CTC interrupt enable input (IEI) is High, the highest priority interrupting channel within the CTC places its interrupt vector on the data bus when $\overline{IORQ}$ goes Low. Two wait states (T_{WA}) are automati-

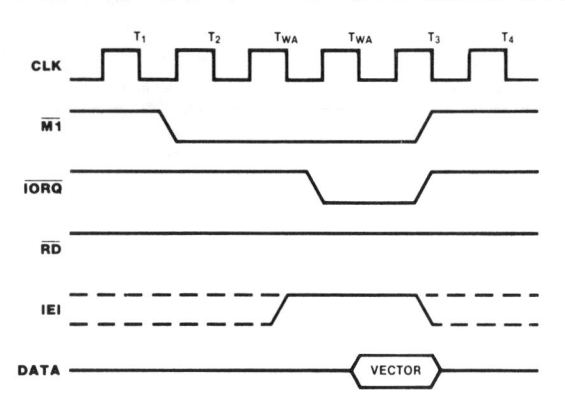

Fig. 8.60 *Interrupt acknowledge timing*

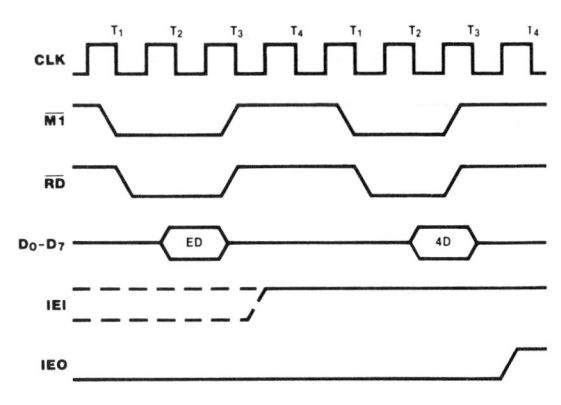

Fig. 8.61 *Return from interrupt timing*

cally inserted at this time to allow the daisy chain to stabilise. Additional wait states may be added.

Return from interrupt timing

At the end of an interrupt service routine the RETI (Return From Interrupt) instruction initialises the daisy chain enable lines for proper control of nested priority interrupt handling. The CTC decodes the 2-byte RETI code internally and determines whether it is intended for a channel being serviced. Fig. 8.61 shows RETI timing.

If several Z80 peripherals are in the daisy chain, IEI settles active (High) on the chip currently being serviced when the opcode ED_{16} is decoded. If the following opcode is $4D_{16}$, the peripheral being serviced is released and its IEO becomes active. Additional wait states are allowed.

Further data

Table 8.16 gives a.c. characteristics and Fig. 8.62 shows the a.c. timing diagram. D.C. characteristics, maximum ratings and capacitance are given in Tables 8.17–8.19.

The characteristics given apply for the following test conditions, unless otherwise noted. All voltages are referenced to GND (0 V). Positive current flows into the referenced pin. Available operating temperature range is:

$$E = -40\,°C \text{ to } +85\,°C, +4.50\,V \leqslant V_{cc} \leqslant 5.50\,V$$

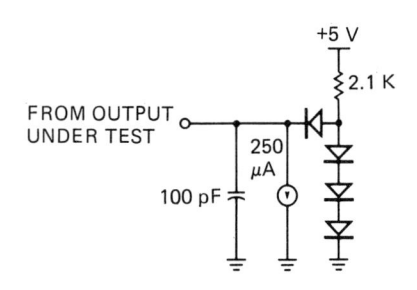

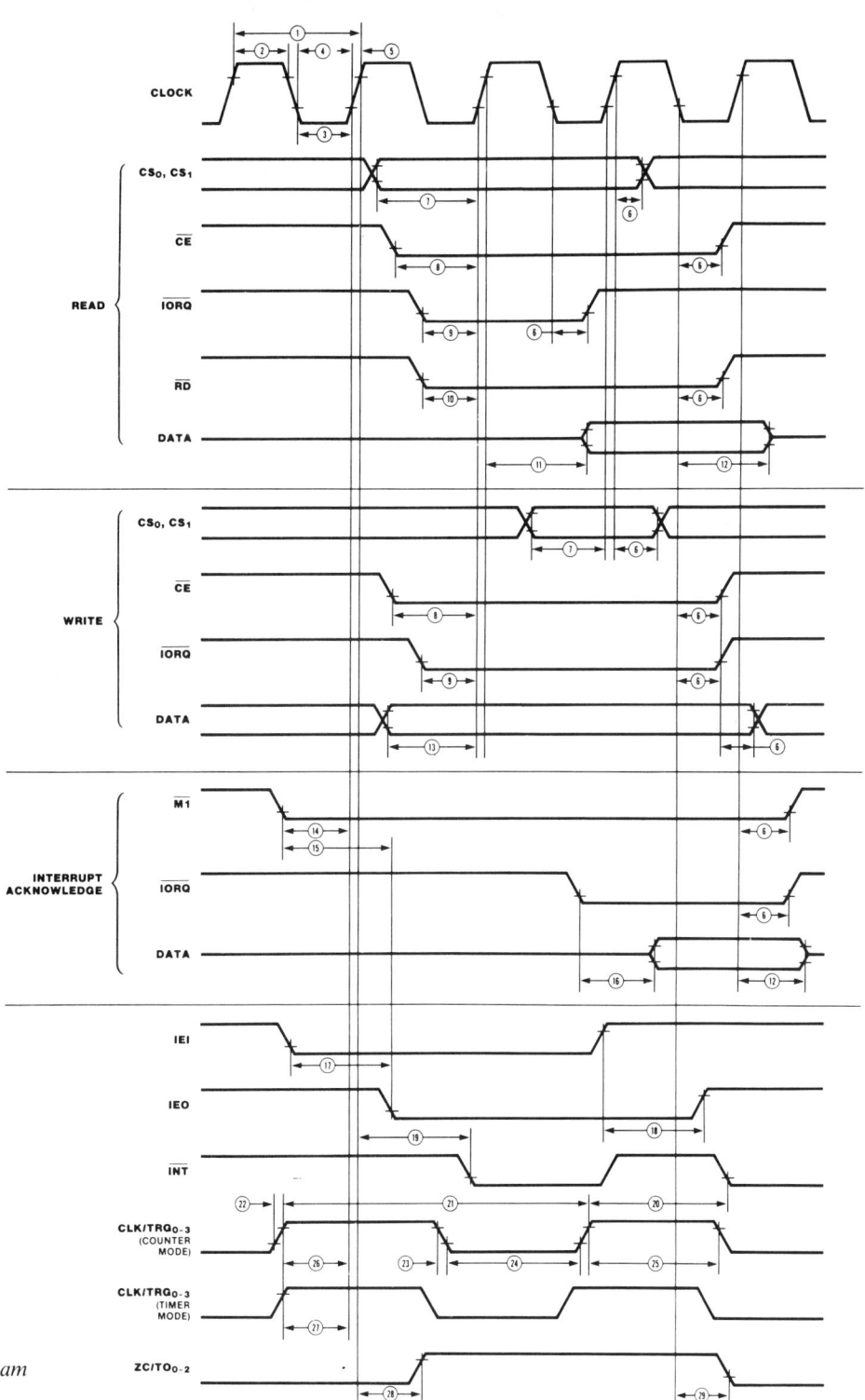

Fig. 8.62 A.C. timing diagram for the Z80 CTC

Table 8.16 A.C. Characteristics of the Z80 CTC

Number (Fig. 8.62)	Symbol	Parameter	Z84C30-4 Min (ns)	Z84C30-4 Max (ns)	Z84C30-6 Min (ns)	Z84C30-6 Max (ns)	Notes*
1	TcC	Clock cycle time	250	DC[1]	165	DC[1]	
2	TwCh	Clock pulse width (high)	105	DC	65	DC	
3	TwCl	Clock pulse width (low)	105	DC	65	DC	
4	TfC	Clock fall time		30		20	
5	TrC	Clock rise time		30		20	
6	Th	All hold times	0		0		
7	TsCS(C)	$\overline{CS}$ to Clock ↑ Setup Time	160		100		
8	TsCE(C)	$\overline{CE}$ to Clock ↑ Setup Time	150		100		
9	TsIO(C)	$\overline{IORQ}$ ↓ to Clock ↑ Setup Time	115		70		
10	TsRD(C)	$\overline{RD}$ ↓ to Clock ↑ Setup Time	115		70		
11	TdC(DO)	Clock ↑ to Data Out Delay		200		130	[2]
12	TdC(DOz)	Clock ↓ to Data Out Float Delay		110		90	
13	TsDI(C)	Data in to Clock ↑ Setup Time	50		40		
14	TsM1(C)	$\overline{M1}$ to Clock ↑ Setup Time	90		70		
15	TdM1(IEO)	$\overline{M1}$ ↓ IEO ↓ Delay (Interrupt immediately preceding $\overline{M1}$)		190		130	[3]
16	TdIO(DOI)	$\overline{IORQ}$ ↓ to Data Out Delay (INTA cycle)		160		110	[2], [6]
17	TdIEI(IEOf)	IEI ↓ to IEO ↓ Delay		130		100	[3]
18	TdIEI(IEOr)	IEI ↑ to IEO ↑ Delay (after ED Decode)		160		110	[3]
19	TdC(INT)	Clock ↑ to $\overline{INT}$ ↓ Delay		(TcC + 140)		(TcC + 120)	[4]

Number (Fig. 8.62)	Symbol	Parameter	Z84C30-4 Min (ns)	Z84C30-4 Max (ns)	Z84C30-6 Min (ns)	Z84C30-6 Max (ns)	Notes*
20	TdCLK(INT)	CLK/TRG↑ to INT̄ ↓ tsCTR(C) satisfied		(19) + (26)		(19) + (26)	[5]
		tsCTR(C) not satisfied		(1) + (19) + (26)		(1) + (19) + (26)	[5]
21	TcCTR	CLK/TRG cycle time	(2TcC)		(2TcC)		[5]
22	TrCTR	CLK/TRG rise time		50		40	
23	TfCTR	CLK/TRG fall time		50		40	
24	TwCTRl	CLK/TRG width (low)	200		120		
25	TwCTRh	CLK/TRG width (high)	200		120		
26	TsCTR(Cs)	CLK/TRG ↑ to Clock ↑ Setup Time for Immediate Count	210		150		[5]
27	TsCTR(Ct)	CLK/TRG ↑ to Clock ↑ Setup Time for enabling of Prescaler on following clock ↑	210		150		•[4]
28	TdC(ZC/TOr)	Clock ↑ to ZC/TO ↑ Delay		190		140	
29	TdC(ZC/TOf)	Clock ↓ to ZC/TO ↓ Delay		190		140	

* RESET must be active for a minimum of 3 clock cycles.
[1] TcC = TwCh + TwCl + TrC + TfC.
[2] Increase delay by 10 ns for each 50 pF increase in loading, 200 pF maximum for data lines, and 100 pF for control lines.
[3] Increase delay by 2 ns for each 10 pF increase in loading. 100 pF maximum.
[4] Timer mode.
[5] Counter mode.
[6] 2.5 TcC > (n − 2) TDIEI(IEOf) + TdM1(IEO) + TsIEI(IO) + TTL buffer delay, if any.

Table 8.17 D.C. characteristics of the Z80 CTC

Symbol	Parameter	Min	Max	Typ	Unit	Test Condition
V_{ILC}	Clock input low voltage	-0.3	$+0.45$		V	
V_{IHC}	Clock input high voltage	$V_{CC}-0.6$	$V_{CC}+0.3$		V	
V_{IL}	Input low voltage	-0.3	$+0.8$		V	
V_{IH}	Input high voltage	$+2.2$	V_{CC}		V	
V_{OL}	Output low voltage		$+0.4$		V	$I_{OL} = 2.0\,\text{mA}$
V_{OH_1}	Output high voltage	$+2.4$			V	$I_{OH} = -1.6\,\text{mA}$
V_{OH_2}	Output high voltage	$V_{CC}-0.8$			V	$I_{OH} = -250\,\mu\text{A}$
I_{LI}	Input leakage current		± 10		μA	$V_{IN} = 0.4$ to V_{CC}
I_{LO}	3-State output leakage current in float		± 10		μA	$V_{OUT} = 0.4$ to V_{CC}
I_{CC_1}	Power supply current		7	3	mA	$V_{CC} = 5\,\text{V}$
I_{CC_2}	Standby supply current		10	0.5	μA	CLK = 4 MHz, $V_{IH} = V_{CC} - 0.2\,\text{V}$, $V_{IL} = 0.2\,\text{V}$, $V_{CC} = 5\,\text{V}$, CLK = (0)
I_{OHD}	Darlington drive current	-1.5	-5.0		mA	$V_{IH} = V_{CC} - 0.2\,\text{V}$, $V_{IL} = 0.2\,\text{V}$, $V_{OH} - 1.5\,\text{V}$, $R_{EXT} - 1.1\,\text{k}\Omega$

Over specified temperature and voltage range.

Table 8.18 Absolute maximum ratings for the Z80 CTC

Voltages on V_{CC} with respect to V_{SS}	$-0.3\,\text{V}$ to $+7.0\,\text{V}$
Voltages on all inputs with respect to V_{SS}	$-0.3\,\text{V}$ to $V_{CC} + 0.3\,\text{V}$
Storage temperature	$-65°\text{C}$ to $+150°\text{C}$

Table 8.19 Capacitance data for the Z80 CTC

Symbol	Parameter	Max
CLK	Clock capacitance	20 pF
C_{IN}	Input capacitance	5 pF
C_{OUT}	Output capacitance	15 pF

$T_A = 25°\text{C}, f = 1\,\text{MHz}$
Unmeasured pins returned to ground.

Hardware design 239

Address decoding

Address decoding diagrams are shown in Figs. 8.63–8.65.

Interrupts

Interrupt circuits are shown in Fig. 8.66. Fig. 8.67 illustrates multiple interrupts.

(a)

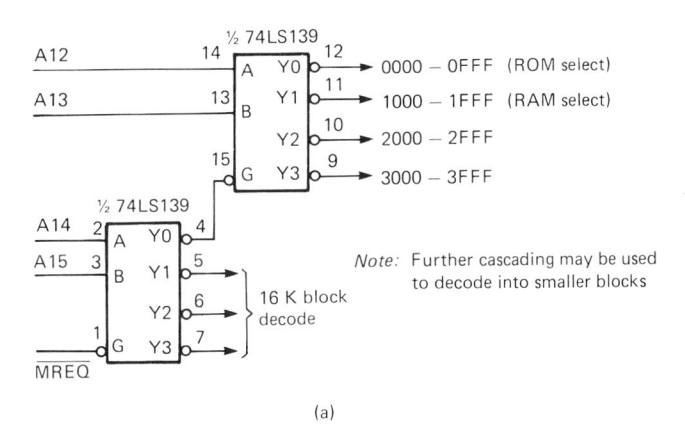

Fig. 8.63 *(a) Address decoding using a 74LSI39 2-line to 4-line decoder*
(b) Address decoding using a 74LSI54 4-line to 16-line decoder (larger systems)
(c) Address decoding using discrete logic gates (small system only)

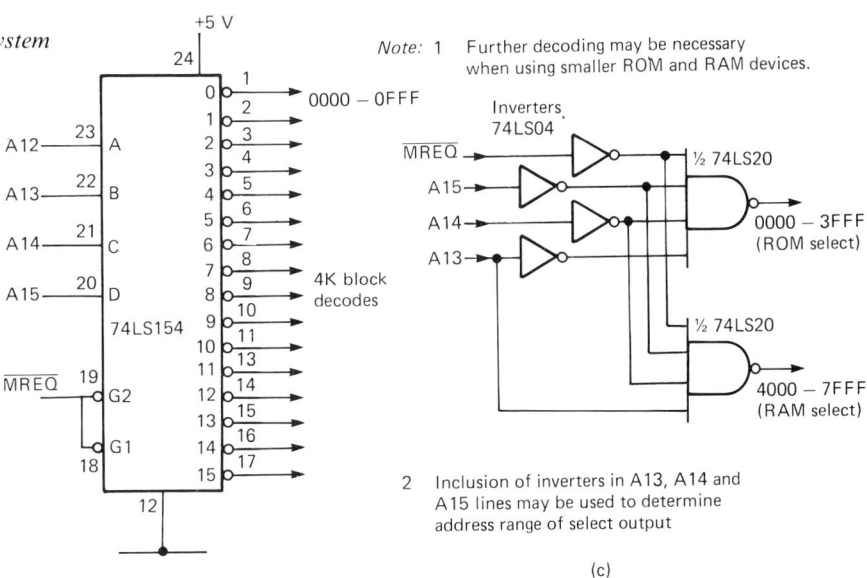

(b)

(c)

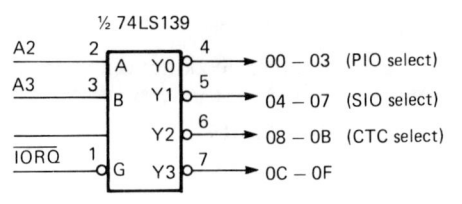

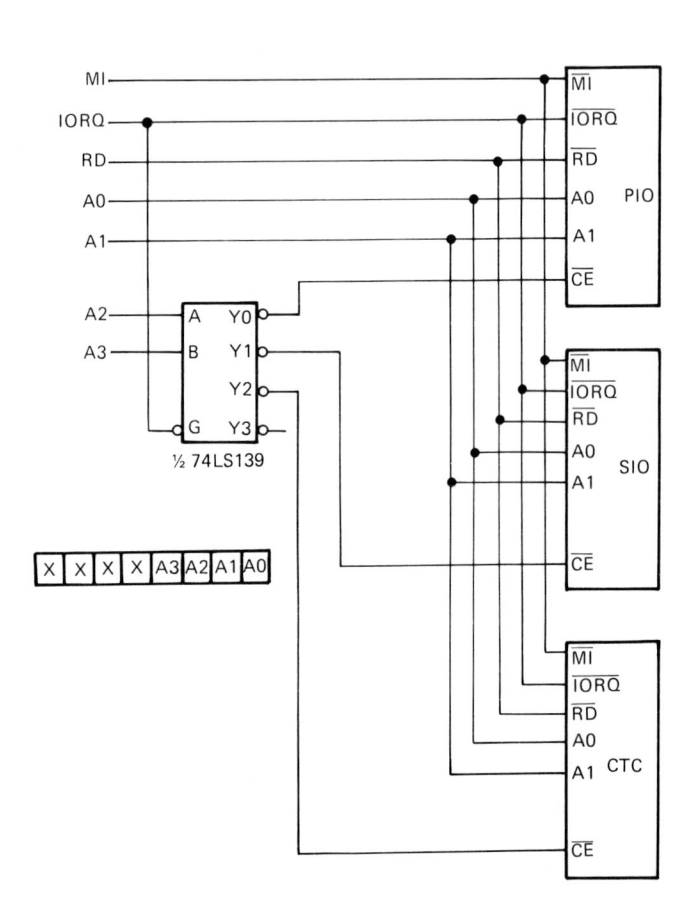

Fig. 8.64 *I/O address decoding. This arrangement is suitable for many small systems where only four I/O devices are required. Higher addresses repeatedly select the same four I/O devices*

Hardware design 241

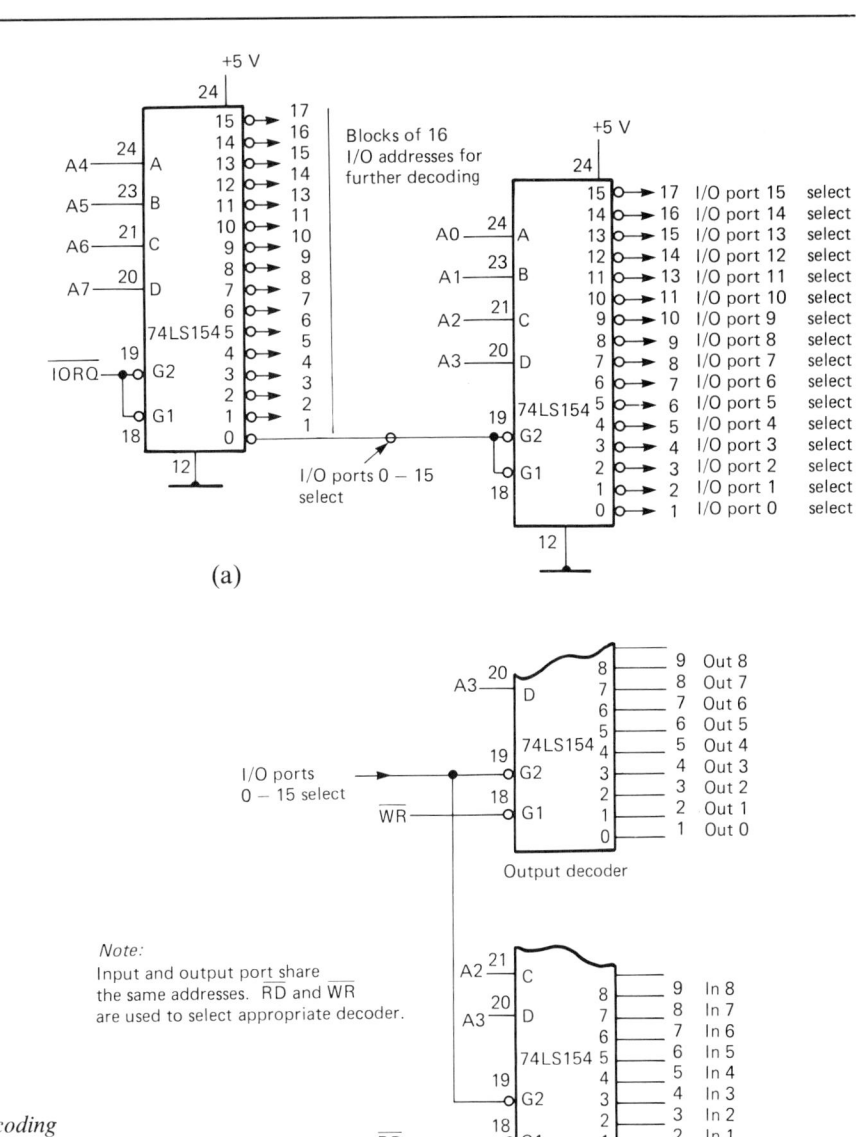

(a)

(b)

Fig. 8.65 *I/O address decoding to single port level*
(a) Use of 74154 4-line to 16-line decoder to provide full I/O decoding
(b) Maintenance of separate input and output ports

Note:
Input and output port share the same addresses. $\overline{RD}$ and $\overline{WR}$ are used to select appropriate decoder.

242 *Microprocessor based systems*

Fig. 8.66 *Interrupt circuits*

Z80 mode 0 interrupts using restarts (RST)

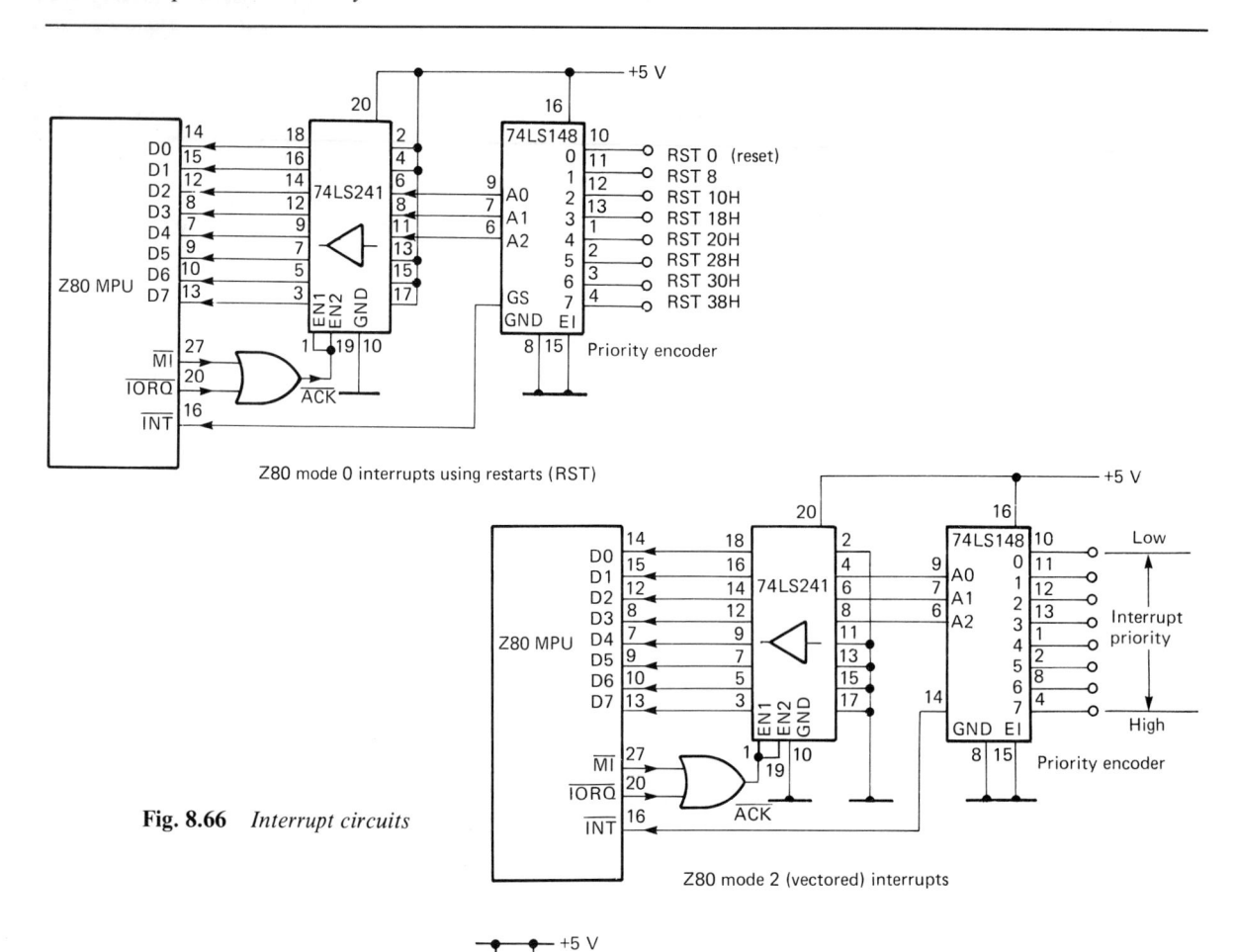

Z80 mode 2 (vectored) interrupts

Fig. 8.67 *Multiple interrupts*

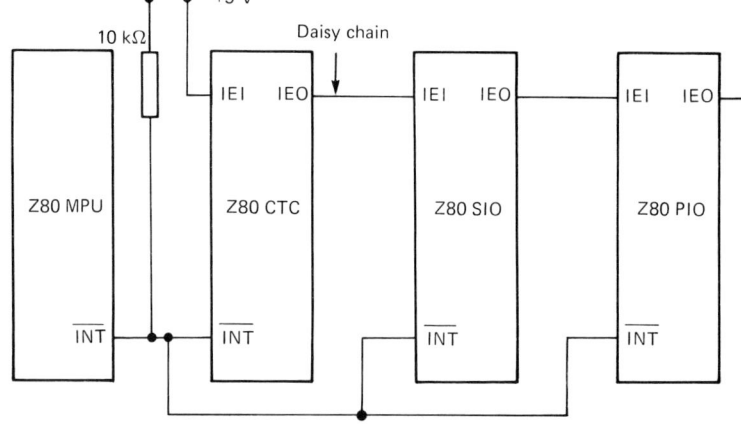

Notes: 1 Open collector techniques allow $\overline{INT}$ outputs of all devices to be 'wire ORed'

2 Priority depends upon orders of chaining. CTC has highest priority in this example

Problems

1. Draw a circuit to show how two 2 K EPROMS and two 2 K RAMs may be connected to a Z80 microprocessor so that they are located in memory as follows:

    RAM 2   1800–1FFF
    RAM 1   1000–17FF
    EPROM 2 0800–0FFF
    EPROM 1 0000–07FF

    (partial address decoding may be used)

2. Draw a circuit to show how a Z80 CTC and a Z80 PIO may be connected to a Z80 microprocessor so that they are located at the following I/O addresses:

    CTC   00 to 03
    PIO   04 to 07

    (partial I/O decoding may be used)

3. (a) Draw a circuit to show how four LEDs may be directly interfaced to the data bus of a microcomputer without using a programmable I/O device.
   (b) Describe the operation of the circuit given for (a).

4. (a) Draw a circuit to show how four single pole switches may be directly interfaced to the data bus of a microcomputer without using a programmable I/O device.
   (b) Describe the operation of the circuit given for (a).

5. A circuit is required for a microprocessor-based industrial controller with the following specification:
   (i)   Z80 MPU,
   (ii) 2K EPROM (2516) located 0000 to 07FF
   (iii) 1K RAM (6116) located 0800 to 0BFF,
   (iv) 2 MHz XTAL Clock,
   (v)   separate address and I/O decoding with 74LS139 decoders,
   (vi) four switched inputs at address 00, and
   (vii) four isolated switched outputs at address 01.

    Draw a suitable circuit to meet the required specification.

9 Hardware/Software Integration

Introduction

Upon completion of both hardware and software design for a system, the problem of integrating these two major elements must be faced. Although interaction between hardware and software in the final system should have been considered during each of the design stages, this does not necessarily imply that a fully functional system will result once the two are integrated.

For example, software will no doubt have been developed in the RAM of a tried and tested host environment that is free from bus conflicts and timing problems. Once this software is installed in its new environment, it may cease to function correctly for a variety of reasons, e.g. lack of provision of an adequate stack in RAM or use of partial address decoding in the target hardware; relocation errors in the software.

Originally the method used for integration was to commit the final code to EPROM and carry out any further debugging of hardware or software with the aid of a logic analyser (see Chapter 10). The major disadvantage of this method as far as software debugging is concerned is that each fault can be remedied only by correcting the source code, reassembling and preparing another EPROM. This is a somewhat time-consuming process, therefore in-circuit emulation (I.C.E.) techniques are preferred which do not rely on EPROMs as a means of transferring software into the target system.

Principle of in-circuit emulation

An in-circuit emulator is basically a specialised computer (or *host* system) which contains an identical MPU to that proposed for the system under development (the *target* system). In use, the emulator MPU replaces the target MPU and is connected to the target system by means of a 40-way ribbon cable/D.I.L. plug, as shown in Fig. 9.1.

There may at first seem little point in replacing one MPU with another identical MPU remote from the target system, however this arrangement does allow the emulator to intercept signals passing between the target system and the emulator MPU, and thus monitor or control the operation of the target system.

Hardware/software integration 245

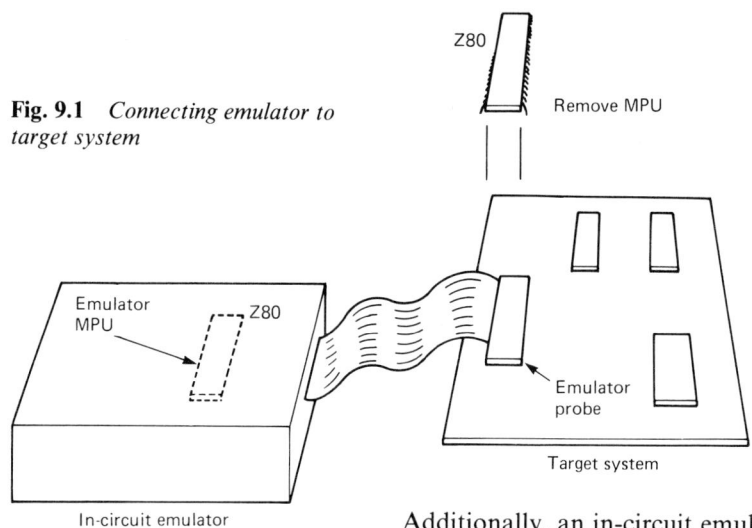

Fig. 9.1 *Connecting emulator to target system*

Additionally, an in-circuit emulator contains a large amount of RAM (typically 64K bytes) which may be configured to fully or partially emulate the target memory system. A process known as 'mapping' may be used to designate blocks of this RAM as being target, emulator or non-existent memory. It is also possible to define any of these blocks as read-write (RAM) or read-only (ROM) memory. An emulator often contains its own logic analyser so that real-time hardware traces of the target may be obtained in order to obtain information relating to all MPU signals and additional external signals during program execution. The general organisation of a typical in-circuit emulator is shown in Fig. 9.2.

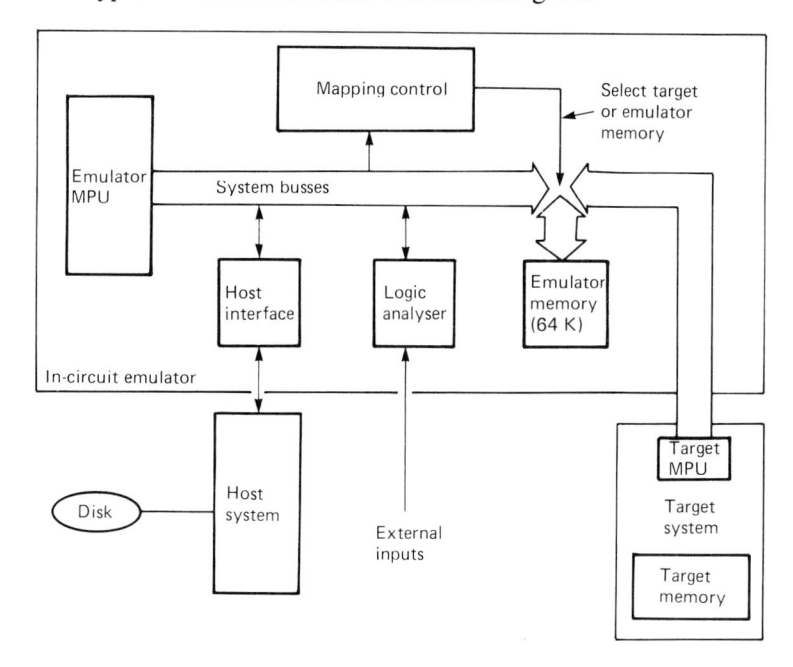

Fig. 9.2 *Organisation of an in-circuit emulator*

DICE in-circuit emulator

The author has made extensive use of the DICE emulator which is manufactured by DUX (Kokusai Data Machinesystems Inc.), and the following information is based upon experience with this equipment.

System configuration

Some development systems have in-circuit emulation facilities which form an integral part of the system. The DICE emulator is a self-contained unit which may be connected to an RS-232C terminal or to a host computer to provide comprehensive facilities for integrating hardware and software. The following configurations are possible:

Stand-alone mode

In the 'stand alone' mode, the emulator may be controlled from an RS-232C terminal device. This frees the development system for other work, but suffers from the disadvantage that it is not possible to transfer hex format object code files between emulator memory and disk.

Other modes

Transparent, master and console modes are available which differ in the manner in which the console, emulator and host computer are interconnected. These configurations allow file transfers between the emulator memory and host disk system to take place, and in addition enable the extended commands available with SICEZ.COM software to be supported. They are shown in Fig. 9.3.

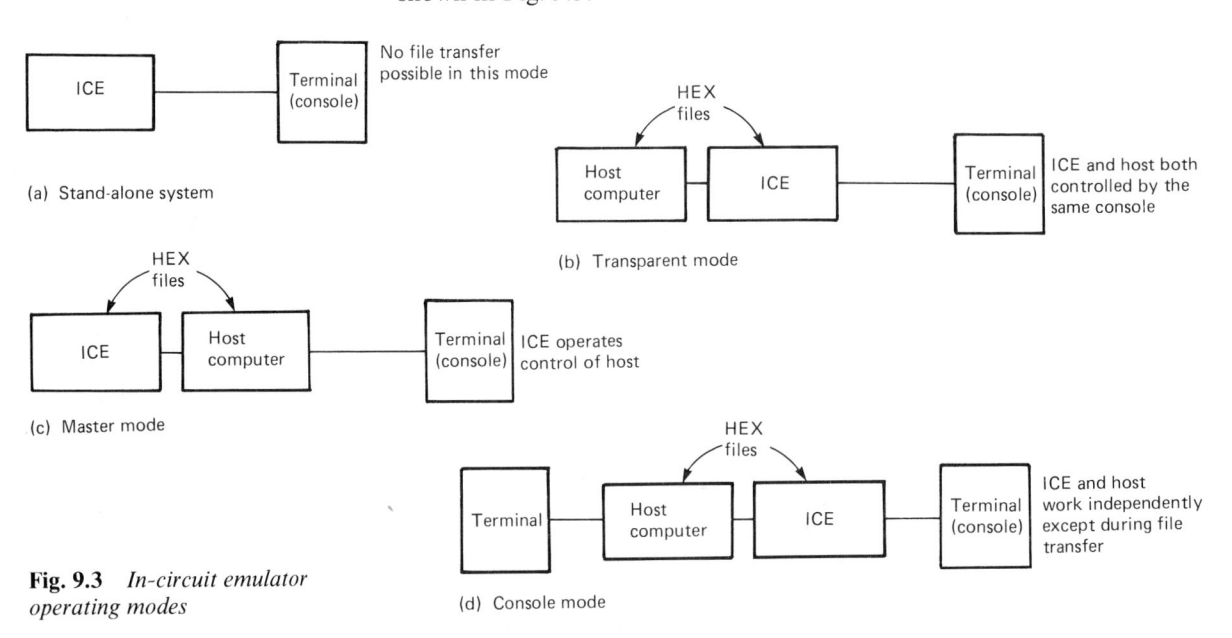

Fig. 9.3 *In-circuit emulator operating modes*

(a) Stand-alone system

(b) Transparent mode

(c) Master mode

(d) Console mode

Debugging facilities

An in-circuit emulator should provide debugging facilities similar to those already studied in Chapter 7 so that programs loaded into emulator memory may be executed under controlled conditions. The DICE emulator uses commands based upon ZSID, thus offering the advantage that the user does not need to become familiar with a different set of commands. Additional commands are provided which are not available with ZSID, many of which relate to the emulation process. The full list of commands is as follows:

A	in-line assembly,
B	enable/disable breakpoints,
C	set/display emulation conditions,
D	display memory contents in hexadecimal and ASCII,
E	display/initialise/set emulation mode,
F	fill selected memory locations with data,
G	begin program execution with optional breakpoint,
H	carry out hexadecimal addition/subtraction, hexadecimal to decimal and ASCII conversion,
L	disassemble memory contents,
M	move block of memory to another area of memory,
MM	display/set memory map base and size,
MS	search memory for specified data,
N	disable verify function during memory write,
O	set offset value to relative address register,
P	access I/O port,
Q	return to CP/M (quit),
R	read Intel hex format file from disk to memory,
S	examine/alter memory contents,
T	selective tracing of program execution,
U	trace program without display of intermediate steps,
V	verify object file with memory contents,
W	save memory contents on disk as object file,
X	examine/alter register contents,
TM	display/set conditions of real-time trace monitor,
TML	trace memory list, provides history of bus activity during a real-time trace,
TSD	trace signal dump, sends content of external signal trace to analogue output terminal (logic analyser capability),
ITL	internal trace list, lists contents of internal signal trace,
ZH	extended command: HELP command,
ZY	extended command: load symbol file from disk,
ZS	extended command: display symbol table,
ZL	extended command: define symbol,
ZK	extended command: disable symbol table, and
ZB	extended command: read BAT file for batch processing.

The extended commands are available when using a host computer with appropriate software (SICEZ.COM) i.e. not in the 'stand-alone' mode.

Emulation modes

Three modes of emulation are available, selectable by means of commands EM0, EM1 or EM2.

(i) *Mode 0*

All target systems are invalid and the emulator clock is used. This mode of operation is suitable for the development of target I/O where isolated I/O is employed.

(ii) *Mode 1*

All target systems are valid, and memory may be mapped to the target or to the emulator as selected by the user. The target clock is used and must be operational.

(iii) *Mode 2*

Target clock and target memories are used. Emulator functions as monitored MPU only.

The user normally starts in Mode 0, and as system development proceeds, switches to Modes 1 and 2 at appropriate times.

Memory mapping

Initially, target system software executes entirely within the emulation memory, but as soon as each block of target memory becomes fully operational, the corresponding block within the emulator memory is disabled. This process continues block by block until eventually the software executes entirely in target memory, all emulation memory having been disabled.

The ability to construct a target memory system within the emulator is therefore central to the emulation process. Emulation memory may be enabled or disabled as required (typically 1K to 4K blocks) by hardware or software means depending upon the type of emulator. The DICE emulator provides software controlled switching of memory in 1K blocks, with the user designating blocks as follows:

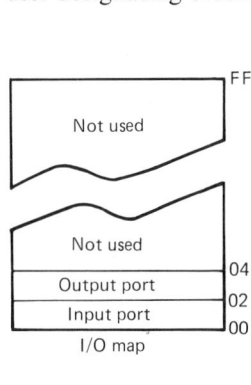

Fig. 9.4 *Memory map for a small micro-controller*

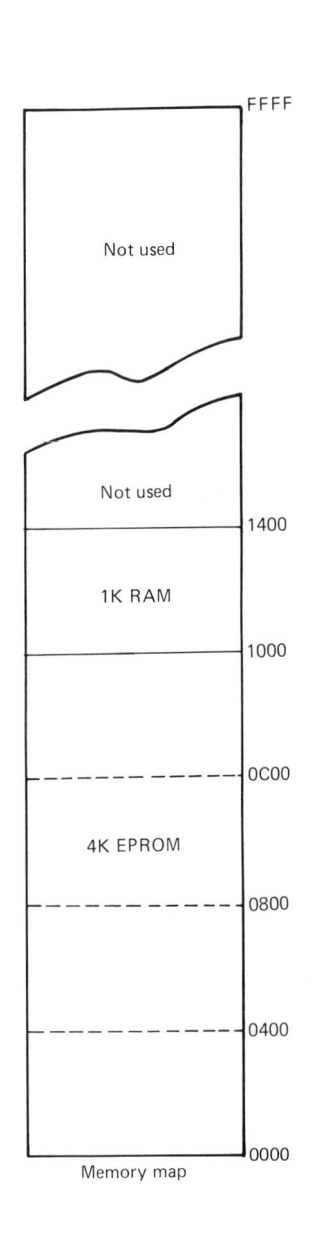

(i) system (ICE) memory/user (target) memory
(ii) existent memory/non-existent memory
(iii) ROM/RAM

The memory map may be displayed or altered by means of an 'MM' command with one of the following formats:-

(i) MM   *display current mapping status*,
(ii) MM*ms,e*   memory from address *s* to *e* is mapped in 1K blocks to *m*, where *m* represents either:

      U: user (target) memory,
   m S: system (emulator) memory,
      R: read-only memory,
      N: non-existent memory, or
      W: read-write memory.

The current mapping status is displayed using the following format:

```
ADRS    000    400    800    C00
0000    -SR-   -SR-   -SR-   -SR-   ←system read-only
1000    -SR-   -SR-   -SR-   -SR-
2000    -S--   -S--   -S--   -S--   ←system read-write
3000    -S--   -S--   -S--   -S--
4000    U---   U---   U---   U---   ←user read-write
5000    U---   U---   U---   U---
6000    U-R-   U-R-   U-R-   U-R-   ←user read-only
7000    U-R-   U-R-   U-R-   U-R-
8000    U--N   U--N   U--N   U--N   ←user non-existent
9000    U--N   U--N   U--N   U--N
A000    U--N   U--N   U--N   U--N
B000    U--N   U--N   U--N   U--N
C000    U--N   U--N   U--N   U--N
D000    U--N   U--N   U--N   U--N
E000    U--N   U--N   U--N   U--N
F000    U--N   U--N   U--N   U--N
```

Typical emulation sequence

The manner in which an in-circuit emulator is used to integrate hardware and software may best be illustrated by considering the development of a small micro-controller which consists of 4K bytes of program in EPROM, 1K bytes of RAM for the stack, system variables and collected data, and two 8-bit I/O ports (I/O mapped). The memory map for this system is shown in Fig. 9.4.

(i) Software debugging

With the emulator set to Mode 0, target software may be down-loaded from the host system using a command with the following format:

R*filename,d*   [RETURN]

where the file is assumed to be in Intel hex format, and *d* is a 'bias' value which may be required to locate the software in the correct place in memory.

Software may then be debugged using the ZSID type of commands available with the emulator. It may be argued that software debugging should have been completed before this stage is reached, and normally this will be the case. However, valid reasons may exist, e.g. no suitable Z80 debugger available with some CP/M systems.

This stage requires no interconnection between target and emulator.

(ii) **I/O testing**

Remaining in Mode 0, the emulation probe may be connected to the MPU socket on the target system. All Z80 signals are available on the target system, and the I/O ports may be tested using the 'P' (port) command. This command has the following form:

P*a*[RETURN], or
P*a,d1,d2,....,dn*   [RETURN]

The first of these commands reads data from an I/O port at address *a* (00 to FFH).

Once hardware adjustments have been made (if necessary), and satisfactory operation has been obtained, appropriate sections of target software may be executed in order to test the I/O under dynamic conditions.

(iii) **Software testing in target memory model**

The target software may now be tested with the I.C.E. configured so that it emulates the target memory system exactly. This ensures that the software is not attempting to write to memory blocks designated as ROM, or attempting data transfers with non-existent memory. The I.C.E. must be changed to Mode 1 for this form of testing, and this also means that the program executes under the control of the target clock.

The following sequence of commands must be issued to emulate the target system memory:

```
EM1 [RETURN]              select emulation mode 1
MMR0,0FFF [RETURN]        read-only memory
MMW,1000,13FF [RETURN]    read-write memory
MMN,1400,FFFF [RETURN]    non-existent memory
MM [RETURN]               display memory map
```

After the last of these commands, the following display should be obtained:

```
ADRS   000    400    800    C00
0000   -SR-   -SR-   -SR-   -SR-    ←system read-only (4K)
1000   -S--   -S-N   -S-N   -S-N    ←system read-write (1K)
2000   -S-N   -S-N   -S-N   -S-N
3000   -S-N   -S-N   -S-N   -S-N
4000   -S-N   -S-N   -S-N   -S-N
5000   -S-N   -S-N   -S-N   -S-N
6000   -S-N   -S-N   -S-N   -S-N
7000   -S-N   -S-N   -S-N   -S-N
8000   -S-N   -S-N   -S-N   -S-N
9000   -S-N   -S-N   -S-N   -S-N
A000   -S-N   -S-N   -S-N   -S-N
B000   -S-N   -S-N   -S-N   -S-N
C000   -S-N   -S-N   -S-N   -S-N
D000   -S-N   -S-N   -S-N   -S-N
E000   -S-N   -S-N   -S-N   -S-N
F000   -S-N   -S-N   -S-N   -S-N
```

The system may now be fully tested to see if the software functions satisfactorily with the proposed hardware. If not, then changes may be necessary in either software or hardware.

Upon successful completion of this stage, the designer is sure that the target system will operate as intended and all that remains is to install each of the memory blocks into the target. The order for this is not normally critical.

(iv) **RAM installation**

Once the 1K RAM chip is installed on the circuit board, this function may be handed over to the target system for testing. Should the system then cease to function correctly, then attention must be paid to the RAM wiring and associated address decoder.

The RAM is mapped into the target with the following command:

MMU1000,13FF   [RETURN]

The memory map should now look as follows:

```
ADRS   000    400    800    C00
0000   -SR-   -SR-   -SR-   -SR-    ←system read-only (4K)
1000   -U--   -S-N   -S-N   -S-N    ←user read-write (1K)
2000   -S-N   -S-N   -S-N   -S-N
3000   -S-N   -S-N   -S-N   -S-N
4000   -S-N   -S-N   -S-N   -S-N
5000   -S-N   -S-N   -S-N   -S-N
6000   -S-N   -S-N   -S-N   -S-N
7000   -S-N   -S-N   -S-N   -S-N
8000   -S-N   -S-N   -S-N   -S-N
```

```
9000    -S-N    -S-N    -S-N    -S-N
A000    -S-N    -S-N    -S-N    -S-N
B000    -S-N    -S-N    -S-N    -S-N
C000    -S-N    -S-N    -S-N    -S-N
D000    -S-N    -S-N    -S-N    -S-N
E000    -S-N    -S-N    -S-N    -S-N
F000    -S-N    -S-N    -S-N    -S-N
```

(v) **ROM installation**

On the assumption that the software is satisfactory, having been previously tested in the emulator, it may now be committed to EPROM and tested in the target system.

Although the EPROM specified is a single 4K × 8 bit device, it is still possible to map it in 1K blocks into the target system using the emulator. Once the first 1K block is functional, it may be assumed that connections to the data bus are correct, but faults in the connection of the higher order address lines may still exist. Mapping of the remaining blocks one after another should enable any further faults to be eliminated.

This is achieved by the following sequence in which the memory map is shortened in each case to show just the relevant information:

```
MMUC00,FFF  [RETURN]
    ADRS    000     400     800     C00
    0000    -SR-    -SR-    -SR-    -UR-    ←system/user R,0,(4K)
    1000    -U--    -S-N    -S-N    -S-N    ←user read-write (1K)

MMU800,BFF  [RETURN]
    ADRS    000     400     800     C00
    0000    -SR-    -SR-    -UR-    -UR-    ←system/user R,0,(4K)
    1000    -U--    -S-N    -S-N    -S-N    ←user read-write (1K)

MMU400,7FF  [RETURN]
    ADRS    000     400     800     C00
    0000    -SR-    -UR-    -UR-    -UR-    ←system/user R,0,(4K)
    1000    -U--    -S-N    -S-N    -S-N    ←user read-write (1K)

MMU0,3FF    [RETURN]
    ADRS    000     400     800     C00
    0000    -UR-    -UR-    -UR-    -UR-    ←user read-only (4K)
    1000    -U--    -S-N    -S-N    -S-N    ←user read-write (1K)
```

(vi) **Final emulation**

Once the preceding stages have been successfully completed, final emulation may take place during which time the target clock, target I/O and all target memories are used, and the emulator acts as a fully controlled and monitored MPU. This requires the emulator to be operated in Mode 2, and this is achieved by means of the following command:

EM2 [RETURN]

It may be assumed that if the target system functions correctly under final emulation, the emulator probe may be removed and be replaced with an appropriate MPU. The target system then performs as a totally independent microprocessor based system.

Additional items which are included in many emulators, and which may be of use in the final testing states are the 'real time trace', 'hardware trace' and 'breakpoint monitor' facilities.

Real time trace and hardware trace

Whilst the target system is running in real time, it is possible to capture trace information in a high speed memory for subsequent analysis. In this respect the emulator has 'logic analyser' capabilities (see Chapter 10).

The real time trace captures information concerning the MPU data, address and control lines, whilst the hardware trace captures data from user-selectable trace points in the target system, using external probes, as shown in Fig. 9.5.

The user may therefore study the hardware conditions prevailing in the target system whilst executing the software in real time, thus isolating any timing problems, particularly in interrupt driven systems.

Sampling start/stop conditions

The user may select when tracing starts by specifying conditions in the trace monitor command line. Similarly, the user may control the point at which tracing is terminated by means of a command containing the terminal conditions, or by specifying a 'trace volume' (maximum number of samples). Typical sampling start/stop conditions are:
(i) emulation start/break,
(ii) opcode fetch,
(iii) memory read,
(iv) memory write,
(v) I/O port access, or
(vi) external signals.

Therefore entering DICE commands TMSMO100 and TMEMR120 would cause sampling to start on an opcode fetch at address 100H, and cease on a memory read of address 120H. A command TMV3FF would cause 3FFH samples to be taken before termination.

Sample trigger signals

A trigger signal is required to determine when trace data is written into the real-time trace buffer.

Possible sample trigger signals are:
(i) MPU clock,
(ii) rising edge of external signal, or
(iii) falling edge of external signal.

A 32-bit real-time counter may be enabled which counts MPU clock cycles during program execution. This may be used to determine the running times of traced sections of program.

Trace memory display

The contents of a real-time trace buffer may be displayed, and the information is shown in the following way:

```
              |* CPU status *|              |*=== probe data ===*|
       T,POS  A,BUS STAT D,BUS  INSTRUCTION  XD 8 7 6 5 4 3 2 1 0 B
       #2047  0300  M1   D3     OUT (55),A      1 1 1 1 1 1 1 1 1 1
       #2046  0301  MR   55                     1 1 1 1 1 1 1 1 1 1
       #2045  0255  IOW  02                     1 1 1 1 1 1 1 1 1 1
       #2044  0302  M1   C3     JP  0400        1 1 1 1 1 1 1 1 1 1
       #2043  0303  MR   00                     1 1 1 1 1 1 1 1 1 1
       #2042  0304  MR   04                     1 1 1 1 1 1 1 1 1 1
       #2041  0400  M1   31     LD  SP,3000     1 1 1 1 1 1 1 1 1 1
       #2040  0401  MR   00                     1 1 1 1 1 1 1 1 1 1
       #2039  0402  MR   00                     1 1 1 1 1 1 1 1 1 1
       *** COMMAND ABORTED
```

Breakpoint monitor

Hardware breakpoints allow the emulation process to be terminated when pre-defined conditions occur. An emulation break may be requested when any of the following conditions occur:
(i)   specified address,
(ii)   opcode fetch cycle,
(iii) specified pass count,
(iv)   specified I/O port,
(v)   external signal (BRK probe),
(vi)   attempt to write to memory designated as either ROM or non-existent, or
(vii) interrupt.

Software breakpoints may also be set in a program, and these cause emulation to cease after the breakpoint address has been accessed a number of times specified by the user.

Program storage in EPROM

Once satisfactory testing of system software has been achieved with the target ROM being emulated, it is necessary to transfer the software into EPROM. Mask programmed ROM may be used for volume production once satisfactory evaluation of EPROM prototypes has been achieved.

EPROM characteristics

A range of EPROMs are currently available, using both NMOS and

Hardware/software integration 255

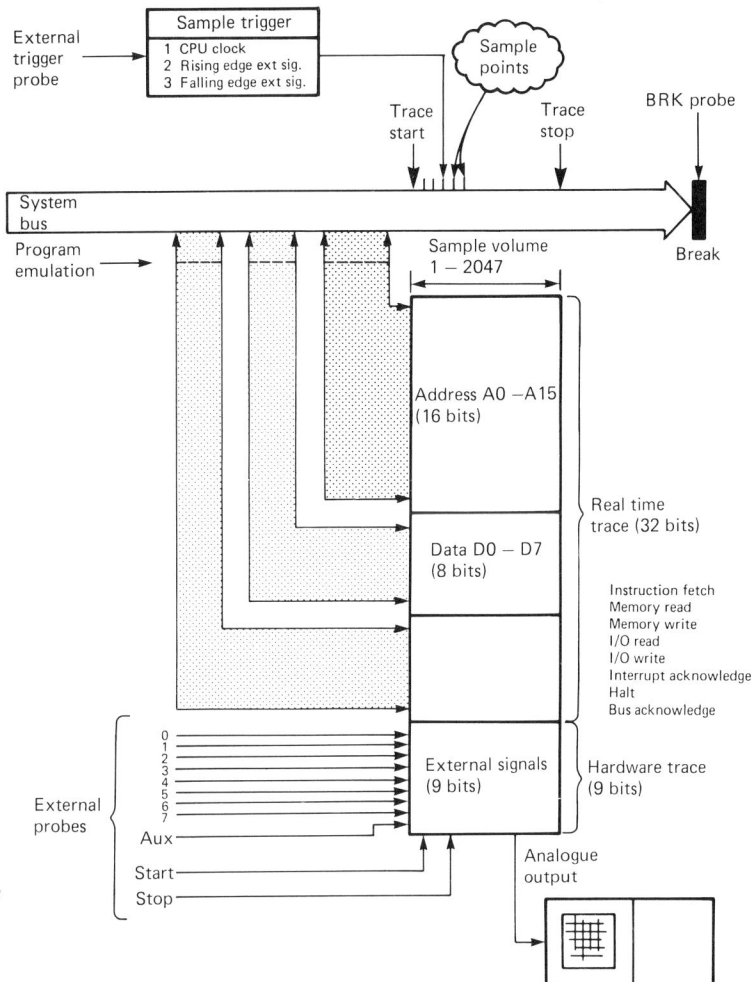

Fig. 9.5 *Real time and hardware trace*

CMOS technology, which provide between 2K and 32K bytes of storage per device. Pin-compatibility is virtually maintained throughout the range, and compatibility with similar capacity ROM and RAM devices is also achieved with minor changes, thus offering considerable flexibility in use. The following device types are commonly available:

SIZE	NMOS	CMOS
2K × 8 bits	2516/2716	27C16
4K × 8 bits	2532/2732	27C32
8K × 8 bits	2564/2764	27C64
16K × 8 bits	27128	
32K × 8 bits	27256	27C256

256 Microprocessor based systems

Pin-out connections for these devices are shown in Fig. 9.6.

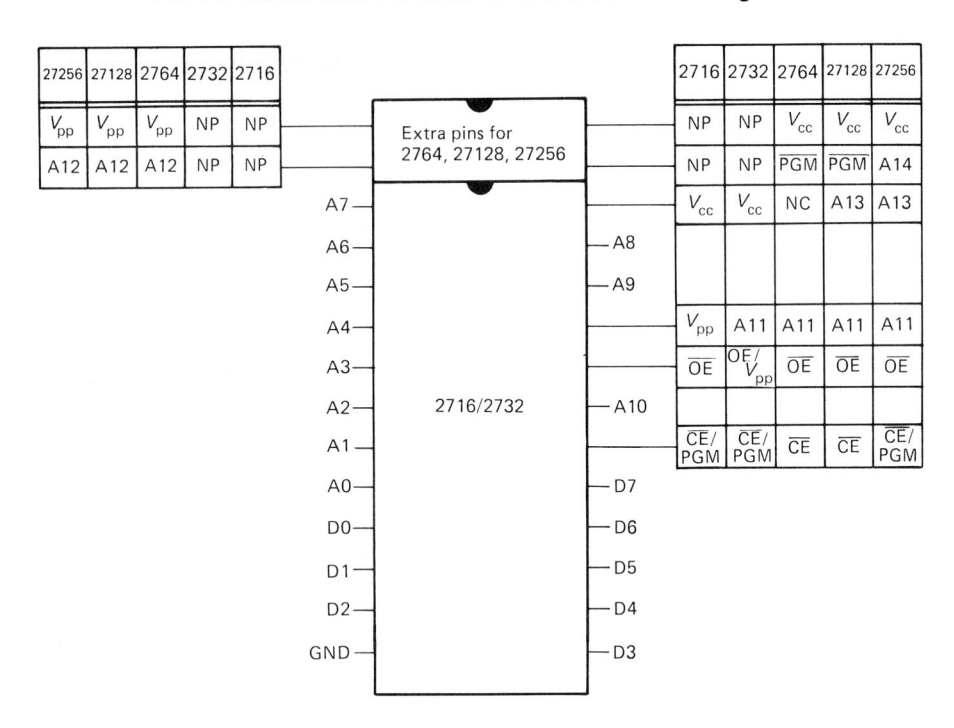

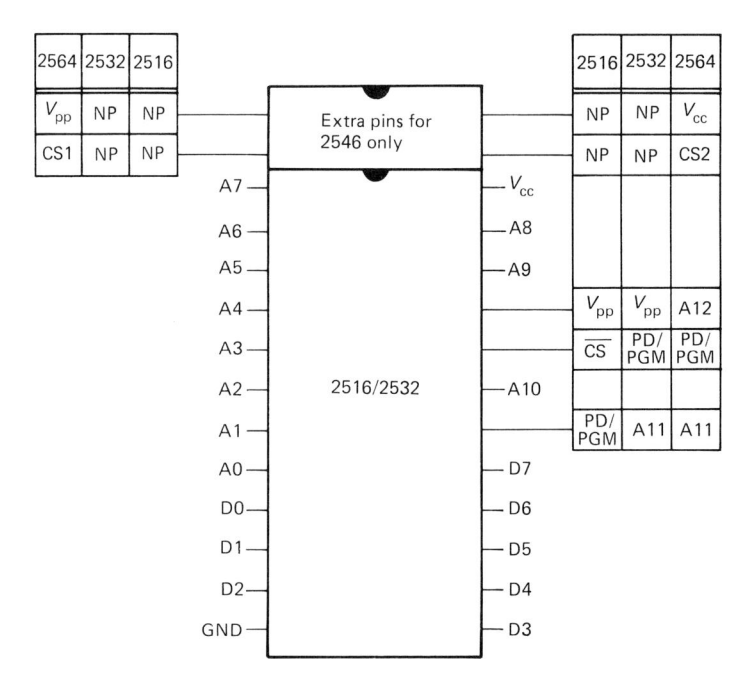

27256	27128	2764	2732	2716
V_{pp}	V_{pp}	V_{pp}	NP	NP
A12	A12	A12	NP	NP

2716	2732	2764	27128	27256
NP	NP	V_{cc}	V_{cc}	V_{cc}
NP	NP	$\overline{PGM}$	$\overline{PGM}$	A14
V_{cc}	V_{cc}	NC	A13	A13

Extra pins for 2764, 27128, 27256

Chip 2716/2732 pinout:
- A7, A6, A5, A4, A3, A2, A1, A0, D0, D1, D2, GND (left side)
- A8, A9, A10, D7, D6, D5, D4, D3 (right side)

	2716	2732	2764	27128	27256
	V_{pp}	A11	A11	A11	A11
	$\overline{OE}$	$\overline{OE}/V_{pp}$	$\overline{OE}$	$\overline{OE}$	$\overline{OE}$
	$\overline{CE}/\overline{PGM}$	$\overline{CE}/\overline{PGM}$	$\overline{CE}$	$\overline{CE}$	$\overline{CE}/\overline{PGM}$

2564	2532	2516
V_{pp}	NP	NP
$\overline{CS1}$	NP	NP

2516	2532	2564
NP	NP	V_{cc}
NP	NP	$\overline{CS2}$

Extra pins for 2546 only

Chip 2516/2532 pinout:
- A7, A6, A5, A4, A3, A2, A1, A0, D0, D1, D2, GND (left side)
- V_{cc}, A8, A9, A10, D7, D6, D5, D4, D3 (right side)

	2516	2532	2564
	V_{pp}	V_{pp}	A12
	$\overline{CS}$	$\overline{PD}/\overline{PGM}$	$\overline{PD}/\overline{PGM}$
	$\overline{PD}/\overline{PGM}$	A11	A11

Fig. 9.6 *EPROM chip pin-outs*

EPROM programming

The sequence of events required to program data into an EPROM cell may be determined from the timing diagram shown in Fig. 9.7.

A typical sequence consists of the following steps:
(i) raise V_{pp} from $+5$ V to $+25$ V (or 12 to 21 V depending upon type),
(ii) connect $\overline{OE}$ to $+5$ V to disable the outputs,
(iii) apply address of location to be programmed to the address inputs,
(iv) using the data output pins as inputs, apply data to be programmed into the selected cell,
(v) apply a pulse to the PGM input to program in the data (1 ms to 50 ms, depending upon type),
(vi) verify that correct data has been programmed, and
(vii) repeat for next location to be programmed.

This sequence is normally carried out using an EPROM programmer which may be attached to one of I/O ports of a development system, or which may be a 'stand alone' system. Software is usually provided with the EPROM programmer which enables a binary file to be copied into an EPROM and generate control signals for correct timing of the programming process. A file is first transferred into an intermediate buffer RAM before being copied into EPROM, therefore the software also provides facilities for inspecting this buffer and for making minor changes. When attached to a development system, the development system memory may be used for buffering purposes, but a 'stand alone' programmer must contain its own buffer unless it is used for EPROM copying only.

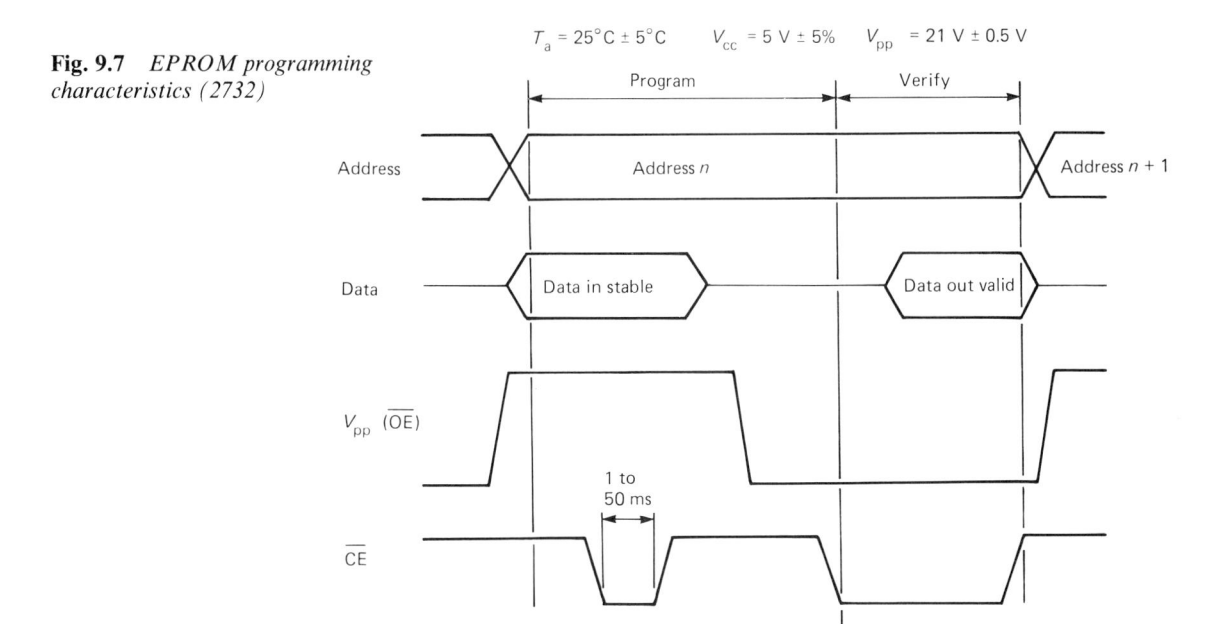

Fig. 9.7 *EPROM programming characteristics (2732)*

EPROM erasure

One of the advantages of using EPROMs is that they may be erased and reprogrammed at a later stage. Erasure is accomplished by exposing the entire memory chip to ultra-violet light of wavelength 2537 Å for a period of 10 to 20 minutes.

Problems

1. Describe the problems likely to be encountered when integrating hardware and software in a microprocessor based system.
2. Describe the principle of operation of an in-circuit emulator.
3. A microprocessor based system contains the following components:
   - (i) 4 K EPROM (address 0 to 0FFFH),
   - (ii) 2 K RAM (address 1000H to 17FFH), and
   - (iii) Z80 PIO (I/O address 20H to 23H).

   With the aid of suitable diagrams, describe how emulation techniques may be used to integrate hardware and software.
4. (a) Explain how 'traces' may be used to locate problems when integrating hardware and software.
   (b) Describe the difference between hardware and software traces.
5. (a) Describe the principle used for data storage in an EPROM,
   (b) List the sequence of operations necessary to program data into an EPROM, and
   (c) Describe fully the procedure for erasing an EPROM.

10 Fault Location

Introduction

The location of faults within a microprocessor based system is a task which an electronics technician may frequently be asked to perform. Faults may need locating and rectifying in prototypes during the initial development work or in production models which have subsequently failed. The former task is perhaps the more daunting, since prototype equipment may never have worked due to a fundamental design fault, whereas it is known that production equipment was performing satisfactorily prior to developing a fault. This chapter describes some of the fault location techniques available to the technician, although it must be stated that the ability to locate faults is an acquired skill and requires much practice in interpreting symptoms and test results.

Typical faults in microprocessor based systems

Although the symptoms produced by faults in microprocessor based equipment may be many and varied, the actual fault will probably fall into one of the following categories:
(i) chip failure,
(ii) open circuit interconnection,
(iii) bridging or short circuit interconnection,
(iv) externally induced interference, or
(v) original software bugs.

Chip failure

Digital integrated circuits are on the whole inherently reliable, provided that they are operated within the manufacturer's limits. Nevertheless they inevitably do fail occasionally, and typical modes of failure include the following:
(a) input(s) open circuit,
(b) input(s) shorted to ground,
(c) two or more inputs shorted together,
(d) output stuck high,
(e) output stuck low,
(f) incorrect or partial operation due to internal open or short circuit, and
(g) sequential logic faults (wrong count, wrong reset, etc.).

Open circuit interconnection

Included in this category are faults which cause a break in any signal or power line. Typical sources of such faults include the following:
(a) unsoldered or faulty soldered joint,
(b) fracture of a printed circuit track,
(c) faulty contact on a connector, e.g. edge connector or IC holder, and
(d) breaks in cables, particularly at their point of attachment to the circuit or cable connector.

Connectors are often a weak link in the chain, particularly if of dubious quality, subject to abuse or if equipment is repeatedly dismantled. The environment in which equipment is used may also have a profound effect upon such components, and often gold plated (non-tarnishable) connectors must be used.

Bridging or short circuit interconnection

Modern printed circuit boards are becoming ever more compact. One outcome of this is that printed circuit tracks and associated connections are in much closer proximity to one another with the result that it becomes very easy to form bridging contacts. A major source of such unwanted contacts is surplus solder, the effects of which may not become apparent until much later. Short circuit connections may also occur in closely spaced cables, e.g. ribbon cables where attached to a connector.

Externally induced interference

Since the signals in a microcomputer consist of sequences of pulses, it follows that any externally induced pulses will affect its operation, causing programs to 'crash', since these pulses will be interpreted by the system as valid digital signals. Such pulses frequently enter a microcomputer via the mains supply (mains 'spikes'), and are generated when other equipment is switched on or off (particularly large inductive loads such as electric motors). The only practical solution to this problem is to remove such spikes before they can enter the system by fitting filters in series with the mains supply to a microcomputer. In extreme cases, damage to components may occur due to mains-borne interference, e.g. buffer chip failure. It is also possible for interference signals to be directly induced into a microcomputer, although generally such signals would need to be large in amplitude.

Original software bugs

Despite prolonged and exhaustive testing of newly developed software, it is still possible for logical errors, or 'bugs' to exist. These errors may go undetected for months or even years, only becoming apparent when a particular set of inputs or operating conditions are established which hitherto have not been used. Long, complicated programs may well contain original software bugs, since it is quite easy for a software writer to concentrate on the normal, and hence obvious, operating conditions, and to overlook, and therefore fail to test, the more obscure operating conditions. In fact, when writing very complex programs it may not be feasible to test for every possible combination of operating conditions, and feedback from the software user then becomes essential. The maintenance and support for software requires that updated versions are released to registered users each time that serious bugs are eliminated.

Conventional fault-finding techniques

Certain fault finding techniques have evolved over the years since electronic circuits were first introduced. Some of these techniques are still valid for microprocessor based systems fault finding, although often to a lesser degree. Examples of these techniques are as follows:
(i)   visual inspection,
(ii) d.c. test, and
(iii) oscilloscope (CRO).

Visual inspection

Visual inspection of a faulty microcomputer system may reveal the source of a fault, and is certainly worth carrying out before attempting further investigations. By this means it is possible to locate simple faults such as loose connectors, ICs loose in their holders or cracked PCBs. Sometimes the temperature of components helps to isolate a fault, e.g. a voltage regulator which runs cool may mean that it is faulty. It should be noted, however, that many modern components dissipate quite a lot of heat during normal operation, and excessive heat may not always indicate a fault.

D.C. test

This form of test, using a multimeter to measure d.c. potentials or resistance, is of limited use in microprocessor based systems, but may be satisfactory for checking power supplies to each device, or for checking for short or open circuit interconnections.

Oscilloscope

The use of an oscilloscope is really limited to those applications in which repetitive signals can be obtained, e.g. clock signals. Most of the signals in a microprocessor based system are not repetitive, and depend upon the program being executed at the time. This limits the use of an oscilloscope, unless a microprocessor can be made to generate repetitive signals, for example by '*free-running*' it, or running very short looping programs.

Special test equipment

Certain items of test equipment have been developed to enable faults to be more readily isolated in digital, and sometimes, more specifically, in microprocessor based equipment. The following equipment is included in this category:

(i)   logic probe
(ii) logic pulser
(iii) current tracer
(iv) logic clip
(v)   logic comparator
(vi) logic analyser
(vii) signature analyser

Logic probe

A logic probe is a hand-held instrument which is used to detect and indicate 'high' and 'low' logic levels in all types of logic circuits, including TTL and CMOS. In addition, a logic probe should be capable of detecting and indicating 'bad' logic levels, open circuits and pulse inputs. The method used to indicate the detected logic level varies. Some logic probes, e.g. Hewlett-Packard™ 545A, use a lamp near the logic probe tip which gives the following four indications:

(i)   off   —— below logical 0 threshold,
(ii) dim   —— bad level or open circuit,
(iii) bright   —— above logical 1 threshold, and
(iv) flashing —— pulsating input.

Other types of logic probe use three different coloured LEDs, typically red, yellow and green, which give the following indications:

(i)   green only   —— below logical 0 threshold,
(ii) red only   —— above logical 1 threshold,
(iii) red and yellow   —— pulsing 1 to 0,
(iv) green and yellow   —— pulsing 0 to 1, and
(v)   red, green and yellow —— square wave.

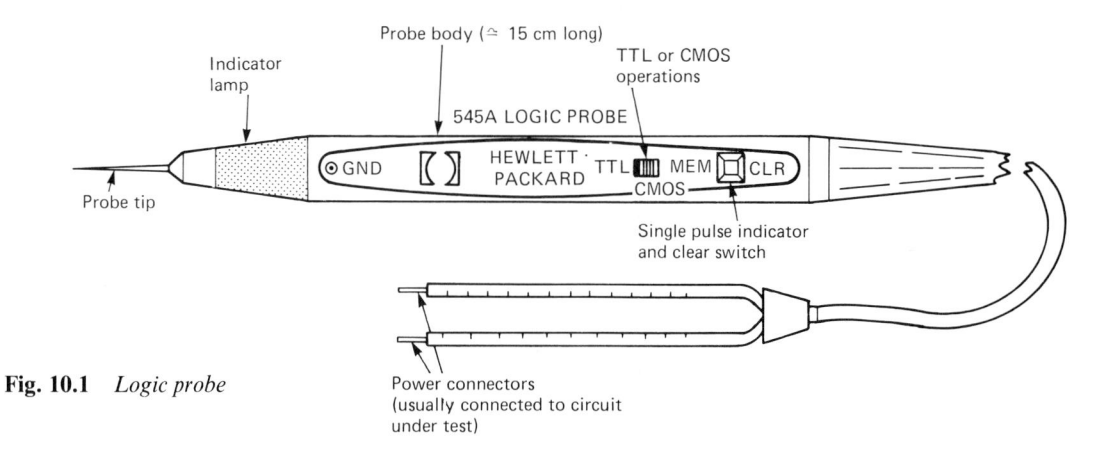

Fig. 10.1 *Logic probe*

Fault location

A pulse stretching circuit is often included in a logic probe to enable even very short pulses to cause a noticeable change at the probe indicator lamp, thus giving the user a visual indication of their presence.

The inclusion of a memory circuit for detecting a single pulse, e.g. a chip enable signal, is also an advantage. This consists of a resettable latch with an indicator lamp connected to its output. The probe is applied to the circuit node being tested, and the 'memory clear' (reset) button is pressed to turn off the indicator lamp. Any change in logic level will then be detected and turn on the indicator lamp.

Power supplies for a logic probe are normally taken from the circuit under test and should therefore not impose excessive demands.

Physically a logic probe should be of slim construction with a fine probe tip for ease of handling when taking measurements on modern compact circuits (see Fig. 10.1). Unfortunately, many of the cheaper instruments do not meet this requirement.

Logic pulser

A logic pulser is a hand-held instrument which is used to stimulate digital circuits by the injection of controlled pulses. Typically a single pulse from a low impedance output source is generated, which swings between both logic levels. The duration of this pulse is kept deliberately short to avoid damage to the circuit under test.

In use, the pulser tip is applied to a circuit node (input or output of a digital I.C.) and a button is pressed on the pulser body to generate a pulse and cause the node to be forced to its opposite logic state, thus exercising the circuit. A logic probe is often used to determine the effect of exercising a circuit node.

Examples of the use of a logic pulser and probe are shown in Fig. 10.2.

Some logic pulsers, e.g. Hewlett-Packard™ 546A, provide additional outputs such as continuous pulses and bursts of pulses. A pulser is usually powered from the circuit under test, and, as for the logic probe, its physical construction should be such as to provide ease of handling.

Fig. 10.2 *Use of logic pulser*

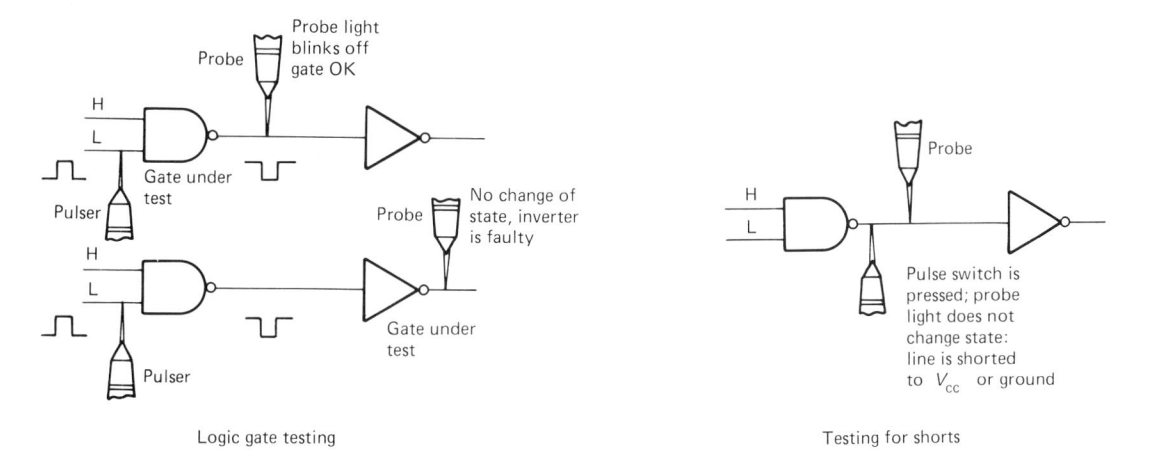

Fig. 10.3 *Use of current tracer*

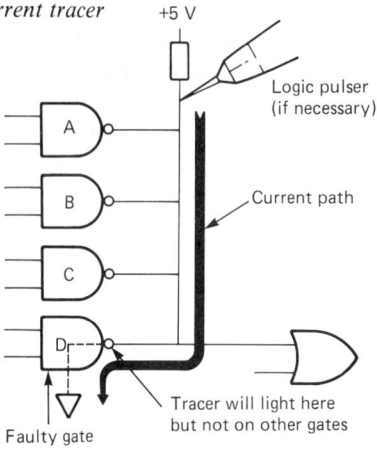

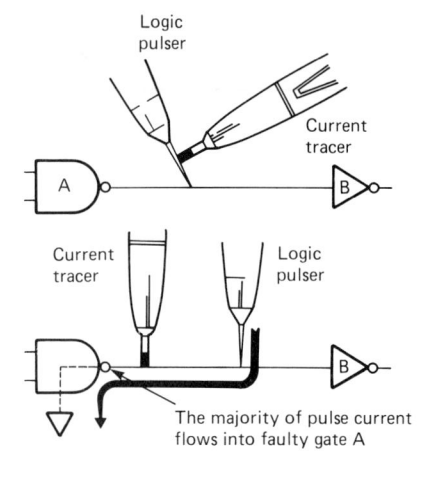

Wire-AND node fault

Gate-to-gate faults

Fig. 10.4 *Logic chip*

Current tracer

A current tracer is used to locate the source of a low impedance path without the necessity of removing components from the circuit. The tip of a current tracer is magnetically sensitive and is used to detect the magnetic field which surrounds a conductor when carrying a pulsating current. The presence of a pulsating current is indicated by a lamp whose brightness is adjustable by means of a sensitivity control. If the circuit does not produce the pulsating current internally, then current pulses must be provided from an external source such as a logic pulser.

In use, a current tracer must first be aligned with the printed circuit track where tracing is to begin, and its sensitivity control is adjusted so that the indicator lamp glows faintly. The current tracer tip is then moved along the track, and along all branches leading off the track, until the source of abnormal current flow is detected.

Examples of typical uses for a current tracer are shown in Fig. 10.3.

Logic clip

A logic clip consists of a spring-loaded assembly which clips onto dual-in-line I.C. packages, and which contains one LED for each pin of the I.C. under test (see Fig. 10.4). This enables the logic states of all pins of an I.C. to be simultaneously monitored, which is an advantage when checking the operation of logic gates, flip-flops, or counters. A logic clip is usually able to monitor 16 pin packages, but is equally suitable for 8 and 14 pin devices.

Logic comparator

A logic comparator is used for checking faulty nodes in digital circuits, often associated with faulty I.Cs. It operates on the principle of comparing a known-good or *reference* I.C. with one that is suspected of being faulty.

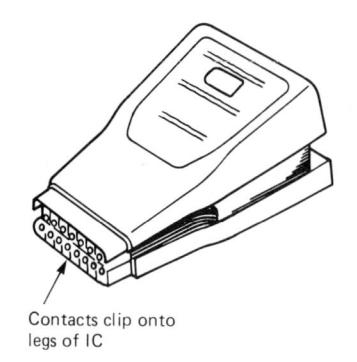

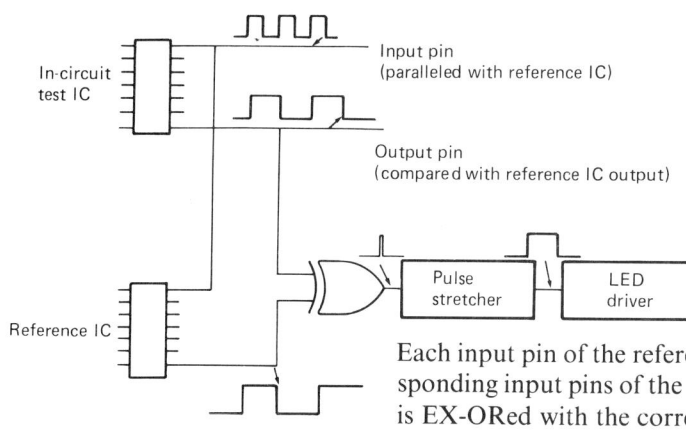

Fig. 10.5 *Operation of a logic comparator*

Each input pin of the reference I.C. is connected in parallel with the corresponding input pins of the suspected I.C. Each output of the reference I.C. is EX-ORed with the corresponding output on the I.C. under test. A difference between any two corresponding outputs generates a logical 1 level on one of the EX-OR gate outputs, and this is used to activate an error indicator LED (see Fig. 10.5).

Physically a logic comparator is connected to the I.C. under test by means of a flying lead with a 16 pin I.C. connector clip. Each reference I.C. is mounted onto a small printed circuit board which may be plugged into the instrument.

The main advantage of using this instrument is that testing may be carried out at normal operating speeds without needing to remove the suspect I.C. from circuit.

Logic analyser

One problem associated with checking the operation of a microprocessor based system is that data on the bus and control lines changes rapidly as the program executes the programs at its normal speed. It is not normally possible to follow this data in real time and, since the bus signals are seldom repetitive, a single event may occur within one or two microseconds and go undetected.

A logic analyser allows the logic states of bus and control signals to be captured at specified times and stored in a 'first-in-first-out' (FIFO)

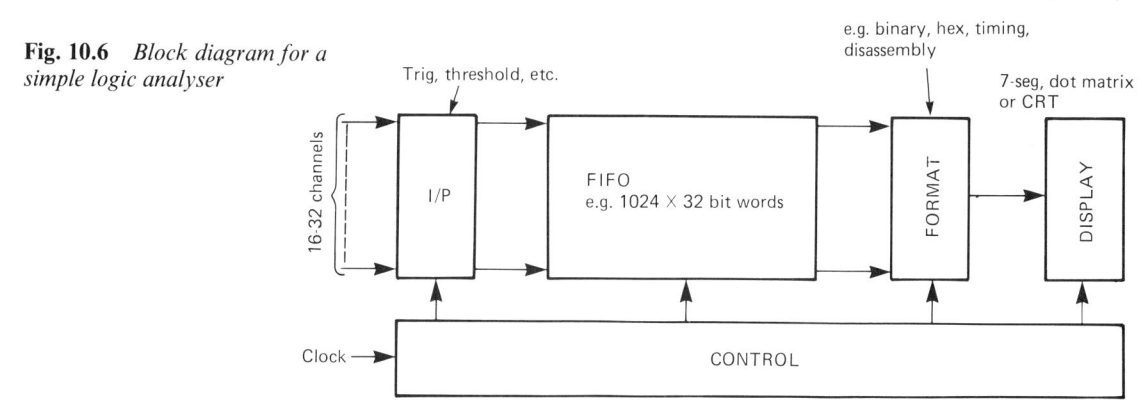

Fig. 10.6 *Block diagram for a simple logic analyser*

memory, so that they may be viewed later at leisure. The block diagram for a simple logic analyser is shown in Fig. 10.6.

FIFO

The data storage provided by a logic analyser is organised as a 'first-in-first-out' (FIFO) memory which has typically 1024 to 2048 individual storage locations, each 32 bits wide. Some logic analysers allow this memory to be re-configured by the user to obtain a larger number of storage locations, but of reduced width, i.e. the locations/width product is a constant. Each of the 32 bits of a word is used to store the instantaneous logic state of a bus or control line, and all 32 bits are clocked into the FIFO simultaneously, using either internally generated or externally derived clock signals. As each new data word is clocked into the FIFO, all previously captured data is shifted one place to make room for it. The data word shifted out from the opposite end of the FIFO is lost. Therefore at any instant, the FIFO contains a record of the logic states on the bus and control lines during the previous 1024 or 2048 clock periods.

Trigger word

The point in a program where data capture starts or finishes must be selectable by the user. This is achieved by setting up a 'trigger word' in the logic analyser which is compared with the incoming data (see Fig. 10.7). The

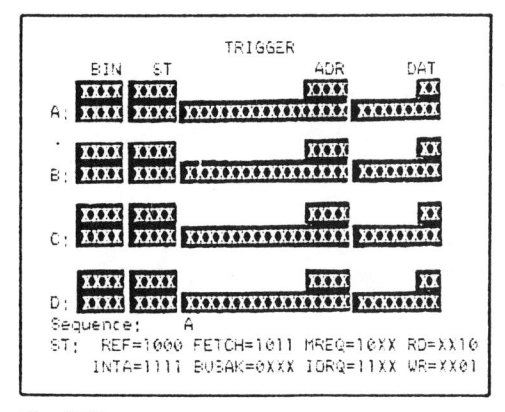

Fig. 10.7

Fig. 10.8

trigger word may contain 'don't care' characters (X) which enable data with unknown elements to be specified, for example, an address whose contents are unknown. Once a match is found between the incoming data and the trigger word, data capture continues for a predetermined number of clock pulses, and is then terminated. This arrangement allows the user to study events leading up to the trigger point as well as those immediately following it. A logic analyser is frequently set up so that equal numbers of pre-trigger and post-trigger words are captured, but the user may specify a different arrangement if the logic analyser possesses a 'delay' facility (see Fig. 10.8). For example, the user may only be interested in events leading up to the appearance of the trigger condition, in which case a larger number of pre-trigger events may be studied if data capture terminates once the trigger word arrives. Some logic analysers allow several different trigger words to be specified which are then combined in various ways to form trigger sequences (see Fig. 10.9).

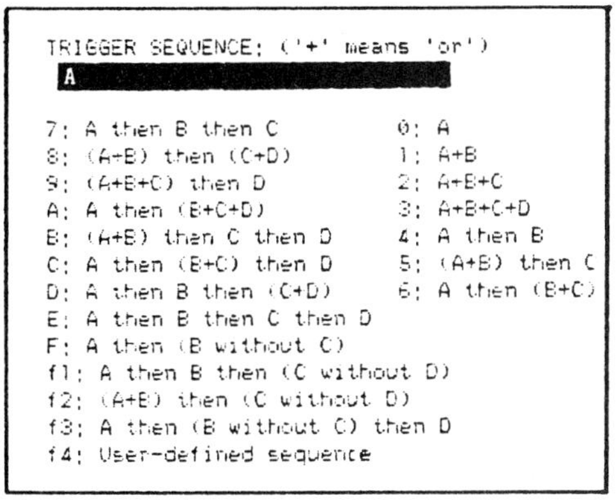

```
TRIGGER SEQUENCE: ('+' means 'or')
 A

 7: A then B then C           0: A
 8: (A+B) then C              1: A+B
 9: (A+B+C) then D            2: A+B+C
 A: A then (B+C+D)            3: A+B+C+D
 B: (A+B) then C then D       4: A then B
 C: A then (B+C) then D       5: (A+B) then C
 D: A then B then (C+D)       6: A then (B+C)
 E: A then B then C then D
 F: A then (B without C)
 f1: A then B then (C without D)
 f2: (A+B) then (C without D)
 f3: A then (B without C) then D
 f4: User-defined sequence
```

Fig. 10.9

```
              CLOCK

SOURCE (0=internal,1=external): External

INTERNAL:
 Clock period (10 ns - 200 ms): 0800  nsec
   (f1=nsec, f2=usec, f3=msec)
 Clock rate              : 12.5 MHz
 Record time             : 80.0 usecs

EXTERNAL:
 Clock edge (0=fall, 1=rise) : rising
 Qualifier valid                always
   (0=low, 1=high, 2=always)
```

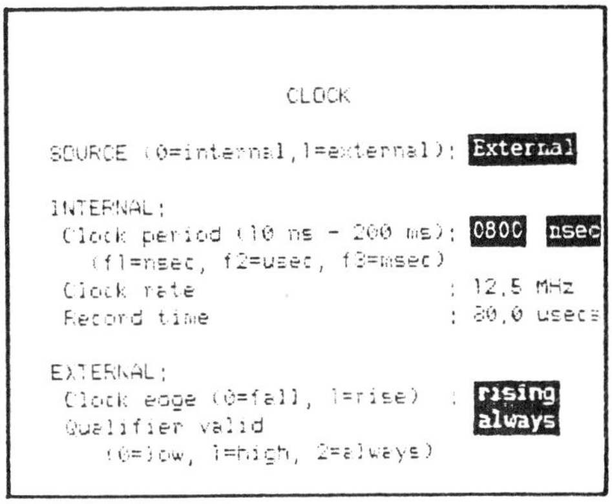

Fig. 10.10

Clock signals

A logic analyser must be told at which instants to capture data from the bus and control lines. Therefore a clock signal is used to shift data into the FIFO memory which may operate asynchronously or synchronously with the clock of the circuit under test.

A high speed asynchronous clock signal with user selectable frequencies may be generated by the logic analyser itself. This type of clock can operate at much higher frequencies than are used in the system under test, thus enabling a logic analyser to perform high speed sampling of signals for solving hardware, logic and timing problems.

A low speed synchronous clock signal is derived from the system under test, using such signals as $\overline{RD}$, $\overline{WR}$, $\overline{MREQ}$, $\overline{IORQ}$ etc as the source. This type of clock is useful for debugging software. The user may select which edge of the clock is used to transfer data into the FIFO memory (see Fig. 10.10).

Clock qualifier

A logic analyser is usually provided with an external clock qualifier input which must be active before data can be clocked into the FIFO memory. The active level for this input (1, 0 or don't care) is user selectable, and is obtained from the circuit under test. This enables data to be selectively accepted or rejected under the control of an external signal.

Data qualifier

Data qualification may be used to enable specified blocks of data to be recorded. Combinational data qualification allows all incoming data which matches a specified trigger word to be either accepted ('only' qualifier) or rejected ('all but' qualifier), thus enabling a user to separate out unwanted data. State data qualification enables the recording process to be started and stopped between limits set by specified trigger words.

Display format

The outputs from the FIFO memory may be formatted by a logic analyser to provide one of the following user selectable displays:
(i) list or state
(ii) timing
(iii) disassembly

The user may have control over the format of the displays, as shown in Fig. 10.11.

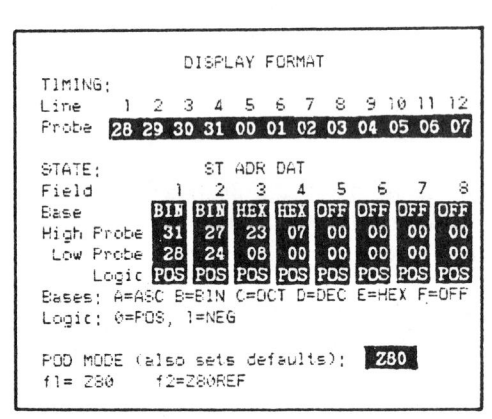

Fig. 10.11

Fig. 10.12

State display

A list or state display shows the contents of a logic analyser memory as a sequence of binary, octal, decimal or hexadecimal codes. Cheap logic analysers use LED matrix devices for this purpose, but suffer from the disadvantage that it is only possible to view single words. Logic analysers with CRT display devices are preferred since they allow the user to view long sequences of records for comparison purposes. Often a display of ASCII equivalents is provided for easier identification of certain records. A typical state display is shown in Fig. 10.12.

Timing display

A timing display allows data captured from a limited number of channels to be displayed in correct time sequence as digital waveforms. A display of this type is shown in Fig. 10.13. Since these waveforms are constructed from data stored in memory, they do not represent the true shape of the original waveforms and are used for timing comparisons only. Cheap logic analy-

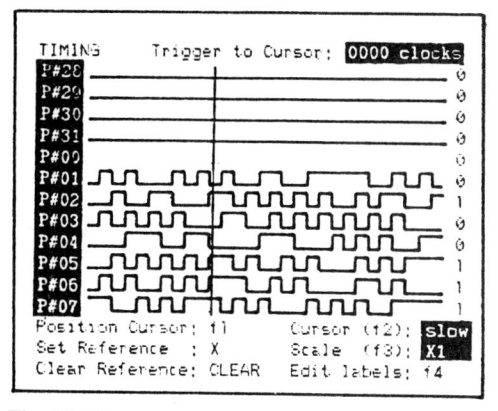

Fig. 10.13

Fig. 10.14

sers often provide formatting for this type of display, but require the addition of an oscilloscope as the display unit. More advanced logic analysers allow the user to expand the display, set cursor references and set up special labels for each timing channel.

Disassembly

Many logic analysers allow captured data to be displayed as disassembled assembly language mnemonics. For each different type of microprocessor supported, a logic analyser requires the addition of a personality module or 'pod' and the installation of associated software. The pod simply clips onto the microprocessor, automatically making all of the necessary connections. A typical display of this type is shown in Fig. 10.14.

Signature analysis

Signature analysis is a technique which has been evolved to simplify fault location on complex microprocessor based systems. Faced with the complexities of modern equipment, a manufacturer may often adopt a modular form of construction in order to simplify testing and subsequent fault location. This means that personnel need only be trained in the specialised areas of the complete system with which they are to be concerned. The major disadvantage of this approach is that it requires a large number of interlinking connectors which add to the cost of equipment and provide an additional source for possible faults.

The technique used for fault location using signature analysis is similar to that adopted for analogue circuits, in which a circuit diagram is provided which is marked up with appropriate waveforms and voltage readings. By tracing back from the output, waveforms and voltages obtained from the equipment under test may be compared with those on the circuit diagram until a discrepancy is found, thus enabling the faulty component to be located. This technique is not possible with digital circuits, since all waveforms look very similar on an oscilloscope, and are therefore not included on a circuit diagram. With microprocessor based equipment there is a further problem in that it is no longer possible to relate functions performed by a circuit to individual stages within that circuit, i.e. most functions require the use of all of the system on a time shared basis.

Deriving signatures

Signatures are a compressed 'fingerprint' of the digital information at any point in the circuit. They are taken at different points of the circuit and are compared with the correct signature which is printed on the circuit diagram as shown in Fig. 10.15. Any discrepancies should lead the technician back to the source of the trouble.

Fig. 10.15 *Circuit diagram*

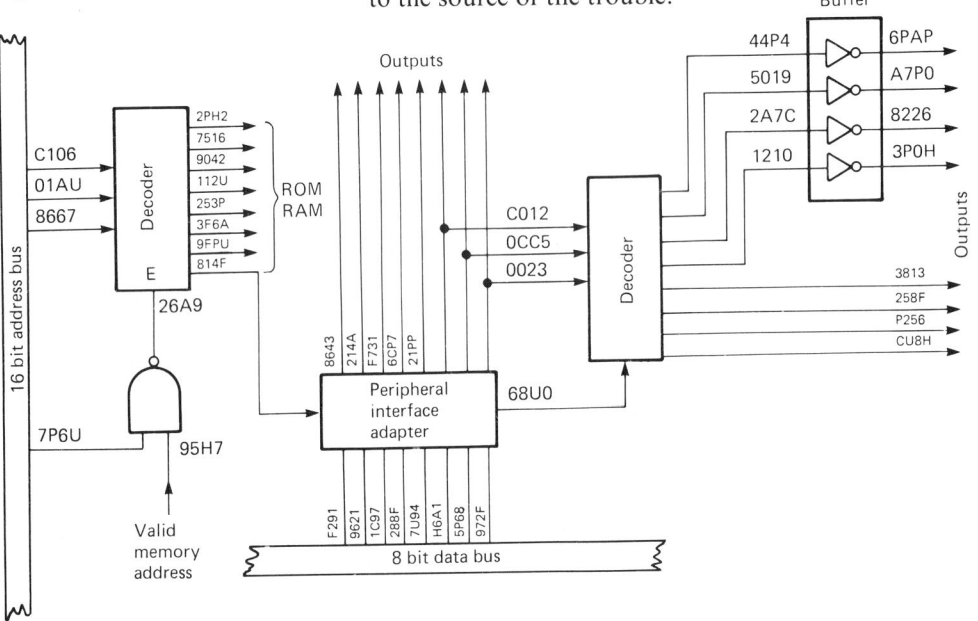

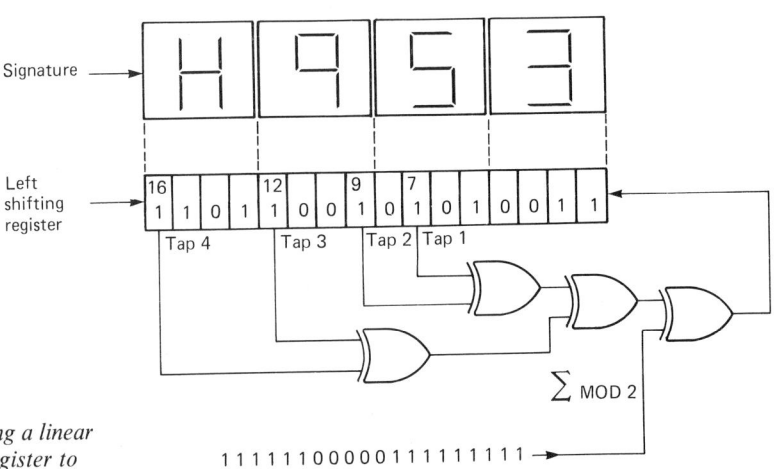

Fig. 10.16 *Using a linear feedback shift register to generate a signature*

A signature is generated by using a linear feedback shift register, configured as shown in Fig. 10.16.

The bit sequences being measured are added to the feedback information before being clocked into the shift register. The effect of this is that some bits are inverted before being clocked into the shift register, depending upon what has happened previously. The bit streams may be any length, but only the residue in the shift register at the end of the measurement is used. These 16 bits, displayed in hexadecimal, are the signature of the measured data stream. A non-standard hexadecimal character set is used to avoid ambiguity when using 7-segment displays, and this is:

0,1,2,3,4,5,6,7,8,9,A,C,F,H,P,U

Table 10.1 (page 272) shows how the register generates a signature from the 20-bit input sequence:

1 1 1 1 1 1 0 0 0 0 0 1 1 1 1 1 1 1 1 1

For the first eight time periods (0 to 7), the circuit performs as an ordinary shift register, but at time 7 the first '1' of the sequence has reached the first tap of the shift register. The result of this is that the next input bit, which is a logical '0' is inverted before being clocked into the shift register. This process continues until the end of the measurement when the 16-bit residue remaining is:

1 1 0 1 1 0 0 1 0 1 0 1 0 0 1 1

Taking signatures

In order to take signatures, a signature analyser requires START and STOP signals to define the measurement *window*. A CLOCK signal is also required, and these signals are obtained from the circuit under test at points defined in the service manual. Typical points for obtaining the START and STOP signals are the high order address lines, whilst the CLOCK may be obtained from the 'read' or 'write' lines or from the chip selects. The signature analyser probe is then used to obtain signatures from each node point in the circuit.

Accuracy of signature analysis

With a register length of 16, the error will always be less than 1 in 2^{16}, regardless of the length of the data stream measured. This gives rise to a 99.998% certainty of detecting an error should one be present. There is no such thing as a 'nearly correct' signature, and if only one pulse is missing, the resultant signature will be totally wrong.

Designing-in signature analysis

Building signature analysis into an item of equipment requires only two items, and these are:

Table 10.1 Generation of a signature from a 20-bit input sequence

Time	Contents of shift register	Next input to shift register	Next input sequence bit
0	0 0 0 0 0 0 0 0 0 0 0 0 0 0 0 0	1	1
1	0 0 0 0 0 0 0 0 0 0 0 0 0 0 0 1	1	1
2	0 0 0 0 0 0 0 0 0 0 0 0 0 0 1 1	1	1
3	0 0 0 0 0 0 0 0 0 0 0 0 0 1 1 1	1	1
4	0 0 0 0 0 0 0 0 0 0 0 0 1 1 1 1	1	1
5	0 0 0 0 0 0 0 0 0 0 0 1 1 1 1 1	1	1
6	0 0 0 0 0 0 0 0 0 0 1 1 1 1 1 1	0	0
7	0 0 0 0 0 0 0 0 0 1 1 1 1 1 1 0	1	0
8	0 0 0 0 0 0 0 0 1 1 1 1 1 1 0 1	1	0
9	0 0 0 0 0 0 0 1 1 1 1 1 1 0 1 1	0	0
10	0 0 0 0 0 0 1 1 1 1 1 1 0 1 1 0	0	0
11	0 0 0 0 0 1 1 1 1 1 1 0 1 1 0 0	1	1
12	0 0 0 0 1 1 1 1 1 1 0 1 1 0 0 1	0	1
13	0 0 0 1 1 1 1 1 1 0 1 1 0 0 1 0	1	1
14	0 0 1 1 1 1 1 1 0 1 1 0 0 1 0 1	0	1
15	0 1 1 1 1 1 1 0 1 1 0 0 1 0 1 0	1	1
16	1 1 1 1 1 1 0 1 1 0 0 1 0 1 0 1	0	1
17	1 1 1 1 1 0 1 1 0 0 1 0 1 0 1 0	0	1
18	1 1 1 1 0 1 1 0 0 1 0 1 0 1 0 0	1	1
19	1 1 1 0 1 1 0 0 1 0 1 0 1 0 0 1	1	1
20	1 1 0 1 1 0 0 1 0 1 0 1 0 0 1 1	—	—

(i) the ability to break the data bus feedback, and
(ii) a short S.A. program in ROM to stimulate the circuit nodes, arranged as shown in Fig. 10.17.

These two items add a small cost to the production of equipment, but this is more than offset by the savings obtained by no longer needing to use modular construction, and the ease with which fault finding can be accomplished.

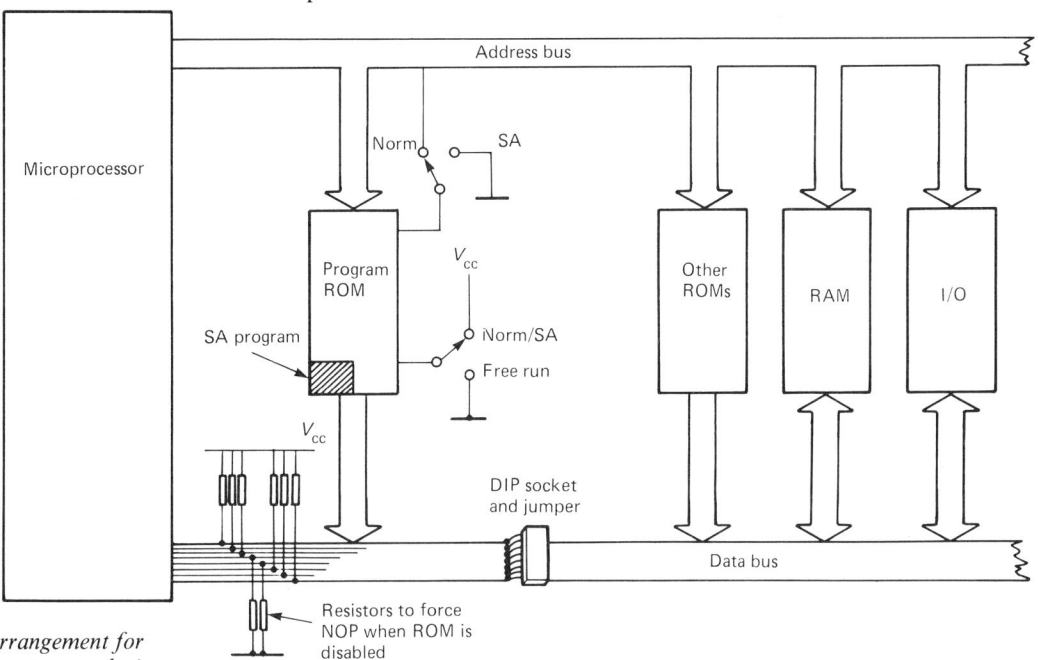

Fig. 10.17 *Arrangement for designed-in signature analysis*

The method used to find faults with signature analysis varies according to whether the fault lies in the 'kernel' (microprocessor plus minimal circuitry to operate it), or in the remainder of the circuit. For faults in the kernel, the data bus is broken and a 'no operation' (NOP) instruction is hard wired to the microprocessor data inputs. The microprocessor is then allowed to *free run* which causes the program counter to cycle through the address field, executing NOPs at each address. Signatures are then taken under these conditions.

For faults which lie in the remainder of the circuit, the S.A. program in ROM is executed. This program serves only to exercise various parts of the system to enable signatures to be taken.

Software diagnostics

If a microcomputer is partially working, then it may be possible to use software diagnostics (resident or non-resident) so that it checks itself for correct functioning. The following examples show how software may be used for this purpose:

(i) Software loops

Short programs may be developed which generate repetitive sequences, thus allowing investigation of the circuit with an oscilloscope. For example, the following program may be used to test the $\overline{RD}$, $\overline{WR}$ and $\overline{CE}$ signals of a microcomputer for correct operation:

```
       ORG  100H
       ;
       LD   HL,0500H    ;point to memory block
LOOP:  LD   A,(HL)      ;read data
       LD   (HL),A      ;write data
       JR   LOOP        ;repeat indefinitely
```

Repetitive traces may be obtained on an oscilloscope with this program, and monitoring the $\overline{RD}$, $\overline{WR}$ and $\overline{CE}$ signals should provide traces similar to those shown in Fig. 10.18.

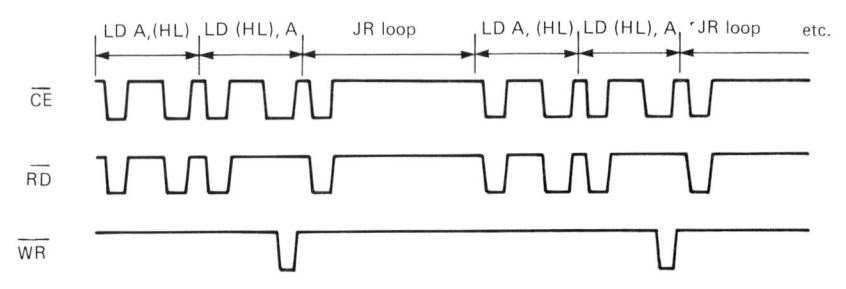

Fig. 10.18 *Traces from repetitive sequences: most oscilloscopes will display only any two of these waveforms simultaneously*

Other $\overline{CE}$ signals may be tested (for correct address decoder action) by loading HL with different values.

(ii) RAM test

Due to the large number of memory locations in a microcomputer, it is almost impossible to test each location by manual means. Therefore it is normal to use a test program to check out blocks of memory, and this may form part of the start-up sequence for a microcomputer when it is first switched on.

A full memory test would involve attempting to store all possible binary combinations into every memory location, in sequence, and then reading back each value stored to check that it corresponds to the data sent. Such a program would invariably take a long time to execute, therefore a much simpler test, called a 'checker board' test is normally adopted. This test involves storing data patterns in which adjacent bits are at opposite logic levels, i.e. 55_{16} and AA_{16}.

```
55 ---)   0 1 0 1 0 1 0 1     location 1
AA ---)   1 0 1 0 1 0 1 0     location 2
55 ---)   0 1 0 1 0 1 0 1     location 3
AA ---)   1 0 1 0 1 0 1 0     location 4
              etc
```

The following program is an example of this type of test:

```
;%%%%%%%%%%%%%%%%%%%%%%%%%%%%%%%%%%%
;RAM TEST PROGRAM
;
;TESTS A 2K BLOCK OF RAM FROM ADDRESS
;1000H TO 17FFH USING A CHECKER-BOARD
;PATTERN (55H FOLLOWED BY AAH)
;%%%%%%%%%%%%%%%%%%%%%%%%%%%%%%%%%%%
;
0100                ORG     100H            ;start of TPA
1000 =      RMSTRT  EQU     1000H           ;start of RAM for test
0005 =      BDOS    EQU     5               ;primary BDOS entry
0000 =      BOOT    EQU     0               ;warm boot
            ;
0100 210010         LD      HL,RMSTRT       ;pointer to start of RAM
0103 3E55   TEST:   LD      A,55H           ;01010101 pattern
0105 77             LD      (HL),A          ;store it in RAM
0106 BE             CP      (HL)            ;check if stored OK
0107 2011           JR      NZ,ERR          ;if not, RAM faulty
0109 3EAA           LD      A,0AAH          ;10101010 pattern
010B 77             LD      (HL),A          ;store it in RAM
010C BE             CP      (HL)            ;check if stored OK
010D 200B           JR      NZ,ERR          ;if not, RAM faulty
010F 23             INC     HL              ;move pointer
0110 3E18           LD      A,18H           ;check for RAMTOP+1
0112 BC             CP      H               ;end of RAM?
0113 20EE           JR      NZ,TEST         ;keep testing if not
0115 112501         LD      DE,MSG1         ;RAM OK message
0118 1803           JR      PRINT           ;print it!
011A 112D01 ERR:    LD      DE,MSG2         ;RAM fault message
011D 0E09   PRINT:  LD      C,9             ;BDOS print string
011F CD0500         CALL    BDOS            ;routine
0122 C30000         JP      BOOT            ;reboot CP/M
0125 52414D20 MSG1: DEFM    'RAM OK!$'
012D 52414D20 MSG2: DEFM    'RAM FAULT!$'


0005 BDOS     0000 BOOT     011A ERR     0125 MSG1     012D MSG2
011D PRINT    1000 RMSTRT   0103 TEST

No errors
```

One major disadvantage of this type of test is that it is unable to check for short circuits between bits which are separated by an even number of places. For this reason, if a RAM fails this test then it certainly is faulty, but if it passes this test, the best that can be said is that it may be free from faults.

(iii) ROM test

The checker board test cannot be applied to ROM, since it is not possible for a microprocessor to write data into a ROM whilst in circuit. The usual test applied to a ROM is to process its data in a predefined manner, e.g. total all of its data, and then compare the result with data stored in a specified ROM location (often the highest address in ROM). This is known as a 'checksum' test, and the byte in ROM used for comparison purposes is known as a 'check byte'. A checksum test may be performed as part of the start-up sequence when a microcomputer is first switched on.

A typical checksum algorithm may add together all bytes stored in a ROM, retaining just the 8-bit residue after each addition, as shown in the following example:

Address	Data	
0000	0 E	←data bytes stored in ROM
0001	0 2	
0002	1 E	
0003	3 F	
0004	C D	
0005	0 5	
0006	0 0	
0007	C 9	
ignore → 2	0 8	← checksum = 08

When all bytes in the ROM have been added, the result (the checksum) is then stored in the last location. Each time that a ROM is tested, the checksum algorithm is repeated, and the result is checked against the value of the stored checksum. If the two values do not coincide, a 'checksum error' results which indicates that the ROM is faulty. If the two values do coincide, then the ROM may be free from errors, although since it is possible for two or more errors to cancel each other out, this is far from certain. The program on page 277 is an example of a checksum ROM test.

Problems

1. A fault has developed in the circuit shown in Fig. 10.19 such that a short circuit appears at point X.
   Describe how a logic pulser and current tracer may be used to locate this fault.
2. Describe the principle of operation of a current tracer.
3. Explain why a logic analyser is more suitable for locating faults in a microprocessor based system than an ordinary oscilloscope.

Fault location

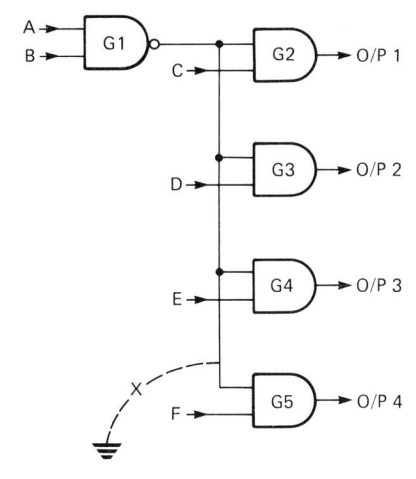

Fig. 10.19

```
;XXXXXXXXXXXXXXXXXXXXXXXXXXXXXXXXX
;ROM TEST PROGRAM
;
;TESTS ROM ADDRESSES F000H TO F7FFH
;PERFORMS SIMPLE ADDITION OF ALL
;BYTES IN A 2K ROM, AND COMPARES
;THE 8-BIT RESIDUE WITH A CHECKSUM
;BYTE STORED AT ADDRESS 07FFH
;XXXXXXXXXXXXXXXXXXXXXXXXXXXXXXXXX
;
0100                    ORG     100H            ;start of TPA
F000 =          ROM     EQU     0F000H          ;start of ROM for test
0005 =          BDOS    EQU     5               ;primary BDOS entry
0000 =          BOOT    EQU     0               ;warm boot
                ;
0100 2100F0             LD      HL,ROM          ;ROM pointer
0103 86         SUM:    ADD     A,(HL)          ;add byte to sum in A
0104 23                 INC     HL              ;point to next address
0105 4F                 LD      C,A             ;temp save sum in C
0106 3EF8               LD      A,0F8H          ;check for ROMTOP+1
0108 BC                 CP      H               ;end of ROM?
0109 79                 LD      A,C             ;get sum back into A
010A 20F7               JR      NZ,SUM          ;and keep on adding
010C 2B                 DEC     HL              ;too far!
010D 96                 SUB     (HL)            ;subtract checksum byte
010E BE                 CP      (HL)            ;should halve the sum!
010F 2005               JR      NZ,ERR          ;error if not half
0111 112101             LD      DE,MSG1         ;ROM OK! message
0114 1803               JR      PRINT           ;print it!
0116 112901     ERR:    LD      DE,MSG2         ;ROM fault message
0119 0E09       PRINT:  LD      C,9             ;BDOS print string
011B CD0500             CALL    BDOS            ;routine
011E C30000             JP      BOOT            ;reboot CP/M
0121 524F4D20   MSG1:   DEFM    'ROM OK!$'
0129 524F4D20   MSG2:   DEFM    'ROM FAULT!$'


0005 BDOS    0000 BOOT    0116 ERR    0121 MSG1    0129 MSG2
0119 PRINT   F000 ROM     0103 SUM

No errors
```

4. A 16-channel logic analyser is connected to the address and data busses of a Z80 based microprocessor system in the following manner:

```
<---- Address Bus ---->     <----- Data Bus ----->

A  A  A  A    A  A  A  A    D  D  D  D    D  D  D  D    M1
7  6  5  4    3  2  1  0    7  7  5  4    3  2  1  0    |
↓  ↓  ↓  ↓    ↓  ↓  ↓  ↓    ↓  ↓  ↓  ↓    ↓  ↓  ↓  ↓    ↓
15 14 13 12  11 10  9  8    7. 6  5  4    3  2  1  0   CLOCK

<---------- Logic analyser input channel ---------->
```

If the trigger word 9BDB is used, determine the first six data words captured after the trigger when executing the following program:

```
                ;****************************************
                ;Motor and heater control program
                ;****************************************
                ;
0C90            ORG    0C90H
0004 =          PORT   EQU    4           ;Z80 PIO addr
                ;
0C90 3ECF       LD     A,0CFH             ;Port A bit mode
0C92 D306       OUT    (PORT+2),A
0C94 3EC0       LD     A,0C0H             ;config data
0C96 D306       OUT    (PORT+2),A
0C98 AF         XOR    A                  ;clear acc
0C99 D304       OUT    (PORT),A
0C9B DB04  POLL: IN    A,(PORT)           ;read the port
0C9D CB7F       BIT    7,A                ;test motor switch
0C9F CBC7       SET    0,A                ;switch on motor
0CA1 2802       JR     Z,MTR              ;leave motor on
0CA3 CB87       RES    0,A                ;or switch it off
0CA5 CB77  MTR:  BIT    6,A               ;test heater switch
0CA7 CBCF       SET    1,A                ;switch on heater
0CA9 2802       JR     Z,HTR              ;leave heater on
0CAB CB8F       RES    1,A                ;or switch it off
0CAD D304  HTR:  OUT   (PORT),A           ;control data out
0CAF 18EA       JR     POLL               ;keep it going
```

5. If $\overline{RD}$ is used as a clock signal in Q4 instead of $\overline{M1}$, determine the first six data words captured, assuming that the trigger word is unchanged.
6. State the advantages of using signature analysis as a means of locating faults in a microprocessor based system.
7. Describe the facilities which must be included in microprocessor based equipment to allow signature analysis to be used.
8. The circuit shown in Fig. 10.20 is tested using signature analysis. Signatures are shown for working, and faulty conditions. Determine the most likely fault.

Fig. 10.20

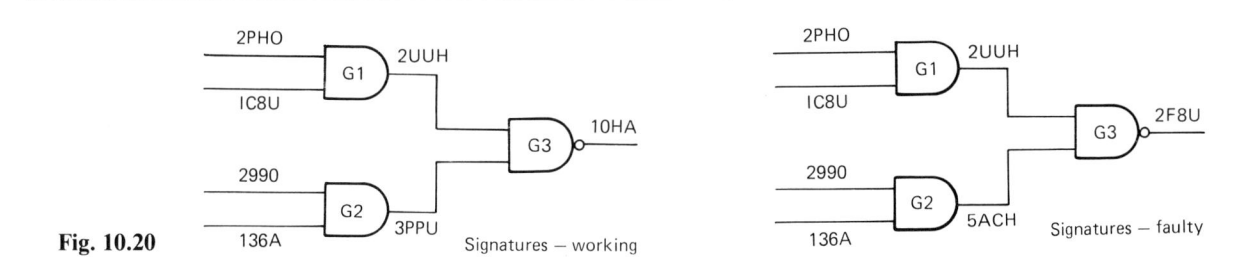

Signatures — working

Signatures — faulty

Solutions

Chapter 2

5 (b)

(i)
```
;**********************************
;Console input routine
;BDOS function 1
;**********************************
;
BDOS    EQU     5
RDCHR   EQU     1
        ;
        LD      C,RDCHR  ;sel. BDOS fn.
        CALL    BDOS     ;BDOS entry
        RET
```

(ii)
```
;**********************************
;Console output routine
;BDOS function 2
;**********************************
;
BDOS    EQU     5
WCHR    EQU     2
        ;
        LD      E,'X'    ;display 'X'
        LD      C,WCHR   ;sel. BDOS fn.
        CALL    BDOS     ;BDOS entry
        RET
```

(iii)
```
;**********************************
;Print string routine
;BDOS Function 9
;string terminator = $
;**********************************
;
BDOS    EQU     5
PSTR    EQU     9
        ;
        LD      DE,TEXT  ;DE= text pointer
        LD      C,9
        CALL    BDOS
        RET
TEXT:   DEFM    'This is the string$'
```

Chapter 4

5. (i) EQU, ORG, and END
   (ii) CHECK, NEXT, and EXIT
   (iii) START, BUFF, COUNT, and BUFLEN
   (iv) COUNT   EQU   BUFF+BUFLEN,
        JR   NZ,CHECK   ;null count?, and
        JR   Z,EXIT   ;exit when found

6. A = data at address 0202H
   B = 16H
   C = 08
   D = 03
   E = 50H

7.

```
;*************************************
;Audio alarm signal generator
;produces 1 KHz tone for 2 second
;duration (Z80 clock at 2 MHz)
;1T = 0.5µs
;Each pass = (68 x 14) + 45 ≃ 0.5 ms
;Total      = 4000 x 0.5 ms = 2 s
;*************************************
;
PA      EQU     4           ;I/O port address
        ORG     100H
;
        LD      HL,4000 ;(4T) 4000 x 0.5 ms = 2 s
PULSE:  LD      A,C     ;(7T) pass o/p via A
        AND     1       ;(7T) only bit 0
        OUT     (PA),A  ;(11T) drive port
        LD      B,68    ;(7T) inner loop count
DLY:    DEC     B       ;(4T) ((68x14)+45) x 0.5
        JP      NZ,DLY  ;(10T) ≃ 0.5 ms
        INC     C       ;(4T) toggle bit 0
        JR      PULSE   ;(12T) repeat
        RET
```

8(b).

```
;*************************************
;Display driver subroutine
;Suitable for 7-segment common anode
;and ASCII coded dot matrix displays
;ENTRY: A = numeric code to display
;EXIT:  A = display code
;*************************************
;
TRUE    EQU     0FFFFH
FALSE   EQU     NOT TRUE
SEG7    EQU     FALSE   ;alternative - TRUE
DOTM    EQU     NOT SEG7
;
        ORG     100H
;
        COND    SEG7    ;assemble for 7-seg
        LD      HL,SEGTAB ;segments table
        ADD     A,L       ;determine table
        LD      L,A       ;element for number
        LD      A,(HL)    ;get segments code
        ENDC
;
        COND    DOTM    ;assemble for dot
        AND     0FH     ;mask high 4 bits
        OR      30H     ;convert to ASCII
        ENDC
;
        RET
        COND    SEG7
SEGTAB: DEFB    3FH,6,5BH,4FH ;segment codes
        DEFB    66H,6DH,7DH,7 ;for display
        DEFB    7FH,67H
        ENDC
```

Chapter 5

5(i).

```
        .Z80
;***************************************
;Macro to provide multiplication instruction
;for the Z80 microprocessor
;Allows any 8-bit register to be multiplied
;by a constant in the range 0 - 255
;Product is stored in the HL pair
;***************************************
;
MULT    MACRO   REG,NUM
        LOCAL   SHIFT,NOADD
        LD      H,REG
        LD      DE,NUM AND 255
        LD      L,0
        LD      B,8
SHIFT:  ADD     HL,HL
        JR      NC,NOADD
        ADD     HL,DE
NOADD:  DJNZ    SHIFT
        ENDM
```

5(ii).   .Z80
;***
;Macro to provide a division instruction
;for the Z80 microprocessor
;Allows any 8-bit register to be divided by
;a constant in the range 0 - 255
;Quotient is left in the register specified
;for division, and remainder is left in H
;***
;
```
DIV     MACRO   REG,NUM
        LOCAL   SHIFT,NOADD
        LD      L,REG
        LD      DE,NUM SHL 8
        LD      H,0
        LD      B,8
SHIFT:  ADD     HL,HL
        SBC     HL,DE
        JR      NC,NOADD
        ADD     HL,DE
NOADD:  RLA
        DJNZ    SHIFT
        CPL
        LD      REG,A
        ENDM
```

5(iii). .Z80
;***
;Macro provides an instruction to shift the
;contents of any 8-bit register to the
;right a specified number of places
;***
;
```
SHR     MACRO   REG,NUM
        LD      A,REG
        LD      B,NUM
SHIFTR: SRL     A
        DJNZ    SHIFTR
        LD      REG,A
        ENDM
```

5(iv).   .Z80
;***
;Macro provides an instruction to shift the
;contents of any 8-bit register to the left
;a specified number of places
;***
;
```
SHL     MACRO   REG,NUM
        LD      A,REG
        LD      B,NUM
SHIFTL: SLA     A
        DJNZ    SHIFTL
        LD      REG,A
        ENDM
```

6(v).   .Z80
;***
;Macro to convert lb to kg
;(approximate)
;***
;
```
LBTOKG  MACRO   LB
        LD      A,LB
        MULT    A,22
        DIV     A,10
        ENDM
```

6(vi).   .Z80
;***
;Macro to convert kg to lb
;(approximate)
;***
;
```
KGTOLB  MACRO   KG
        LD      A,KG
        MULT    A,10
        DIV     A,22
        ENDM
```

Chapter 6

```
3.  0004 =                  PORT    EQU     4
                            ;
    0100 1E08               LD      E,8
    0102 211301             LD      HL,TABLE
    0105 7E         SEND:   LD      A,(HL)
    0106 D304               OUT     (PORT),A
    0108 23                 INC     HL
    0109 CD1B01             CALL    WAIT
    010C 1D                 DEC     E
    010D C20501             JP      NZ,SEND
    0110 C30000             JP      0
    0113            TABLE:  DEFS    8
                            ;
    011B 0680       WAIT:   LD      B,80H
    011D 05         DLY:    DEC     B
    011E C21D01             JP      NZ,DLY
    0121 C9                 RET
```

```
4(b).  0004                            PORT     EQU     4
                                       ;
       0000'                           CSEG
                                       ;configure PIO
                                       ;
       0000'   06 05                   LD       B,5
       0002'   21 0000"                LD       HL,CTRLB
       0005'   7E              CONFIG: LD       A,(HL)
       0006'   D3 06                   OUT      (PORT+2),A
       0008'   23                      INC      HL
       0009'   10 FA                   DJNZ     CONFIG
                                       ;
       000B'                           DSEG
       0000"   CF 29 20 B7     CTRLB:  DEFB     0CFH,29H,20H,0B7H,0D6H
       0004"   D6
                                       ;
       0005"                           CSEG
                                       ;interrupt vector
                                       ;
       000B'   3E 0D                   LD       A,0DH
       000D'   ED 47                   LD       I,A
       000F'   21 0D25                 LD       HL,0D25H
       0012'   22 0005"                LD       (INTVEC),HL
                                       ;
```

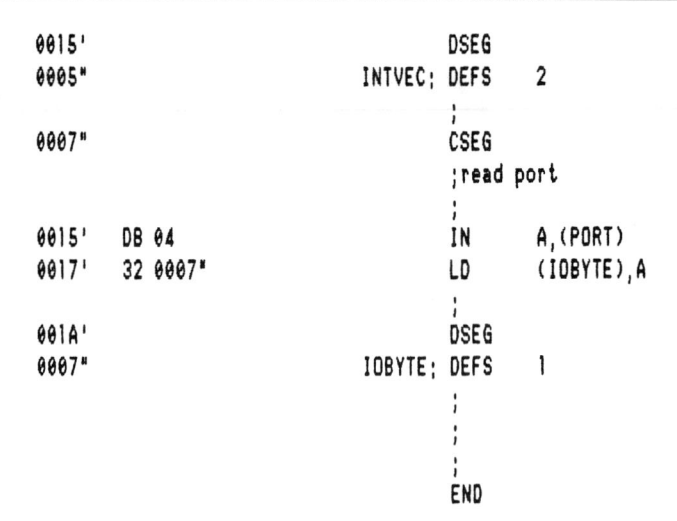

```
0015'                           DSEG
0005"                  INTVEC:  DEFS    2
                                ;
0007"                           CSEG
                                ;read port
                                ;
0015'    DB 04                  IN      A,(PORT)
0017'    32 0007"               LD      (IOBYTE),A
                                ;
001A'                           DSEG
0007"                  IOBYTE:  DEFS    1
                                ;
                                ;
                                ;
                                END
```

Chapter 10

4. DB,CB,7F,CB,C7,28
5. DB,04,**,CB,7F,CB   (** = data read in from the port)
8. G2 faulty.

Index

Absolute segment, 108
Address decoding, 239
Ambiguous filename (afn), 20
Arithmetic operator, 50
ASEG directive, 108
Assembler, 43
Assembler directives, 49
Assembly language, 4, 6, 48

Back-up copy, 33
Base page, 17
Basic disk operating system (BDOS), 15
Basic I/O system (BIOS), 15
Binary constant, 50
Blocks (disk), 19
Breakpoint monitor (emulator) 254
Bug, 133
Built-in commands, 16, 22

Character pointer, 33
Checksum (ROM test), 276
Chip failure, 259
Clock (logic analyser), 267
Clock circuit, 168
Clock qualifier (logic analyser), 267
Close file, 30
Code conversion subroutine, 62
Code segment, 108
Commands (text editor), 40
Comments (assembly language), 52
COMMON directive, 115
Console command processor (CCP), 15
Cost effectiveness, 3
CP/M, 14
Cross-assembler, 44
Cross-reference (symbols), 129
CSEG directive, 108
Current tracer, 264
Cursor, 33

Data qualifier (logic analyser), 267
Data segment, 111
Data sort subroutine, 65
Debug run, 145

Debugger, 133
Decimal constant, 50
Default radix, 50
DEFB directive, 52, 56
DEFM directive, 52, 57
DEFS directive, 52, 57
DEFW directive, 52, 56
Design sequence, 1
Development system (MDS), 10
Diagnostics (software), 273
DICE (emulator), 246
DIR command, 23
Directive (assembler), 49, 52
Directory, 19
Disassembly (logic analyser), 269
Disk directory, 19
Disk errors (assembler), 59
Disk files, 18
Disk storage, 17
Display format (logic analyser), 268
Division subroutine, 60
Documentation (assembly language), 59
Drive reference, 22
DSEG directive, 111
Dummy parameter (macro), 77

ED text editor, 36
Edit buffer, 30
ELSE directive, 52, 55
Emulation, 9
Emulation modes, 248
Emulation sequence, 249
Emulator (debugging facilities), 247
END directive, 52, 53
ENDIF directive, 52, 54
ENDM pseudo-op, 76, 83
EPROM (characteristics), 254
EPROM (erasure), 258
EPROM (programming), 257
EQU directive, 52, 53
ERA command, 23
Error messages (assembler), 58
Error messages (linker), 125
Error messages (loader), 127
Errors (assembly), 58

Index

Examine register command (debugger), 144
EXITM pseudo-op, 83
Extent (disk), 20
External references, 120
EXTRN directive, 120

Fault conditions, 259
Fault location, 259
Field (assembly language), 48
FIFO, 266
File control block (FCB), 30
File type, 21
Filename, 19
Files, 18
Floppy disks, 17
Forward reference, 45

Go/execute command (debugger), 139

Hand assembly, 41
Hardware, 164
Hardware design, 1
Hardware trace (emulator), 253
HEX file, 46
Hexadecimal constant, 50
High level language, 4, 7
Histogram utility, 157
Host system, 11, 244

I.C.E., 244
I/O, 165, 188
IF directive, 52, 54
In-circuit emulation, 244
In-line assembly command (debugger), 137
In-line macro, 70
INCLUDE Directive, 52, 57
Initial specification, 2
Input command (debugger), 139
Install (text editor), 38
Integration (hardware/software), 244
Interrupts, 239
IRP pseudo-op, 75
IRPC pseudo op, 73

Jump table, 16

Labe, 48
LIB (library manager), 128
Library manager, 127
Line editor, 33
Line number (assembly language), 48
LINK, 123
Linking, 101, 122

Linking loader, 122
List/disassemble command (debugger), 140
LOAD/HEXCOM, 127
Loading 101, 122, 126
LOCAL pseudo-op, 86
Logic analyser, 265
Logic clip, 264
Logic comparator, 264
Logic probe, 262
Logic pulser, 263
Logical errors (assembler), 58
Logical operator, 50

M80 (macro-assembler), 105
Machine language, 4
MACLIB, 89
Macro, 70
Macro application programs, 95
Macro-assembler, 70
Macro library (traffic lights), 90
MACRO pseudo-op, 76
Make file, 30
Memory dump command (debugger), 137
Memory fill command (debugger), 138
Memory mapping, 256, 248
Menu (text editor), 41
Mnemonics, 49
Monitor program, 13
Move command (debugger), 141
MPU clock circuit, 168
MPU kernel circuit, 166
MPU reset circuit, 169
Multiplication subroutine, 60

Non-document file, 36
Numeric constants, 50

Octal constant, 50
On-screen editor, 33
Open file, 30
Operand, 49
Operating system, 13
ORG directive, 52

Pass counter command (debugger), 141
Power supply, 167
Precedence (of operators), 51
Primary filename, 20
PRN file, 46
Program flowchart, 4
Program testing, 9
Program writing, 4

Index

Pseudo-op, 49, 52
PUBLIC directive, 121

RADIX (pseudo-op), 50
RAM (size), 165
RAM test, 274
Read file command (debugger), 141
Read sequential, 32
Real-time trace (emulator), 253
Record counter, 32
Records (disk), 18
REL file, 105
Relocatable code, 45
Relocatable modules, 105
REN command, 24
REPT pseudo-op, 71
Reserved word, 50
Reset circuit, 169
ROM (size), 165
ROM test, 276
ROM/RAM circuits, 186

SAVE command, 24
Sectors (disk), 18
Set command (debugger), 142
Signature analysis, 269
Software design, 1
Software development sequence, 4
Software diagnostics, 273
Software loop testing, 274
Sort subroutine, 65
Source code, 28
State display (logic analyser), 268
Stored macro, 70, 76
String constants, 50
Switches (linker), 124
Switches (macro assembler), 107
SYM file, 46
Symbol tables, 157
Syntax errors (assembler), 58
System flowchart, 4

Target system, 11, 244
Temporary file, 33
Text editor, 28
Timing display (logic analyser), 268
TPA, 15
Trace command (debugger), 143
Trace utility, 159
Tracks (disk), 18
Transient commands, 16, 25
Trigger word, 266
Two-pass assembler, 45
TYPE command, 25

Unambiguous filename (ufn), 20
Untrace command (debugger), 144
USER command, 25
Utility program, 157

Wildcards, 21
Word processor, 38
WordStar, 38

XREF (cross referencer), 129

Z80 (a.c. characteristics), 180
Z80 (d.c. characteristics), 184
Z80 (instruction set), 174
Z80 (timing), 173
Z80 CTC (a.c. characteristics), 236
Z80 CTC (d.c. characteristics), 238
Z80 CTC (programming), 226
Z80 CTC (technical data), 222
Z80 PIO (a.c. characteristics), 195
Z80 PIO (d.c. characteristics), 198
Z80 P1O (programming), 193
Z80 PIO (technical data), 187
Z80 PIO (timing), 191
Z80 SIO (a.c. characteristics), 219
Z80 SIO (d.c. characteristics), 222
Z80 SIO (programming), 214
Z80 SIO (technical data), 199
Z80 SIO (timing), 216
ZSID (debugger), 134

SANDWELL COLLEGE OF FURTHER
AND HIGHER EDUCATION